# A PASSION TO LEAD

# CONTENTS

*Sterling Signature*
NEW YORK

An Imprint of Sterling Publishing
387 Park Avenue South
New York, NY 10016

ISBN 978-1-4027-8735-5 (hardcover)
ISBN 978-1-4027-9615-9 (ebook)
ISBN 978-1-4549-0385-7 (book club)

Distributed in Canada by Sterling Publishing
$c/o$ Canadian Manda Group, 165 Dufferin Street
Toronto, Ontario, Canada M6K 3H6
Distributed in the United Kingdom by GMC Distribution Services
Castle Place, 166 High Street, Lewes, East Sussex, England BN7 1XU
Distributed in Australia by Capricorn Link (Australia) Pty. Ltd.
P.O. Box 704, Windsor, NSW 2756, Australia

Designed by: Matt Rue, Miko McGinty Inc.
Photo research by: Susan Oyama and Edward Goodman

For information about custom editions, special sales, and premium and corporate purchases,
please contact Sterling Special Sales at 800-805-5489 or specialsales@sterlingpublishing.com.

Manufactured in China

2  4  6  8  10  9  7  5  3  1

www.sterlingpublishing.com

*page ii: Rough Riders* LIEUTENANT-COLONEL THEODORE ROOSEVELT
*and* COLONEL LEONARD WOOD, *San Antonio, Texas, 1898.*

# A PASSION TO LEAD
## THEODORE ROOSEVELT IN HIS OWN WORDS

### HOW ONE EXTRAORDINARY MAN
### LED FROM THE FRONT
### AND CHANGED AMERICA FOREVER

*Edited by Laura Ross*

*Sterling Signature*
NEW YORK

# "THIS IS A GOOD DAY FOR AMERICA"

O N JULY 1, 1898, exposed as the only man on horseback as his troops surged below him on foot, Colonel Theodore Roosevelt led his "Rough Riders" in charges at Kettle Hill and San Juan Heights in Cuba.

Those who fought by his side, both above and below him in rank, extolled his bravery and leadership in that pivotal battle, and he was recommended for the Medal of Honor, an award that all concerned (including Roosevelt himself) believed he deserved. But the Colonel was denied the accolade at least in part because of his outspokenness over the treatment of the troops after the war was over.

More than one hundred years later, Roosevelt would finally be recognized for his wartime bravery. In a ceremony (conducted, appropriately, in the Roosevelt Room of the White House) on January 16, 2001, President William J. Clinton presented the nation's highest military award to Theodore Roosevelt posthumously. Roosevelt's great grandson, Tweed Roosevelt, received the Medal on behalf of the family. Clinton's remarks on that day provide an apt starting point as we embark upon Roosevelt's extraordinary journey from a child of urban privilege to one of the most influential leaders in our country's history.

In 1782, George Washington created the Badge of Military Merit. It was the first medal awarded by our nation's Armed Forces. But soon it fell into oblivion, and for decades no new medals were established. It was thought that a medal was too much like a European aristocratic title, while to fight for one's country in America was simply doing your

THEODORE ROOSEVELT *in his Rough Rider uniform, 1898.*

democratic duty. So when the Medal of Honor was instituted during the Civil War it was agreed it would be given only for gallantry, at the risk of one's life above and beyond the call of duty. That's an extraordinarily high standard, one that precious few ever meet.

The Medal of Honor is our highest military decoration.

I award [it] today for the bravery of Lt. Colonel Theodore Roosevelt on July 1, 1898.

That was the day he led his volunteer troops, the Rough Riders, in taking San Juan Hill, which changed the course of the battle and the Spanish–American War. We are greatly honored to be joined today by members of the Roosevelt family, including Tweed Roosevelt, here to accept the Medal of Honor on behalf of his great-grandfather.

This is the thirty-seventh Medal of Honor I have presented, but the first I present in the recipient's old office, in front of a portrait of him in full battle gear. It is a tradition in the Roosevelt Room that when a Democrat is in the White House, a portrait of Franklin Roosevelt hangs above the mantle, and when a Republican is here, Teddy Roosevelt occupies the hallowed spot.

I chose to break with the tradition these last eight years because I figured if we could have even half the luck and skill leading America into the twenty-first century that Theodore Roosevelt did in leading America into the twentieth century, our nation would do just fine. TR was a larger-than-life figure who gave our nation a larger-than-life vision of our place in the world. Part of that vision was formed on San Juan Hill. His Rough Riders were made up of all kinds of Americans from all walks of life. They were considered unpolished and undisciplined, but they were true citizen soldiers. By taking San Juan Hill, eventually they forced the enemy fleet into the Battle of Santiago Bay, where it was routed. This led to the Spanish surrender and opened the era of America as a global power.

Twenty-two people won the Medal of Honor for actions that day. Two high-ranking military officers who had won the Medal of Honor in earlier wars and who saw Theodore Roosevelt's bravery recommended him for the medal, too.

For some reason, the War Department never acted on the recommendation. Some say he didn't get it because of the bias the War Department had against volunteers. Others say it was because he ran afoul of the Secretary of War, who after the war was reluctant to allow the return of a number of American servicemen afflicted with Yellow Fever.

Roosevelt publicly called for America to bring its heroes home, where they had a far better chance to recover. The administration had to reverse course and it proved embarrassing to the Secretary. But while opinions about why he didn't receive the medal are mixed, opinion that he should have received it long ago is unanimous . . . .

Here's what he said, way back then: "We know there are dangers ahead, as we know there are evils to fight and overcome. But stout of heart, we see across the dangers the great future that lies beyond, and we rejoice."

Let these words continue to guide as, as we go forth into a new century. May we continue to live up to the ideals for which . . . Theodore Roosevelt risked [his life].

CITATION awarding the Medal of Honor to Theodore Roosevelt:
The President of the United States of America, authorized by Act of Congress, March 3, 1863, has awarded in the name of The Congress the Medal of Honor to:

LIEUTENANT COLONEL THEODORE ROOSEVELT
UNITED STATES ARMY

for conspicuous gallantry and intrepidity at the risk of his life above and beyond the call of duty.

Lieutenant Colonel Theodore Roosevelt distinguished himself by acts of bravery on 1 July 1898, near Santiago de Cuba, Republic of Cuba, while leading a daring charge up San Juan Hill. Lieutenant Colonel Roosevelt, in total disregard for his personal safety, and accompanied by only four or five men, led a desperate and gallant charge up San Juan Hill, encouraging his troops to continue the assault through withering enemy fire over open countryside. Facing the enemy's heavy fire, he displayed extraordinary bravery throughout the charge, and was the first to reach the enemy trenches, where he quickly killed one of the enemy with his pistol, allowing his men to continue the assault. His leadership and valor turned the tide in the Battle for San Juan Hill. Lieutenant Colonel Roosevelt's extraordinary heroism and devotion to duty are in keeping with the highest traditions of military service and reflect great credit upon himself, his unit, and the United States Army.

Thank you all very much for being here today. This has been a very moving ceremony. Again, I want to thank the large delegation from the Congress, and former members who have come, and families and folks in the Pentagon who worked hard to get this done. This is a good day for America.

# INTRODUCTION

**B**ENJAMIN FRANKLIN FAMOUSLY SAID, "Either write something worth reading or do something worth writing." Theodore Roosevelt can surely be credited with having done both, to a degree never equaled among U.S. Presidents (or perhaps anyone else). His life story includes death-defying adventures, battlefield bravery, audacious political maneuvering, visionary social and environmental legislation, and literary accomplishment. His awards include a Nobel Peace Prize and a Medal of Honor. To say he was larger than life is in itself reductive, because he was also very much engaged in life—leading by example, amassing firsthand experience in all that interested him, setting high standards and then demonstrating that they could be met by anyone willing to put forth energy and commitment.

It is no wonder that Roosevelt has been the subject of dozens of biographies—or that new ones continue to come out even nearly 100 years after his death. His life and influence can be viewed from myriad angles and are sure to be revisited and reassessed for decades to come.

What particular combination of qualities and circumstances formed the character of this unique figure? The simple facts are as follows. Born into a wealthy New York family in 1858, young Roosevelt overcame a sickly constitution to hold his own in athletic endeavors while excelling in the study of science. After graduating from Harvard (where, among other things, he completed most of the work on the first of 30 books he would write in his lifetime), he turned his back on the idea of life as a scientist and briefly studied law at Columbia University.

THEODORE ROOSEVELT *at his home in Oyster Bay, New York.*

His political career began with two terms as a New York State Assemblyman, but when sudden widowhood and political setbacks dispirited him, he took off for a life of cattle ranching in the West. After a couple of years, a second chance at marital happiness and the siren song of politics drew him back into the fray, and—though he was unsuccessful in his 1866 bid for New York City Mayor—he soon decamped for Washington, D.C., and a job on the U.S. Civil Service Commission.

A stint as New York City Police Commissioner plunged Roosevelt into urban social realities and city politics. His successful campaigning efforts helped get William McKinley elected as U.S. President, who in turn appointed him Assistant Secretary of the Navy. From that platform, Roosevelt advocated for war against Spain, and when it came, he put himself on the line, leading his "Rough Riders" to victory in Cuba.

As a returning war hero, Roosevelt easily won the Governorship of New York, attacking the job with his usual reformist zeal. Just as he was wearing out his welcome in his home state by butting heads with his party's bosses, he moved on to become Vice President during McKinley's second term—until an assassin's bullet took McKinley's life, hastening Roosevelt's ascendancy to Chief Executive. (After completing McKinley's term, he was elected President in his own right in 1904.) Throughout his eventful presidency, Roosevelt moved the United States onto the world stage as never before, while simultaneously undertaking numerous life- (and wildlife-) changing domestic initiatives.

His post-presidential life included an African safari and an expedition into uncharted realms of the South American wilderness, as well as a failed bid for re-election as a representative of his own Bull Moose Party. No doubt hastened by the illness and injury he suffered in South America, Roosevelt died in 1919. ✻ ✻ ✻

Though his accomplishments were astonishingly numerous and diverse, certain qualities characterized everything Roosevelt did, from his early academic and athletic efforts to his final wilderness forays. First and foremost, he was a born leader, unhesitatingly stepping forward to take charge, influence all who would listen, make policy at home and abroad, change what needed changing, and safeguard what needed protecting. Call it ego if you will, or selflessness, or even compulsion—but one thing is clear. He had a passion to lead, and he exercised it at every opportunity.

Roosevelt believed in the square deal, American might, and personal merit as the one and only criterion that mattered when filling any post, from foot soldier to cabinet member. He always led from the front, never expecting others to do jobs that he himself wasn't able or willing to take on. He spoke his mind and followed his heart always—regardless of the personal or political consequences. No cause or endeavor was too big for him to tackle, and no opponent, special interest, or natural obstacle (mountain, river, ferocious animal) could make him back down or soften his attack. It has been argued that it is these very qualities that ultimately killed his career—and led to his death at the relatively young age of 61—but few would deny that he left the world a richer place, with America's role in it a bigger and more vigorous one.

What is the best way to get to know Roosevelt today? As noted, there are enough biographies to shake one of his "big sticks" at. But why not go right to the source? Roosevelt was the most prolific writers of any of our Presidents, turning out works of history, biography, and memoir, as well as books on military strategy and travel, collections of speeches and articles—even a children's book. And of the reportedly 150,000 letters he wrote, many survive and are available for our perusal.

Any attempt to put together a representative selection of Roosevelt's writings is daunting by virtue of the sheer volume and breadth of his work—and yet we feel that the best way to get to the heart of the Roosevelt legacy is through his own words. What you will find in this volume is a variety of excerpts and complete works that touch on his numerous passions and preoccupations. Pieces from his autobiography address the influence of his father, the virtues of physical exercise, the rights of women, and other topics. Sections from his adventure memoirs carry us to the heart of the American West and the farthest reaches of the Amazon. His *Rough Riders*, included here in slightly abridged form, transports us to the Cuban battleground of the Spanish–American War. And numerous speeches, articles, and letters reveal Roosevelt at his most public and most private, making pronouncements for the ages and offering small talk and jokes to calm and amuse his children.

Accompanying this array of Roosevelt's most vivid writing are images and ephemera (some items never-before published) that bring his world and career to life, revealing a man with a voracious appetite for knowledge and experience, a deep-seated calling to public service, and a ferocious love of his country and the world. Whether you are a scholar of American history or simply captivated by the mythology surrounding the twenty-sixth President of the United States, you are sure to find much to surprise, enlighten, and enthrall you within the pages of *A Passion to Lead.*

# 1.

# PRIVILEGE AND PROMISE

THE SECOND OF FOUR CHILDREN, Theodore Roosevelt was born on October 27, 1858, into an eminent and wealthy family that had been in New York since the mid-1700s. The family home at the time was a well-appointed brownstone on Manhattan's East 20th Street.

Roosevelt's father, also named Theodore, helped run the family glass-importing business and was well known for his philanthropy. During the Civil War, Theodore Sr. was a staunch supporter of Abraham Lincoln and the Union, while his wife, the former Martha Bulloch, came from a slave-owning southern family and retained her Confederate sympathies. One can only imagine the dinner-table conversations "Teedie" (as young Theodore was known within the family) overheard as a child. He surely learned the value of sticking to one's guns in the face of opposition.

Roosevelt's young life was plagued by illness, including chronic asthma, but he was loath to let his physical infirmities slow him down; his inquiring mind and restless spirit were evident from a very early age. Roosevelt was home-schooled for most of his childhood, which left him timid and prone to becoming lost in his own imagination. But his father, aware that he needed both socialization and physical activity, built him a gym, encouraged him to take up boxing, and took him on vacations to

*overleaf:* THE PORCELLIAN CLUB, *Harvard University, c. 1876–80. Theodore Roosevelt is sitting on the floor to the right of the table. The exclusive final club was founded in 1791 and counts Henry Cabot Lodge and Oliver Wendell Holmes Jr. among its members.*

*opposite:* LIBRARY OF THE ROOSEVELT HOME *at 6 West 57th Street, New York City, where the family moved in 1873.*

*left:* LETTER FROM THEODORE ROOSEVELT TO "BAMIE" *(his older sister Anna), August 6, 1876. Written at Oyster Bay the summer before Theodore was to begin his first year at Harvard, the letter describes the days as being full of "ornithological enjoyment and reptilian rapture."*

THE FAMILY RESIDENCE *at 28 East 20th Street in New York City, where Theodore Roosevelt was born in 1858.*

THEODORE ROOSEVELT, *age 11, in a carte de visite portrait taken in Paris, 1870.*

Europe and the Middle East. Somewhere along the way, Roosevelt, who could have led a cosseted life of scholarly pursuit or entered an already-thriving family business, developed a drive to assert his independence, excel at a variety of physical endeavors, and ultimately become a leader of men and a nation.

Roosevelt's unconventional early education did not dampen his chances for a top-notch college career: he entered Harvard in the fall of 1876, already particularly proficient in history and the natural sciences. At the time, he had no particular inclination toward politics and shunned the study of elocution and debate. "I am exceedingly glad that I did not take part in the type of debate in which stress is laid, not upon getting a speaker to think rightly, but on getting him to talk glibly on the side to which he is assigned, without regard either to what his convictions are or to what they ought to be." It was certainly the fervency of his convictions, along with a deep-seated sense that he was meant to lead, that eventually drew Roosevelt into political life, in spite of his chronic disillusionment with it—and drew him back to it when he attempted veer onto other paths.

The death of his father in 1878 caused Roosevelt great pain, but he maintained his position in the top tenth of his Harvard class and nurtured his ambition to be a scientist. "I left college and entered the big world owing more than I can express to the training I had received, especially in my own home," he wrote later. "But with much else also to learn if I were to become really fitted to do my part in the work that lay ahead for the generation of Americans to which I belonged."

PORTRAIT OF THE ROOSEVELT FAMILY *during their trip to Egypt in 1872–73. Theodore Roosevelt is the second child from the right seated in the front row.*

Theodore and Alice Hathaway Lee became engaged in January 1880, while he was still at Harvard, working on his senior thesis, "The Practicability of Equalizing Men and Women Before the Law." They were married the following October, after he graduated (Number 21 in his class of 177), and they moved into the family home on West 57th Street. Surprisingly, since he'd professed his utmost dedication to science, he began studying the law at Columbia University.

*In front of the* **HARVARD BOAT HOUSE** *in a sculling outfit, c. 1877.*

In spite—or perhaps because—of warnings from his doctors that he should severely limit his physical activities due to congenital heart problems, Roosevelt seized every opportunity to hunt, climb, camp, and explore the outdoors. While on a grand tour of Europe with Alice the summer after they married, he even climbed the Matterhorn. Upon his return to New York, he was wooed away from law school by the prospect of becoming the Republican candidate for State Assemblyman in the 21st District. He won the race handily, and immediately became a vociferous reformer within that body.

In his two terms as Assemblyman, Roosevelt wrote more bills than any other New York legislator and set the tone for his entire political life, remaining fiercely independent even under pressure from his closest allies to adapt his views to the politically expedient ones of the moment. In 1883, he was elected Republican minority leader, though he failed to win back that spot for the following year. His refusal to march in lockstep with his colleagues may very well have been the reason—but this was not a lesson he was inclined to learn.

Perhaps attempting to compensate for the wealth and ease into which he was born, Roosevelt was instrumental in the passage of many social reform initiatives, reaching across the aisle to work with Democratic governor Grover Cleveland when necessary.

When the 1883 Assembly session went into recess, Roosevelt and his wife made plans to build a house in Oyster Bay, but his love for the West beckoned, and in early September, he traveled out to the Dakota Badlands to hunt Buffalo. Impulsively, he purchased two cattle ranches, before returning to his pregnant wife and the new Assembly session that began on January 1.

On February 12, 1884, Alice Lee Roosevelt was born. Two days later, suffering from a case of kidney failure that had gone undiagnosed because of her pregnancy, Roosevelt's wife Alice passed way—just hours after his mother had succumbed to typhoid fever.

Roosevelt carried on bravely in the Assembly, but found himself more and more disillusioned with party politics. He decided that he would forgo renomination to the Assembly and traveled out to the Badlands, where he began building a house on one of the parcels of land he'd purchased. Declaring his political aspirations completely behind him, he wanted nothing more than to retire to the West, he said—though that retirement would not last long.

EDISON'S LIGHT.

The Great Inventor's Triumph in Electric Illumination.

A SCRAP OF PAPER.

It Makes a Light, Without Gas or Flame, Cheaper Than Oil.

TRANSFORMED IN THE FURNACE

Complete Details of the Perfected Carbon Lamp.

FIFTEEN MONTHS OF TOIL.

Story of His Tireless Experiments with Lamps, Burners and Generators.

SUCCESS IN A COTTON THREAD.

The Wizard's Byplay, with Bodily Pain and Gold "Tailings."

NEW YORK HERALD
Dec. 21. 1879.

Theodore Roosevelt in mountaineering costume; his first wife Alice Hathaway Lee (1861-1884). Above: Sagamore Hill, which was not equipped with the new-fangled light for many years.

SCRAPBOOK PAGE *from the Roosevelt family albums. Most captions were written by Eleanor Butler Roosevelt, wife of Teddy Jr. Top: Sagamore Hill, the house in Oyster Bay, New York, that was built for Roosevelt (bottom left) and his first wife, Alice Hathaway Lee (bottom right).*

IN *AN AUTOBIOGRAPHY*, published in 1913 when Roosevelt was 55, he looked back on his early years—his childhood, his education, his formative political experiences, and his dawning love of the West. In the first three excerpts that follow, Roosevelt reflects on early memories of his father's benevolent spirit, his own budding interest in natural history—and books of every kind—and his first experience of world travel. (Note his reference to "Smike" at the end of the third piece, an allusion to a character in Charles Dickens's *Nicholas Nickleby*. Even at age 14, Roosevelt was integrating the great books he read into his view of the world.)

# Boyhood and Youth

My father, Theodore Roosevelt, was the best man I ever knew. He combined strength and courage with gentleness, tenderness, and great unselfishness. He would not tolerate in us children selfishness or cruelty, idleness, cowardice, or untruthfulness. As we grew older he made us understand that the same standard of clean living was demanded for the boys as for the girls; that what was wrong in a woman could not be right in a man. With great love and patience, and the most understanding sympathy and consideration, he combined insistence on discipline. He never physically punished me but once, but he was the only man of whom I was ever really afraid. I do not mean that it was a wrong fear, for he was entirely just, and we children adored him. We used to wait in the library in the evening until we could hear his key rattling in the latch of the front hall, and then rush out to greet him; and we would troop into his room while he was dressing, to stay there as long as we were permitted, eagerly examining anything which came out of his pockets which could be regarded as an attractive novelty. Every child has fixed in his memory various details which strike it as of grave importance. The trinkets he used to keep in a little box on his dressing-table we children always used to speak of as "treasures." The word, and some of the trinkets themselves, passed on to the next generation. My own children, when small, used to troop into my room while I was dressing, and the gradually accumulating trinkets in the "ditty-box"—

THEODORE "THEE" ROOSEVELT SR. *(1831–78), a philanthropist and partner in his family's business, Roosevelt & Son, a glass-importing firm founded in 1797.*

the gift of an enlisted man in the navy—always excited rapturous joy. On occasions of solemn festivity each child would receive a trinket for his or her "very own." My children, by the way, enjoyed one pleasure I do not remember enjoying myself. When I came back from riding, the child who brought the bootjack would itself promptly get into the boots, and clump up and down the room with a delightful feeling of kinship with Jack of the seven-league strides. ✱ ✱ ✱

**WHILE STILL A SMALL BOY** I began to take an interest in natural history. I remember distinctly the first day that I started on my career as zoölogist. I was walking up Broadway, and as I passed the market to which I used sometimes to be sent before breakfast to get strawberries I suddenly saw a dead seal laid out on a slab of wood. That seal filled me with every possible feeling of romance and adventure. I asked where it was killed, and was informed in the harbor. I had already begun to read some of Mayne Reid's books and other boys' books of adventure, and I felt that this seal brought all these adventures in realistic fashion before me. As long as that seal remained there I haunted the neighborhood of the market day after day. I measured it, and I recall that, not having a tape measure, I had to do my best to get its girth with a folding pocket foot-rule, a difficult undertaking. I carefully made a record of the utterly useless measurements, and at once began to write a natural history of my own, on the strength of that seal. This, and subsequent natural histories, were written down in blank books in simplified spelling, wholly unpremeditated and unscientific. I had vague aspirations of in some way or another owning and preserving that seal, but they never got beyond the purely formless stage. I think, however, I did get the seal's skull, and with two of my cousins promptly started what we ambitiously called the "Roosevelt Museum of Natural History." The collections were at first kept in my room, until a rebellion on the part of the chambermaid received the approval of the higher authorities of the household and the collection was moved up to a kind of bookcase

in the back hall upstairs. It was the ordinary small boy's collection of curios, quite incongruous and entirely valueless except from the standpoint of the boy himself. My father and mother encouraged me warmly in this, as they always did in anything that could give me wholesome pleasure or help to develop me.

CHILDHOOD DRAWINGS *of observations of the natural world by Theodore Roosevelt.*

The adventure of the seal and the novels of Mayne Reid together strengthened my instinctive interest in natural history. I was too young to understand much of Mayne Reid, excepting the adventure part and the natural history part—these enthralled me. But of course my reading was not wholly confined to natural history. There was very little effort made to compel me to read books, my father and mother having the good sense not to try to get me to read anything I did not like, unless it was in the way of study. I was given the chance to read books that they thought I ought to read, but if I did not like them I was then given some other good book that I did like. There were certain books that were taboo. For instance, I was not allowed to read dime novels. I obtained some surreptitiously and did read them, but I do not think

that the enjoyment compensated for the feeling of guilt. I was also forbidden to read the only one of Ouida's books which I wished to read—"Under Two Flags." I did read it, nevertheless, with greedy and fierce hope of coming on something unhealthy; but as a matter of fact all the parts that might have seemed unhealthy to an older person made no impression on me whatever. I simply enjoyed in a rather confused way the general adventures. ✳ ✳ ✳

**WHEN I WAS FOURTEEN YEARS OLD,** in the winter of '72 and '73, I visited Europe for the second time, and this trip formed a really useful part of my education. We went to Egypt, journeyed up the Nile, traveled through the Holy Land and part of Syria, visited Greece and Constantinople; and then we children spent the summer in a German family in Dresden. My first real collecting as a student of natural history was done in Egypt during this journey. By this time I had a good working knowledge of American bird life from the superficially scientific standpoint. I had no knowledge of the ornithology of Egypt, but I picked up in Cairo a book by an English clergyman, whose name I have now forgotten, who described a trip

up the Nile, and in an appendix to his volume gave an account of his bird collection. I wish I could remember the name of the author now, for I owe that book very much. Without it I should have been collecting entirely in the dark, whereas with its aid I could generally find out what the birds were. My first knowledge of Latin was obtained by learning the scientific names of the birds and mammals which I collected and classified by the aid of such books as this one.

The birds I obtained up the Nile and in Palestine represented merely the usual boy's collection. Some years afterward I gave them, together with the other ornithological specimens I had gathered, to the Smithsonian Institution in Washington, and I think some of them also to the American Museum of Natural History in New York. I am told that the skins are to be found yet in both places and in other public collections. I doubt whether they have my original labels on them. With great pride the directors of the "Roosevelt Museum," consisting of myself and the two cousins aforesaid, had printed a set of Roosevelt Museum labels in pink ink preliminary to what was regarded as my adventurous trip to Egypt.

*Roosevelt collected this* SPUR-WINGED LAPWING, EGYPTIAN PLOVER, AND WHITE-TAILED LAPWING *during the trip to Egypt in the winter of 1872–73 and presented them to the American Museum of Natural History in New York, c. 1882.*

ACCESSION RECORD *for Roosevelt's gift of mammal specimens to the National Museum (The Smithsonian) in Washington, D.C., May 26, 1882.*

This bird-collecting gave what was really the chief zest to my Nile journey. I was old enough and had read enough to enjoy the temples and the desert scenery and the general feeling of romance; but this in time would have palled if I had not also had the serious work of collecting and preparing my specimens. Doubtless the family had their moments of suffering—especially on one occasion when a well-meaning maid extracted from my taxidermist's outfit the old tooth-brush with which I put on the skins the arsenical soap necessary for their preservation, partially washed it, and left it with the rest of my wash kit for my own personal use. I suppose that all growing boys tend to be grubby; but the ornithological small boy, or indeed the boy with the taste for natural history of any kind, is generally the very grubbiest of all. An added element in my case was the fact that while in Egypt I suddenly started to grow. As there were no tailors up the Nile, when I got back to Cairo I needed a new outfit. But there was one suit of clothes too good to throw away, which we kept for a "change," and which was known as my "Smike suit," because it left my wrists and ankles as bare as those of poor Smike himself. ✶ ✶ ✶

**HERE, ROOSEVELT OFFERS MORE MEMORIES** of his father's influence on his values and goals. From Theodore Sr. he learned that hard and good work was paramount, whatever type of work it might be. While a life of pure science was not in the cards for Roosevelt, it remained an intense avocation throughout his life, even as his passion for politics took root.

I was a reasonably good student in college, standing just within the first tenth of my class, if I remember rightly; although I am not sure whether this means the tenth of the whole number that entered or of those that graduated. I was given a Phi Beta Kappa "key." My chief interests were scientific. When I entered college, I was devoted to out-of-doors natural history, and my ambition was to be a scientific man of the Audubon, or Wilson, or Baird, or Coues type—a man like Hart Merriam, or Frank Chapman, or Hornaday, to-day. My father had from the earliest days instilled into me the knowledge that I was

to work and to make my own way in the world, and I had always supposed that this meant that I must enter business. But in my freshman year (he died when I was a sophomore) he told me that if I wished to become a scientific man I could do so. He explained that I must be

> "I fully intended to make science my life-work. I did not, for the simple reason that at that time Harvard . . . utterly ignored the possibilities of the faunal naturalist, the outdoor naturalist and observer of nature."

sure that I really intensely desired to do scientific work, because if I went into it I must make it a serious career; that he had made enough money to enable me to take up such a career and do non-remunerative work of value if I intended to do the very best work there was in me; but that I must not dream of taking it up as a dilettante. He also gave me a piece of advice that I have always remembered, namely, that, if I was not going to earn money, I must even things up by not spending it. As he expressed it, I had to keep the fraction constant, and if I was not able to increase the numerator, then I must reduce the denominator. In other words, if I went into a scientific career, I must definitely abandon all thought of the enjoyment that could accompany a money-making career, and must find my pleasures elsewhere.

After this conversation I fully intended to make science my life-work. I did not, for the simple reason that at that time Harvard, and I suppose our other colleges, utterly ignored the possibilities of the faunal naturalist, the outdoor naturalist and observer of nature. They treated biology as purely a science of the laboratory and the microscope, a science whose adherents were to spend their time in the study of minute forms of marine life, or

# HARVARD COLLEGE.

### CERTIFICATE OF ADMISSION.

CAMBRIDGE, *July 3, 1876.*

*T. Roosevelt* is admitted to the FRESHMAN Class in Harvard College, but can become a candidate for a degree only on condition of passing a satisfactory examination in the studies named below.

*Chas L. Dunbar*
*Dean of the Faculty.*

The examination required above will be in

*Greek Poetry (no book),*
*Plane Trigonometry,*
*Botany.*

A student who has received an admission condition may obtain its removal, within the year after his entrance, by excellence of College work in the special subject in which he was conditioned. Conditions not so removed can be made up only at the beginning of some subsequent academic year, at the regular examination for admission, or at such special examinations as may be authorized by the Faculty.

**THEODORE ROOSEVELT'S ACCEPTANCE LETTER** *to Harvard University in 1876.*

---

## 1878-79.

# HARVARD COLLEGE.

By the regulations of the Faculty I am directed to print, at the end of each Academic Year, the names of all students who have attained seventy-five per cent of the maximum mark in any elective study, or seventy per cent in any prescribed study, and to send a copy of this publication to the father or other guardian of each student. A list of the members of the **Junior** CLASS of 1878-79 who attained these percentages in any study will be found on the following pages.

The studies pursued by *T. Roosevelt* in which he did not attain these percentages, will be found among those below with the percentage attained by him in each.

☞ His per cent on the work of the Junior year is *above* seventy. *Average 87+*

C. J. WHITE,
*Registrar of the Faculty.*

| | Per cent. | | Per cent. | | Per cent. | | Per cent. |
|---|---|---|---|---|---|---|---|
| SANSKRIT | | ENGLISH V. | | PHILOSOPHY I. | | PHYSICS (Post-Graduate) | |
| CLASSICS | | GERMAN I. | | PHILOSOPHY II. | | CHEMISTRY I. | |
| GREEK II. | | GERMAN II. | | PHILOSOPHY V. | | CHEMISTRY II. | |
| GREEK IV. | | GERMAN III. | | PHILOSOPHY VI. | | CHEMISTRY III. | |
| GREEK V. | | GERMAN IV. | | PHILOSOPHY VII. | 89 | CHEMISTRY IV. | |
| GREEK VI. | | GERMAN VI. | | PHILOSOPHY (Post-Grad.) | | NATURAL HISTORY I. | 92 |
| GREEK VII. | | GERMAN VII. | | *Logic* | | NATURAL HISTORY II. | |
| GREEK VIII. | | GERMAN VIII. | 82 | HISTORY II. | | NATURAL HISTORY III. | 97 |
| GREEK IX. | | FRENCH I. | | HISTORY III. | | NATURAL HISTORY IV. | |
| LATIN I. | | FRENCH II. | | HISTORY IV. | | NATURAL HISTORY VI. | |
| LATIN II. | | FRENCH III. | | HISTORY VI. | | NATURAL HISTORY VII. | |
| LATIN III. | | FRENCH IV. | | HISTORY VII. | | MUSIC I. | |
| LATIN IV. | | FRENCH VI. | | HISTORY (Post-Grad.) | | MUSIC II. | |
| LATIN V. | | ITALIAN I. | 82 | *Historical Sources* | | MUSIC III. | |
| LATIN VI. | | ITALIAN II. | | *Roman Law* | | MUSIC IV. | |
| LATIN VII. | | SPANISH I. | | MATHEMATICS I. | | FINE ARTS I. | |
| LATIN VIII. | | SPANISH II. | | MATHEMATICS V. | | FINE ARTS II. | |
| ENGLISH I. | | THEMES | 76 | MATHEMATICS VI. | | FINE ARTS III. | |
| ENGLISH II. | | FORENSICS | 66 | MATHEMATICS VII. | | | |
| ENGLISH III. | | PRESCRIBED LOGIC | 85 | PHYSICS I. | | | |
| ENGLISH IV. | | PRESC. METAPHYSICS | 87 | PHYSICS II. | | | |

*Roosevelt was* **ACTIVE IN MANY CLUBS AND SOCIETIES** *at Harvard, including the Alpha Delta Phi literary society, the Delta Kappa Epsilon fraternity, and the Porcellian Club.*

else in section-cutting and the study of the tissues of the higher organisms under the microscope. This attitude was, no doubt, in part due to the fact that in most colleges then there was a not always intelligent copying of what was done in the great German universities. The sound revolt against superficiality of study had been carried to an extreme; thoroughness in minutiæ as the only end of study had been erected into a fetish. There was a total failure to understand the great variety of kinds of work that could be done by naturalists, including what could be done by outdoor naturalists—the kind of work which Hart Merriam and his assistants in the Biological Survey have carried to such a high degree of perfection as regards North American mammals. In the entirely proper desire to be thorough and to avoid slipshod methods, the tendency was to treat as not serious, as unscientific, any kind of work that was not carried on with laborious minuteness in the laboratory. My taste was specialized in a totally different direction, and I had no more desire or ability to be a microscopist and section-cutter than to be a mathematician. Accordingly I abandoned all thought of becoming a scientist. Doubtless this meant that I really did not have the intense devotion to science which I thought I had; for, if I had possessed such devotion, I would have carved out a career for myself somehow without regard to discouragements.

As regards political economy, I was of course while in college taught the laissez-faire doctrines—one of them being free trade—then accepted as canonical. Most American boys of my age were taught both by their surroundings and by their studies certain principles which were very valuable from the standpoint of National interest, and certain others which were very much the reverse. The political economists were not especially to blame for this; it was the general attitude of the writers who wrote for us of that generation. Take my beloved *Our Young Folks*, the magazine which taught me much more than any of my text-books. Everything in this magazine instilled the individual virtues, and the necessity of character as the chief factor in any man's success—a teaching

in which I now believe as sincerely as ever, for all the laws that the wit of man can devise will never make a man a worthy citizen unless he has within himself the right stuff, unless he has self-reliance, energy, courage, the power of insisting on his own rights and the sympathy that makes him regardful of the rights of others. All this individual morality I was taught by the books I read at home and the books I studied at Harvard. But there was almost no teaching of the need for collective action, and of the fact that in addition to, not as a substitute for, individual responsibility, there is a collective responsibility. Books such as Herbert Croly's "Promise of American Life" and Walter E. Weyl's "New Democracy" would generally at that time have been treated either as unintelligible or else as pure heresy. ✶ ✶ ✶

"I NEVER WON ANYTHING WITHOUT HARD LABOR and the exercise of my best judgment and careful planning and working long in advance," insists Roosevelt in his autobiography. Excelling at that which comes easily is commendable, he admits, but excelling at that which is difficult is soul satisfying—and within the grasp of each of us.

There are two kinds of success, or rather two kinds of ability displayed in the achievement of success. There is, first, the success either in big things or small things which comes to the man who has in him the natural power to do what no one else can do, and what no amount of training, no perseverance or will power, will enable any ordinary man to do. This success, of course, like every other kind of success, may be on a very big scale or on a small scale. The quality which the man possesses may be that which enables him to run a hundred yards in nine and three-fifths seconds, or to play ten separate games of chess at the same time blindfolded, or to add five columns of figures at once without effort, or to write the "Ode to a Grecian Urn," or to deliver the Gettysburg speech, or to show the ability of Frederick at Leuthen or Nelson at Trafalgar. No amount of training of body or mind would enable any good ordinary man to perform any one of these feats. Of course the proper performance of each

## A WRITER IS BORN

While still an undergraduate, Roosevelt began work on what would become the first of 30 books he'd publish during his lifetime. *The Naval War of 1812* marked the beginning of his fascination with military strategy, and naval warfare in particular. His meticulously researched book, which included intricate drawings, charts, and analyses, still stands as a paragon in the genre, and helped establish him as a serious historian. The Department of the Navy placed a copy of it in the library of every ship in its fleet. Fifteen years after its 1882 publication, Roosevelt would become the Assistant Secretary (and, for a time, Acting Secretary) of the U.S. Navy.

ROOSEVELT *as a sophomore at Harvard, 1878.*

implies much previous study or training, but in no one of them is success to be attained save by the altogether exceptional man who has in him the something additional which the ordinary man does not have.

This is the most striking kind of success, and it can be attained only by the man who has in him the quality which separates him in kind no less than in degree from his fellows. But much the commoner type of success in every walk of life and in every species of effort is that which comes to the man who differs from his fellows not by the kind of quality which he possesses but by the degree of development which he has given that quality. This kind of success is open to a large number of persons, if only they seriously determine to achieve it. It is the kind of success which is open to the average man of sound body and fair mind, who has no remarkable mental or physical attributes, but who gets just as much as possible in the way of work out of the aptitudes that he does possess. It is the only kind of success that is open to most of us. Yet some of the greatest successes in history have been those of this second class—when I call it second class I am not running it down in the least, I am merely pointing out that it differs in kind from the first class. To the average man it is probably more useful to study this second type of success than to study the first. From the study of the first he can learn inspiration, he can get uplift and lofty enthusiasm. From the study of the second he can, if he chooses, find out how to win a similar success himself.

I need hardly say that all the successes I have ever won have been of the second type. I never won anything without hard labor and the exercise of my best judgment and careful planning and working long in advance. Having been a rather sickly and awkward boy, I was as a young man at first both nervous and distrustful of my own prowess. I had to train myself painfully and laboriously not merely as regards my body but as regards my soul and spirit.

Left to right: standing, John Ellis Roosevelt, his wife (Nannie Vance), Elliott Roosevelt. Seated on chairs: Corinne Roosevelt (later Mrs Douglas Robinson,) Anna Roosevelt (later Mrs William S. Cowles). Seated on step: Theodore Roosevelt, -------Iselin.

**TWO MORE EXCERPTS FROM AN AUTOBIOGRAPHY**, dealing with Roosevelt's early experiences in the legislature, offer a window into the formation of his life's calling as a leader. As he came to understand—and disdain—"practical politics," he resolved to perform his duties without regard to how his actions might affect his own career—and to step in vigorously wherever he felt he might make a difference.

# Practical Politics

Like most young men in politics, I went through various oscillations of feeling before I "found myself." At one period I became so impressed with the virtue of complete independence that I proceeded to act on each case purely as I personally viewed it, without paying any heed to the principles and prejudices of others. The result was that I speedily and deservedly lost all power of accomplishing anything at all; and I thereby learned the invaluable lesson that in the practical activities of life no man can render the highest service unless he can act in combination with his fellows, which means a certain amount of give-and-take between him and them. Again, I at one period began to believe that I had a future before me, and that it behooved me to be very far-sighted and scan each action carefully with a view to its possible effect on that future. This speedily made me useless to the public and an object of aversion to myself; and I then made up my mind that I would try not to think of the future at all, but would proceed on the assumption that each office I held would be the last I ever should hold, and that I would confine myself to trying to do my work as well as possible while I held that office. I found that for me personally this was the only way in which I could either enjoy myself or render good service to the country, and I never afterwards deviated from this plan. ✴ ✴ ✴

**THE SPEAKERSHIP CONTEST** enlightened me as regards more things than the attitude of the bosses. I had already had some exasperating experiences with the "silk stocking" reformer type, as Abraham Lincoln called it, the gentlemen who were very nice, very refined, who shook their heads over political corruption and discussed it in drawing-rooms and parlors, but who were wholly unable to grapple with real men in real life. They were apt vociferously to demand "reform" as if it were some concrete substance, like cake, which could be handed out at will, in tangible masses, if only the demand were urgent enough. These parlor reformers made up for inefficiency in action by zeal in criticising; and they delighted in criticising the men who really were doing the things which they said ought to be done, but which they lacked the sinewy power to do. They often upheld ideals which were not merely impossible but highly undesirable, and thereby played into the hands of the very politicians to whom they professed to be most hostile. Moreover, if they believed that their own interests, individually or as a class, were jeoparded, they were apt to show no higher standards than did the men they usually denounced.

One of their shibboleths was that the office should seek the man and not the man the office. This is entirely true of certain offices at certain times. It is entirely untrue when the circumstances are different. It would have been unnecessary and undesirable for Washington to have sought the Presidency. But if Abraham Lincoln had not sought the Presidency he never would have been nominated. The objection in such a case as this lies not to seeking the office, but to seeking it in any but an honorable and proper manner.

"Tranquillity", summer home at Oyster Bay of Mr and Mrs Theodore Roosevelt (1) 1872. Left to right: on the verandah, Mrs Roosevelt, Mr Roosevelt. On the lawn, Edith Kermit Carow (later Mrs Theodore Roosevelt 2), Corinne Roosevelt, (later Mrs Douglas Robinson).

The Plaza, New York, about 1875.

Above: Theodore Roosevelt.

Right: Alice Hathaway Lee, her cousin, and Theodore Roosevelt.

Below: Alice Hathaway Lee.

**SCRAPBOOK PAGE** *from the Roosevelt family photo albums. Top left:* **ROOSEVELT** *as an Assemblyman; top right:* **ALICE HATHAWAY LEE, HER COUSIN, AND THEODORE;** *bottom left:* **ALICE;** *bottom right:* **BABY ALICE LEE ROOSEVELT** *at one year, 1885.*

Alice Lee Roosevelt (later Mrs Nicholas Longworth) at one year; daughter of Theodore Roosevelt and Alice Hathaway Lee, born 1884.

**THE FOUR PASSAGES FROM HIS AUTOBIOGRAPHY** that follow reveal an aspect of Roosevelt's nature that is as key to understanding him as any study of his political accomplishments: his love of the West. Never is he more heartfelt or expressive in his writings than when describing his life "in cowboy land." It is a testament to his strong commitment to public service that he didn't follow through on his threat to leave politics altogether in favor of the ranching life. In fact, his experiences of frontier justice and mercy helped form his ideas about how to lead.

# In Cowboy Land

Though I had previously made a trip into the then Territory of Dakota, beyond the Red River, it was not until 1883 that I went to the Little Missouri, and there took hold of two cattle ranches, the Chimney Butte and the Elkhorn. It was still the Wild West in those days, the Far West, the West of Owen Wister's stories and Frederic Remington's drawings, the West of the Indian and the buffalo-hunter, the soldier and the cow-puncher. That land of the West has gone now, "gone, gone with lost Atlantis," gone to the isle of ghosts and of strange dead memories. It was a land of vast silent spaces, of lonely rivers, and of plains where the wild game stared at the passing horseman. It was a land of scattered ranches, of herds of long-horned cattle, and of reckless riders who unmoved looked in the eyes of life or of death. In that land we led a free and hardy life, with horse and with rifle. We worked under the scorching midsummer sun, when the wide plains shimmered and wavered in the heat; and we knew the freezing misery of riding night guard round the cattle in the late fall round-up. In the soft springtime the stars were glorious in our eyes each night before we fell asleep; and in the winter we rode through blinding blizzards, when the driven snow-dust burned our faces. There were monotonous days, as we guided the trail cattle or the beef herds, hour after hour, at the slowest of

**PRAIRIE AT THE EDGE OF THE BADLANDS**, *looking west to the Little Missouri.*

*opposite:* **THEODORE ROOSEVELT** *in a deer-skin hunting suit holding a rifle, photographed by George Grantham Bain, 1885.*

walks; and minutes or hours teeming with excitement as we stopped stampedes or swam the herds across rivers treacherous with quicksands or brimmed with running ice. We knew toil and hardship and hunger and thirst; and we saw men die violent deaths as they worked among the horses and cattle, or fought in evil feuds with one another; but we felt the beat of hardy life in our veins, and ours was the glory of work and the joy of living.

It was right and necessary that this life should pass, for the safety of our country lies in its being made the country of the small home-maker. The great unfenced ranches, in the days of "free grass," necessarily represented a temporary stage in our history. The large migratory flocks of sheep, each guarded by the hired shepherds of absentee owners, were the first enemies of the cattlemen; and owing to the way they ate out the grass and destroyed all other vegetation, these roving sheep bands represented little of permanent good to the country. But the homesteaders, the permanent settlers, the men who took up each his own farm on which he lived and brought up his family, these represented from the National standpoint the most desirable of all possible users of, and dwellers on, the soil. Their advent meant the breaking up of the big ranches; and the change was a National gain, although to some of us an individual loss. ✳ ✳ ✳

I OWE MORE THAN I can ever express to the West, which of course means to the men and women I met in the West. There were a few people of bad type in my neighborhood—that would be true of every group of men, even in a theological seminary—but I could not speak with too great affection and respect of the great majority of my friends, the hard-working men and women who dwelt for a space of perhaps a hundred and fifty miles along the Little Missouri. I was always as welcome at their houses as they were at mine. Everybody worked, everybody was willing to help everybody else, and yet nobody asked any favors. The same thing was true of the people whom I got to know fifty miles east and fifty miles west of my own range, and of the men I met on the round-ups. They soon

accepted me as a friend and fellow-worker who stood on an equal footing with them, and I believe the most of them have kept their feeling for me ever since. No guests were ever more welcome at the White House than these old friends of the cattle ranches and the cow camps—the men with whom I had ridden the long circle and eaten at the tail-board of a chuck-wagon—whenever they turned up at Washington during my Presidency. . . .

Not only did the men and women whom I met in the cow country quite unconsciously help me, by the insight which working and living with them enabled me to get into the mind and soul of the average American of the right type, but they helped me in another way. I made up my mind that the men were of just the kind whom it would be well to have with me if ever it became necessary to go to war. When the Spanish War came, I gave this thought practical realization.

Fortunately, Wister and Remington, with pen and pencil, have made these men live as long as our literature lives. I have sometimes been asked if Wister's "Virginian" is not overdrawn. . . . Half of the men I worked with or played with and half of the men who soldiered with me afterwards in my regiment might have walked out of Wister's stories or Remington's pictures. ✳ ✳ ✳

THERE WAS ONE BIT of frontier philosophy which I should like to see imitated in more advanced communities. Certain crimes of revolting baseness and cruelty were never forgiven. But in the case of ordinary offenses, the man who had served his term and who then tried to make good was given a fair chance; and of course this was equally true of the women. Every one who has studied the subject at all is only too well aware that the world offsets the readiness with which it condones a crime for which a man escapes punishment, by its unforgiving relentlessness to the often far less guilty man who is punished, and who therefore has made his atonement. On the frontier, if the man honestly tried to behave himself there was generally a disposition to give

THE COWBOY *by Frederic Remington, c. 1897.*

FOUR MEN ON HORSEBACK, *probably near Medora, North Dakota, photographed by Theodore Roosevelt.*

him fair play and a decent show. Several of the men I knew and whom I particularly liked came in this class. There was one such man in my regiment, a man who had served a term for robbery under arms, and who had atoned for it by many years of fine performance of duty. I put him in a high official position, and no man under me rendered better service to the State, nor was there any man whom, as soldier, as civil officer, as citizen, and as friend, I valued and respected—and now value and respect—more.

Now I suppose some good people will gather from this that I favor men who commit crimes. I certainly do not favor them. I have not a particle of sympathy with the sentimentality—as I deem it, the mawkishness—which overflows with foolish pity for the criminal and cares not at all for the victim of the criminal. I am glad to see wrong-doers punished. The punishment is an absolute necessity from the standpoint of society; and I put the reformation of the criminal second to the welfare of society. But I do desire to see the man or woman who has paid the penalty and who wishes to reform given a helping hand—surely every one of us who knows his own heart must know that he too may stumble, and should be anxious to help his brother or sister who has stumbled. When the criminal has been punished, if he then shows a sincere desire to lead a decent and upright life, he should be given the chance, he should be helped and not hindered; and if he makes good, he should receive that respect from others which so often aids in creating self-respect—the most invaluable of all possessions.

# TRAGEDY
# KNOCKS TWICE

Roosevelt's mother died on the same day as his first wife—February 14, 1884, making it possibly the worst Valentine's Day in U.S. history. He was so devastated by these twin tragedies that he placed a large, black X on that date in his personal diary and wrote, "the light has gone out of my life." After that, he abhorred the nickname Teddy, which had been given him by his late wife Alice, calling it "an outrageous impertinence."

*left:* **THEODORE ROOSEVELT'S LOVING LETTER** *to his wife Alice from Albany, New York, February, 5, 1884.*

*right:* **ROOSEVELT'S DIARY ENTRY** *for February 14, 1884, the day he lost both his wife and his mother.*

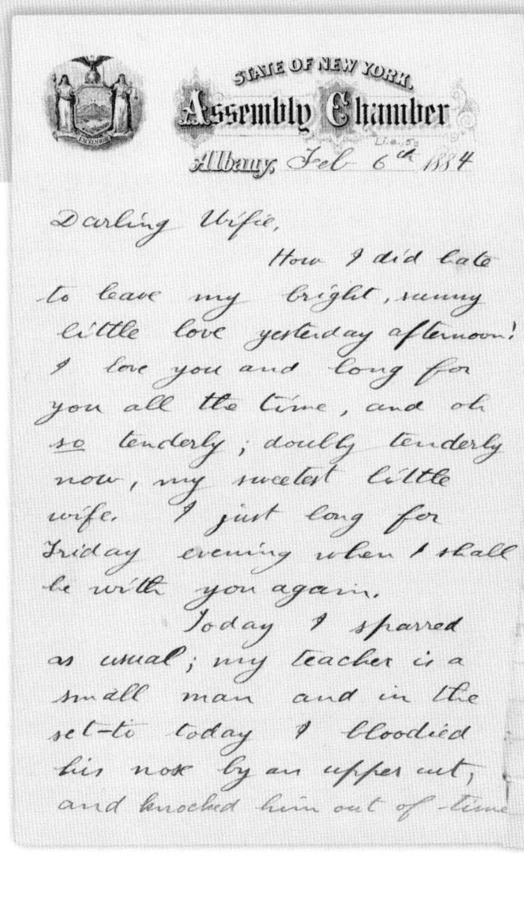

STATE OF NEW YORK.
**Assembly Chamber**
Albany, Feb 6th 1884

Darling Wife,

How I did late to leave my bright, sunny little love yesterday afternoon! I love you and long for you all the time, and oh so tenderly; doubly tenderly now, my sweetest little wife. I just long for Friday evening when I shall be with you again.

Today I sparred as usual; my teacher is a small man and in the set-to today I bloodied his nose by an upper cut, and knocked him out of time

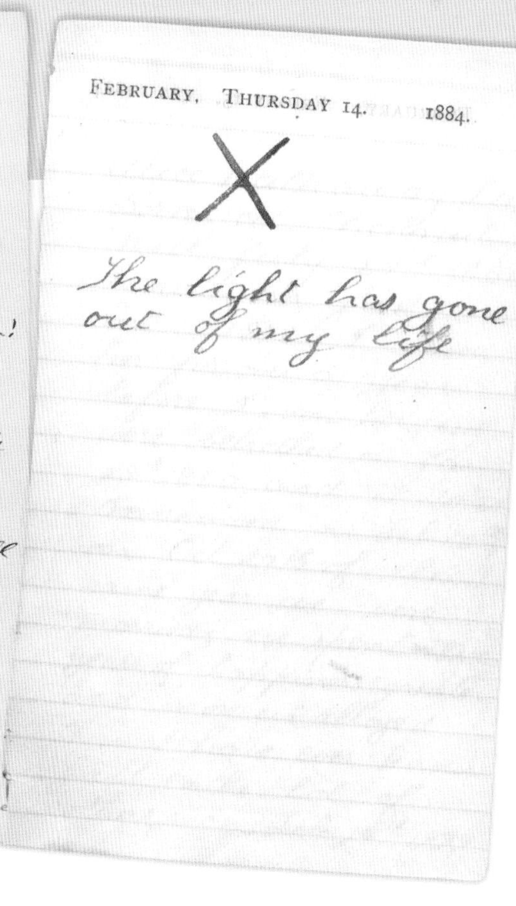

FEBRUARY, THURSDAY 14. 1884.

X

The light has gone out of my life

# 2.

# THE LURE OF
# THE WEST

BY JUNE 1885, the Oyster Bay house that Roosevelt and Alice had looked forward to living in was finished, but it must have felt empty to the silently grieving Roosevelt. His sister Anna took up residence there with his baby daughter, and Roosevelt paid them a two-month visit before heading west again. (He'd travel back and forth several more times that year.) The trip coincided with the publication of a new book born of his passion for the West: *Hunting Trips of a Ranchman.* For a brief period, it did seem possible that Roosevelt's political career was behind him.

In North Dakota, Roosevelt became a consummate cowboy (though he insisted on the modesty of his roping skills)—and a deputy sheriff. "I do not believe there ever was any life more attractive to a vigorous young fellow than life on a cattle ranch in those days," he wrote. One exploit from that period that biographers are as fond of relating as Roosevelt himself was is the story of his capture of three men who had stolen his boat. He contemplated hanging the thieves on the spot, but, in accordance with his better nature, opted to remain within the law and transport them to the nearest town where they could stand trial. This involved guarding them single-handedly for more than 40 hours. He read Tolstoy to keep himself awake, and when he'd exhausted his own library, dipped into a commercial western novel he found on one of his charges.

*overleaf:* **THEODORE ROOSEVELT** *on the round-up near Medora, North Dakota, in 1885.*

*opposite:* **GROUP OF BAD LANDS CITIZENS**, *thought to be taken near Medora, North Dakota, c. 1885.*

*left:* **ILLUSTRATIONS OF ROOSEVELT'S CATTLE BRANDS** *for both of his ranches, Chimney Butte and Elkhorn Ranch, c. 1884.*

On his September 1885 visit to his family in New York, he ran into a childhood sweetheart, Edith Carow, and by November, they were engaged (though they kept this news between them). Roosevelt soon returned to his ranch, but fate clearly had more in store for him than the life of a crime-fighting cowboy.

Whether it was Edith's siren song or other longings that drew him, Roosevelt allowed himself to be lured back into the political arena,

ELKHORN RANCH,
MEDORA, DAKOTA Sept 20th 1886

Darling Bamie,

On returning from the mountains I was savagely irritated by seeing in the papers the statement that I was engaged to Edith Carow; from what source it could have originated I can not possibly conceive.

But the statement itself is true. I am engaged to Edith and before Christmas I shall cross the ocean and marry her. You are the first person to whom I have breathed one word on the subject; I am absolutely sure that I have never betrayed myself in any way, unless some servant has seen the address on the letters I wrote. When as the Republican candidate for mayor of New York City. Alas, "the Cowboy of the Dakotas" was roundly defeated, coming in behind both Democrat Abram Hewitt and independent Labor candidate Henry George, respectively.

Immediately following the election, Roosevelt sailed to London and married Edith, taking her on an extended honeymoon in Europe, during which he somehow managed to find the time to summit Mont Blanc. The couple returned to New York in March of '87—to bad news about the ranch. The previous winter had been a punishing one, and Roosevelt had lost his entire herd of cattle. It proved to be a turning point. He threw in the towel on the ranching business (though he would return to his land for periodic hunting trips) and moved into the Oyster Bay mansion, dubbed Sagamore Hill, with Edith and Alice. It's unlikely that the ladies in his life shed many tears over the loss of Roosevelt's cattle concern. In September of 1887, his first son, Theodore Jr., was born.

Perhaps to carry a bit of his beloved wilderness to the city, Roosevelt founded the Boone and Crockett Club, dedicated to the hunting, study, and conservation of American big game. He remained its president until 1894, and the club is still active today. Between 1887 and '89, Roosevelt published five books, including biographies of the painter Thomas Hart Benton and American founding father Gouverneur Morris, another memoir of ranch life, and the first two volumes in his mammoth history, *The Winning of the West*. Another son, Kermit, came along in October 1889.

RK, SUNDAY, OCTOBER 31, 1886.     26 PAGES.

THE HEWITT MAYORALTY LOCOMOTIVE MOVING GRANDLY ON.

*A Very Simple Little Story of the Political Plains Plainly Told.*

*"The Hewitt Mayoralty Locomotive Moving Grandly On," October 31, 1886. This political cartoon depicts Democratic candidate, ABRAM HEWITT, as an unstoppable locomotive. Independent candidate, Henry George, blocks the track with his book, "How to Prevent Progress", while Republican candidate, Theodore Roosevelt, attempts to stop the Hewitt train with his lasso.*

*HUNTING TRIPS OF A RANCHMAN* (along with another book that grew out of his western experiences during the period, *The Wilderness Hunter*) features some of Roosevelt's most vivid and evocative writing. His tales of tracking a 1,200-pound grizzly bear through the pine forests of the Bighorn Mountains, as well as his asides on the flora and fauna of the Badlands and the simple pleasures of ranch life, have entered the realm of classic American folklore—and stand today as some of our most detailed records of that time and place. The excerpts from *Hunting Trips* that follow exemplify Roosevelt's eye for detail, his love of the landscape and its denizens, and his gift for storytelling.

# Ranching in the Bad Lands

The northern cattle plains occupy the basin of the Upper Missouri; that is, they occupy all of the land drained by the tributaries of that river, and by the river itself, before it takes its long trend to the southeast. They stretch from the rich wheat farms of Central Dakota to the Rocky Mountains, and southward to the Black Hills and the Big Horn chain, thus including all of Montana, Northern Wyoming, and extreme Western Dakota. The character of this rolling, broken, plains country is everywhere much the same. It is a high, nearly treeless region, of light rainfall, crossed by streams which are sometimes rapid torrents and sometimes merely strings of shallow pools. In places it stretches out into deserts of alkali and sage brush, or into nearly level prairies of short grass, extending for many miles without a break; elsewhere there are rolling hills, sometimes of

JOHNNY GOODALL *mounted on horseback and two unidentified men leaning against a wagon, probably near Medora, North Dakota, photographed by Theodore Roosevelt, c. 1880s.*

*above:* During a September 1883 buffalo hunting trip to the Badlands, Roosevelt became a partner in the MALTESE CROSS RANCH, *an open-range cattle operation shown here in an 1883 photo. The cabin was constructed from ponderosa pine logs that were brought to the building site by way of the Little Missouri River, and it featured three rooms: a kitchen, living room, and bedroom.*

*left:* THE MALTESE CROSS RANCH HOUSE, *shown here weathering a recent winter, has been preserved by the National Parks Service. Roosevelt once said, "I would not have been President, had it not been for my experience in North Dakota."*

considerable height; and in other places the ground is rent and broken into the most fantastic shapes, partly by volcanic action and partly by the action of water in a dry climate. These latter portions form the famous Bad Lands. Cotton-wood trees fringe the streams or stand in groves on the alluvial bottoms of the rivers; and some of the steep hills and canyon sides are clad with pines or stunted cedars. In the early spring, when the young blades first sprout, the land looks green and bright; but during the rest of the year there is no such appearance of freshness, for the short bunch grass is almost brown, and the gray-green sage bush, bitter and withered-looking, abounds everywhere, and gives a peculiarly barren aspect to the landscape.

It is but little over half a dozen years since these lands were won from the Indians. They were their only remaining great hunting-grounds, and towards the end of the last decade all of the northern plains tribes went on the war-path in a final desperate effort to preserve them. After bloody fighting and protracted campaigns they were defeated, and the country thrown open to the whites, while the building of the Northern Pacific Railroad gave immigration an immense impetus. There were great quantities of game, especially buffalo, and the hunters who thronged in to pursue the huge herds of the latter were the rough forerunners of civilization. No longer dreading the Indians, and having the railway on which to transport the robes, they followed the buffalo in season and out, until in 1883 the herds were practically destroyed. But meanwhile the cattle-men formed the vanguard of the white settlers. * * *

**IN THE NORTHERN COUNTRY** the ranches vary greatly in size; on some there may be but a few hundred head, on others ten times as many thousand. The land is still in great part unsurveyed, and is hardly anywhere fenced in, the cattle roaming over it at will. The small ranches are often quite close to one another, say within a couple of miles; but the home ranch of a big outfit will not have another building within ten or twenty miles of it, or, indeed, if the country is dry, not within fifty. The ranch-house may be only a mud dugout, or a "shack" made of logs stuck upright into the ground; more often it is a fair-sized, well-made building of hewn logs, divided into several rooms. Around it are grouped the other buildings—log-stables, cow-sheds, and hay-ricks, an out-house in which to store things, and on large ranches another house in which the cowboys sleep. The strongly made, circular horse-corral, with a snubbing-post in the middle, stands close by; the larger cow-corral, in which the stock is branded, may be some distance off. A small patch of ground is usually enclosed as a vegetable garden, and a very large one, with water in it, as a pasture to be used only in special cases. All the work is done on horseback, and the quantity of ponies is thus of necessity very great, some of the large outfits numbering them by hundreds; on my own ranch there are eighty. Most of them are small, wiry beasts, not very speedy, but with good bottom, and able to pick up a living under the most adverse circumstances. There are usually a few large, fine horses kept for the special use of the ranchman or foremen. The best are those from Oregon; most of them come from Texas, and many are bought from the Indians. They are broken in a very rough manner, and many are in consequence vicious brutes, with the detestable habit of bucking. . . .

The cattle rove free over the hills and prairies, picking up their own living even in winter, all the animals of each herd having certain distinctive brands on them. But little attempt is made to keep them within definite bounds, and they wander whither they wish, except that the ranchmen generally combine to keep some of their cowboys riding lines to prevent them straying away altogether. The missing ones are generally recovered in the annual round-ups, when the calves are branded. These round-ups, in which many outfits join together, and which cover hundreds of miles of territory, are the busiest period of the year for the stockmen, who then, with their cowboys, work from morning till night. In winter little is done except a certain amount of line riding. * * *

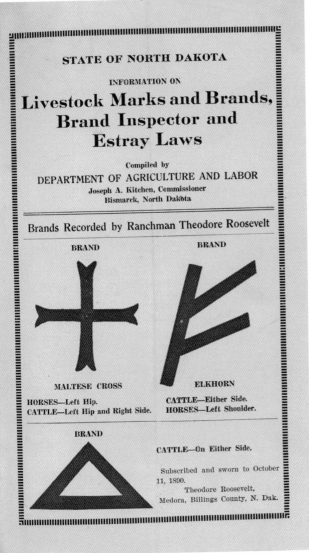

THEODORE ROOSEVELT'S CATTLE BRAND MARKS, *as recorded by the State of North Dakota Information on Livestock Marks and Brands, c. 1884.*

MY OWN RANCHES, the Elkhorn and the Chimney Butte, lie along the eastern border of the cattle country, where the Little Missouri flows through the heart of the Bad Lands. This, like most other plains rivers, has a broad, shallow bed, through which in times of freshets runs a muddy torrent, that neither man nor beast can pass; at other seasons of the year it is very shallow, spreading out into pools, between which the trickling water may be but a few inches deep. . . .

In spite of their look of savage desolation, the Bad Lands make a good cattle country, for there is plenty of nourishing grass and excellent shelter from the winter storms. The cattle keep close to them in the cold months, while in the summer time they wander out on the broad prairies stretching back of them, or come down to the river bottoms.

My home ranch-house stands on the river brink. From the low, long veranda, shaded by leafy cotton-woods, one looks across sand bars and shallows to a strip of meadowland, behind which rises a line of sheer cliffs and grassy plateaus. This veranda is a pleasant place in the summer evenings when a cool breeze stirs along the river and blows in the faces of the tired men, who loll back in their rocking-chairs (what true American does not enjoy a rocking-chair?), book in hand—though they do not often read the books, but rock gently to and fro, gazing sleepily out at the weird-looking buttes opposite, until their sharp outlines grow indistinct and purple in the after-glow of the sunset. The story-high house of hewn logs is clean and neat, with many rooms, so that one can be alone if one wishes to. The nights in summer are cool and pleasant, and there are plenty of bear-skins and buffalo robes, trophies of our own skill, with which to bid defiance to the bitter cold of winter. In summer time we are not much within doors, for we rise before dawn and work hard enough to be willing to go to bed soon after nightfall. The long winter evenings are spent sitting round the hearthstone, while the pine logs roar and crackle, and the men play checkers or chess, in the fire light. The rifles stand in the corners of the room or

A ROOSEVELT RANCH ROUND-UP *with two men on horses driving cattle near Medora, North Dakota, c. 1884.*

rest across the elk antlers which jut out from over the fireplace. From the deer horns ranged along the walls and thrust into the beams and rafters hang heavy overcoats of wolf-skin or coon-skin, and otter-fur or beaver-fur caps and gauntlets. Rough board shelves hold a number of books, without which some of the evenings would be long indeed. No ranchman who loves sport can afford to be without Van Dyke's "Still Hunter," Dodge's "Plains of the Great West," or Caton's "Deer and Antelope of America"; and Coues' "Birds of the Northwest" will be valued if he cares at all for natural history. A western

plainsman is reminded every day, by the names of the prominent landmarks among which he rides, that the country was known to men who spoke French long before any of his own kinsfolk came to it, and hence he reads with a double interest Parkman's histories of the early Canadians. As for Irving, Hawthorne, Cooper, Lowell, and the other standbys, I suppose no man, east or west, would willingly be long without them; while for lighter reading there are dreamy Ike Marvel, Burroughs' breezy

*overleaf:* THE LITTLE MISSOURI RIVER *near Elkhorn Ranch, c. 1919.*

above: ELKHORN RANCH HOUSE
with hunting "trophies" scattered
about, 1886.

right: UNTITLED (HIGH PRAIRIE,
SAGEBRUSH AND MOUNTAINS)
by Frederic Remington. Currently
in the collection of the Buffalo Bill
Historical Center in Cody,
Wyoming.

pages, and the quaint, pathetic character-sketches of the Southern writers—Cable, Cradock, Macon, Joel Chandler Harris, and sweet Sherwood Bonner. And when one is in the Bad Lands he feels as if they somehow look just exactly as Poe's tales and poems sound. ✴ ✴ ✴

> "This veranda is a pleasant place in the summer evenings when a cool breeze stirs along the river and blows in the faces of the tired men . . . until their sharp outlines grow indistinct and purple in the after-glow of the sunset."

**THE WOLF IS NOT VERY COMMON** with us; nothing like as plentiful as the little coyote. A few years ago both wolves and coyotes were very numerous on the plains, and as Indians and hunters rarely molested them, they were then very unsuspicious. But all this is changed now. When the cattle-men came in they soon perceived in the wolves their natural foes, and followed them unrelentingly. They shot at and chased them on all occasions, and killed great numbers by poisoning; and as a consequence the comparatively few that are left are as wary and cunning beasts as exist anywhere. ✴ ✴ ✴

**THE COUGAR IS HARDLY EVER SEEN** round my ranch; but toward the mountains it is very destructive both to horses and horned cattle. The ranchmen know it by the name of mountain lion; and it is the same beast that in the east is called panther or "painter." The cougar is the same size and build as the Old World leopard, and with very much the same habits. One will generally lie in wait for the heifers or young steers as they come down to water, and singling out an animal, reach it in a couple of bounds and fasten its fangs in the throat or neck. I have seen quite a large cow that had been killed by a cougar; and on another occasion, while out hunting over light snow, I came across a place where two bucks, while fighting, had been stalked up to by a cougar which pulled down one and tore him in pieces. The cougar's gait is silent and stealthy to an extraordinary degree; the look of the animal when creeping up to his prey has been wonderfully caught by the sculptor, Kemeys, in his bronzes: "The Still Hunt" and "The Silent Footfall."

I have never myself killed a cougar, though my brother shot one in Texas, while still-hunting some deer, which the cougar itself was after. It never attacks man, and even when hard pressed and wounded turns to bay with extreme reluctance, and at the first chance again seeks safety in flight. This was certainly not the case in old times, but the nature of the animal has been so changed by constant contact with rifle-bearing hunters, that timidity toward them has become a hereditary trait deeply engrained in its nature. When the continent was first settled, and for long afterward, the cougar was quite as dangerous an antagonist as the African or Indian leopard, and would even attack men unprovoked. ✴ ✴ ✴

**UNTIL RECENTLY** all sporting on the plains was confined to army officers, or to men of leisure who made extensive trips for no other purpose; leaving out of consideration the professional hunters, who trapped and shot for their livelihood. But with the incoming of the cattle-men, there grew up a class of residents, men with a stake in the welfare of the country, and with a regular business carried on in it, many of whom were keenly devoted to sport—a class whose members were in many respects closely akin to the old Southern planters. . . . Still, ranch life undoubtedly offers more chance to a man to get sport than is now the case with any other occupation in America, and those who follow it are apt to be men of game spirit, fond of excitement and adventure, who perforce lead an open-air life, who must needs ride well, for they are often in the saddle from sunrise to sunset, and who naturally take kindly to that noblest of weapons, the rifle. With such men hunting is one of the chief of pleasures; and they follow it eagerly when their work will allow them. And with some of them it is at times more than a pleasure. On many of the ranches—on my own, for instance—the supply of fresh meat depends mainly on the skill of the riflemen, and so, both for pleasure and profit, most ranchmen do a certain amount of hunting each season. The buffalo are now gone forever, and the elk are rapidly sharing their fate; but antelope and deer are still quite plenty, and will remain so for some years; and these are the common game of the plainsman. Nor is it likely that the game will disappear much before ranch life itself is a thing of the past. It is a phase of American life as fascinating as it is evanescent, and one well deserving an historian. ✶ ✶ ✶

THE OLD HUNTERS were a class by themselves. They penetrated, alone or in small parties, to the farthest and wildest haunts of the animals they followed, leading a solitary, lonely life, often never seeing a white face for months and even years together. They were skilful shots, and were cool, daring, and resolute to the verge of recklessness. On any thing like even terms they very greatly overmatched the Indians by whom they were surrounded, and with whom they waged constant and ferocious war. In the government expeditions against the plains tribes they were of absolutely invaluable assistance as scouts. They rarely had regular wives or white children, and there are none to take their places, now that the greater part of them have gone. For the men who carry on hunting as a business where it is perfectly safe have all the vices of their prototypes, but, not having to face the dangers that beset the latter, so neither need nor possess the stern, rough virtues that were required in order to meet and overcome them. The ranks of the skin-hunters and meat-hunters contain some good men; but as a rule they are a most unlovely race of beings, not excelling even in the pursuit which they follow because they are too shiftless to do any thing else; and the sooner they vanish the better.

# A Trip on the Prairie

The antelope is a queer-looking rather than a beautiful animal. The curious pronged horns, great bulging eyes, and strange bridle-like marks and bands on the face and throat are more striking, but less handsome, than the delicate head and branching antlers of a deer; and it entirely lacks the latter animal's grace of movement. In its form and look, when standing still, it is rather angular and goat-like, and its movements merely have the charm that comes from lightness, speed, and agility. Its gait is singularly regular and even, without any of the bounding, rolling movement of a deer; and it is, consequently, very easy to hit running, compared with other kinds of game.

Antelope possess a most morbid curiosity. The appearance of any thing out of the way, or to which they are not accustomed, often seems to drive them nearly beside themselves with mingled fright and desire to know what it is, a combination of feelings that throws them into a perfect panic, during whose continuance they will at times seem utterly unable to take care of themselves. In very remote, wild places, to which no white man often penetrates, the appearance of a white-topped wagon will be enough to excite this feeling in the pronghorn, and in such cases it is not unusual for a herd to come up and circle round the strange object heedless of rifle-shots. . . .

No other kind of plains game, except the big-horn, is as shy and sharp-sighted as the antelope; and both its own habits and the open nature of the ground on which it is found render it peculiarly difficult to stalk.

*top:* THEODORE ROOSEVELT'S BOOT SPURS. *The top spur features the Maltese Cross and the bottom spur features the Elkhorn Ranch symbol.*

*bottom:* RIFLE, SHOT-GUN, AND SIX-SHOOTER *used by Roosevelt during his ranch days, c. 1884.*

BUFFALO ON THE PLAINS *by Albert Bierstadt, c. 1890.*

# The Lordly Buffalo

Gone forever are the mighty herds of the lordly buffalo. A few solitary individuals and small bands are still to be found scattered here and there in the wilder parts of the plains; and though most of these will be very soon destroyed, others will for some years fight off their doom and lead a precarious existence either in remote and almost desert portions of the country near the Mexican frontier, or else in the wildest and most inaccessible fastnesses of the Rocky Mountains; but the great herds, that for the first three quarters of this century formed the distinguishing and characteristic feature of the Western plains, have vanished forever.

It is only about a hundred years ago that the white man, in his march westward, first encroached upon the lands of the buffalo, for these animals had never penetrated in any number to the Appalachian chain of mountains. Indeed, it was after the beginning of the century before the inroads of the whites upon them grew at all serious. Then, though constancy driven westward, the diminution in their territory, if sure, was at least slow, although growing progressively more rapid. Less than a score of years ago the great herds, containing many millions of individuals, ranged over a vast expanse of country that stretched in an unbroken line from near Mexico to far into British America; in fact, over almost all the plains that are now known as the cattle region. But since that time their destruction has gone on with appalling rapidity and thoroughness; and the main factors in bringing it about have been the railroads, which carried hordes of hunters into the land and gave them means to transport their spoils to market. Not quite twenty years since, the range was broken in two, and the buffalo herds in the middle slaughtered or thrust aside; and thus there resulted two ranges, the northern and the southern. The latter was the larger, but being more open to the hunters, was the sooner to be depopulated; and the last of the great southern herds was destroyed in 1878, though scattered bands escaped and wandered into the desolate wastes to the southwest. Meanwhile equally savage war was waged on the northern herds, and five years later the last of these was also destroyed or broken up. The bulk of this slaughter was done in the dozen years from 1872 to 1883; never before in all history were so many large wild animals of one species slain in so short a space of time.

The extermination of the buffalo has been a veritable tragedy of the animal world. Other races of animals have been destroyed within historic times, but these have been species of small size, local distribution, and limited numbers, usually found in some particular island or group of islands; while the huge buffalo, in countless myriads, ranged over the greater part of a continent. Its nearest relative, the Old World aurochs, formerly found all through the forests of Europe, is almost as near the verge of extinction, but with the latter the process has been slow, and has extended over a period of a thousand years, instead of being compressed into a dozen. The destruction of the various larger species of South African game is much more local, and is proceeding at a much slower rate. It may truthfully be said that the sudden and complete extermination of the vast herds of the buffalo is without a parallel in historic times.

> "The extermination of the buffalo has been a veritable tragedy of the animal world."

No sight is more common on the plains than that of a bleached buffalo skull; and their countless numbers attest the abundance of the animal at a time not so very long past. On those portions where the herds made their last stand, the carcasses, dried in the clear, high air, or the mouldering skeletons, abound. . . .

The most striking characteristics of the buffalo, and those which had been found most useful in maintaining the species until the white man entered upon the scene, were

its phenomenal gregariousness—surpassed by no other four-footed beast, and only equalled, if equalled at all, by one or two kinds of South African antelope—its massive bulk, and unwieldy strength. The fact that it was a plains and not a forest or mountain animal was at that time also greatly in its favor. Its toughness and hardy endurance fitted it to contend with purely natural forces: to resist cold and the winter blasts, or the heat of a thirsty summer, to wander away to new pastures when the feed on the old was exhausted, to plunge over broken ground, and to plough its way through snow-drifts or quagmires. But one beast of prey existed sufficiently powerful to conquer it when full grown and in health; and this, the grizzly bear, could only be considered an occasional foe. The Indians were its most dangerous enemies, but they were without horses, and their weapons, bows and arrows, were only available at close range; so that a slight degree of speed enabled buffalo to get out of the way of their human foes when discovered, and on the open plains a moderate development of the senses was sufficient to warn them of the approach of the latter before they had come up to the very close distance required for their primitive weapons to take effect. Thus the strength, size, and gregarious habits of the brute were sufficient for a protection against most foes; and a slight degree of speed and moderate development of the senses served as adequate guards against the grizzlies and bow-bearing foot Indians. Concealment and the habit of seeking lonely and remote places for a dwelling would have been of no service.

WILMOT DOW, WILLIAM SEWALL, AND MR. TOMPKINS *with an elk carcass in a wagon, probably near Medora, North Dakota, c. 1885.*

## Still-Hunting Elk on the Mountains

After the buffalo the elk are the first animals to disappear from a country when it is settled. This arises from their size and consequent conspicuousness, and the eagerness with which they are followed by hunters; and also because of their gregariousness and their occasional fits of stupid panic during whose continuance hunters can now and then work great slaughter in a herd. Five years ago elk were abundant in the valley of the Little Missouri, and in fall were found wandering in great bands of over a hundred individuals each. But they have now vanished completely, except that one or two may still lurk in some of the most remote and broken places, where there are deep, wooded ravines.

Formerly the elk were plentiful all over the plains, coming down into them in great bands during the fall months and traversing their entire extent. But the incoming of hunters and cattle-men has driven them off the ground as completely as the buffalo; unlike the latter, however, they are still very common in the dense woods that cover the Rocky Mountains and the other great western chains. In the old days running elk on horseback was a highly esteemed form of plains sport; but now that it has become a beast of the timber and the craggy ground, instead of a beast of the open, level prairie, it is followed almost solely on foot and with the rifle. Its sense of smell is very acute, and it has good eyes and quick ears; and its wariness makes it under ordinary circumstances very difficult to approach. But it is subject to fits of panic folly, and during their continuance great numbers can be destroyed. A band places almost as much reliance upon the leaders as does a flock of sheep; and if the leaders are shot down, the others will huddle together in a terrified mass, seemingly unable to make up their minds in which direction to flee. When one, more bold than the rest, does at last step out, the hidden hunter's at once shooting it down will produce a fresh panic; I have known of twenty elk (or wapiti, as they are occasionally called) being thus procured out of one band. And at times they show a curious indifference to danger, running up on a hunter who is in plain sight, or standing still for a few fatal seconds to gaze at one that unexpectedly appears. In spite of its size and strength and great branching antlers, the elk is but little more dangerous to the hunter than is an ordinary buck. . . .

The elk is unfortunately one of those animals seemingly doomed to total destruction at no distant date. Already its range has shrunk to far less than one half its former size. . . .

The gradual extermination of this, the most stately and beautiful animal of the chase to be found in America, can be looked upon only with unmixed regret by every sportsman and lover of nature. Excepting the moose, it is the largest and, without exception, it is the noblest of the deer tribe. No other species of true deer, in either the Old or the New World, comes up to it in size and in the shape, length, and weight of its mighty antlers; while the grand, proud carriage and lordly bearing of an old bull make it perhaps the most majestic-looking of all the animal creation. The open plains have already lost one of their great attractions, now that we no more see the long lines of elk trotting across them; and it will be a sad day when the lordly, antlered beasts are no longer found in the wild rocky glens and among the lonely woods of towering pines that cover the great western mountain chains.

## Old Ephraim

But few bears are found in the immediate neighborhood of my ranch; and though I have once or twice seen their tracks in the Bad Lands, I have never had any experience with the animals themselves except during the elk-hunting trip on the Bighorn Mountains. . . .

The grizzly bear undoubtedly comes in the category of dangerous game, and is, perhaps, the only animal in the United States that can be fairly so placed, unless we

count the few jaguars found north of the Rio Grande. But the danger of hunting the grizzly has been greatly exaggerated, and the sport is certainly very much safer than it was at the beginning of this century. The first hunters who came into contact with this great bear were men belonging to that hardy and adventurous class of backwoodsmen which had filled the wild country between the Appalachian Mountains and the Mississippi. These men carried but one weapon: the long-barrelled, small-bored pea-rifle, whose bullets ran seventy to the pound, the amount of powder and lead being a little less than that contained in the cartridge of a thirty-two calibre Winchester. In the Eastern States almost all the hunting was done in the woodland; the shots were mostly obtained at short distance, and deer and black bear were the largest game; moreover, the pea-rifles were marvellously accurate for close range, and their owners were famed the world over for their skill as marksmen. Thus these rifles had so far proved plenty good enough for the work they had to do, and indeed had done excellent service as military weapons in the ferocious wars that the men of the border carried on with their Indian neighbors, and even in conflict with more civilized foes, as at the battles of King's Mountain and New Orleans. But when the restless frontiersmen pressed out over the Western plains, they encountered in the grizzly a beast of far greater bulk and more savage temper than any of those found in the Eastern woods, and their small-bore rifles were utterly inadequate weapons with which to cope with him. . . . No grizzly will assail a man now unprovoked, and one will almost always rather run than fight; though if he is wounded or thinks himself cornered he will attack his foes with a headlong, reckless fury that renders him one of the most dangerous of wild beasts. The ferocity of all wild animals depends largely upon the amount of resistance they are accustomed to meet with, and the quantity of molestation to which they are subjected.

*View of the* LITTLE MISSOURI RIVER *at Elkhorn Ranch, near Medora, North Dakota, c. 1919.*

# CRUSADER AND REFORMER

ONCE BACK EAST, Roosevelt was not about to let his defeat in the New York City mayoral race deter him from playing his part in history, nor was he one to rest on his literary laurels or his family wealth. Before the year 1887 was out, he had rented a house in Washington, D.C., and was soon joined by his wife and children.

The couple plunged themselves into Washington's social whirl, and were soon entertaining the likes of Henry Cabot Lodge (already a friend and political ally), John Hay, House Speaker Thomas Reed, and Henry Adams. President Harrison, for whom Roosevelt had campaigned, reciprocated by appointing him to the U.S. Civil Service Commission, a post he would hold until 1895. Not surprisingly, he took an active role in attempting to reform that body, calling for the dismissal of office holders he believed to be corrupt. Such was the force of his righteous zeal that his friend and first biographer, Joseph Bucklin Bishop, characterized him as "a bull in a china shop." What's most interesting about Roosevelt's tenure as a crusading Commissioner is that Harrison's successor, Grover Cleveland—a Democrat that Roosevelt had helped Harrison campaign against—reappointed him to the same post. It is difficult to imagine such a thing happening today, under any circumstances.

*overleaf:* ITALIAN IMMIGRANT FAMILIES *in New York on Jersey Street, living in shacks, photographed by Jacob Riis, 1897.*

*opposite:* ASSISTANT SECRETARY OF THE NAVY THEODORE ROOSEVELT *writing at his desk, c. 1897–98, Washington, D.C.*

*left: "We are not a nation of swindlers." This* POLITICAL CARTOON, *published in Puck on October 21, 1896, features a group of men that includes Grover Cleveland, Benjamin Harrison, and William McKinley in the foreground, with McKinley holding up flag that says "The national honor must be upheld!"*

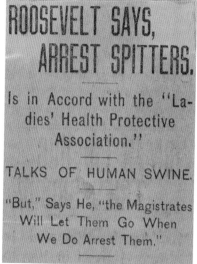

WHILE SERVING AS CIVIL SERVICE COMMISSIONER *in the early 1890s, Theodore Roosevelt lived with his family in this residence at 1215 19th St. N.W., in Washington, D.C.*

*This* 1895 NEWS CLIPPING *shows that no matter was too small for his concern as Police Commissioner in New York City.*

*opposite:* SCRAPBOOK PAGE *from the Roosevelt family albums.*

Lest you think Roosevelt was neglecting his literary interests as his political career took shape, note that while he served as Commissioner, he published *History of the City of New York*, *The Wilderness Hunter*, and the third volume of *The Winning of the West*. Roosevelt continued to build his family, as well. Edith gave birth to a daughter, Ethel Carow Roosevelt, in 1891, and two sons, Archibald Bulloch Roosevelt in 1894 and Quentin Roosevelt in 1897.

In 1895, Roosevelt was appointed to the New York City Police Commission by William Strong, the city's reform-minded Republican mayor—and, as usual, Roosevelt vaulted to the top spot when he was elected president of the four-member body. In his brief two-year stint as top cop, Roosevelt attacked the rampant corruption and inefficiency in the department with his usual vigor, establishing new forms of oversight as well as a police bicycle squad to help alleviate growing traffic problems. Firearms inspections and annual physicals for police officers became the new order of the day, telephones were installed in station houses, and 1,600 new recruits were appointed based on their fitness for the job rather than their political connections or leanings.

Always a hands-on manager, Roosevelt was fond of roaming the city at night, checking on the officers walking their beats. While the law-abiding public must have been pleased to find their city becoming safer, one of

Roosevelt's crusades made him more enemies than friends, particularly among the traditionally Republican German-American community: the strict enforcement of the law that kept saloons closed on Sundays.

Perhaps as a respite from his often-frustrating work with the police department, Roosevelt collaborated with his friend, Congressman Henry Cabot Lodge, on a book for children called *Hero Tales from American History*. The fourth and final volume of *The Winning of the West* came out during his last year in the post, 1896.

Roosevelt spent much of the fall of that year on a seven-state campaign swing on behalf of William McKinley, who defeated the 36-year-old William Jennings Bryan by 600,000 votes (and more than 60 percent of the electoral vote) in the November 3rd presidential election. In return, and at the urging of Congressman Lodge, McKinley appointed Roosevelt as Assistant Secretary of the Navy—a post he was well qualified for and eager to take on, by virtue of his avid lifelong interest in maritime affairs. (Remember that he'd literally "written the book" on naval warfare while still a Harvard undergraduate.)

As usual, Roosevelt was soon functionally in charge. In an article published in *The Bookman* in June of 1897, Roosevelt wrote, "No triumph of peace can equal the armed triumph over malice domestic or foreign levy. No qualities called out by a purely peaceful life can stand on a level with those stern and virile virtues which move the men of stout heart and strong hand who uphold the honor of their flag in battle. It is better for a nation to produce one [General Ulysses S.] Grant or one [Admiral David] Farragut than a thousand shrewd manufacturers or successful speculators." Quite the "hawk" and eager to test the troops in battle, he advocated for the rapid expansion of the Navy and for war with Spain, declaring, "It is through strife, or the readiness for strife, that a nation must win greatness."

When the battleship *Maine* was destroyed in Havana harbor, it became clear that he would get the war he yearned for; by April of '98, the official declaration was made and the Spanish–American War was on. Having done his part to prepare the military, Roosevelt resigned his post in order to take a more hands-on role in the effort.

## A MAN OF MANY OFFICES

Here is the astonishing list of offices held by Theodore Roosevelt—all by the age of 42.

| | |
|---|---|
| 1882–84 | New York State Assemblyman |
| 1889–95 | Civil Service Commissioner |
| 1895–96 | New York City Police Commissioner/ President of the Commission |
| 1897–98 | Assistant/Acting Secretary of the Navy |
| 1898 | Deputy/ Regimental Commander of the First U.S. Volunteer Cavalry |
| 1898–1900 | Governor of New York |
| 1901 | Vice President of the United States |
| 1901–03 | Became President of the United States |
| 1904–08 | Elected President in his own right |

**THEODORE ROOSEVELT**, *Civil Service Commissioner, 1889.*

IN THE THREE EXCERPTS from Roosevelt's autobiography that follow, he ruminates on the six years he served as Civil Service Commissioner. It was in this role that he solidified his commitment to "stand with every one while he was right, and to stand against him when he went wrong," no matter the personal political consequences. More important, by the time he ended his service to the Commission, he had come to believe that "mere improvement in political conditions by itself was not enough. . . . [A]n even greater fight must be waged to improve economic conditions, and to secure social and industrial justice, justice as between individuals and justice as between classes." To truly lead, he discovered, it was not enough to be a crusader—one had to be an active reformer as well.

# Applied Idealism

I served six years as Civil Service Commissioner—four years under President Harrison and then two years under President Cleveland. I was treated by both Presidents with the utmost consideration. Among my fellow-Commissioners there was at one time ex-Governor Hugh Thompson, of South Carolina, and at another time John R. Proctor, of Kentucky. They were Democrats and ex-Confederate soldiers. I became deeply attached to both, and we stood shoulder to shoulder in every contest in which the Commission was forced to take part.

Civil Service Reform had two sides. There was, first, the effort to secure a more efficient administration of the public service, and, second, the even more important effort to withdraw the administrative offices of the Government from the domain of spoils politics, and thereby cut out of American political life a fruitful source of corruption and degradation. The spoils theory of politics is that public office is so much plunder which the victorious political party is entitled to appropriate to the use of its adherents . . . . Civil Service Reform is designed primarily to give the average American citizen a fair chance in politics, to give to this citizen the same weight in politics that the "ward heeler" has.

Patronage does not really help a party. It helps the bosses to get control of the machinery of the party—as in 1912 was true of the Republican party—but it does not help the party. On the average, the most sweeping party victories in our history have been won when the patronage was against the victors. All that the patronage does is to help the worst element in the party retain control of the party organization. Two of the evil elements in our Government against which good citizens have to contend are, 1, the lack of continuous activity on the part of these good citizens themselves, and, 2, the ever-present activity of those who have only an evil self-interest in political life. It is difficult to interest the average citizen in any particular movement to the degree of getting him to take an efficient part in it. He wishes the movement well, but he will not, or often cannot, take the time and the trouble to serve it efficiently; and this whether he happens to be a mechanic or a banker, a telegraph operator or a storekeeper. He has his own interests, his own business, and it is difficult for him to spare the time to go around to the primaries, to see to the organization, to see to getting out the vote—in short, to attend to all the thousand details of political management.

On the other hand, the spoils system breeds a class of men whose financial interest it is to take this necessary time and trouble. They are paid for so doing, and they are paid out of the public chest. Under the spoils system a man is appointed to an ordinary clerical or ministerial position in the municipal, Federal, or State

PORTRAIT OF THEODORE ROOSEVELT *as a member of the U.S. Civil Service Commission, c. 1889–95.*

government, not primarily because he is expected to be a good servant, but because he has rendered help to some big boss or to the henchman of some big boss. His stay in office depends not upon how he performs service, but upon how he retains his influence in the party. This necessarily means that his attention to the interests of the public at large, even though real, is secondary to his devotion to his organization, or to the interest of the ward leader who put him in his place. So he and his fellows attend to politics, not once a year, not two or three times a year, like the average citizen, but every day in the year. It is the one thing that they talk of, for it is their bread and butter. They plan about it and they scheme about it. They do it because it is their business. I do not blame them in the least. I blame us, the people, for we ought to make it clear as a bell that the business of serving the people in one of the ordinary ministerial Government positions, which have nothing to do with deciding the policy of the Government, should have no necessary connection with the management of primaries, of caucuses, and of nominating conventions. As a result of our wrong thinking and supineness, we American citizens tend to breed a mass of men whose interests in governmental matters are often adverse to ours, who are thoroughly drilled, thoroughly organized, who make their livelihood out of politics, and who frequently make their livelihood out of bad politics. They know every little twist and turn, no matter how intricate, in the politics of their several wards, and when election day comes the ordinary citizen who has merely the interest that all good men, all decent citizens, should have in political life, finds himself as helpless before these men as if he were a solitary volunteer in the presence of a band of drilled mercenaries on a field of battle. There are a couple of hundred thousand Federal offices, not to speak of State and municipal offices. The men who fill these offices, and the men who wish to fill them, within and without the dominant party for the time being, make a regular army, whose interest it is that the system of bread-and-butter politics shall continue. Against their concrete interest we have merely the generally unorganized sentiment of the community in favor of putting things on a decent basis. The large number of men who believe vaguely in good are pitted against the smaller but still larger number of men whose interest it often becomes to act very concretely and actively for evil; and it is small wonder that the struggle is doubtful. ✳ ✳ ✳

"Under no system will it be possible to do away with all favoritism and brutality and meanness and malice. But at least we can try to minimize the exhibition of these qualities."

YET AGAIN EVEN THE BOSS who really is evil, like the business man who really is evil, may on certain points be sound, and be doing good work. It may be the highest duty of the patriotic public servant to work with the big boss or the big business man on these points, while refusing to work with him on others. In the same way there are many self-styled reformers whose conduct is such as to warrant Tom Reed's bitter remark, that when Dr. Johnson defined patriotism as the last refuge of a scoundrel he was ignorant of the infinite possibilities contained in the word reform. Yet, none the less, it is our duty to work for the reforms these men champion, without regard to the misconduct of the men themselves on other points. I have known in my life many big business men and many big political bosses who often or even generally did evil, but who on some occasions and on certain issues were right. I never hesitated to do battle against these men when they were wrong; and, on the other hand, as long as they were going my way I was glad to have them do so. To have repudiated their aid when they were right and were striving for a right end, and for what was of benefit to the people—no matter what their motives may have been—would have been childish, and moreover would have itself been misconduct against the people.

My duty was to stand with every one while he was right, and to stand against him when he went wrong; and this I have tried to do as regards individuals and as regards groups of individuals. When a business man or labor leader, politician or reformer, is right, I support him; when he goes wrong, I leave him. When Mr. Lorimer upheld the war for the liberation of Cuba, I supported him; when he became United States Senator by improper methods, I opposed him. The principles or methods which the Socialists advocate and which I believe to be in the interest of the people I support, and those which I believe to be against the interest of the people I oppose. Moreover, when a man has done evil, but changes, and works for decency and righteousness, and when, as far as I can see, the change is real and the man's conduct sincere, then I welcome him and work heartily with him, as an equal with an equal. For thirty years after the Civil War the creed of mere materialism was rampant in both American politics and American business, and many, many strong men, in accordance with the prevailing commercial and political morality, did things for which they deserve blame and condemnation; but if they now sincerely change, and strive for better things, it is unwise and unjust to bar them from fellowship. . . .

Every man who has been in practical politics grows to realize that politicians, big and little, are no more all of them bad than they are all of them good. Many of these men are very bad men indeed, but there are others among them—and some among those held up to special obloquy, too—who, even although they may have done much that is evil, also show traits of sterling worth which many of their critics wholly lack. There are few men for whom I have ever felt a more cordial and contemptuous dislike than for some of the bosses and big professional politicians with whom I have been brought into contact. On the other hand, in the case of some political leaders who were most bitterly attacked as bosses, I grew to know certain sides of their characters which inspired in me a very genuine regard and respect. ✳ ✳ ✳

COMMISSIONERS:
CHARLES LYMAN, *President,*
THEODORE ROOSEVELT,
HUGH S. THOMPSON.

WM. H. WEBSTER, *Chief Examiner.*
JOHN T. DOYLE, *Secretary.*

**United States**
**Civil Service Commission,**
**Washington, D. C.**

Febye 11ᵗʰ '90

Blessed Ted-pod, I send you
a *picture letter* because you
are not old enough yet to
read writing. Will you be glad
to see your papa when he
comes back? Do you want
to go and play in the
barn with him? and go in
swimming on the beach when
it is warm?

Your loving
Father

*A pony and a cow go out to see the world*

*They meet    bear and are much frightened*

*He chases them back just as hard as they can run*

*and when they get home in safety they make up their minds they will never run away again.*

WHEN AWAY FROM HIS CHILDREN, *Roosevelt often sent them letters containing stories that he illustrated himself. In this July 11, 1890, letter to Teddy Jr. (written on U.S. Civil Service Commission letterhead), Roosevelt tells a story of a pony and a cow who "go out to see the world." The pair does not make it far, however, because they are frightened by a bear, which prompts them to return home.*

BY THE TIME that I was ending my career as Civil Service Commissioner I was already growing to understand that mere improvement in political conditions by itself was not enough. I dimly realized that an even greater fight must be waged to improve economic conditions, and to secure social and industrial justice, justice as between individuals and justice as between classes. I began to see that political effort was largely valuable as it found expression and resulted in such social and industrial betterment. I was gradually puzzling out, or trying to puzzle out, the answers to various questions—some as yet unsolvable to any of us, but for the solution of which it is the bounden duty of all of us to work. I had grown to realize very keenly that the duty of the Government to protect women and children must be extended to include the protection of all the crushable elements of labor. I saw that it was the affair of all our people to see that justice obtained between the big corporation and its employees, and between the big corporation and its smaller rivals, as well as its customers and the general public. I saw that it was the affair of all of us, and not only of the employer, if dividends went up and wages went down; that it was to the interest of all of us that a full share of the benefit of improved machinery should go to the workman who used the machinery; and also that it was to the interest of all of us that each man, whether brain worker or hand worker, should do the best work of which he was capable, and that there should be some correspondence between the value of the work and the value of the reward. It is these and many similar questions which in their sum make up the great social and industrial problems of to-day, the most interesting and important of the problems with which our public life must deal. . . .

The selfish individual needs to be taught that we must now shackle cunning by law exactly as a few centuries back we shackled force by law. Unrestricted individualism spells ruin to the individual himself. But so does the elimination of individualism, whether by law or custom. It is a capital error to fail to recognize the vital need of good laws. It is also a capital error to

THEODORE ROOSEVELT, *c. 1889–95.*

believe that good laws will accomplish anything unless the average man has the right stuff in him. The toiler, the manual laborer, has received less than justice, and he must be protected, both by law, by custom, and by the exercise of his right to increase his wage; and yet to decrease the quantity and quality of his work will work only evil. There must be a far greater need of respect and reward for the hand worker than we now give him, if our society is to be put on a sound basis; and this respect and reward cannot be given him unless he is as ambitious to do the best possible work as is the highest type of brain worker, whether doctor or writer or artist. There must be a raising of standards, and not a leveling down to the standard of the poorest and most inefficient. There is urgent need of intelligent governmental action to assist in making the life of the man who tills the soil all that it should be, and to see that the manual worker gets his full share of the reward for what he helps produce; but if either farmer, mechanic, or day laborer is shiftless or lazy, if he shirks downright hard work, if he is stupid or self-indulgent, then no law can save him, and he must give way to a better type. ✳ ✳ ✳

**IN THE CHAPTER OF HIS AUTOBIOGRAPHY** describing his time spent as Civil Service Commissioner, Roosevelt reflects on all manner of reform, mapping out his unswerving devotion to the "merit system" rather than the "spoils system." It isn't surprising that such a staunch meritocrat favored women's suffrage—as long as women understood their responsibilities as well as their rights.

The relationship of man and woman is the fundamental relationship that stands at the base of the whole social structure. Much can be done by law towards putting women on a footing of complete and entire equal rights with man—including the right to vote, the right to hold and use property, and the right to enter any profession she desires on the same terms as a man. Yet when this has been done it will amount to little unless on the one hand the man himself realizes his duty to the woman, and unless on the other hand the woman realizes that she has no claim to rights unless she performs the duties that go with those rights and that alone justify her in appealing to them. A cruel, selfish, or licentious man is an abhorrent member of the community; but, after all, his actions are no worse in the long run than those of the woman who is content to be a parasite on others, who is cold, selfish, caring for nothing but frivolous pleasure and ignoble ease. The law of worthy effort, the law of service for a worthy end, without regard to whether it brings pleasure or pain, is the only right law of life, whether for man or for woman. The man must not be selfish; nor, if the woman is wise, will she let the man grow selfish, and this not only for her own sake but for his. One of the prime needs is to remember that almost every duty is composed of two seemingly conflicting elements, and that overinsistence on one, to the exclusion of the other, may defeat its own end. Any man who studies the statistics of the birth-rate among the native Americans of New England, or among the native French of France, needs not to be told that when prudence and forethought are carried to the point of cold selfishness and self-indulgence, the race is bound to disappear. Taking into account the women who for good reasons do not marry, or who when married are childless or are able to have but one or two children, it is evident that the married woman able to have children must on an average have four or the race will not perpetuate itself. This is the mere statement of a self-evident truth. Yet foolish and self-indulgent people often resent this statement as if it were in some way possible by denunciation to reverse the facts of nature; and, on the other hand, improvident and shiftless people, inconsiderate and brutal people, treat the statement as if it justified heads of families in having enormous numbers of badly nourished, badly brought up, and badly cared for children for whom they make no effort to provide. A man must think well before he marries. He must be a tender and considerate husband and realize that there is no other human being to whom he owes so much of love and regard and consideration as he does to the woman who with pain bears and with labor rears the children that are his. No words can paint the scorn and contempt which must be felt by all right-thinking men, not only for the brutal husband, but for the husband who fails to show full loyalty and consideration to his wife. Moreover, he must work, he must do his part in the world. On the other hand, the woman must realize that she has no more right to shirk the business of wifehood and motherhood than the man has to shirk his business as breadwinner for the household. Women should have free access to every field of labor which they care to enter, and when their work is as valuable as that of a man it should be paid as highly. Yet normally for the man and the woman whose welfare is more important than the welfare of any other human beings, the woman must remain the housemother, the homekeeper, and the man must remain the breadwinner, the provider for the wife who bears his children and for the children she brings into the world. No other work is as valuable or as exacting for either man or woman; it must always, in every healthy society, be for both man and woman the prime work, the most important work;

THEODORE ROOSEVELT AND WIFE, EDITH, *beneath parasol, driving near their home in Oyster Bay, c. 1895.*

THEODORE ROOSEVELT AND DAUGHTER ETHEL *at Sagamore Hill, 1895.*

normally all other work is of secondary importance, and must come as an addition to, not a substitute for, this primary work. The partnership should be one of equal rights, one of love, of self-respect, and unselfishness, above all a partnership for the performance of the most vitally important of all duties. The performance of duty, and not an indulgence in vapid ease and vapid pleasure, is all that makes life worth while.

Suffrage for women should be looked on from this standpoint. Personally I feel that it is exactly as much a "right" of women as of men to vote. But the important point with both men and women is to treat the exercise of the suffrage as a duty, which, in the long run, must be well performed to be of the slightest value. I always favored woman's suffrage, but only tepidly, until my association with women like Jane Addams and Frances Kellor, who desired it as one means of enabling them to render better and more efficient service, changed me into a zealous instead of a lukewarm adherent of the cause—in spite of the fact that a few of the best women

of the same type, women like Mary Antin, did not favor the movement. A vote is like a rifle: its usefulness depends upon the character of the user. The mere possession of the vote will no more benefit men and women not sufficiently developed to use it than the possession of rifles will turn untrained Egyptian fellaheen into sol-

> "A vote is like a rifle: its usefulness depends upon the character of the user."

diers. This is as true of woman as of man—and no more true. Universal suffrage in Hayti has not made the Haytians able to govern themselves in any true sense; and woman suffrage in Utah in no shape or way affected the problem of polygamy. I believe in suffrage for women in America, because I think they are fit for it. I believe for women, as for men, more in the duty of fitting one's self to do well and wisely with the ballot than in the naked right to cast the ballot.

**WHEN HE WAS APPOINTED** Police Commissioner of New York City, Roosevelt attacked the new role with his usual bravado—all the while knowing that his life of privilege was no benefit when it came to understanding the working people of the city. To help fill the gaps in his experience, he relied on his friend Jacob Riis. These two pieces from his autobiography offer glimpses of his expanding social conscience, as he dealt with the constant conflict between justice and order inherent in his job.

# The New York Police

The man who was closest to me throughout my two years in the Police Department was Jacob Riis. By this time, as I have said, I was getting our social, industrial, and political needs into pretty fair perspective. I was still ignorant of the extent to which big men of great wealth played a mischievous part in our industrial and social life, but I was well awake to the need of making ours in good faith both an economic and an industrial as well as a political democracy. I already knew Jake Riis, because his book "How the Other Half Lives" had been to me both an enlightenment and an inspiration for which I felt I could never be too grateful. Soon after it was written I had called at his office to tell him how deeply impressed I was by the book, and that I wished to help him in any practical way to try to make things a little better. I have always had a horror of words that are not translated into deeds, of speech that does not result in action—in other words, I believe in realizable ideals and in realizing them, in preaching what can be practiced and then in practicing it. Jacob Riis had drawn an indictment of the things that were wrong, pitifully and dreadfully wrong, with the tenement homes and the tenement lives of our wage-workers. In his book he had pointed out how the city government, and especially those connected with the departments of police and health, could aid in remedying some of the wrongs.

As President of the Police Board I was also a member of the Health Board. In both positions I felt that with Jacob Riis's guidance I would be able to put a goodly number of

THEODORE ROOSEVELT *in his office at the New York City Board of Police Commissioners, c. 1895–97.*

During his two years on the Police Commission, Roosevelt developed a close comradeship with Jacob Riis, the activist newspaperman and author of the groundbreaking book *How the Other Half Lives,* which Roosevelt credited as "both an enlightenment and an inspiration for which I felt I could never be too grateful." Never willing to stay within the comfort zone that his own familial circumstances had provided him, Roosevelt enlisted Riis's help in understanding the lives of the working men and women whose interests he was now bound to protect.

"Jacob Riis had drawn an indictment of the things that were wrong, pitifully and dreadfully wrong, with the tenement homes and the tenement lives of our wage workers," he wrote. With Riis, Roosevelt (who was also an ex officio member of the Health Board) visited many of the city's most notorious tenements, talked to the residents, and ultimately launched a variety of legislation to improve living conditions for New York's poorest citizens. "I have always had a horror of words that are not translated into deeds, of speech that does not result in action," he wrote. For his part, Riis said of Roosevelt, "No one ever helped as he did. . . . For the first time, a moral purpose came into the street."

*left:* JACOB RIIS, *c. 1900.*

*right:* JACOB RIIS, THEODORE ROOSEVELT, AND JOHN HEYL VINCENT *(a Methodist Episcopal bishop) at Higgins Memorial Hall, Chautauqua, New York, August 11, 1905.*

his principles into actual effect. He and I looked at life and its problems from substantially the same standpoint. Our ideals and principles and purposes, and our beliefs as to the methods necessary to realize them, were alike. After the election in 1894 I had written him a letter which ran in part as follows:

> *It is very important to the city to have a business man's Mayor, but it is more important to have a workingman's Mayor; and I want Mr. Strong to be that also. . . . It is an excellent thing to have rapid transit, but it is a good deal more important, if you look at matters with a proper perspective, to have ample playgrounds in the poorer quarters of the city, and to take the children off the streets so as to prevent them growing up toughs. In the same way it is an admirable thing to have clean streets; indeed, it is an essential thing to have them; but it would be a better thing to have our schools large enough to give ample accommodation to all who should be pupils and to provide them with proper playgrounds.*

And I added, while expressing my regret that I had not been able to accept the street-cleaning commissionership, that "I would have been delighted to smash up the corrupt contractors and put the street-cleaning force absolutely out of the domain of politics."

This was nineteen years ago, but it makes a pretty good platform in municipal politics even to-day—smash corruption, take the municipal service out of the domain of politics, insist upon having a Mayor who shall be a workingman's Mayor even more than a business man's Mayor, and devote all attention possible to the welfare of the children. ✶ ✶ ✶

MY EXPERIENCE in the Police Department taught me that not a few of the worst tenement-houses were owned by wealthy individuals, who hired the best and most expensive lawyers to persuade the courts that it was "unconstitutional" to insist on the betterment of conditions. These business men and lawyers were very adroit in using a word with fine and noble associations to cloak their opposition to vitally necessary movements for industrial fair play and decency. They made it evident that they valued the Constitution, not as a help to righteousness, but as a means for thwarting movements against unrighteousness. After my experience with them I became more set than ever in my distrust of those men, whether business men or lawyers, judges, legislators, or executive officers, who seek to make of the Constitution a fetich for the prevention of the work of social reform, for the prevention of work in the interest of those men, women, and children on whose behalf we should be at liberty to employ freely every governmental agency.

Occasionally during the two years we had to put a stop to riotous violence, and now and then on these occasions some of the labor union leaders protested against the actions of the police. By this time I was becoming a strong believer in labor unions, a strong believer in the rights of labor. For that very reason I was all the more bound to see that lawlessness and disorder were put down, and that no rioter was permitted to masquerade under the guise of being a friend of labor or a sympathizer with labor. I was scrupulous to see that the labor men had fair play; that, for instance, they were allowed to picket just so far as under the law picketing could be permitted, so that the strikers had ample opportunity peacefully to persuade other labor men not to take their places. But I made it clearly and definitely understood that under no circumstances would I permit violence or fail to insist upon the keeping of order. If there were wrongs, I would join with a full heart in striving to have them corrected. But where there was violence all other questions had to drop until order was restored. This is a democracy, and the people have the power, if they choose to exercise it, to make conditions as they ought to be made, and to do this strictly within the law; and therefore the first duty of the true democrat, of the man really loyal to the principles of popular government, is to see that law is enforced and order upheld. It was a peculiar gratification to me that so many of the labor leaders with whom I was thrown in contact grew cordially to accept this view.

# LETTER OF RESIGNATION
## AS THE NEW YORK CITY POLICE COMMISSIONER
New York, April 17, 1897

**ROOSEVELT'S TERM** as one of three Police Commissioners was bound to be a short one; a nation on the brink of war awaited him—and, in any case, he had never been cut out for sharing a job. In his deeply respectful resignation letter, Roosevelt pays tribute to the Mayor who appointed him as well as the rank and file of New York's hard-working police force, and cites the many strides that were made during his tenure. His suggestion that the city would be better off with a sole Police Commissioner was soon heeded.

To the Mayor.

*My Dear Mr. Mayor:* I herewith tender you my resignation to take effect on April 19 in accordance with our understanding.

I wish to take this opportunity, sir, to thank you for appointing me, and to express my very deep appreciation of your attitude toward me and toward the force, the direction of which you in part intrusted to my care. We have been very intimately associated with your work, and I know, as all men who have been associated with you do know, the devotion with which you have given all of your time and all of your efforts to the betterment of our civic conditions and the single-mindedness with which at every crisis you have sought merely the good of the city. I have been able to work so zealously under you because you have never required of me anything but loyal service to what you conceived to be the best interest of New York City, and I well know that had I followed any other course it would have met with instant and sharp rebuke from you. I know also the almost incredible difficulties with which you have been surrounded, and the impossibility of your acting so as to please every one. Nevertheless, I firmly believe that people are now realizing that you have given us far and away the best administration which this city has ever had. In this department we, as well as you, have been hampered by unwise legislation, and the so-called bipartisan law, under which the department itself is administered, is of such absurdly foolish character that it has been impossible to achieve the results which would have been achieved had you had your hands free with reference to your appointees, and had your appointees in turn possessed full and proper power over the force.

THEODORE ROOSEVELT *as President of the Board of Police Commissioners, New York City, 1895–97.*

Nevertheless, very much has been accomplished. For the first time the police force has been administered without regard to politics, and with an honest and resolute purpose to enforce the laws equitably, and show favor to no man. The old system of blackmail and corruption has been almost entirely broken up; we have greatly improved the standard of discipline; we have preserved complete order; and we have warred against crime and vice more effectively than ever before. The fact that we have come short in any measure is due simply to the folly of the law which deprives us of the full measure of power over our subordinates which could alone guarantee the best results. We have administered the civil-service law in spirit and in letter, so as to show that there is not the slightest excuse for wishing to get rid of it, or for claiming that it does not produce the best possible results when honestly enforced. About two-fifths of the patrolmen have been appointed by us under the operation of the civil-service law, and they make the best body of recruits that have ever come into the service. This is about four times the number of appointments that have ever before been made in the same period; and we have also made many more promotions. In promotions and appointments alike we have disregarded wholly all considerations of political or religious creed; we have treated all men alike on their merits, rewarding the good and punishing the bad without reference to outside consideration. This was the course followed so long as the board had control over all promotions; and it has been followed in the promotions actually made. I have joined with Commissioner Andrews in refusing to take part in any offer to promote men or appoint them on other terms. I cannot resist expressing my appreciation of the high-mindedness, disinterestedness, courage, and fidelity to duty which Commissioner Andrews has brought to the performance of every official action.

During my term of service we have striven especially to make the police force not only the terror of the burglar, the rioter, the tough, the lawbreaker, and criminal of every kind, but also the ready ally of every movement for good. One of my pleasantest experiences has been working with all men, rich and poor, priests and laymen, Catholics and Protestants, Jews and Gentiles, who are striving to make our civil conditions better, who are striving to raise the standard of living, of morality, and of comfort among our less fortunate brethren. We have endeavored to make all men and all societies engaged in such work feel that the police were their natural allies. We have endeavored to make the average private citizen feel that the officer of the law was to be dreaded only by the lawbreaker, and was ever ready to treat with courtesy, and to befriend, any one who needed his aid.

The man in the ranks, the man with the night-stick, has been quick to respond to our efforts, quick to recognize honesty of purpose in his superiors. You have in the police force a body of men, brave, able, and zealous; under proper leadership they can at any time be depended upon to do the best possible work. I have bitterly regretted that the law under which the force is administered is so bad that it has been impossible to make of this splendid body of men all that could be made, if the board had one responsible head with complete power and absolute singleness of purpose to do right.

Again thanking you for having appointed me, and for your treatment of me during my term of service, I am, with much gratitude and great respect, very faithfully yours,

*Theodore Roosevelt*

Theodore Roosevelt

# NAVAL WAR COLLEGE ADDRESS

Newport, Rhode Island

June 2, 1897

---

**PRESIDENT MCKINLEY** appointed Roosevelt Assistant Secretary of the Navy in April 1897, but it wasn't long before he would take a leading role in the organization. This speech, widely reported on at the time, calls in no uncertain terms for the rapid expansion of the Navy and a willingness (some would say an eagerness) to wage war whenever and wherever necessary.

A century has passed since Washington wrote "To be prepared for war is the most effectual means to promote peace." We pay to this maxim the lip loyalty we so often pay to Washington's words; but it has never sunk deep into our hearts. Indeed of late years many persons have refused it even the poor tribute of lip loyalty, and prate about the iniquity of war as if somehow that was a justification for refusing to take the steps which can alone in the long run prevent war or avert the dreadful disasters it brings in its train. The truth of the maxim is so obvious to everyman of really far-sighted patriotism that its mere statement seems trite and useless; and it is not over-creditable to either our intelligence or our love of country that there should be, as there is, need to dwell upon and amplify such a truism.

In this country there is not the slightest danger of an over-development of warlike spirit, and there never has been any such danger. In all our history there has never been a time when preparedness for war was any menace to peace. On the contrary, again and again we have owed peace to the fact that we were prepared for war; and in the only contest which we have had with a European power since the Revolution, the War of 1812, the struggle and all its attendant disasters were due solely to the fact that we were not prepared to face, and were not ready instantly to resent, an attack upon our honor and interest; while the glorious triumphs at sea which redeemed that war were due to the few preparations which we had actually made. We are a great peaceful nation; a nation of merchants and manufacturers, of farmers and mechanics; a nation of workingmen, who labor incessantly with head or hand. It is idle to talk of such a nation ever being led into a course of wanton aggression or conflict with military powers by the possession of a sufficient navy.

The danger is of precisely the opposite character. If we forget that in the last resort we can only secure peace by being ready and willing to fight for it,

THEODORE ROOSEVELT, *Assistant Secretary of the Navy (1897–98), at his desk.*

we may someday have bitter cause to realize that a rich nation which is slothful, timid, or unwieldy is an easy prey for any people which still retains those most valuable of all qualities, the soldierly virtues. We but keep to the traditions of Washington, to the traditions of all the great Americans who struggled for the real greatness of America, when we strive to build up those fighting qualities for the lack of which in a nation, as in an individual, no refinement, no culture, no wealth, no material prosperity, can atone.

Preparation for war is the surest guaranty for peace. Arbitration is an excellent thing, but ultimately those who wish to see this country at peace with foreign nations will be wise if they place reliance upon a first-class fleet of first-class battleships rather than on any arbitration treaty which the wit of man can devise. Nelson said that the British fleet was the best negotiator in Europe, and there was much truth in the saying. Moreover, while we are sincere and earnest in our advocacy of peace, we must not forget that an ignoble peace is worse than any war. . . .

Peace is a goddess only when she comes with sword girt on thigh. The ship of state can be steered safely only when it is possible to bring her against any foe with "her leashed thunders gathering for the leap." A really great people, proud and high-spirited, would face all the disasters of war rather than purchase that base prosperity which is bought at the price of national honor. All the great masterful races have been fighting races, and the minute that a race loses the hard fighting virtues, then, no matter what else it may retain, no matter how skilled in commerce and finance, in science or art, it has lost its proud right to stand as the equal of the best. Cowardice in a race, as in an individual, is the unpardonable sin, and a willful failure to prepare for any danger may in its effects be as bad as cowardice. The timid man who cannot fight, and the selfish, short-sighted, or foolish man who will not take the steps that will enable him to fight, stand on almost the same plane. . . .

This nation cannot stand still if it is to retain its self-respect, and to keep undimmed the honorable traditions inherited from the men who with the sword founded it and by the sword preserved it. . . . No nation should ever wage war wantonly, but no nation should ever avoid it at the cost of the loss of national honor. A nation should never fight unless forced to; but it should always be ready to fight. The mere fact that it is ready will generally spare it the necessity of fighting. . . .

If in the future we have war, it will almost certainly come because of some action, or lack of action, on our part in the way of refusing to accept responsibilities at the proper time, or failing to prepare for war when war does not threaten. An ignoble peace is even worse than an unsuccessful war; but an unsuccessful war would leave behind it a legacy of bitter memories which would hurt our national development for a generation to come.

BEING A LEADER TAKES on a new meaning during war time—at least for someone such as Roosevelt. It was not something he believed he could do from his position as Naval Secretary. "As soon as war was upon us . . . I began to try for a chance to go to the front," he writes in the excerpts from his autobiography that follow. In his view, a strong country must always be prepared for war—and effective leadership happens from the front line.

# The War of America the Unready

Soon after I began work as Assistant Secretary of the Navy I became convinced that the war would come. The revolt in Cuba had dragged its weary length until conditions in the island had become so dreadful as to be a standing disgrace to us for permitting them to exist. There is much that I sincerely admire about the Spanish character; and there are few men for whom I have felt greater respect than for certain gentlemen of Spain whom I have known. But Spain attempted to govern her colonies on archaic principles which rendered her control of them incompatible with the advance of humanity and intolerable to the conscience of mankind. In 1898 the so-called war in Cuba had dragged along for years with unspeakable horror, degradation, and misery. It was not "war" at all, but murderous oppression. Cuba was devastated.

During those years, while we continued at "peace," several hundred times as many lives were lost, lives of men, women, and children, as were lost during the three months' "war" which put an end to this slaughter and opened a career of peaceful progress to the Cubans. Yet there were misguided professional philanthropists who cared so much more for names than for facts that they preferred a "peace" of continuous murder to a "war" which stopped the murder and brought real peace. Spain's humiliation was certain, anyhow; indeed, it was more certain without war than with it, for she could not permanently keep the island, and she minded yielding to the Cubans more than yielding to us. Our own direct interests were great, because of the Cuban tobacco and sugar, and especially because of Cuba's relation to the

THEODORE ROOSEVELT *as Assistant Secretary of the Navy in New York City, c. 1897–98.*

projected Isthmian Canal. But even greater were our interests from the standpoint of humanity. Cuba was at our very doors. It was a dreadful thing for us to sit supinely and watch her death agony. It was our duty, even more from the standpoint of National honor than from the standpoint of National interest, to stop the devastation and destruction. Because of these considerations I favored war; and to-day, when in retrospect it is easier to see things clearly, there are few humane and honorable men who do not believe that the war was both just and necessary. ✶ ✶ ✶

WHEN THE MAINE WAS BLOWN UP in Havana Harbor, war became inevitable. A number of the peace-at-any-price men of course promptly assumed the position that she had blown herself up; but investigation showed that the explosion was from outside. And, in any event, it would have been impossible to prevent war. The enlisted men of the navy, who often grew bored to the point of desertion in peace, became keyed up to a high pitch of efficiency, and crowds of fine young fellows, from the interior as well as from the seacoast, thronged to enlist. The navy officers showed alert ability and unwearied industry in getting things ready. There was one deficiency, however, which there was no time to remedy, and of the very existence of which, strange to say, most of our best men were ignorant. Our navy had no idea how low our standard of marksmanship was. We had not realized that the modern battle-ship had become such a complicated piece of mechanism that the old methods of training in marksmanship were as obsolete as the old muzzle-loading broadside guns themselves. Almost the only man in the navy who fully realized this was our naval attaché at Paris, Lieutenant Sims. He wrote letter after letter pointing out how frightfully backward we were in marksmanship. I was much impressed by his letters; but Wainwright was about the only other man who was. And as Sims proved to be mistaken in his belief that the French had taught the Spaniards how to shoot, and as the Spaniards proved to be much worse even than we were, in the service generally Sims was treated as an alarmist. But although I at first partly acquiesced in this view, I grew uneasy when I studied the small proportion of hits to shots made by our vessels in battle. When I was President I took up the matter, and speedily became convinced that we needed to revolutionize our whole training

THE U.S.S. MAINE BATTLESHIP, *which had been sent to Havana, Cuba, to protect U.S. interests during the Cuban revolt against Spain, suddenly exploded and sank on the evening of February 15, 1898. Nearly three quarters of her crew were killed..*

THE MAST AND WRECKAGE *of the sunken* U.S.S. Maine *battleship in Havana Harbor, 1898.*

**THEODORE ROOSEVELT'S** *muster-in roll, 1898.*

in marksmanship. Sims was given the lead in organizing and introducing the new system; and to him more than to any other one man was due the astonishing progress made by our fleet in this respect, a progress which made the fleet, gun for gun, at least three times as effective, in point of fighting efficiency, in 1908, as it was in 1902. The shots that hit are the shots that count!

Like the people, the Government was for a long time unwilling to prepare for war, because so many honest but misguided men believed that the preparation itself tended to bring on the war. I did not in the least share this feeling, and whenever I was left as Acting Secretary I did everything in my power to put us in readiness. I knew that in the event of war Dewey could be slipped like a wolf-hound from a leash; I was sure that if he were given half a chance he would strike instantly and with telling effect; and I made up my mind that all I could do to give him that half-chance should be done. I was in the closest touch with Senator Lodge throughout this period, and either consulted him about or notified him

of all the moves I was taking. By the end of February I felt it was vital to send Dewey (as well as each of our other commanders who were not in home waters) instructions that would enable him to be in readiness for immediate action. . . .

All that was needed with Dewey was to give him the chance to get ready, and then to strike, without being hampered by orders from those not on the ground. Success in war depends very largely upon choosing a man fit to exercise such powers, and then giving him the powers.

It would be instructive to remember, if only we were willing to do so, the fairly comic panic which swept in waves over our seacoast, first when it became evident that war was about to be declared, and then when it was declared. The public waked up to the sufficiently obvious fact that the Government was in its usual state—perennial unreadiness for war. Thereupon the people of the seaboard district passed at one bound from unreasoning confidence that war never could come to unreasoning

THEODORE ROOSEVELT AND LEONARD WOOD *in Tampa with camp tents, 1898. Wood was a physician who, with Roosevelt, organized the 1st Cavalry known as the Rough Riders. After the war, he was appointed Governor of Cuba (1899–1902).*

For years we had been saying, just as any number of our people now say, that no nation would venture to attack us. Then when we did go to war with an exceedingly feeble nation, we, for the time being, rushed to the other extreme of feeling, and attributed to this feeble nation plans of offensive warfare which it never dreamed of making, and which, if made, it would have been wholly unable to execute. Some of my readers doubtless remember the sinister intentions and unlimited potentialities for destruction with which the fertile imagination of the yellow press endowed the armored cruiser *Viscaya* when she appeared in American waters just before war was declared. The state of nervousness along much of the seacoast was funny in view of the lack of foundation for it; but it offered food for serious thought as to what would happen if we ever became engaged with a serious foe. ✴ ✴ ✴

**AS SOON AS WAR WAS UPON US,** Wood and I began to try for a chance to go to the front. Congress had authorized the raising of three National Volunteer Cavalry regiments, wholly apart from the State contingents. Secretary Alger of the War Department was fond of me personally, and Wood was his family doctor. Alger had been a gallant soldier in the Civil War, and was almost the only member of the Administration who felt all along that we would have to go to war with Spain over Cuba. He liked my attitude in the matter, and because of his remembrance of his own experiences he sympathized with my desire to go to the front. Accordingly he offered me the command of one of the regiments. I told him that after six weeks' service in the field I would feel competent to handle the regiment, but that I would not know how to equip it or how to get it into the first action; but that Wood was entirely competent at once to take command, and that if he would make Wood colonel I would accept the lieutenant-colonelcy. General Alger thought this an act of foolish

*overleaf:* THE ROUGH RIDERS IN TRAINING *in San Antonio, Texas, 1898*

fear as to what might happen now that it had come. That acute philosopher Mr. Dooley proclaimed that in the Spanish War we were in a dream, but that the Spaniards were in a trance. This just about summed up the facts. Our people had for decades scoffed at the thought of making ready for possible war. Now, when it was too late, they not only backed every measure, wise and unwise, that offered a chance of supplying a need that ought to have been met before, but they also fell into a condition of panic apprehension as to what the foe might do.

*This **ROOSEVELT POLITICAL CARTOON** was accompanied by a poem that declared, "Will he fight? Will ducks go swimming? Fight? He'd rather fight than eat!"*

self-abnegation on my part—instead of its being, what it was, the wisest act I could have performed. He told me to accept the colonelcy, and that he would make Wood lieutenant-colonel, and that Wood would do the work anyway; but I answered that I did not wish to rise on any man's shoulders; that I hoped to be given every chance that my deeds and abilities warranted; but that I did not wish what I did not earn, and that above all I did not wish to hold any position where any one else did the work.

He laughed at me a little and said I was foolish, but I do not think he really minded, and he promised to do as I wished. True to his word, he secured the appointment of Wood as colonel and of myself as lieutenant-colonel of the First United States Volunteer Cavalry. This was soon nicknamed, both by the public and by the rest of the army, the Rough Riders, doubtless because the bulk of the men were from the Southwestern ranch country and were skilled in the wild horsemanship of the great plains.

> "This was soon nicknamed . . . the Rough Riders, doubtless because the bulk of the men were from the Southwestern ranch country and were skilled in the wild horsemanship of the great plains."

Wood instantly began the work of raising the regiment. He first assembled several old non-commissioned officers of experience, put them in office, and gave them blanks for requisitions for the full equipment of a cavalry regiment. He selected San Antonio as the gathering-place, as it was in a good horse country, near the Gulf from some port on which we would have to embark, and near an old arsenal and an old army post from which we got a good deal of stuff—some of it practically condemned, but which we found serviceable at a pinch, and much better than nothing. He organized a horse board in Texas, and began purchasing all horses that were not too big and were sound. A day or two after he was commissioned he wrote out in the office of the Secretary of War, under his authority, telegrams to the Governors of Arizona, New Mexico, Oklahoma, and Indian Territory, in substance as follows:

*The President desires to raise—volunteers in your Territory to form part of a regiment of mounted riflemen to be commanded by Leonard Wood, Colonel; Theodore Roosevelt, Lieutenant-Colonel. He desires that the men selected should be young, sound, good shots and good riders, and that you expedite by all means in your power the enrollment of these men.*
*(Signed) R. A. ALGER, Secretary of War*

As soon as he had attended to a few more odds and ends he left Washington, and the day after his arrival in San Antonio the troops began to arrive.

For several weeks before I joined the regiment, to which Wood went ahead of me, I continued as Assistant Secretary of the Navy, trying to get some coherence of plan between the War Department and the Navy Department; and also being used by Wood to finish getting the equipment for the regiment. As regards finding out what the plans of the War Department were, the task was simple. They had no plans. Even during the final months before the outbreak of hostilities very little was done in the way of efficient preparation. On one occasion, when every one knew that the declaration of war was sure to come in a few days, I went on military business to the office of one of the highest line generals of the army, a man who at that moment ought to have been working eighteen hours out of the twenty-four on the vital problems ahead of him. What he was actually doing was trying on a new type of smart-looking uniform on certain enlisted men; and he called me in to ask my advice as to the position of the pockets in the blouse, with a view to making it look attractive. An aide of this general—funnily enough a good fighting man in actual service—when I consulted him as to what my uniform for the campaign should be, laid special stress upon my purchasing a pair of black top boots for full dress, explaining that they were very effective on hotel piazzas and in parlors. I did not intend to be in any hotel if it could possibly be avoided; and as things turned out, I had no full-dress uniform, nothing but my service uniform, during my brief experience in the army.

I suppose that war always does bring out what is highest and lowest in human nature. The contractors who furnish poor materials to the army or the navy in time of war stand on a level of infamy only one degree above that of the participants in the white slave traffic themselves. But there is conduct far short of this which yet seems inexplicable to any man who has in him any spirit of disinterested patriotism combined with any power of imagination. Respectable men, who I suppose lack the imagination thoroughly to realize what they are doing, try to make money out of the Nation's necessities in war at the very time that other men are making every sacrifice, financial and personal, for the cause. In the closing weeks of my service as Assistant Secretary of the Navy we were collecting ships for auxiliary purposes. Some men, at cost to their own purses, helped us freely and with efficiency; others treated the affair as an ordinary business transaction; and yet others endeavored, at some given crisis when our need was great, to sell us inferior vessels at exorbitant prices, and used every pressure, through Senators and Congressmen, to accomplish their ends. In one or two cases they did accomplish them too, until we got a really first-class board established to superintend such purchases. A more curious experience was in connection with the point chosen for the starting of the expedition against Cuba. I had not supposed that any human being could consider this matter save from the standpoint of military need. But one morning a very wealthy and influential man, a respectable and upright man according to his own lights, called on me to protest against our choice of Tampa, and to put in a plea for a certain other port, on the ground that his railroad was entitled to its share of the profit for hauling the army and equipment! I happened to know that at this time this very man had kinsfolk with the army, who served gallantly, and the circumstances of his coming to me were such as to show that he was not acting secretly, and had no idea that there was anything out of the way in his proposal. I think the facts were merely that he had been trained to regard business as the sole object in life, and that he lacked the imagination to enable him to understand the real nature of the request that he was making; and, moreover, he had good reason to believe that one of his business competitors had been unduly favored.

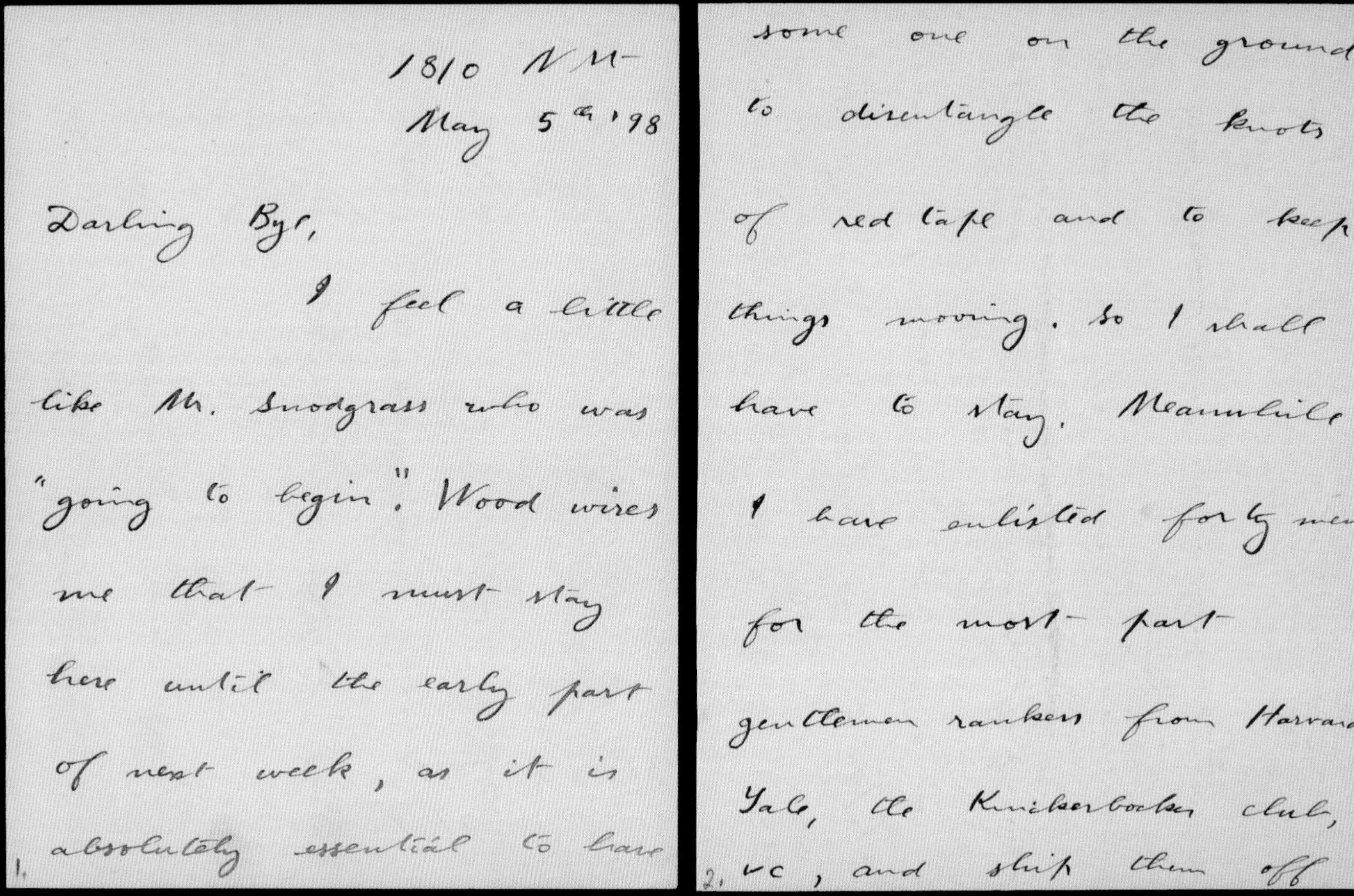

1810 N M—
May 5th '98

Darling Bys,

I feel a little like Mr. Snodgrass who was "going to begin". Wood wires me that I must stay here until the early part of next week, as it is absolutely essential to have

1.

some one on the ground to disentangle the knots of red tape and to keep things moving. So I shall have to stay. Meanwhile I have enlisted forty men for the most part gentlemen rankers from Harvard Yale, the Knickerbocker club, &c, and ship them off

2.

In this 1898 LETTER FROM NEW MEXICO to his sister, Theodore Roosevelt tells her, "I have enlisted forty men for the most part gentlemen rankers from Harvard, Yale, Knickerbocker Club . . . and ship them off tomorrow night. . . . The Harvard contingent is particularly good. Love to Alice. . . ."

tomorrow night. Good Bob goes with them, seemingly very happy; and at any rate he has a nice set of companions. The Harvard contingent is particularly good.

Did you send me some excellent spurs?

Tell Will to drop me a line as to whether he likes the Topeka and what battery he'll have aboard her.

Edith keeps improving, but of course the worry over my going, and over what this entails on her in the way of work about the house, &c, tells on her. Love to Alice,

Your loving brother
T. R.

# LETTERS SENT HOME DURING THE SPANISH-AMERICAN WAR

**A SOLDIER'S LETTERS TO HIS FAMILY** are always moving, and Roosevelt's are no exception. These were written during preparations for the Rough Riders' Cuban campaign. (Edith was still recovering from major surgery to repair an abdominal abscess—but clearly, she was a trooper in her own right.) In spite of their father's attempts at levity, the children must have been feeling extremely unsettled as he prepared to lead his troops into battle.

**TROOP K** *in transport cars in the railroad yard, Tampa, Florida, 1898.*

*Camp at Tampa, May 6th, '98.*

Blessed Bunnies,
It has been a real holiday to have darling mother here. Yesterday I brought her out to the camp, and she saw it all—the men drilling, the tents in long company streets, the horses being taken to water, my little horse Texas, the colonel and the majors, and finally the mountain lion and the jolly little dog Cuba, who had several fights while she looked on. The mountain lion is not much more than a kitten as yet, but it is very cross and treacherous.

I was very much interested in Kermit's and Ethel's letters to-day.

We were all, horses and men, four days and four nights on the cars coming here from San Antonio, and were very tired and very dirty when we arrived. I was up almost all of each night, for it happened always to be at night when we took the horses out of the cars to feed and water them.

Mother stays at a big hotel about a mile from camp. There are nearly thirty thousand troops here now, besides the sailors from the war-ships in the bay. At night the corridors and piazzas are thronged with officers of the army and navy; the older ones fought in the great Civil War, a third of a century ago, and now they are all going to Cuba to war against the Spaniards. Most of them are in blue, but our rough-riders are in brown. Our camp is on a great flat, on sandy soil without a tree, though round about are pines and palmettos. It is very hot, indeed, but there are no mosquitoes. Marshall is very well, and he takes care of my things and of the two horses. A general was out to inspect us when we were drilling to-day. ✶ ✶ ✶

*Off Santiago, 1898.*

Darling Ethel:
We are near shore now and everything is in a bustle, for we may have to disembark to-night, and I do not know when I shall have another chance to write to my three blessed children, whose little notes please me so. This is only a line to tell you all how much father loves you. The Pawnee Indian drew you the picture of the little dog, which runs everywhere round the ship, and now and then howls a little when the band plays. ✶ ✶ ✶

*A battalion of the* **2D U.S. INFANTRY** *embarks for Cienfuegos, Cuba, upon U.S. Transport Crook in Savannah, Georgia, 1898.*

*Near Santiago, May 20, 1898.*

Darling Ethel:

I loved your little letter. Here there are lots of funny little lizards that run about in the dusty roads very fast, and then stand still with their heads up. Beautiful red cardinal birds and tanagers flit about in the woods, and the flowers are lovely. But you never saw such dust. Sometimes I lie on the ground outside and sometimes in the tent. I have a mosquito net because there are so many mosquitoes. ✳ ✳ ✳

*Camp near Santiago, July 15, 1898.*

Darling Ethel:

When it rains here—and it's very apt to rain here every day—it comes down just as if it was a torrent of water. The other night I hung up my hammock in my tent and in the middle of the night there was a terrific storm, and my tent and hammock came down with a run. The water was running over the ground in a sheet, and the mud was knee-deep; so I was a drenched and muddy object when I got to a neighboring tent, where I was given a blanket, in which I rolled up and went to sleep.

There is a funny little lizard that comes into my tent and is quite tame now; he jumps about like a little frog and puffs his throat out. There are ground-doves no bigger than big sparrows, and cuckoos almost as large as crows.

✳ ✳ ✳

OUTDOOR MESS KITCHEN *of the 5th Army Corps camp in Tampa, Florida, 1898.*

# THE ROUGH RIDERS

**W**HEN THE *MAINE* WENT DOWN in Havana harbor and war with Spain became inevitable, Roosevelt eagerly made the transition from statesman to soldier. Joining forces with his friend, U.S. Army Colonel Leonard Wood, he formed the first U.S. Volunteer Cavalry Regiment, recruiting everyone he could think of, from his Dakota cowboy friends to his New York society cronies. (The colorful moniker "Rough Riders" was dreamed up by the press. At first Roosevelt resisted it, but it wasn't long before he was using the term himself.) His official rank was Lieutenant Colonel, while Wood was appointed Regimental Commander. By the middle of June, the company had set sail for Cuba, where they saw action almost immediately. Wood soon ascended to the role of Brigade Commander, and Roosevelt to Regimental Commander.

On July 1, Roosevelt led the Rough Riders in a series of successful campaigns, including the battle for San Juan Heights—and it was for this heroic turn, as much as for anything in his career, that he is remembered. Leading his foot soldiers on horseback until his horse could go no further, always at the front of the regiment, Roosevelt urged the troops onward up San Juan and Kettle Hills, though he'd received no specific orders to do so, until the city of Santiago fell.

By August, Roosevelt was losing more troops to Malaria than in the fighting, and he and the other officers demanded that the soldiers be permitted to return home. For his bravery and the success of his

*overleaf:* **COLONEL ROOSEVELT AND HIS MEN** *in the trenches on San Juan Hill in front of Santiago, Cuba, 1898.*

*opposite:* **THEODORE ROOSEVELT** *on horseback Camp Wikoff, Montauk, New York, 1898.*

*left: An illustration of the* **EXPLOSION OF THE U.S.S. MAINE** *off the coast of Cuba on February 15, 1898.*

initiatives on July 1, Roosevelt was nominated for the National Medal of Honor—the country's highest military accolade—but, perhaps because of his outspokenness in the aftermath of those battles (or simply his out-spokenness in general), he would not receive it in his lifetime. Armistice came on August 12, with Spain ceding Cuba, Puerto Rico, Guam, and the Philippines to the United States. The troops headed home via the port at Montauk, Long Island, officially mustering out on September 15.

Roosevelt's rousing book on the period, *The Rough Riders*, has done much to immortalize the events of that moment, which he came to refer to as "the great day of my life" and "my crowded hour." Vivid descriptions of the heat of battle alternate with acute portraits of the men he commanded and the trying conditions that tested their strength and resolve. A slightly abridged version of the book follows here. Many consider it to be his crowning literary legacy, and it certainly offers the clearest portrait of a man driven to lead.

*left: Detail of a portrait of* **THEODORE ROOSEVELT** *in his Rough Riders uniform by Charles Dana Gibson, 1898. Despite the uniform's cowboyish look, Roosevelt had his tailored by Brooks Brothers in Boston.*

*right:* **THEODORE ROOSEVELT'S STETSON ROUGH RIDERS HAT AND PISTOL** *(possibly a Colt). While campaigning for Vice President on McKinley's ticket in 1900, Roosevelt often wore his hat to solidify his war hero image.*

# Raising the Regiment

During the year preceding the outbreak of the Spanish War, I was Assistant Secretary of the navy. While my party was in opposition, I had preached, with all the fervor and zeal I possessed, our duty to intervene in Cuba, and to take this opportunity of driving the Spaniard from the Western World. Now that my party had come to power, I felt it incumbent on me, by word and deed, to do all I could to secure the carrying out of the policy in which I so heartily believed; and from the beginning I had determined that, if a war came, somehow or other, I was going to the front.

Meanwhile, there was any amount of work at hand in getting ready the navy, and to this I devoted myself.

Naturally, when one is intensely interested in a certain cause, the tendency is to associate particularly with those who take the same view. A large number of my friends felt very differently from the way I felt, and looked upon the possibility of war with sincere horror. But I found plenty of sympathizers, especially in the navy, the army, and the Senate Committee on Foreign Affairs. Commodore Dewey, Captain Evans, Captain Brownson, Captain Davis—with these and the various other naval officers on duty at Washington I used to hold long consultations, during which we went over and over, not only every question of naval administration, but specifically everything necessary to do in order to put the navy in trim to strike quick and hard if, as we believed would be the case, we went to war with Spain. Sending an ample quantity of ammunition to the Asiatic squadron and providing it with coal; getting the battle-ships and the armored cruisers on the Atlantic into one squadron, both to train them in maneuvering together, and to have them ready to sail against either the Cuban or the Spanish coasts; gathering the torpedo-boats into a flotilla for practice; securing ample target exercise, so conducted as to raise the standard of our marksmanship; gathering in the small ships from European and South American waters; settling on the number and kind of craft needed as auxiliary cruisers—every one of these points was threshed over in conversations with officers who were present in Washington, or in correspondence with officers who, like Captain Mahan, were absent.

As for the Senators, of course Senator Lodge and I felt precisely alike; for to fight in such a cause and with such an enemy was merely to carry out the doctrines we had both of us preached for many years. Senator Davis, Senator Proctor, Senator Foraker, Senator Chandler, Senator Morgan, Senator Frye, and a number of others also took just the right ground; and I saw a great deal of them, as

HENRY CABOT LODGE, *in an 1890 painting (detail) by John Singer Sargent, was an influential senator from Massachusetts and a proponent of the Spanish–American War.*

New York and Cuba Mail Steamship Company

NEW YORK
TO
HAVANA
MATANZAS, CARDENAS,
SAGUA LA GRANDE,

NASSAU
SANTIAGO DE CUBA
CIENFUEGOS.

NEW YORK
TO
VERA CRUZ
PROGRESO
CAMPECHE
FRONTERA
TAMPICO
TUXPAM

JAMES E. WARD & CO., Agents.
113 Wall Street.

S.S. _____

_____ 189_

Secnav —
    Washington, D.C.

Maine blown up in Havana Harbor at
nine forty two night and destroyed. Many
wounded and doubtless more killed or drowned.
Wounded and others on board Spanish man-
of war and Ward Line Steamer. ~~City of Washington~~
Send Light House Tenders from Key West —
~~and the vicinity of the ~~off to~~
~~total muscle equipment for vessel, of~~
~~which is about water~~ for crew and
the few pieces of equipment above water. No one
has clothing other than that upon him —
Public Opinion should be suspended until
further report — All Officers believed to
be saved. Jenkins and Merritt not yet
accounted for — ~~Spanish~~ Representative of ~~General~~
Many Spanish officers including representative
of General Blanco now with me express sympath—
Sigsbee

well as of many members of the House, particularly those from the West, where the feeling for war was strongest.

Naval officers came and went, and Senators were only in the city while the Senate was in session; but there was one friend who was steadily in Washington. This was an army surgeon, Dr. Leonard Wood. I only met him after I entered the navy department, but we soon found that we had kindred tastes and kindred principles. He had served in General Miles' inconceivably harassing campaigns against the Apaches, where he had displayed such courage that he won that most coveted of distinctions—the Medal of Honor; such extraordinary physical strength and endurance that he grew to be recognized as one of the two or three white men who could stand fatigue and hardship as well as an Apache; and such judgment that toward the close of the campaigns he was given, though a surgeon, the actual command of more than one expedition against the bands of renegade Indians. Like so many of the gallant fighters with whom it was later my good fortune to serve, he combined, in a very high degree, the qualities of entire manliness with entire uprightness and cleanliness of character. It was a pleasure to deal with a man of high ideals, who scorned everything mean and base, and who also possessed those robust and hardy qualities of body and mind, for the lack of which no merely negative virtue can ever atone. He was by nature a soldier of the highest type, and, like most natural soldiers, he was, of course, born with a keen longing for adventure; and, though an excellent doctor, what he really desired was the chance to lead men in some kind of hazard. To every possibility of such adventure he paid quick attention. For instance, he had a great desire to get me to go with him on an expedition into the Klondike in midwinter, at the time when it was thought that a relief party would have to be sent there to help the starving miners.

TELEGRAM FROM CAPTAIN CHARLES D. SIGSBEE, *Commander of the U.S.S. Maine, sent to the Secretary of the Navy detailing the attack, February 15, 1898.*

In the summer he and I took long walks together through the beautiful broken country surrounding Washington. In winter we sometimes varied these walks by kicking a football in an empty lot, or, on the rare occasions when there was enough snow, by trying a couple of sets of skis or snow-skates, which had been sent me from Canada.

But always on our way out to and back from these walks and sport, there was one topic to which, in our talking, we returned, and that was the possible war with Spain. We both felt very strongly that such a war would be as righteous as it would be advantageous to the honor and the interests of the nation; and after the blowing up of the *Maine,* we felt that it was inevitable. We then at once began to try to see that we had our share in it. The president and my own chief, Secretary Long, were very firm against my going, but they said that if I was bent upon going they would help me. Wood was the medical adviser of both the president and the secretary of war, and could count upon their friendship. So we started with the odds in our favor.

At first we had great difficulty in knowing exactly what to try for. We could go on the staff of any one of several generals, but we much preferred to go in the line. Wood hoped he might get a commission in his native State of Massachusetts; but in Massachusetts, as in every other State, it proved there were ten men who wanted to go to the war for every chance to go. Then we thought we might get positions as field-officers under an old friend of mine, Colonel—now General—Francis V. Greene, of New York, the Colonel of the Seventy-first; but again there were no vacancies.

Our doubts were resolved when Congress authorized the raising of three cavalry regiments from among the wild riders and riflemen of the Rockies and the Great Plains. During Wood's service in the Southwest he had commanded not only regulars and Indian scouts, but also white frontiersmen. In the Northwest I had spent much of my time, for many years, either on my ranch or in long hunting trips, and had lived and worked for

# A SUCCESS IN ALL COUNTRIES.

## ✳ ANNIE OAKLEY ✳
### America's Representative Lady Shot.

For eleven years next to
BUFFALO BILL
the attraction with the
Wild West.
The wonder and talk of
the American Exhibitions
London '87,
Paris Exhibition, '89,
Horticultural Exhibition
London '92,
World's Fair, Chicago,'93

RUSSIA BELGIUM AMERICA ENGLAND FRANCE SPAIN ITALY AUSTRIA GERMANY HOLLAND

Miss Oakley,
has appeared before all
the Royalty and Nobility
of Europe, including
their R. H. the
Prince and Princess
of Wales
before whom she has
given fine exhibitions.

*Hon Wm McKinley President*

*Dear Sir I for one feel Confident that your good judgment will carry America safely through without war But in case of such an event I am ready to place a company of fifty lady sharpshooters at your disposal. Every one of them will be an American and as they will furnish their own Arms and Ammunition will be little if any expense to the government*

*Very Truly Annie Oakley*

---

*In this April 5, 1898,* LETTER TO PRESIDENT MCKINLEY, *legendary sharpshooter and star of Buffalo Bill Cody's Wild West Show Annie Oakley offers "a company of 50 lady sharpshooters" to help in the Spanish-American War effort: "Every one of them will be an American, and as they will furnish their own arms and ammunition, will be little, if any, expense to the government." Her offer was turned down.*

months together with the cowboy and the mountain hunter, faring in every way precisely as they did.

Secretary Alger offered me the command of one of these regiments. If I had taken it, being entirely inexperienced in military work, I should not have known how to get it equipped most rapidly, for I should have spent valuable weeks in learning its needs, with the result that I should have missed the Santiago campaign, and might not even have had the consolation prize of going to Porto Rico. Fortunately, I was wise enough to tell the secretary that while I believed I could learn to command the regiment in a month, yet that it was just this very month which I could not afford to spare, and that therefore I would be quite content to go as Lieutenant-Colonel, if he would make Wood Colonel.

This was entirely satisfactory to both the president and secretary, and, accordingly, Wood and I were speedily commissioned as Colonel and Lieutenant-Colonel of the First United States Volunteer Cavalry. This was the official title of the regiment, but for some reason or other the public promptly christened us the Rough Riders. At first we fought against the use of the term, but to no purpose; and when finally the Generals of Division and Brigade began to write in formal communications about our regiment as the Rough Riders, we adopted the term ourselves.

> "I was wise enough to tell the secretary that while I believed I could learn to command the regiment in a month, yet that it was just this very month which I could not afford to spare, and that therefore I would be quite content to go as Lieutenant-Colonel, if he would make Wood Colonel."

The mustering-places for the regiment were appointed in New Mexico, Arizona, Oklahoma, and Indian Territory. The difficulty in organizing was not in selecting, but in rejecting men. Within a day or two after it was announced that we were to raise the regiment, we were literally deluged with applications from every quarter of the Union. Without the slightest trouble, so far as men went, we could have raised a brigade or even a division. The difficulty lay in arming, equipping, mounting, and disciplining the men we selected. Hundreds of regiments were being called into existence by the National Government, and each regiment was sure to have innumerable wants to be satisfied. To a man who knew the ground as Wood did, and who was entirely aware of our national unpreparedness, it was evident that the ordnance and quartermaster's bureaus could not meet, for some time to come, one-tenth of the demands that would be made upon them; and it was all-important to get in first with our demands. Thanks to his knowledge of the situation and promptness, we immediately put in our requisitions for the articles indispensable for the equipment of the regiment; and then, by ceaseless worrying of excellent bureaucrats, who had no idea how to do things quickly or how to meet an emergency, we succeeded in getting our rifles, cartridges, revolvers, clothing, shelter-tents, and horse gear just in time to enable us to go on the Santiago expedition. Some of the State troops, who were already organized as National Guards, were, of course, ready, after a fashion, when the war broke out; but no other regiment which had our work to do was able to do it in anything like as quick time, and therefore no other volunteer regiment saw anything like the fighting which we did.

Wood thoroughly realized what the Ordnance Department failed to realize, namely, the inestimable advantage of smokeless powder; and, moreover, he was bent upon our having the weapons of the regulars, for this meant that we would be brigaded with them, and it was evident that they would do the bulk of the fighting if the war were short. Accordingly, by acting with the utmost vigor and promptness, he succeeded in getting our regiment armed with the Krag-Jorgensen carbine used by the regular cavalry.

It was impossible to take any of the numerous companies which were proffered to us from the various States. The only organized bodies we were at liberty to accept were those from the four Territories. But owing to the fact that the number of men originally allotted to us, seven hundred eighty, was speedily raised to one thousand, we were given a chance to accept quite a number of eager volunteers who did not come from the Territories, but who possessed precisely the same temper that distinguished our Southwestern recruits, and whose presence materially benefited the regiment.

We drew recruits from Harvard, Yale, Princeton, and many another college; from clubs like the Somerset, of Boston, and Knickerbocker, of New York; and from among the men who belonged neither to club nor to college, but in whose veins the blood stirred with the same impulse which once sent the Vikings over sea. Four of the policemen who had served under me, while I was President of the New York Police Board, insisted on coming—two of them to die, the other two to return unhurt after honorable and dangerous service. It seemed to me that almost every friend I had in every State had some one acquaintance who was bound to go with the Rough Riders, and for whom I had to make a place. Thomas Nelson Page, General Fitzhugh Lee, Congressman Odell of New York, Senator Morgan; for each of these, and for many others, I eventually consented to accept some one or two recruits, of course only after a most rigid examination into their physical capacity, and after they had shown that they knew how to ride and shoot. I may add that in no case was I disappointed in the men thus taken.

Harvard being my own college, I had such a swarm of applications from it that I could not take one in ten. What particularly pleased me, not only in the Harvard but the Yale and Princeton men, and, indeed, in these recruits from the older States generally, was that they did not ask for commissions. With hardly an exception they entered upon their duties as troopers in the spirit which they held

THEODORE ROOSEVELT *and his Rough Riders.*

to the end, merely endeavoring to show that no work could be too hard, too disagreeable, or too dangerous for them to perform, and neither asking nor receiving any reward in the way of promotion or consideration. The Harvard contingent was practically raised by Guy Murchie, of Maine. He saw all the fighting and did his duty with the utmost gallantry, and then left the service as he had entered it, a trooper, entirely satisfied to have done his duty—and no man did it better. So it was with Dudley Dean, perhaps the best quarterback who ever played on a Harvard Eleven; and so with Bob Wrenn, a quarterback whose feats rivalled those of Dean's, and who, in addition, was the champion tennis player of America, and had, on two different years, saved this championship from going to an Englishman. So it was with Yale men like Waller, the high jumper, and Garrison and Girard; and with Princeton men like Devereux and Channing, the football players; with Lamed, the tennis player; with Craig Wadsworth, the steeplechase rider; with Joe Stevens, the crack polo player; with Hamilton Fish, the ex-captain of the Columbia crew, and with scores of others whose names are quite as worthy of mention as any of those I have given. Indeed, they all sought entry into the ranks of the Rough Riders as eagerly as if it meant something widely different from hard work, rough fare, and the possibility of death; and the reason why they turned out to be such good soldiers lay largely in the fact that they were men who had thoroughly counted the cost before entering, and who went into the regiment because they believed that this offered their best chance for seeing hard and dangerous service. Mason Mitchell, of New York, who had been a chief of scouts in the Riel Rebellion, traveled all the way to San Antonio to enlist; and others came there from distances as great.

Some of them made appeals to me which I could not possibly resist. Woodbury Kane had been a close friend of mine at Harvard. During the eighteen years that had passed since my graduation I had seen very little of him, though, being always interested in sport, I occasionally met him on the hunting field, had seen him on the deck of the *Defender* when she vanquished the *Valkyrie,* and knew the part he had played on the *Navajoe,* when, in her most important race, that otherwise unlucky yacht vanquished her opponent, the Prince of Wales' *Britannia.* When the war was on, Kane felt it his duty to fight for his country. He did not seek any position of distinction. All he desired was the chance to do whatever work he was put to do well, and to get to the front; and

he enlisted as a trooper. When I went down to the camp at San Antonio he was on kitchen duty, and was cooking and washing dishes for one of the New Mexican troops; and he was doing it so well that I had no further doubt as to how he would get on.

My friend of many hunts and ranch partner, Robert Munro Ferguson, of Scotland, who had been on Lord

**REGIMENTAL DRILL OF THE ROUGH RIDERS** *at San Antonio, Texas, 1898. Leonard Wood, front left; Theodore Roosevelt, front right; James Robb Church, second row, far right; and Alexander O. Brodie, second row, second from the left. Church won the Medal of Honor for his actions during the war, and Brodie was later appointed Governor of Arizona Territory (1902–05).*

Aberdeen's staff as a Lieutenant but a year before, likewise could not keep out of the regiment. He, too, appealed to me in terms which I could not withstand, and came in like Kane to do his full duty as a trooper, and like Kane to win his commission by the way he thus did his duty.

I felt many qualms at first in allowing men of this stamp to come in, for I could not be certain that they had counted the cost, and was afraid they would find it very hard to serve—not for a few days, but for months—in the ranks, while I, their former intimate associate, was a field-officer; but they insisted that they knew their minds, and the events showed that they did. We enlisted about fifty of them from Virginia, Maryland, and the North-eastern States, at Washington. Before allowing them to be sworn in, I gathered them together and explained that if they went in they must be prepared not merely to fight, but to perform the weary, monotonous labor incident to the ordinary routine of a soldier's life; that they must be ready to face fever exactly as they were to face bullets; that they were to obey unquestioningly, and to do their

**SEVERAL ROUGH RIDERS** *in San Antonio, Texas, 1898. Despite the fact that the Rough Riders were an odd-seeming combination of Ivy League graduates, cowboys, prospectors, and Native Americans, they all had superior skills when it came to riding horses and shooting guns.*

duty as readily if called upon to garrison a fort as if sent to the front. I warned them that work that was merely irksome and disagreeable must be faced as readily as work that was dangerous, and that no complaint of any kind must be made; and I told them that they were entirely at liberty not to go, but that after they had once signed there could then be no backing out.

Not a man of them backed out; not one of them failed to do his whole duty.

These men formed but a small fraction of the whole. They went down to San Antonio, where the regiment was to gather and where Wood preceded me, while I spent a week in Washington hurrying up the different bureaus

and telegraphing my various railroad friends, so as to ensure our getting the carbines, saddles, and uniforms that we needed from the various armories and storehouses. Then I went down to San Antonio myself, where I found the men from New Mexico, Arizona, and Oklahoma already gathered, while those from Indian Territory came in soon after my arrival.

These were the men who made up the bulk of the regiment, and gave it its peculiar character. They came from the Four Territories which yet remained within the boundaries of the United States; that is, from the lands that have been most recently won over to white civilization, and in which the conditions of life are nearest those that obtained on the frontier when there still was a frontier. They were a splendid set of men, these Southwesterners—tall and sinewy, with resolute, weather-beaten faces, and eyes that looked a man straight in the face without flinching. They included in their ranks men of every occupation; but the three types were those of the cowboy, the hunter, and the mining prospector—the man who wandered hither and thither, killing game for a living, and spending his life in the quest for metal wealth.

In all the world there could be no better material for soldiers than that afforded by these grim hunters of the mountains, these wild rough riders of the plains. They were accustomed to handling wild and savage horses; they were accustomed to following the chase with the rifle, both for sport and as a means of livelihood. Varied though their occupations had been, almost all had, at one time or another, herded cattle and hunted big game. They were hardened to life in the open, and to shifting for themselves under adverse circumstances. They were used, for all their lawless freedom, to the rough discipline of the round-up and the mining company. Some of them came from the small frontier towns; but most were from the wilderness, having left their lonely hunters' cabins and shifting cow-camps to seek new and more stirring adventures beyond the sea.

They had their natural leaders—the men who had shown they could master other men, and could more than hold their own in the eager driving life of the new settlements.

The Captains and Lieutenants were sometimes men who had campaigned in the regular army against Apache, Ute, and Cheyenne, and who, on completing their term of service, had shown their energy by settling in the new communities and growing up to be men of mark. In other cases they were sheriffs, marshals, deputy-sheriffs, and deputy-marshals—men who had fought Indians, and still more often had waged relentless war upon the bands of white desperadoes. There was Bucky O'Neill, of Arizona, Captain of Troop A, the Mayor of Prescott, a famous sheriff throughout the West for his feats of

victorious warfare against the Apache, no less than against the white road-agents and mankillers. His father had fought in Meagher's Brigade in the Civil War; and he was himself a born soldier, a born leader of men. He was a wild, reckless fellow, soft spoken, and of dauntless courage and boundless ambition; he was staunchly loyal to his friends, and cared for his men in every way. There was Captain Llewellen, of New Mexico, a good citizen, a political leader, and one of the most noted peace-officers of the country; he had been shot four times in pitched fights with red marauders and white outlaws. There was Lieutenant Ballard, who had broken up the Black Jack gang of ill-omened notoriety, and his Captain, Curry, another New Mexican sheriff of fame. The officers from the Indian Territory had almost all served as marshals and deputy-marshals; and in the Indian Territory, service as a deputy-marshal meant capacity to fight stand-up battles with the gangs of outlaws.

Three of our higher officers had been in the regular army. One was Major Alexander Brodie, from Arizona, afterward Lieutenant-Colonel, who had lived for twenty years in the Territory, and had become a thorough

MAJOR ALEXANDER O. BRODIE, *Camp Wikoff, Montauk, New York, 1898.*

Westerner without sinking the West Pointer—a soldier by taste as well as training, whose men worshipped him and would follow him anywhere, as they would Bucky O'Neill or any other of their favorites. Brodie was running a big mining business; but when the *Maine* was blown up, he abandoned everything and telegraphed right and left to bid his friends get ready for the fight he saw impending.

Then there was Micah Jenkins, the Captain of Troop K, a gentle and courteous South Carolinian, on whom danger acted like wine. In action he was a perfect gamecock, and he won his majority for gallantry in battle.

Finally, there was Allyn Capron, who was, on the whole, the best soldier in the regiment. In fact, I think he was the ideal of what an American regular army officer should be. He was the fifth in descent from father to son who had served in the army of the United States, and in body and mind alike he was fitted to play his part to perfection. Tall and lithe, a remarkable boxer and walker, a first-class rider and shot, with yellow hair and piercing blue eyes, he looked what he was, the archetype of the fighting man. He had under him one of the two companies from the Indian Territory; and he so soon impressed

CAPTAIN ALLYN CAPRON.

A GROUP PORTRAIT OF ROUGH RIDERS *with Colt machine guns, San Antonio, Texas, 1898.*

himself upon the wild spirit of his followers, that he got them ahead in discipline faster than any other troop in the regiment, while at the same time taking care of their bodily wants. His ceaseless effort was so to train them, care for them, and inspire them as to bring their fighting efficiency to the highest possible pitch. He required instant obedience, and tolerated not the slightest evasion of duty; but his mastery of his art was so thorough and his performance of his own duty so rigid that he won at once not merely their admiration, but that soldierly affection so readily given by the man in the ranks to the superior who cares for his men and leads them fearlessly in battle.

All—Easterners and Westerners, Northerners and Southerners, officers and men, cowboys and college graduates, wherever they came from, and whatever their social position—possessed in common the traits of hardihood and a thirst for adventure. They were to a man born adventurers, in the old sense of the word.

The men in the ranks were mostly young; yet some were past their first youth. These had taken part in the killing of the great buffalo herds, and had fought Indians when the tribes were still on the war-path. The younger ones, too, had led rough lives; and the lines in their faces told of many a hardship endured, and many a danger silently faced with grim, unconscious philosophy. Some were originally from the East, and had seen strange adventures in different kinds of life, from sailing round the Horn to mining in Alaska. Others had been born and bred in the West, and had never seen a larger town than Santa Fé or a bigger body of water than the Pecos in flood. Some of them went by their own name; some had changed their names; and yet others possessed but half a name, colored by some adjective, like Cherokee Bill, Happy Jack of Arizona, Smoky Moore, the bronco-buster, so named because cowboys often call vicious horses "smoky" horses, and Rattlesnake Pete, who had lived among the Moquis and taken part in the snake dances. Some were professional gamblers, and, on the other hand, no less than four were or had been Baptist or Methodist clergymen—and

proved first-class fighters, too, by the way. Some were men whose lives in the past had not been free from the taint of those fierce kinds of crime into which the lawless spirits who dwell on the borderland between civilization and savagery so readily drift. A far larger number had served at different times in those bodies of armed men with which the growing civilization of the border finally puts down its savagery.

There was one characteristic and distinctive contingent which could have appeared only in such a regiment as ours. From the Indian Territory there came a number of Indians—Cherokees, Chickasaws, Choctaws, and Creeks. Only a few were of pure blood. The others shaded off until they were absolutely indistinguishable from their white comrades; with whom, it may be mentioned, they all lived on terms of complete equality.

Not all of the Indians were from the Indian Territory. One of the gamest fighters and best soldiers in the regiment was Pollock, a full-blooded Pawnee. He had been educated, like most of the other Indians, at one of those admirable Indian schools which have added so much to the total of the small credit account with which the White race balances the very unpleasant debit account of its dealings with the Red. Pollock was a silent, solitary fellow—an excellent penman, much given to drawing pictures. When we got down to Santiago he developed into the regimental clerk. I never suspected him of having a sense of humor until one day, at the end of our stay in Cuba, as he was sitting in the Adjutant's tent working over the returns, there turned up a trooper of the First who had been acting as barber. Eyeing him with immovable face Pollock asked, in a guttural voice: "Do you cut hair?" The man answered "Yes"; and Pollock continued, "Then you'd better cut mine," muttering, in an explanatory soliloquy: "Don't want to wear my hair long like a wild Indian when I'm in civilized warfare."

Another Indian came from Texas. He was a brakeman on the Southern Pacific, and wrote telling me he was an American Indian, and that he wanted to enlist. His name was Colbert, which at once attracted my attention; for

**A GROUP OF BRONCO BUSTERS:** *Thomas Darnell; William Wood; probably Roscoe Moore; probably Morris J. Storms; and probably Levi Jones, a Cherokee Indian, Camp Wikoff, Montauk, New York, 1898.*

I was familiar with the history of the Cherokees and Chickasaws during the eighteenth century, when they lived east of the Mississippi. Early in that century various traders, chiefly Scotchmen, settled among them, and the half-breed descendants of one named Colbert became the most noted chiefs of the Chickasaws. I summoned the applicant before me, and found that he was an excellent man, and, as I had supposed, a descendant of the old Chickasaw chiefs.

He brought into the regiment, by the way, his "partner," a white man. The two had been inseparable companions for some years, and continued so in the regiment. Every man who has lived in the West knows that, vindictive though the hatred between the white man and the Indian is when they stand against one another in what may be called their tribal relations, yet that men of Indian blood, when adopted into white communities, are usually treated precisely like anyone else.

Colbert was not the only Indian whose name I recognized. There was a Cherokee named Adair, who, upon inquiry, I found to be descended from the man who, a century and a half ago, wrote a ponderous folio, to this day of great interest, about the Cherokees, with whom he had spent the best years of his life as a trader and agent.

I don't know that I ever came across a man with a really sweeter nature than another Cherokee named

Holderman. He was an excellent soldier, and for a long time acted as cook for the headquarters mess. He was a half-breed, and came of a soldier stock on both sides and through both races. He explained to me once why he had come to the war; that it was because his people always had fought when there was a war, and he could not feel happy to stay at home when the flag was going into battle. ✳ ✳ ✳

**THERE WERE OTHER INDIANS** of much wilder type, but their wildness was precisely like that of the cowboys with whom they were associated. One or two of them needed rough discipline; and they got it, too. Like the rest of the regiment, they were splendid riders. I remember one man, whose character left much to be desired in some respects, but whose horsemanship was unexceptionable. He was mounted on an exceedingly bad bronco, which would bolt out of the ranks at drill. He broke it of this habit by the simple expedient of giving it two tremendous twists, first to one side and then to the other, as it bolted, with the result that, invariably, at the second bound its legs crossed and over it went with a smash, the rider taking the somersault with unmoved equanimity.

The life histories of some of the men who joined our regiment would make many volumes of thrilling adventure. ✳ ✳ ✳

**WHAT WAS NECESSARY** was to teach them to act together, and to obey orders. Our special task was to make them ready for action in the shortest possible time. We were bound to see fighting, and therefore to be with the first expedition that left the United States; for we could not tell how long the war would last.

I had been quite prepared for trouble when it came to enforcing discipline, but I was agreeably disappointed. There were plenty of hard characters who might by themselves have given trouble, and with one or two of whom we did have to take rough measures; but the bulk of the men thoroughly understood that without disci-

pline they would be merely a valueless mob, and they set themselves hard at work to learn the new duties. Of course, such a regiment, in spite of, or indeed I might almost say because of, the characteristics which made the individual men so exceptionally formidable as soldiers, could very readily have been spoiled. Any weakness in the commander would have ruined it. On the other hand, to treat it from the standpoint of the martinet and military pedant would have been almost equally fatal. From the beginning we started out to secure the essentials of discipline, while laying just as little stress as possible on the nonessentials. The men were singularly quick to respond to any appeal to their intelligence and patriotism. The faults they committed were those of ignorance merely. When Holderman, in announcing dinner to the colonel and the three majors, genially remarked, "If you fellars don't come soon, everything'll get cold," he had no thought of other than a kindly and respectful regard for their welfare, and was glad to modify his form of address on being told that it was not what could be described as conventionally military. When one of our sentinels, who had with much labor learned the manual of arms, saluted with great pride as I passed, and added, with a friendly nod, "Good evening, Colonel," this variation in the accepted formula on such occasions was meant, and was accepted, as mere friendly interest. In both cases the needed instruction was given and received in the same kindly spirit.

One of the new Indian Territory recruits, after twenty-four hours' stay in camp, during which he had held himself distinctly aloof from the general interests, called on the colonel in his tent, and remarked, "Well, Colonel, I want to shake hands and say we're with you. We didn't know how we would like you fellars at first; but you're all right, and you know your business, and you mean business, and you can count on us every time!"

That same night, which was hot, mosquitoes were very annoying; and shortly after midnight both the colonel and I came to the doors of our respective tents, which adjoined one another. The sentinel in front was also fighting mosquitoes. As we came out we saw him pitch his gun about ten feet off, and sit down to attack some of the pests that had swarmed up his trousers' legs. Happening to glance in our direction, he nodded pleasantly and, with unabashed and friendly feeling, remarked, "Ain't they bad?"

It was astonishing how soon the men got over these little peculiarities. They speedily grew to recognize the fact that the observance of certain forms was essential to the maintenance of proper discipline. They became scrupulously careful in touching their hats, and always came to attention when spoken to. They saw that we did not insist upon the observance of these forms to humiliate them; that we were as anxious to learn our own duties as we were to have them learn theirs, and as scrupulous in paying respect to our superiors as we were in exacting the acknowledgment due our rank from those below us; moreover, what was very important, they saw that we were careful to look after their interests in every way, and were doing all that was possible to hurry up the equipment and drill of the regiment, so as to get into the war.

Rigid guard duty was established at once, and everyone was impressed with the necessity for vigilance and watchfulness. The policing of the camp was likewise attended to with the utmost rigor. As always with new troops, they were at first indifferent to the necessity for cleanliness in camp arrangements; but on this point Colonel Wood brooked no laxity, and in a very little while the hygienic conditions of the camp were as good as those of any regular regiment. Meanwhile the men were being drilled, on foot at first, with the utmost assiduity. Every night we had officers' school, the noncommissioned officers of each troop being given similar schooling by the Captain or one of the Lieutenants of the troop; and every day we practiced hard, by squad, by troop, by squadron and battalion. The earnestness and intelligence with which the men went to work rendered the task of instruction much less difficult than would be supposed. It soon grew easy to handle the regiment in all the simpler forms of close

and open order. When they had grown so that they could be handled with ease in marching, and in the ordinary maneuvers of the drill-ground, we began to train them in open-order work, skirmishing and firing. Here their woodcraft and plainscraft, their knowledge of the rifle, helped us very much. Skirmishing they took to naturally, which was fortunate, as practically all our fighting was done in open order.

Meanwhile we were purchasing horses. Judging from what I saw I do not think that we got heavy enough animals, and of those purchased certainly a half were nearly unbroken. It was no easy matter to handle them on the picket-lines, and to provide for feeding and watering; and the efforts to shoe and ride them were at first productive of much vigorous excitement. Of course, those that were wild from the range had to be thrown and tied down before they could be shod. Half the horses of the regiment bucked, or possessed some other of the amiable weaknesses incident to horse life on the great ranches; but we had abundance of men who were utterly unmoved by any antic a horse might commit. Every animal was speedily mastered, though a large number remained to the end mounts upon which an ordinary rider would have felt very uncomfortable.

My own horses were purchased for me by a Texas friend, John Moore, with whom I had once hunted peccaries on the Nueces. I only paid fifty dollars apiece, and the animals were not showy; but they were tough and hardy, and answered my purpose well.

Mounted drill with such horses and men bade fair to offer opportunities for excitement; yet it usually went off smoothly enough. Before drilling the men on horseback they had all been drilled on foot, and having gone at their work with hearty zest, they knew well the simple movements to form any kind of line or column. Wood was busy from morning till night in hurrying the final details of the equipment, and he turned the drill of the men over to me. To drill perfectly needs long practice, but to drill roughly is a thing very easy to learn indeed. We were not always right about our intervals, our lines were somewhat

**TROOP K ROUGH RIDERS** *mounted on horses, 1898. In front, from left to right: Woodbury Kane, Joseph A. Carr, and Horace K. Devereaux.*

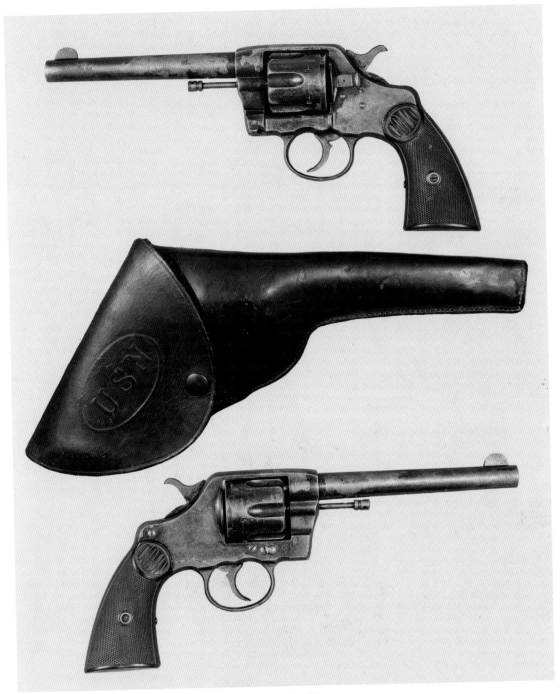

*The* COLT REVOLVER *used by Colonel Roosevelt in the Spanish-American War.*

irregular, and our more difficult movements were executed at times in rather a haphazard way; but the essential commands and the essential movements we learned without any difficulty, and the men performed them with great dash. When we put them on horseback, there was, of course, trouble with the horses; but the horsemanship of the riders was consummate. In fact, the men were immensely interested in making their horses perform each evolution with the utmost speed and accuracy, and in forcing each unquiet, vicious brute to get into line and stay in line, whether he would or not. The guidon-bearers held their plunging steeds true to the line, no matter what they tried to do; and each wild rider brought his wild horse into his proper place with a dash and ease which showed the natural cavalryman.

In short, from the very beginning the horseback drills were good fun, and everyone enjoyed them. We marched out through the adjoining country to drill wherever we found open ground, practicing all the different column formations as we went. On the open ground we threw out the line to one side or the other, and in one position and the other, sometimes at the trot, sometimes at the gallop. As the men grew accustomed to the simple evolutions, we tried them more and more in skirmish drills, practicing them so that they might get accustomed to advance in open order and to skirmish in any country, while the horses were held in the rear.

Our arms were the regular cavalry carbine, the "Krag," a splendid weapon, and the revolver. A few carried their favorite Winchesters, using, of course, the new model, which took the Government cartridge. We felt very strongly that it would be worse than a waste of time to try to train our men to use the sabre—a weapon utterly alien to them; but with the rifle and revolver they were already thoroughly familiar. Many of my cavalry friends in the past had insisted to me that the revolver was a better weapon than the sword—among them Basil Duke, the noted Confederate cavalry leader, and Captain Frank Edwards, whom I had met when elk-hunting on the headwaters of the Yellowstone and the Snake. Personally, I knew too little to decide as to the comparative merits of the two arms; but I did know that it was a great deal better to use the arm with which our men were already proficient. They were therefore armed with what might be called their natural weapon, the revolver.

As it turned out, we were not used mounted at all, so that our preparations on this point came to nothing. In a way, I have always regretted this. We thought we should at least be employed as cavalry in the great campaign against Havana in the fall; and from the beginning I began to train my men in shock tactics for use against hostile cavalry. My belief was that the horse was really the weapon with which to strike the first blow. I felt that if my men could be trained to hit their adversaries with their horses, it was a matter of small amount whether, at the moment when the onset occurred, sabres, lances, or revolvers were used; while in the subsequent mêlée I believed the revolver would outclass cold steel as a weapon. But this is all guesswork, for we never had occasion to try the experiment.

It was astonishing what a difference was made by two or three weeks' training. The mere thorough performance of guard and police duties helped the men very rapidly to become soldiers. The officers studied hard, and both officers and men worked hard in the drill-field. It was, of course, rough and ready drill; but it was very efficient, and it was suited to the men who made up the regiment. Their uniform also suited them. In their slouch hats, blue flannel shirts, brown trousers, leggings and boots, with handkerchiefs knotted loosely around their necks, they looked exactly as a body of cowboy cavalry should look. The officers speedily grew to realize that they must not be over-familiar with their men, and yet that they must care for them in every way. The men, in return, began to acquire those habits of attention to soldierly detail which mean so much in making a regiment. Above all, every man felt, and had constantly instilled into him, a keen pride of the regiment, and a resolute purpose to do his whole duty uncomplainingly, and, above all, to win glory by the way he handled himself in battle.

# To Cuba

Up to the last moment we were spending every ounce of energy we had in getting the regiment into shape. Fortunately, there were a good many vacancies among the officers, as the original number of seven hundred eighty men was increased to one thousand; so that two companies were organized entirely anew. This gave the chance to promote some first-rate men.

One of the most useful members of the regiment was Dr. Robb Church, formerly a Princeton football player. He was appointed as Assistant Surgeon, but acted throughout almost all the Cuban campaign as the Regimental Surgeon. It was Dr. Church who first gave me an idea of Bucky O'Neill's versatility, for I happened to overhear them discussing Aryan word-roots together, and then sliding off into a review of the novels of Balzac, and a discussion as to how far Balzac could be said to be the founder of the modern realistic school of fiction. Church had led almost as varied a life as Bucky himself, his career including incidents as far apart as exploring and elk-hunting in the Olympic Mountains, cooking in a lumber-camp, and serving as doctor on an emigrant ship.

Woodbury Kane was given a commission, and also Horace Devereux, of Princeton. Kane was older than the other college men who entered in the ranks; and as he had the same good qualities to start with, this resulted in his ultimately becoming perhaps the most useful soldier in the regiment. He escaped wounds and serious sickness, and was able to serve through every day of the regiment's existence.

Two of the men made Second Lieutenants by promotion from the ranks while in San Antonio were John Greenway, a noted Yale football player and catcher on her baseball nine, and David Goodrich, for two years captain of the Harvard crew. They were young men,

Goodrich having only just graduated; while Greenway, whose father had served with honor in the Confederate Army, had been out of Yale three or four years. They were natural soldiers, and it would be wellnigh impossible to overestimate the amount of good they did the regiment. They were strapping fellows, entirely fearless, modest, and quiet. Their only thought was how to perfect themselves in their own duties, and how to take care of the men under them, so as to bring them to the highest point of soldierly perfection. I grew steadily to rely upon them, as men who could be counted upon with absolute certainty, not only in every emergency, but in all routine work. They were never so tired as not to respond with eagerness to the slightest suggestion of doing something new, whether it was dangerous or merely difficult and laborious. They not merely did their duty, but were always on the watch to find out some new duty which they could construe to be theirs. Whether it was policing camp, or keeping guard, or preventing straggling on the march, or procuring food for the men, or seeing that they took care of themselves in camp, or performing some feat of unusual hazard in the fight—no call was ever made upon them to which they did not respond with eager thankfulness for being given the chance to answer it. Later on I worked them as hard as I knew how, and the regiment will always be their debtor.

Greenway was from Arkansas. We could have filled up the whole regiment many times over from the South Atlantic and Gulf States alone, but were only able to accept a very few applicants. One of them was John McIlhenny, of Louisiana; a planter and manufacturer, a big-game hunter and booklover, who could have had a commission in the Louisiana troops, but who preferred to go as a trooper in the Rough Riders because he believed we would surely see fighting. He could have commanded any influence, social or political, he wished; but he never

*In this May 1898 photograph,* **THEODORE ROOSEVELT, LEONARD WOOD, AND ALEXANDER O. BRODIE** *sit in front of camp tents in San Antonio, where the Rough Riders trained before deploying to Cuba by way of Tampa.*

asked a favor of any kind. He went into one of the New Mexican troops, and by his high qualities and zealous attention to duty speedily rose to a sergeancy, and finally won his lieutenancy for gallantry in action.

The tone of the officers' mess was very high. Everyone seemed to realize that he had undertaken most serious work. They all earnestly wished for a chance to distinguish themselves, and fully appreciated that they ran the risk not merely of death, but of what was infinitely worse—namely, failure at the crisis to perform duty well; and they strove earnestly so to train themselves, and the men under them, as to minimize the possibility of such disgrace. Every officer and every man was taught continually to look forward to the day of battle eagerly, but with an entire sense of the drain that would then

be made upon his endurance and resolution. They were also taught that, before the battle came, the rigorous performance of the countless irksome duties of the camp and the march was demanded from all alike, and that no excuse would be tolerated for failure to perform duty. Very few of the men had gone into the regiment lightly, and the fact that they did their duty so well may be largely attributed to the seriousness with which these eager, adventurous young fellows approached their work. This seriousness, and a certain simple manliness which accompanied it, had one very pleasant side. During our entire time of service, I never heard in the officers' mess a foul story or a foul word; and though there was occasional hard swearing in moments of emergency, yet even this was the exception.

SHOEING A BRONCO *at camp, San Antonio, Texas, 1898.*

"Every officer and every man was taught continually to look forward to the day of battle eagerly, but with an entire sense of the drain that would then be made upon his endurance and resolution."

The regiment attracted adventurous spirits from everywhere. Our chief trumpeter was a native American, our second trumpeter was from the Mediterranean—I think an Italian—who had been a soldier of fortune not only in Egypt, but in the French Army in Southern China. Two excellent men were Osborne, a tall Australian, who had been an officer in the New South Wales Mounted Rifles; and Cook, an Englishman, who had served in South Africa. Both, when the regiment disbanded, were plaintive in expressing their fond regret that it could not be used against the Transvaal Boers!

One of our best soldiers was a man whose real and assumed names I, for obvious reasons conceal. He usually went by a nickname which I will call Tennessee. He was a tall, gaunt fellow, with a quiet and distinctly sinister eye, who did his duty excellently, especially when a fight was on, and who, being an expert gambler, always contrived to reap a rich harvest after pay day. When the regiment was mustered out, he asked me to put a brief memorandum of his services on his discharge certificate, which I gladly did. He much appreciated this, and added, in explanation, "You see, Colonel, my real name isn't Smith, it's Yancy. I had to change it, because three or four years ago I had a little trouble with a gentleman, and—er—well, in fact, I had to kill him; and the district attorney, he had it in for me, and so I just skipped the country; and now, if it ever should be brought up against me, I should like to show your certificate as to my character!" The course of frontier justice sometimes moves in unexpected zigzags; so I did not express the doubt I felt as to whether my certificate that he had been a good soldier would help him much if he was tried for a murder committed three or four years previously.

The men worked hard and faithfully. As a rule, in spite of the number of rough characters among them, they behaved very well. One night a few of them went on a spree, and proceeded "to paint San Antonio red." One was captured by the city authorities, and we had to leave him behind us in jail. The others we dealt with ourselves, in a way that prevented a repetition of the occurrence.

The men speedily gave one another nicknames, largely conferred in a spirit of derision, their basis lying in contrast. A brave but fastidious member of a well-known Eastern club, who was serving in the ranks, was christened "Tough Ike"; and his bunkie, the man who shared his shelter-tent, who was a decidedly rough cowpuncher, gradually acquired the name of "The Dude." One unlucky and simpleminded cowpuncher, who had never been east of the great plains in his life, unwarily boasted that he had an aunt in New York, and ever afterward went by the name of "Metropolitan Bill." A huge red-headed Irishman was named "Sheeny Solomon." A young Jew who developed into one of the best fighters in the regiment accepted, with entire equanimity, the name of "Pork chop." We had quite a number of professional gamblers, who, I am bound to say, usually made good soldiers. One, who was almost abnormally quiet and gentle, was called "Hell Roarer"; while another, who in point of language and deportment was his exact antithesis, was christened "Prayerful James."

While the officers and men were learning their duties, and learning to know one another, Colonel Wood was straining every nerve to get our equipments—an effort which was complicated by the tendency of the Ordnance Bureau to send whatever we really needed by freight instead of express. Finally, just as the last rifles, revolvers, and saddles came, we were ordered by wire at once to proceed by train to Tampa.

Instantly, all was joyful excitement. We had enjoyed San Antonio, and were glad that our regiment had been organized in the city where the Alamo commemorates the death fight of Crockett, Bowie, and their famous band of frontier heroes. All of us had worked hard, so that we had had no time to be homesick or downcast; but we were glad to leave the hot camp, where every day the strong wind sifted the dust through everything, and to start for the gathering place of the army which was to invade Cuba. Our horses and men were getting into good shape. We were well enough equipped to warrant our starting on the campaign, and every man was filled with dread of being out of the fighting. We had a pack-train of one hundred fifty mules, so we had close on to one thousand two hundred animals to carry. * * *

**EVERYWHERE THE PEOPLE CAME OUT** to greet us and cheer us. They brought us flowers; they brought us watermelons and other fruits, and sometimes jugs and pails of milk—all of which we greatly appreciated. We were travelling through a region where practically all the older men had served in the Confederate Army, and where the younger men had all their lives long drunk in the endless tales told by their elders, at home, and at the crossroads taverns, and in the court-house squares, about the cavalry of Forrest and Morgan and the infantry of Jackson and Hood. The blood of the old men stirred to the distant breath of battle; the blood of the young men leaped hot with eager desire to accompany us. The older women, who remembered the dreadful misery of war—the misery that presses its iron weight most heavily on the wives and the little ones—looked sadly at us; but the young girls drove down in bevies, arrayed in their finery, to wave flags in farewell to the troopers and to beg cartridges and buttons as mementos. Everywhere we saw the Stars and Stripes, and everywhere we were told, half-laughing, by grizzled ex-Confederates that they had never dreamed in the bygone days of bitterness to greet the old flag as they now were greeting it, and to send their sons, as now they were sending them, to fight and die under it.

It was four days later that we disembarked, in a perfect welter of confusion. Tampa lay in the pine-covered sand-flats at the end of a one-track railroad, and everything connected with both military and railroad matters was in an almost inextricable tangle. There was no one to meet us or to tell us where we were to camp, and no one to issue us food for the first twenty-four hours; while the railroad people unloaded us wherever they pleased, or rather wherever the jam of all kinds of trains rendered it possible. We had to buy the men food out of our own pockets, and to seize wagons in order to get our spare baggage taken to the camping ground which we at last found had been allotted to us.

Once on the ground, we speedily got order out of confusion. Under Wood's eye the tents were put up in long streets, the picket-line of each troop stretching down its side of each street. The officers' quarters were at the

**ROUGH RIDERS** *sleeping on the rails waiting for a train to take them to Port Tampa to embark for Cuba, June 6, 1898.*

*overleaf:* **THE BAGGAGE TRAM** *of the Rough Riders, 1898.*

upper ends of the streets, the company kitchens and sinks at the opposite ends. The camp was strictly policed, and drill promptly begun. For thirty-six hours we let the horses rest, drilling on foot, and then began the mounted drill again. The regiments with which we were afterward to serve were camped near us, and the sandy streets of the little town were thronged with soldiers, almost all of them regulars; for there were but one or two volunteer organizations besides ourselves. The regulars wore the canonical dark blue of Uncle Sam. Our own men were clad in dusty brown blouses, trousers and leggings being of the same hue, while the broad-brimmed soft hat was of dark gray; and very workmanlike they looked as, in column of fours, each troop trotted down its company street to form by squadron or battalion, the troopers sitting steadily in the saddles as they made their half-trained horses conform to the movement of the guidons.

Over in Tampa town the huge winter hotel was gay with general officers and their staffs, with women in pretty dresses, with newspaper correspondents by the score, with military attachés of foreign powers, and with onlookers of all sorts; but we spent very little time there.

We worked with the utmost industry, special attention being given by each troop-commander to skirmish-drill in the woods. Once or twice we had mounted drill of the regiment as a whole. The military attachés came out to look on—English, German, Russian, French, and Japanese. With the Englishman, Captain Arthur Lee, a capital fellow, we soon struck up an especially close friendship; and we saw much of him throughout the campaign. So we did of several of the newspaper correspondents— Richard Harding Davis, John Fox, Jr., Caspar Whitney, and Frederic Remington. On Sunday Chaplain Brown, of Arizona, held service, as he did almost every Sunday during the campaign.

There were but four or five days at Tampa, however. We were notified that the expedition would start for destination unknown at once, and that we were to go with it; but that our horses were to be left behind, and only

THE 3RD CAVALRY *during a training drill in Tampa, Florida, 1898.*

eight troops of seventy men each taken. Our sorrow at leaving the horses was entirely outweighed by our joy at going; but it was very hard indeed to select the four troops that were to stay, and the men who had to be left behind from each of the troops that went. Colonel Wood took Major Brodie and myself to command the two squadrons, being allowed only two squadron commanders. The men who were left behind felt the most bitter heartburn. To the great bulk of them I think it will be a lifelong sorrow. I saw more than one, both among the officers and privates, burst into tears when he found he could not go. No outsider can appreciate the bitterness of the disappointment. Of course, really, those that stayed were entitled to precisely as much honor as those that went. Each man was doing his duty, and much the hardest and most disagreeable duty was to stay. Credit should go with the performance of duty, and not with what is very often the accident of glory. All this and much more we explained, but our explanations could not alter the fact that some had to be chosen and some had to be left. One of the Captains chosen was Captain Maximilian

Luna, who commanded Troop F, from New Mexico. The Captain's people had been on the banks of the Rio Grande before my forefathers came to the mouth of the Hudson or Wood's landed at Plymouth; and he made the plea that it was his right to go as a representative of his race, for he was the only man of pure Spanish blood who bore a commission in the army, and he demanded the privilege of proving that his people were precisely as loyal Americans as any others. I was glad when it was decided to take him.

It was the evening of June 7th when we suddenly received orders that the expedition was to start from Port Tampa, nine miles distant by rail, at daybreak the following morning; and that if we were not aboard our transport by that time we could not go. We had no intention of getting left, and prepared at once for the scramble which was evidently about to take place. As the number

LIEUTENANT WILLIAM TIFFANY AND CORPORAL HENRY W. BULL *of Troop K, Tampa, Florida, 1898.*

and capacity of the transports were known, or ought to have been known, and as the number and size of the regiments to go were also known, the task of allotting each regiment or fraction of a regiment to its proper transport, and arranging that the regiments and the transports should meet in due order on the dock, ought not to have been difficult. However, no arrangements were made in advance; and we were allowed to shove and hustle for ourselves as best we could, on much the same principles that had governed our preparations hitherto.

We were ordered to be at a certain track with all our baggage at midnight, there to take a train for Port Tampa. At the appointed time we turned up, but the train did not. The men slept heavily, while Wood and I and various other officers wandered about in search of information which no one could give. We now and then came across a brigadier-general, or even a major-general; but nobody knew anything. Some regiments got aboard the trains and some did not, but as none of the trains started this made little difference. At three o'clock we received orders to march over to an entirely different track, and away we went. No train appeared on this track either; but at six o'clock some coal-cars came by, and these we seized. By various arguments we persuaded the engineer in charge of the train to back us down the nine miles to Port Tampa, where we arrived covered with coal-dust, but with all our belongings.

The railway tracks ran out on the quay, and the transports, which had been anchored in midstream, were gradually being brought up alongside the quay and loaded. The trains were unloading wherever they happened to be, no attention whatever being paid to the possible position of the transport on which the soldiers were to go. Colonel Wood and I jumped off and started on a hunt, which soon convinced us that we had our work cut out if we were to get a transport at all. From the highest General down, nobody could tell us where to go to find out what transport we were to have. At last we were informed that we were to hunt up the depot quartermaster, Colonel Humphrey. We found his office, where

**LOADING HORSES ON A TRANSPORT** *heading to Cuba from Tampa, Florida, 1898.*

**THE SCENE ON THE DOCKS** *at Port Tampa on the day of the sailing to Cuba, 1898. Only eight out of the twelve companies of Rough Riders were actually deployed to Cuba due to a shortage of room on the ships, and by the time the ships actually set sail, nearly one-fourth of the men who had been trained in San Antonio had been lost, most to diseases such as yellow fever and malaria.*

his assistant informed us that he didn't know where the colonel was, but believed him to be asleep upon one of the transports. This seemed odd at such a time; but so many of the methods in vogue were odd, that we were quite prepared to accept it as a fact. However, it proved not to be such; but for an hour Colonel Humphrey might just as well have been asleep, as nobody knew where he was and nobody could find him, and the quay was crammed with some ten thousand men, most of whom were working at cross purposes.

At last, however, after over an hour's industrious and rapid search through this swarming ant-heap of humanity, Wood and I, who had separated, found Colonel Humphrey at nearly the same time and were allotted a transport—the *Yucatan*. She was out in mid-stream, so Wood seized a stray launch and boarded her. At the same time I happened to find out that she had previously been allotted to two other regiments—the Second Regular Infantry and the Seventy-first New York Volunteers, which latter regiment alone contained more men than could be put aboard her. Accordingly, I ran at full speed to our train; and leaving a strong guard with the baggage, I double-quicked the rest of the regiment up to the boat, just in time to board her as she came

into the quay, and then to hold her against the Second Regulars and the Seventy-first, who had arrived a little too late, being a shade less ready than we were in the matter of individual initiative. There was a good deal of expostulation, but we had possession; and as the ship could not contain half of the men who had been told to go aboard her, the Seventy-first went away, as did all but four companies of the Second. These latter we took aboard. Meanwhile a general had caused our train to be unloaded at the end of the quay farthest from where the ship was; and the hungry, tired men spent most of the day in the labor of bringing down their baggage and the food and ammunition.

The officers' horses were on another boat, my own being accompanied by my colored body-servant, Marshall, the most faithful and loyal of men, himself an old soldier of the Ninth Cavalry. Marshall had been in Indian campaigns, and he christened my larger horse "Rain-in-the-Face," while the other, a pony, went by the name of "Texas."

By the time that night fell, and our transport pulled off and anchored in midstream, we felt we had spent thirty-six tolerably active hours. The transport was overloaded, the men being packed like sardines, not only below but

TRANSPORT NO. 8, YUCATAN, *conveyed Roosevelt's Rough Riders from Tampa to Cuba.*

**THE BOW OF THE *INDIANA*** *with sailors, 1898.*

upon the decks; so that at night it was only possible to walk about by continually stepping over the bodies of the sleepers. The travel rations which had been issued to the men for the voyage were not sufficient, because the meat was very bad indeed; and when a ration consists of only four or five items, which taken together just meet the requirements of a strong and healthy man, the loss of one item is a serious thing. If we had been given canned corned beef we would have been all right, but instead of this the soldiers were issued horrible stuff called "canned fresh beef." There was no salt in it. At the best it was stringy and tasteless; at the worst it was nauseating. Not one-fourth of it was ever eaten at all, even when the men became very hungry. There were no facilities for the men to cook anything. There was no ice for them; the water was not good; and they had no fresh meat or fresh vegetables.

However, all these things seemed of small importance compared with the fact that we were really embarked, and were with the first expedition to leave our shores. But by next morning came the news that the order to sail had been countermanded, and that we were to stay where we were for the time being. What this meant none of us could understand. It turned out later to be due to the blunder of a naval officer who mistook some of our vessels for Spaniards, and by his report caused consternation in Washington, until by vigorous scouting on the part of our other ships the illusion was dispelled.

Meanwhile the troopships, packed tight with their living freight, sweltered in the burning heat of Tampa Harbor. There was nothing whatever for the men to do, space being too cramped for amusement or for more drill than was implied in the manual of arms. In this we drilled them assiduously, and we also continued to hold school for both the officers and the non-commissioned officers. Each troop commander was regarded as responsible for his own noncommissioned officers, and Wood or myself simply dropped in to superintend, just as we did with the manual of arms. In the officers' school Captain Capron was the special instructor, and a most admirable one he was.

The heat, the steaming discomfort, and the confinement, together with the forced inaction, were very irksome; but everyone made the best of it, and there was little or no grumbling even among the men. All, from the highest to the lowest, were bent upon perfecting themselves according to their slender opportunities. Every book of tactics in the regiment was in use from morning until night, and the officers and noncommissioned officers were always studying the problems presented at the schools. About the only amusement was bathing over the side, in which we indulged both in the morning and evening. Many of the men from the Far West had never seen the ocean. One of them who knew how to swim was much interested in finding that the ocean water was not drinkable. Another, who had never in his life before seen any water more extensive than the headstream of the Rio Grande, met with an accident later in the voyage; that is, his hat blew away while we were in mid-ocean, and I heard him explaining the accident to a friend in the following words: "Oh-o-h, Jim! Ma hat blew into the creek!" So we lay for nearly a week, the vessels swinging around on their anchor chains, while the hot water of the bay flowed to and fro around them and the sun burned overhead.

At last, on the evening of June 13th, we received the welcome order to start. Ship after ship weighed anchor and went slowly ahead under half-steam for the distant mouth of the harbor, the bands playing, the flags flying, the rigging black with the clustered soldiers, cheering and shouting to those left behind on the quay and to their fellows on the other ships. The channel was very tortuous; and we anchored before we had gone far down it, after coming within an ace of a bad collision with another transport. The next morning we were all again under way, and in the afternoon the great fleet steamed southeast until Tampa Light sank in the distance. ✷ ✷ ✷

[O]NCE WE WERE WELL TO EASTWARD of Cuba, we ran southwest with the wind behind on our quarter, and we all knew that our destination was Santiago. On the morning of the 20th we were close to the Cuban coast. High mountains rose almost from the water's edge, looking huge and barren across the sea. We sped onward past Guantanamo Bay, where we saw the little picket-ships of the fleet; and in the afternoon we sighted Santiago Harbor, with the great warships standing off and on in front of it, gray and sullen in their war paint.

All next day we rolled and wallowed in the seaway, waiting until a decision was reached as to where we should land. On the morning of June 22nd the welcome order for landing came.

We did the landing as we had done everything else—that is, in a scramble, each commander shifting for himself. The port at which we landed was called Daiquiri, a squalid little village where there had been a railway and iron-works. There were no facilities for landing, and the fleet did not have a quarter the number of boats it should have had for the purpose. All we could do was to stand in with the transports as close as possible, and then row ashore in our own few boats and the boats of the warships. Luck favored our regiment. My former naval aide,

*A general view of the Rough Riders* PALM LEAF SHELTER *at Daiquiri, Cuba.*

while I was Assistant Secretary of the Navy, Lieutenant Sharp, was in command of the *Vixen,* a converted yacht; and everything being managed on the go-as-you-please principle, he steamed by us and offered to help put us ashore. Of course, we jumped at the chance. Wood and I boarded the *Vixen,* and there we got Lieutenant Sharp's black Cuban pilot, who told us he could take our transport right in to within a few hundred yards of the land. Accordingly, we put him aboard; and in he brought her, gaining at least a mile and a half by the maneuver. The other transports followed; but we had our berth, and were all right.

There was plenty of excitement to the landing. In the first place, the smaller war vessels shelled Daiquiri, so as to dislodge any Spaniards who might be lurking in the neighborhood, and also shelled other places along the coast, to keep the enemy puzzled as to our intentions. Then the surf was high, and the landing difficult; so that the task of getting the men, the ammunition, and provisions ashore was not easy. Each man carried three days'

field rations and a hundred rounds of ammunition. Our regiment had accumulated two rapid-fire Colt automatic guns, the gift of Stevens, Kane, Tiffany, and one or two others of the New York men, and also a dynamite gun, under the immediate charge of Sergeant Borrowe. To get these, and especially the last, ashore, involved no little work and hazard. Meanwhile, from another transport, our horses were being landed, together with the mules, by the simple process of throwing them overboard and letting them swim ashore, if they could. Both of Wood's got safely through. One of mine was drowned. The other, little Texas, got ashore all right. While I was superintending the landing at the ruined dock, with Bucky O'Neill, a boatful of colored infantry soldiers capsized, and two of the men went to the bottom; Bucky O'Neill plunging in, in full uniform, to save them, but in vain.

However, by the late afternoon we had all our men, with what ammunition and provisions they could themselves carry, landed, and were ready for anything that might turn up.

# General Young's Fight at Las Guasimas

Just before leaving Tampa we had been brigaded with the First (white) and Tenth (colored) Regular Cavalry under Brigadier-General S. B. M. Young. We were the Second Brigade, the First Brigade consisting of the Third and Sixth (white), and the Ninth (colored) Regular Cavalry under Brigadier-General Sumner. The two brigades of the cavalry division were under Major-General Joseph Wheeler, the gallant old Confederate cavalry commander.

General Young was—and is—as fine a type of the American fighting soldier as a man can hope to see. He had been in command, as Colonel, of the Yellowstone National Park, and I had seen a good deal of him in connection therewith, as I was President of the Boone and Crockett Club, an organization devoted to hunting big game, to its preservation, and to forest preservation. During the preceding winter, while he was in Washington, he had lunched with me at the Metropolitan Club, Wood being one of the other guests. Of course, we talked of the war, which all of us present believed to be impending, and Wood and I told him we were going to make every effort to get in, somehow; and he answered that we must be sure to get into his brigade, if he had one, and he would guarantee to show us fighting. None of us forgot the conversation. As soon as our regiment was raised General Young applied for it to be put in his brigade. We were put in; and he made his word good; for he fought and won the first fight on Cuban soil.

Yet, even though under him, we should not have been in this fight at all if we had not taken advantage of the chance to disembark among the first troops, and if it had not been for Wood's energy in pushing our regiment to the front.

On landing we spent some active hours in marching our men a quarter of a mile or so inland, as boatload by boatload they disembarked. Meanwhile one of the men, Knoblauch, a New Yorker, who was a great athlete and a champion swimmer, by diving in the surf off the dock,

BRIGADIER-GENERAL SAMUEL BALDWIN MARKS YOUNG *served in the Civil War and the Spanish–American War, and was later Chief of Staff of the U.S. Army.*

recovered most of the rifles which had been lost when the boatload of colored cavalry capsized. The country would have offered very great difficulties to an attacking force had there been resistance. It was little but a mass of rugged and precipitous hills, covered for the most part by dense jungle. Five hundred resolute men could have prevented the disembarkation at very little cost to themselves. There had been about that number of Spaniards at Daiquiri that morning, but they had fled even before the ships began shelling. In their place we found hundreds of Cuban insurgents, a crew of as utter tatterdemalions as human eyes ever looked on, armed with every kind of rifle in all stages of dilapidation. It was evident, at a glance, that they would be no use in serious fighting, but it was hoped that they might be of service in scouting. From a variety of causes, however, they turned out to be nearly useless, even for this purpose, so far as the Santiago campaign was concerned. ✳ ✳ ✳

**I HAD SUCCEEDED IN FINDING TEXAS,** my surviving horse, much the worse for his fortnight on the transport and his experience in getting off, but still able to carry me.

It was mid-afternoon and the tropic sun was beating fiercely down when Colonel Wood started our regiment— the First and Tenth Cavalry and some of the infantry regiments having already marched. Colonel Wood himself rode in advance, while I led my squadron, and Major Brodie followed with his. It was a hard march, the hilly jungle trail being so narrow that often we had to go in single file. We marched fast, for Wood was bound to get us ahead of the other regiments, so as to be sure of our place in the body that struck the enemy next morning. If it had not been for his energy in pushing forward, we should certainly have missed the fight. As it was, we did not halt until we were at the extreme front.

The men were not in very good shape for marching, and moreover they were really horsemen, the majority being cowboys who had never done much walking. The heat was intense and their burdens very heavy. Yet there was very little straggling. Whenever we halted they instantly took off their packs and threw themselves on their backs. Then at the word to start they would spring into place again. The captains and lieutenants tramped along, encouraging the men by example and word. A good part of the time I was by Captain Llewellen, and was greatly pleased to see the way in which he kept his men up to their work. He never pitied or coddled his troopers, but he always looked after them. He helped them whenever he could, and took rather more than his full share of hardship and danger, so that his men naturally followed him with entire devotion. Jack Greenway

COLONEL ROOSEVELT'S WAR HORSE "LITTLE TEXAS," *on which he charged up San Juan Hill, and Marshall, Roosevelt's servant, 1898.*

was under him as lieutenant, and to him the entire march was nothing but an enjoyable outing, the chance of fight on the morrow simply adding the needed spice of excitement.

It was long after nightfall when we tramped through the darkness into the squalid coast hamlet of Siboney. As usual when we made a night camp, we simply drew the men up in column of troops, and then let each man lie down where he was. Black thunderclouds were gathering. Before they broke the fires were made and the men cooked their coffee and pork, some frying the hardtack with the pork. The officers, of course, fared just as the men did. Hardly had we finished eating when the rain came, a regular tropic downpour. We sat about, sheltering ourselves as best we could, for the hour or two it lasted; then the fires were relighted and we closed around them, the men taking off their wet things to dry them, so far as possible, by the blaze.

Wood had gone off to see General Young, as General Wheeler had instructed General Young to hit the Spaniards, who were about four miles away, as soon after daybreak as possible. Meanwhile I strolled over to Captain Capron's troop. He and I, with his two lieutenants, Day and Thomas, stood around the fire, together with two or three noncommissioned officers and privates; among the latter were Sergeant Hamilton Fish and Trooper Elliot Cowdin, both of New York. Cowdin, together with two other troopers, Harry Thorpe and Munro Ferguson, had been on my Oyster Bay Polo Team some years before. Hamilton Fish had already shown himself one of the best noncommissioned officers we had. A huge fellow, of enormous strength and endurance and dauntless courage, he took naturally to a soldier's life. He never complained and never shirked any duty of any kind, while his power over his men was great. So good a sergeant had he made that Captain Capron, keen to get the best men under him, took him when he left Tampa— for Fish's troop remained behind. As we stood around the flickering blaze that night I caught myself admiring the splendid bodily vigor of Capron and Fish—the

captain and the sergeant. Their frames seemed of steel, to withstand all fatigue; they were flushed with health; in their eyes shone high resolve and fiery desire. Two finer types of the fighting man, two better representatives of the American soldier, there were not in the whole army. Capron was going over his plans for the fight when we should meet the Spaniards on the morrow, Fish occasionally asking a question. They were both filled with eager longing to show their mettle, and both were rightly confident that if they lived they would win honorable renown and would rise high in their chosen profession. Within twelve hours they both were dead.

I had lain down when toward midnight Wood returned. He had gone over the whole plan with General Young. We were to start by sunrise toward Santiago, General Young taking four troops of the Tenth and four troops of the First up the road which led through the valley; while Colonel Wood was to lead our eight troops along a hill-trail to the left, which joined the valley road about four miles on, at a point where the road went over a spur of the mountain chain and from thence went down hill toward Santiago. The Spaniards had their lines at the junction of the road and the trail.

Before describing our part in the fight, it is necessary to say a word about General Young's share, for, of course, the whole fight was under his direction, and the fight on the right wing under his immediate supervision. General Young had obtained from General Castillo, the commander of the Cuban forces, a full description of the country in front. General Castillo promised Young the aid of eight hundred Cubans, if he made a reconnaissance in force to find out exactly what the Spanish strength was. This promised Cuban aid did not, however, materialize, the Cubans, who had been beaten back by the Spaniards the day before, not appearing on the firing-line until the fight was over.

General Young had in his immediate command a squadron of the First Regular Cavalry, two hundred and forty-four strong, under the command of Major Bell, and a squadron of the Tenth Regular Cavalry, two hundred

and twenty strong, under the command of Major Norvell. He also had two Hotchkiss mountain guns, under Captain Watson of the Tenth. He started at a quarter before six in the morning, accompanied by Captain A. L. Mills, as aide. It was at half-past seven that Captain Mills, with a patrol of two men in advance, discovered the Spaniards as they lay across where the two roads came together, some of them in pits, others simply lying in the heavy jungle, while on their extreme right they occupied a big ranch. Where General Young struck them they held a high ridge a little to the left of his front, this ridge being separated by a deep ravine from the hill-trail still farther to the left, down which the Rough Riders were advancing. That is, their forces occupied a range of high hills in the form of an obtuse angle, the salient being toward the space between the American forces, while there were advance parties along both roads. There were stone breastworks flanked by blockhouses on that part of the ridge where the two trails came together. The place was called Las Guasimas, from trees of that name in the neighborhood.

General Young, who was riding a mule, carefully examined the Spanish position in person. He ordered the canteens of the troops to be filled, placed the Hotchkiss battery in concealment about nine hundred yards from the Spanish lines, and then deployed the white regulars, with the colored regulars in support, having sent a Cuban guide to try to find Colonel Wood and warn him. He did not attack immediately, because he knew that Colonel Wood, having a more difficult route, would require a longer time to reach the position. During the delay General Wheeler arrived; he had been up since long before dawn, to see that everything went well. Young informed him of the dispositions and plan of attack he made. General Wheeler approved of them, and with excellent judgment left General Young a free hand to fight his battle.

So, about eight o'clock Young began the fight with his Hotchkiss guns, he himself being up on the firing-line. No sooner had the Hotchkiss one-pounders opened than the Spaniards opened fire in return, most of the time

GENERAL JOSEPH WHEELER, *in 1898. He served as a Confederate General in the Civil War and as a U.S. General in the Spanish-American War.*

firing by volleys executed in perfect time, almost as on parade. They had a couple of light guns, which our people thought were quick firers. The denseness of the jungle and the fact that they used absolutely smokeless powder, made it exceedingly difficult to place exactly where they were, and almost immediately Young, who always liked to get as close as possible to his enemy, began to push his troops forward. They were deployed on both sides of

the road in such thick jungle that it was only here and there that they could possibly see ahead, and some confusion, of course, ensued, the support gradually getting mixed with the advance. Captain Beck took A Troop of the Tenth in on the left, next Captain Galbraith's troop of the First; two other troops of the Tenth were on the extreme right. Through the jungle ran wire fences here and there, and as the troops got to the ridge they encountered precipitous heights. They were led most gallantly, as American regular officers always lead their men; and the men followed their leaders with the splendid courage always shown by the American regular soldier. There was not a single straggler among them, and in not one instance was an attempt made by any trooper to fall out in order to assist the wounded or carry back the dead, while so cool were they and so perfect their fire discipline, that in the entire engagement the expenditure of ammunition was not over ten rounds per man. Major Bell, who commanded the squadron, had his leg broken by a shot as he was leading his men. Captain Wainwright succeeded to the command of the squadron. Captain Knox was shot in the abdomen. He continued for some time giving orders to his troops, and refused to allow a man in the firing-line to assist him to the rear. His First Lieutenant, Byram, was himself shot, but continued to lead his men until the wound and the heat overcame him and he fell in a faint. The advance was pushed forward under General Young's eye with the utmost energy, until the enemy's voices could be heard in the entrenchments. The Spaniards kept up a very heavy firing, but the regulars would not be denied, and as they climbed the ridges the Spaniards broke and fled.

Meanwhile, at six o'clock, the Rough Riders began their advance. We first had to climb a very steep hill. Many of the men, footsore and weary from their march of the preceding day, found the pace up this hill too hard, and either dropped their bundles or fell out of line, with the result that we went into action with less than five hundred men—as, in addition to the stragglers, a detachment had been left to guard the baggage on shore. At the

time I was rather inclined to grumble to myself about Wood setting so fast a pace, but when the fight began I realized that it had been absolutely necessary, as otherwise we should have arrived late and the regulars would have had very hard work indeed. Tiffany, by great exertions, had corralled a couple of mules and was using them to transport the Colt automatic guns in the rear of the regiment. The dynamite gun was not with us, as mules for it could not be obtained in time.

Captain Capron's troop was in the lead, it being chosen for the most responsible and dangerous position because of Capron's capacity. Four men, headed by Sergeant Hamilton Fish, went first; a support of twenty men followed some distance behind; and then came Capron and the rest of his troop, followed by Wood, with whom General Young had sent Lieutenants Smedburg and Rivers as aides. I rode close behind, at the head of the other three troops of my squadron, and then came Brodie at the head of his squadron. The trail was so narrow that for the most part the men marched in single file, and it was bordered by dense, tangled jungle, through which a man could with difficulty force his way; so that to put out flankers was impossible, for they could not possibly have kept up with the march of the column. Every man had his canteen full. There was a Cuban guide at the head of the column, but he ran away as soon as the fighting began. There were also with us, at the head of the column, two men who did not run away, who, though non-combatants—newspaper correspondents—showed as much gallantry as any soldier in the field. They were Edward Marshall and Richard Harding Davis.

After reaching the top of the hill the walk was very pleasant. Now and then we came to glades or rounded hill-shoulders, whence we could look off for some distance. The tropical forest was very beautiful, and it was a delight to see the strange trees, the splendid royal palms and a tree which looked like a flat-topped acacia, and which was covered with a mass of brilliant scarlet flowers. We heard many bird-notes, too, the cooing of doves and the call of a great brush cuckoo. Afterward we found that

the Spanish guerillas imitated these birdcalls, but the sounds we heard that morning, as we advanced through the tropic forest, were from birds, not guerillas, until we came right up to the Spanish lines. It was very beautiful and very peaceful, and it seemed more as if we were off on some hunting excursion than as if were about to go into a sharp and bloody little fight. ✳ ✳ ✳

**TO THE RIGHT** the jungle was quite thick, and we had barely begun to deploy when a crash in front announced that the fight was on. It was evidently very hot, and L Troop had its hands full; so I hurried my men up abreast of them. So thick was the jungle that it was very difficult to keep together, especially when there was no time for delay, and while I got up Llewellen's troops and Kane's platoon of K Troop, the rest of K Troop under Captain Jenkins which, with Bucky O'Neill's troop, made up the right wing, were behind, and it was some time before they got into the fight at all.

Meanwhile I had gone forward with Llewellen, Greenway, Kane and their troopers until we came out on a kind of shoulder, jutting over a ravine, which separated us from a great ridge on our right. It was on this ridge that the Spaniards had some of their intrenchments, and it was just beyond this ridge that the Valley Road led, up which the regulars were at that very time pushing their attack; but, of course, at the moment we knew nothing of this. The effect of the smokeless powder was remarkable. The air seemed full of the rustling sound of the Mauser bullets, for the Spaniards knew the trails by which we were advancing, and opened heavily on our position. Moreover, as we advanced we were, of course, exposed, and they could see us and fire. But they themselves were entirely invisible. The jungle covered everything, and not the faintest trace of smoke was to be seen in any direction to indicate from whence the bullets came. It was some time before the men fired; Llewellen, Kane, and I anxiously studying the ground to see where our opponents were, and utterly unable to find out.

We could hear the faint reports of the Hotchkiss guns and the reply of two Spanish guns, and the Mauser bullets were singing through the trees over our heads, making a noise like the humming of telephone wires; but exactly where they came from we could not tell. The Spaniards were firing high and for the most part by volleys, and their shooting was not very good, which perhaps was not to be wondered at, as they were a long way off. Gradually, however, they began to get the range and occasionally one of our men would crumple up. In no case did the man make any outcry when hit, seeming to take it as a matter of course; at the outside, making only such a remark as, "Well, I got it that time." With hardly an exception, there was no sign of flinching. I say with hardly an exception, for though I personally did not see an instance, and though all the men at the front behaved excellently, yet there were a very few men who lagged behind and drifted back to the trail over which we had come. The character of the fight put a premium upon such conduct, and afforded a very severe test for raw troops; because the jungle was so dense that as we advanced in open order, every man was, from time to time, left almost alone and away from the eyes of his officers. There was unlimited opportunity for dropping out without attracting notice, while it was peculiarly hard to be exposed to the fire of an unseen foe, and to see men dropping under it, and yet to be, for some time, unable to return it, and also to be entirely ignorant of what was going on in any other part of the field.

It was Richard Harding Davis who gave us our first opportunity to shoot back with effect. He was behaving precisely like my officers, being on the extreme front of the line, and taking every opportunity to study with his glasses the ground where we thought the Spaniards were. I had tried some volley firing at points where I rather doubtfully believed the Spaniards to be, but had stopped firing and was myself studying the jungle-covered mountain ahead with my glasses, when Davis suddenly said: "There they are, Colonel; look over there; I can see their hats near that glade," pointing across the valley to our right. In a minute I, too, made out the hats, and then

CUBAN REVOLUTIONARIES, *1898.*

pointed them out to three or four of our best shots, giving them my estimate of the range. For a minute or two no result followed, and I kept raising the range, at the same time getting more men on the firing-line. Then, evidently, the shots told, for the Spaniards suddenly sprang out of the cover through which we had seen their hats, and ran to another spot; and we could now make out a large number of them.

I accordingly got all of my men up in line and began quick firing. In a very few minutes our bullets began to do damage, for the Spaniards retreated to the left into the jungle, and we lost sight of them. At the same moment a big body of men who, it afterward turned out, were Spaniards, came in sight along the glade, following the retreat of those whom we had just driven from the trenches. We supposed that there was a large force of Cubans with General Young, not being aware that these Cubans had failed to make their appearance,

and as it was impossible to tell the Cubans from the Spaniards, and as we could not decide whether these were Cubans following the Spaniards we had put to flight, or merely another troop of Spaniards retreating after the first (which was really the case) we dared not fire, and in a minute they had passed the glade and were out of sight.

At every halt we took advantage of the cover, sinking down behind any mound, bush, or tree trunk in the neighborhood. The trees, of course, furnished no protection from the Mauser bullets. Once I was standing behind a large palm with my head out to one side, very fortunately; for a bullet passed through the palm, filling my left eye and ear with the dust and splinters.

No man was allowed to drop out to help the wounded. It was hard to leave them there in the jungle, where they might not be found again until the vultures and the land-crabs came, but war is a grim

game and there was no choice. One of the men shot was Harry Heffner of G Troop, who was mortally wounded through the hips. He fell without uttering a sound, and two of his companions dragged him behind a tree. Here he propped himself up and asked to be given his canteen and his rifle, which I handed to him. He then again began shooting, and continued loading and firing until the line moved forward and we left him alone, dying in the gloomy shade. When we found him again, after the fight, he was dead.

At one time, as I was out of touch with that part of my wing commanded by Jenkins and O'Neill, I sent Greenway, with Sergeant Russell, a New Yorker, and trooper Rowland, a New Mexican cow-puncher, down in the valley to find out where they were. To do this the three had to expose themselves to a very severe fire, but they were not men to whom this mattered. Russell was killed; the other two returned and reported to me the position of Jenkins and O'Neill. They then resumed their places on the firing-line. After awhile I noticed blood coming out of Rowland's side and discovered that he had been shot, although he did not seem to be taking any notice of it. He said the wound was only slight, but as I saw he had broken a rib, I told him to go to the rear to the hospital. After some grumbling he went, but fifteen minutes later he was back on the firing-line again and said he could not

*This* POLITICAL CARTOON *depicting a formidable Roosevelt trouncing the Spanish troops in Cuba appeared in the July 27, 1898, issue of* Puck *magazine.*

find the hospital—which I doubted. However, I then let him stay until the end of the fight. ✳ ✳ ✳

> "No man was allowed to drop out to help the wounded. It was hard to leave them there in the jungle, where they might not be found again until the vultures and the land-crabs came, but war is a grim game and there was no choice."

**I HAD NOT SEEN WOOD** since the beginning of the skirmish, when he hurried forward. When the firing opened some of the men began to curse. "Don't swear—shoot!" growled Wood, as he strode along the path leading his horse, and everyone laughed and became cool again. The Spanish outposts were very near our advance guard, and some minutes of the hottest kind of firing followed before they were driven back and slipped off through the jungle to their main lines in the rear.

Here, at the very outset of our active service, we suffered the loss of two as gallant men as ever wore uniform. Sergeant Hamilton Fish at the extreme front, while holding the point up to its work and firing back where the Spanish advance guards lay, was shot and instantly killed; three of the men with him were likewise hit. Captain Capron, leading the advance guard in person, and displaying equal courage and coolness in the way that he handled them, was also struck, and died a few minutes afterward. The command of the troop then devolved upon the First Lieutenant, young Thomas. Like Capron, Thomas was the fifth in line from father to son who had served in the American army, though in his case it was in the volunteer and not the regular service; the four preceding generations had furnished soldiers respectively to the Revolutionary War, the War of 1812, the Mexican War, and the Civil War. In a few minutes Thomas was shot through the leg, and the command devolved upon the Second Lieutenant, Day

(a nephew of "Albemarle" Cushing, he who sunk the great Confederate ram). Day, who proved himself to be one of our most efficient officers, continued to handle the men to the best possible advantage, and brought them steadily forward. L Troop was from the Indian Territory. The whites, Indians, and half-breeds in it, all fought with equal courage. Captain McClintock was hurried forward to its relief with his Troop B of Arizona men. In a few minutes he was shot through the leg and his place was taken by his First Lieutenant, Wilcox, who handled his men in the same soldierly manner that Day did.

Among the men who showed marked courage and coolness was the tall color-sergeant, Wright; the colors were shot through three times.

When I had led G Troop back to the trail I ran ahead of them, passing the dead and wounded men of L Troop, passing young Fish as he lay with glazed eyes under the rank tropic growth to one side of the trail. When I came to the front I found the men spread out in a very thin skirmish line, advancing through comparatively open ground, each man taking advantage of what cover he could, while Wood strolled about leading his horse, Brodie being close at hand. How Wood escaped being hit, I do not see, and still less how his horse escaped. I had left mine at the beginning of the action, and was only regretting that I had not left my sword with it, as it kept getting between my legs when I was tearing my way through the jungle. I never wore it again in action. Lieutenant Rivers was with Wood, also leading his horse. Smedburg had been sent off on the by no means pleasant task of establishing communications with Young.

Very soon after I reached the front, Brodie was hit, the bullet shattering one arm and whirling him around as he stood. He had kept on the extreme front all through, his presence and example keeping his men entirely steady, and he at first refused to go to the rear; but the wound was very painful, and he became so faint that he had to be sent. Thereupon, Wood directed me to take charge of the left wing in Brodie's place, and to bring it forward; so over I went. ✳ ✳ ✳

A PERFECT HAIL OF BULLETS was sweeping over us as we advanced. Once I got a glimpse of some Spaniards, apparently retreating, far in the front, and to our right, and we fired a couple of rounds after them. Then I became convinced, after much anxious study, that we were being fired at from some large red-tiled buildings, part of a ranch on our front. Smokeless powder, and the thick cover in our front, continued to puzzle us, and I more than once consulted anxiously the officers as to the exact whereabouts of our opponents. I took a rifle from a wounded man and began to try shots with it myself. It was very hot and the men were getting exhausted, though at this particular time we were not suffering heavily from bullets, the Spanish fire going high. As we advanced, the cover became a little thicker and I lost touch of the main body under Wood; so I halted and we fired industriously at the ranch buildings ahead of us, some five hundred yards off. Then we heard cheering on the right, and I supposed that this meant a charge on the part of Wood's men, so I sprang up and ordered the men to rush the buildings ahead of us. They came forward with a will. There was a moment's heavy firing from the Spaniards, which all went over our heads, and then it ceased entirely. When we arrived at the buildings, panting and out of breath, they contained nothing but heaps of empty cartridge-shells and two dead Spaniards, shot through the head.

The country all around us was thickly forested, so that it was very difficult to see any distance in any direction. The firing had now died out, but I was still entirely uncertain as to exactly what had happened. I did not know whether the enemy had been driven back or whether it was merely a lull in the fight, and we might be attacked again; nor did I know what had happened in any other part of the line, while as I occupied the extreme left, I was not sure whether or not my flank was in danger. At this moment one of our men who had dropped out, arrived

AFTER THE FIGHT AT LAS GUASIMAS, *Cuba, 1898. From left to right: Richard Harding Davis (lying down, far left), Joseph T. Dickman (writing), Joseph Wheeler, an unidentified man with his back to the camera, Leonard Wood, Henry Ware Lawton, Theodore Roosevelt, and several unidentified men.*

with the information (fortunately false) that Wood was dead. Of course, this meant that the command devolved upon me, and I hastily set about taking charge of the regiment. I had been particularly struck by the coolness and courage shown by Sergeants Dame and McIlhenny, and sent them out with small pickets to keep watch in front and to the left of the left wing. I sent other men to fill the canteens with water, and threw the rest out in a long line in a disused sunken road, which gave them cover, putting two or three wounded men, who had hitherto kept up with the fighting-line, and a dozen men who were suffering from heat exhaustion—for the fighting and running under that blazing sun through the thick dry jungle was heartbreaking—into the ranch buildings. Then I started over toward the main body, but to my delight encountered Wood himself, who told me the fight was over and the Spaniards had retreated. He also informed me that other troops were just coming up. The first to

appear was a squadron of the Ninth Cavalry, under Major Dimick, which had hurried up to get into the fight, and was greatly disappointed to find it over. They took post in front of our lines, so that our tired men were able to get a rest, Captain McBlain, of the Ninth, good-naturedly giving us some points as to the best way to station our outposts. Then General Chaffee, rather glum at not having been in the fight himself, rode up at the head of some of his infantry, and I marched my squadron back to where the rest of the regiment was going into camp, just where the two trails came together, and beyond—that is, on the Santiago side of—the original Spanish lines.

The Rough Riders had lost eight men killed and thirty-four wounded, aside from two or three who were merely scratched and whose wounds were not reported. The First Cavalry, white, lost seven men killed and eight wounded; the Tenth Cavalry, colored, one man killed and ten wounded; so, out of 964 men engaged on our side,

GENERAL ADNA ROMANZA CHAFFEE *on horseback, Tampa, Florida, 1898.*

16 were killed and 52 wounded. The Spaniards were under General Rubin, with, as second in command, Colonel Alcarez. They had two guns, and eleven companies of about a hundred men each: three belonging to the Porto Rico regiment, three to the San Fernandino, two to the Talavero, two being so-called mobilized companies from the mineral districts, and one a company of engineers; over twelve hundred men in all, together with two guns. ✻ ✻ ✻

**THAT AFTERNOON WE MADE CAMP** and dined, subsisting chiefly on a load of beans which we found on one of the Spanish mules which had been shot. We also looked after the wounded. Dr. Church had himself gone out to the firing-line during the fight, and carried to the rear some of the worst wounded on his back or in his arms. Those who could walk had walked in to where the little field-hospital of the regiment was established on the trail. We found all our dead and all the badly wounded. Around one of the latter the big, hideous land-crabs had gathered in a gruesome ring, waiting for life to be extinct. One of our own men and most of the Spanish dead had been found by the vultures before we got to them; and their bodies were mangled, the eyes and wounds being torn.

The Rough Rider who had been thus treated was in Bucky O'Neill's troop; and as we looked at the body, O'Neill turned to me and asked, "Colonel, isn't it Whitman who says of the vultures that 'they pluck the eyes of princes and tear the flesh of kings'?" I answered that I could not place the quotation. Just a week afterward we were shielding his own body from the birds of prey.

One of the men who fired first, and who displayed conspicuous gallantry was a Cherokee half-breed, who was hit seven times, and of course had to go back to the States. Before he rejoined us at Montauk Point he had gone through a little private war of his own; for on his return he found that a cowboy had gone off with his sweetheart, and in the fight that ensued he shot his rival. Another man of L Troop who also showed marked gallantry was Elliot Cowdin. The men of the plains and

mountains were trained by lifelong habit to look on life and death with iron philosophy. As I passed by a couple of tall, lank, Oklahoma cowpunchers, I heard one say, "Well, some of the boys got it in the neck!" to which the other answered with the grim plains proverb of the South: "Many a good horse dies."

Thomas Isbell, a half-breed Cherokee in the squad under Hamilton Fish, was among the first to shoot and be shot at. He was wounded no less than seven times. The first wound was received by him two minutes after he had fired his first shot, the bullet going through his neck. The second hit him in the left thumb. The third struck near his right hip, passing entirely through the body. The fourth bullet (which was apparently from a Remington and not from a Mauser) went into his neck and lodged against the bone, being afterward cut out. The fifth bullet again hit his left hand. The sixth scraped his head and the seventh his neck. He did not receive all of the wounds at the same time, over half an hour elapsing between the first and the last. Up to receiving the last wound he had declined to leave the firing-line, but by that time he had lost so much blood that he had to be sent to the rear. The man's wiry toughness was as notable as his courage.

We improvised litters, and carried the more sorely wounded back to Siboney that afternoon and the next morning; the others walked. One of the men who had been most severely wounded was Edward Marshall, the correspondent, and he showed as much heroism as any soldier in the whole army. He was shot through the spine, a terrible and very painful wound, which we supposed meant that he would surely die; but he made no complaint of any kind, and while he retained consciousness persisted in dictating the story of the fight. A very touching incident happened in the improvised open-air hospital after the fight, where the wounded were lying. They did not groan, and made no complaint, trying to help one another. One of them suddenly began to hum, "My Country 'Tis of Thee," and one by one the others joined in the chorus, which swelled out through the tropic woods, where the victors lay in camp beside their

dead. I did not see any sign among the fighting men, whether wounded or unwounded, of the very complicated emotions assigned to their kind by some of the realistic modern novelists who have written about battles. At the front everyone behaved quite simply and took things as they came, in a matter-of-course way; but there was doubtless, as is always the case, a good deal of panic and confusion in the rear where the wounded, the stragglers, a few of the packers, and two or three newspaper correspondents were, and in consequence the first reports sent back to the coast were of a most alarming character, describing, with minute inaccuracy, how we had run into ambush, etc. The packers with the mules which carried the rapid-fire guns were among those who ran, and they let the mules go in the jungle; in consequence the guns were never even brought to the firing-line, and only Fred Herrig's skill as a trailer enabled us to recover them. By patient work he followed up the mules' tracks in the forest until he found the animals.

Among the wounded who walked to the temporary hospital at Siboney was the trooper, Rowland, of whom I spoke before. There the doctors examined him, and decreed that his wound was so serious that he must go back to the States. This was enough for Rowland, who waited until nightfall and then escaped, slipping out of the window and making his way back to camp with his rifle and pack, though his wound must have made all movement very painful to him. After this, we felt that he was entitled to stay, and he never left us for a day, distinguishing himself again in the fight at San Juan.

Next morning we buried seven dead Rough Riders in a grave on the summit of the trail, Chaplain Brown reading the solemn burial service of the Episcopalians, while the men stood around with bared heads and joined in singing, Rock of Ages. Vast numbers of vultures were wheeling round and round in great circles through the blue sky overhead. There could be no more honorable burial than that of these men in a common grave—Indian and cowboy, miner, packer, and college athlete—the man of unknown ancestry from the lonely Western plains, and the man who carried on his watch the crests of the Stuyvesants and the Fishes, one in the way they had met death, just as during life they had been one in their daring and their loyalty.

On the afternoon of the 25th we moved on a couple of miles, and camped in a marshy open spot close to a

GRAVE OF THE SEVEN ROUGH RIDERS *who were killed in the fight at Las Guasimas.*

beautiful stream. Here we lay for several days. Captain Lee, the British attaché, spent some time with us; we had begun to regard him as almost a member of the regiment. Count von Götzen, the German attaché, another good fellow, also visited us. General Young was struck down with the fever, and Wood took charge of the brigade. This left me in command of the regiment, of which I was very glad, for such experience as we had had is a quick teacher. By this time the men and I knew one another, and I felt able to make them do themselves justice in march or battle. They understood that I paid no heed to where they came from; no heed to their creed, politics, or social standing; that I would care for them to the utmost of my power, but that I demanded the highest performance of duty; while in return I had seen them tested, and knew I could depend absolutely on their courage, hardihood, obedience, and individual initiative.

There was nothing like enough transportation with the army, whether in the way of wagons or mule-trains; exactly as there had been no sufficient number of landing-boats with the transports. The officers' baggage had come up, but none of us had much, and the shelter-tents proved only a partial protection against the terrific downpours of rain. These occurred almost every afternoon, and turned the camp into a tarn, and the trails into torrents and quagmires. We were not given quite the proper amount of food, and what we did get, like most of the clothing issued us, was fitter for the Klondike than for Cuba. We got enough salt pork and hardtack for the men, but not the full ration of coffee and sugar, and nothing else. I organized a couple of expeditions back to the seacoast, taking the strongest and best walkers and also some of the officers' horses and a stray mule or two, and brought back beans and canned tomatoes. These I got partly by great exertions on my part, and partly by the aid of Colonel Weston of the Commissary Department, a particularly energetic man whose services were of great value. A silly regulation forbade my purchasing canned vegetables, etc., except for the officers; and I had no little difficulty in getting round this regulation, and purchasing (with my own money, of course) what I needed for the men.

One of the men I took with me on one of these trips was Sherman Bell, the former Deputy Marshal of Cripple Creek, and Wells-Fargo Express rider. In coming home with his load, through a blinding storm, he slipped and opened the old rupture. The agony was very great and one of his comrades took his load. He himself, sometimes walking, and sometimes crawling, got back to camp, where Dr. Church fixed him up with a spike bandage, but informed him that he would have to be sent back to the States when an ambulance came along. The ambulance did not come until the next day, which was the day before we marched to San Juan. It arrived after nightfall, and as soon as Bell heard it coming, he crawled out of the hospital tent into the jungle, where he lay all night; and the ambulance went off without him. The men shielded him just as schoolboys would shield a companion, carrying his gun, belt, and bedding; while Bell kept out of sight until the column started, and then staggered along behind it. I found him the morning of the San Juan fight. He told me that he wanted to die fighting, if die he must, and I hadn't the heart to send him back. He did splendid service that day, and afterward in the trenches, and though the rupture opened twice again, and on each occasion he was within a hair's breadth of death, he escaped, and came back with us to the United States.

The army was camped along the valley, ahead of and behind us, our outposts being established on either side. From the generals to the privates all were eager to march against Santiago. At daybreak, when the tall palms began to show dimly through the rising mist, the scream of the cavalry trumpets tore the tropic dawn; and in the evening, as the bands of regiment after regiment played the "Star-Spangled Banner," all, officers and men alike, stood with heads uncovered, wherever they were, until the last strains of the anthem died away in the hot sunset air.

# The Cavalry at Santiago

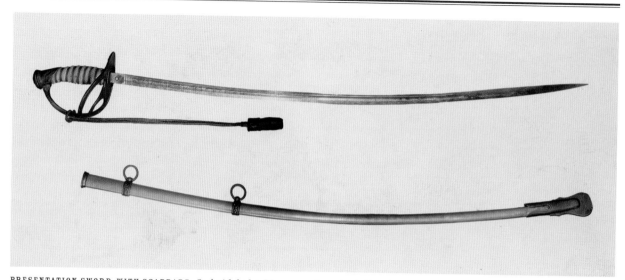

**PRESENTATION SWORD, WITH SCABBARD.** *Steel, nickel, plated, brass mountings. Carried by Colonel Theodore Roosevelt, 1st V.S.V. Cavalry, Santiago, 1898.*

On June 30th we received orders to hold ourselves in readiness to march against Santiago, and all the men were greatly overjoyed, for the inaction was trying. The one narrow road, a mere muddy track along which the army was encamped, was choked with the marching columns. As always happened when we had to change camp, everything that the men could not carry, including, of course, the officers' baggage, was left behind.

About noon the Rough Riders struck camp and drew up in column beside the road in the rear of the First Cavalry. Then we sat down and waited for hours before the order came to march, while regiment after regiment passed by, varied by bands of tatterdemalion Cuban insurgents, and by mule-trains with ammunition. Every man carried three days' provisions. We had succeeded in borrowing mules sufficient to carry along the dynamite gun and the automatic Colts.

At last, toward mid-afternoon, the First and Tenth Cavalry, ahead of us, marched, and we followed. The First was under the command of Lieutenant-Colonel Veile, the Tenth under Lieutenant-Colonel Baldwin. Every few minutes there would be a stoppage in front, and at the halt I would make the men sit or lie down beside the track, loosening their packs. The heat was intense as we passed through the still, close jungle, which formed a wall on either hand. Occasionally we came to gaps or open spaces, where some regiment was camped, and now and then one of these regiments, which apparently had been left out of its proper place, would file into the road, breaking up our line of march. As a result, we finally found ourselves following merely the tail of the regiment ahead of us, an infantry regiment being thrust into the interval. Once or twice we had to wade streams. Darkness came on, but we still continued to march. It was about eight o'clock when we turned to the left and climbed El Paso hill, on whose summit there was a ruined ranch and sugar factory, now, of course, deserted. Here I found General Wood, who was arranging for the camping of the brigade. Our own arrangements for the night were simple. I extended each troop across the road into the jungle, and then the men threw down their belongings where they stood and slept

on their arms. Fortunately, there was no rain. Wood and I curled up under our raincoats on the saddle-blankets, while his two aides, Captain A. L. Mills and Lieutenant W. E. Shipp, slept near us. We were up before dawn and getting breakfast. Mills and Shipp had nothing to eat, and they breakfasted with Wood and myself, as we had been able to get some handfuls of beans, and some coffee and sugar, as well as the ordinary bacon and hardtack.

We did not talk much, for though we were in ignorance as to precisely what the day would bring forth, we knew that we should see fighting. We had slept soundly enough, although, of course, both Wood and I during the night had made a round of the sentries, he of the brigade, and I of the regiment; and I suppose that, excepting among hardened veterans, there is always a certain feeling of uneasy excitement the night before the battle.

Mills and Shipp were both tall, fine-looking men, of tried courage, and thoroughly trained in every detail of their profession; I remember being struck by the quiet, soldierly way they were going about their work early that morning. Before noon one was killed and the other dangerously wounded.

General Wheeler was sick, but with his usual indomitable pluck and entire indifference to his own personal comfort, he kept to the front. He was unable to retain command of the cavalry division, which accordingly devolved upon General Samuel Sumner, who commanded it until mid-afternoon, when the bulk of the fighting was over. General Sumner's own brigade fell to Colonel Henry Carroll. General Sumner led the advance with the cavalry, and the battle was fought by him and by General Kent, who commanded the infantry division, and whose foremost brigade was led by General Hawkins.

As the sun rose the men fell in, and at the same time a battery of field-guns was brought up on the hillcrest just beyond, between us and toward Santiago. It was a fine sight to see the great horses straining under the lash as they whirled the guns up the hill and into position.

Our brigade was drawn up on the hither side of a kind of half basin, a big band of Cubans being off to the left.

As yet we had received no orders, except that we were told that the main fighting was to be done by Lawton's infantry division, which was to take El Caney, several miles to our right, while we were simply to make a diversion. This diversion was to be made mainly with the artillery, and the battery which had taken position immediately in front of us was to begin when Lawton began.

It was about six o'clock that the first report of the cannon from El Caney came booming to us across the miles of still jungle. It was a very lovely morning, the sky of cloudless blue, while the level, shimmering rays from the just-risen sun brought into fine relief the splendid palms which here and there towered above the lower growth. The lofty and beautiful mountains hemmed

STONE FORT AT EL CANEY, *which General Lawton's command fought ten hours to capture. The Spanish fighting trenches were fifty yards down the hillside.*

in the Santiago plain, making it an amphitheatre for the battle.

Immediately our guns opened, and at the report great clouds of white smoke hung on the ridge crest. For a minute or two there was no response. Wood and I were sitting together, and Wood remarked to me that he wished our brigade could be moved somewhere else, for we were directly in line of any return fire aimed by the Spaniards at the battery. Hardly had he spoken when there was a peculiar whistling, singing sound in the air, and immediately afterward the noise of something exploding over our heads. It was shrapnel from the Spanish batteries. We sprung to our feet and leaped on our horses. Immediately afterward a second shot came which burst directly above us; and then a third. From the second shell one of the shrapnel bullets dropped on my wrist, hardly breaking the skin, but raising a bump about as big as a hickory-nut. The same shell wounded four of my regiment, one of them being Mason Mitchell, and two or three of the regulars were also hit, one losing his leg by a great fragment of shell. Another shell exploded right in the middle of the Cubans, killing and wounding a good many, while the remainder scattered like guinea-hens. Wood's lead horse was also shot through the lungs. I at once hustled my regiment over the crest of the hill into the thick underbrush, where I had no little difficulty in getting them together again into column.

Meanwhile the firing continued for fifteen or twenty minutes, until it gradually died away. As the Spaniards used smokeless powder, their artillery had an enormous advantage over ours, and, moreover, we did not have the best type of modern guns, our fire being slow.

As soon as the firing ceased, Wood formed his brigade, with my regiment in front, and gave me orders to follow behind the First Brigade, which was just moving off the ground. In column of fours we marched down the trail toward the ford of the San Juan River. We passed two or three regiments of infantry, and were several times halted before we came to the ford. The First Brigade, which was under Colonel Carroll—Lieutenant-Colonel

SOME OF THE SIXTH INFANTRY *under fire at the bloody angle, 400 yards from San Juan trenches, July 1, 1898.*

Hamilton commanding the Ninth Regiment, Major Wessels the Third, and Captain Kerr the Sixth—had already crossed and was marching to the right, parallel to, but a little distance from, the river. The Spaniards in the trenches and blockhouses on top of the hills in front were already firing at the brigade in desultory fashion. The extreme advance of the Ninth Cavalry was under Lieutenants McNamee and Hartwick. They were joined by General Hawkins, with his staff, who was looking over the ground and deciding on the route he should take his infantry brigade.

Our orders had been of the vaguest kind, being simply to march to the right and connect with Lawton—with whom, of course, there was no chance of our connecting. No reconnaissance had been made, and the exact position and strength of the Spaniards was not known. A captive balloon was up in the air at this moment, but it was worse than useless. A previous proper reconnaissance

*overleaf:* CAPTAIN CAPRON'S BATTERY *in action at El Caney, Cuba, July 1, 1898.*

and proper lookout from the hills would have given us exact information. As it was, Generals Kent, Sumner, and Hawkins had to be their own reconnaissance, and they fought their troops so well that we won anyhow.

I was now ordered to cross the ford, march half a mile or so to the right, and then halt and await further orders; and I promptly hurried my men across, for the fire was getting hot, and the captive balloon, to the horror of everybody, was coming down to the ford. Of course, it was a special target for the enemy's fire. I got my men across before it reached the ford. There it partly collapsed and remained, causing severe loss of life, as it indicated the exact position where the Tenth and the First Cavalry, and the infantry, were crossing. ✶ ✶ ✶

**THE FIGHT WAS NOW ON** in good earnest, and the Spaniards on the hills were engaged in heavy volley firing. The Mauser bullets drove in sheets through the trees and the tall jungle grass, making a peculiar whirring or rustling sound; some of the bullets seemed to pop in the air, so that we thought they were explosive; and, indeed, many of those which were coated with brass did explode, in the sense that the brass coat was ripped off, making a thin plate of hard metal with a jagged edge, which inflicted a ghastly wound. These bullets were shot from a .45-calibre rifle carrying smokeless powder, which was much used by the guerillas and irregular Spanish troops. The Mauser bullets themselves made a small clean hole, with the result that the wound healed in a most astonishing manner. One or two of our men who were shot in the head had the skull blown open, but elsewhere the wounds from the minute steel-coated bullet, with its very high velocity, were certainly nothing like as serious as those made by the old large-calibre, low-power rifle. If a man was shot through the heart, spine, or brain he was, of course, killed instantly; but very few of the wounded died—even under the appalling conditions which prevailed, owing to the lack of attendance and supplies in the field-hospitals with the army.

While we were lying in reserve we were suffering nearly as much as afterward when we charged. I think

that the bulk of the Spanish fire was practically unaimed, or at least not aimed at any particular man, and only occasionally at a particular body of men; but they swept the whole field of battle up to the edge of the river, and man after man in our ranks fell dead or wounded, although I had the troopers scattered out far apart, taking advantage of every scrap of cover. ✶ ✶ ✶

**THE MOST SERIOUS LOSS** that I and the regiment could have suffered befell just before we charged. Bucky O'Neill was strolling up and down in front of his men, smoking his cigarette, for he was inveterately addicted to the habit. He had a theory that an officer ought never to take cover—a theory which was, of course, wrong, though in a volunteer organization the officers should certainly expose themselves very fully, simply for the effect on the men; our regimental toast on the transport running, "The officers; may the war last until each is killed, wounded, or promoted." As O'Neill moved to and fro, his men begged him to lie down, and one of the sergeants said, "Captain, a bullet is sure to hit you." O'Neill took his cigarette out of his mouth, and blowing out a cloud of smoke laughed and said, "Sergeant, the Spanish bullet isn't made that will kill me." A little later he discussed for a moment with one of the regular officers the direction from which the Spanish fire was coming. As he turned on his heel a bullet struck him in the mouth and came out at the back of his head; so that even before he fell his wild and gallant soul had gone out into the darkness.

My orderly was a brave young Harvard boy, Sanders, from the quaint old Massachusetts town of Salem. The work of an orderly on foot, under the blazing sun, through the hot and matted jungle, was very severe, and finally the heat overcame him. He dropped; nor did he ever recover fully, and later he died from fever. In his place I summoned a trooper whose name I did not know. Shortly afterward, while sitting beside the bank, I directed him to go back and ask whatever general he came across if I could not advance, as my men were being much cut up. He stood up to salute and then pitched forward across

**COLONEL ROOSEVELT AND HIS ROUGH RIDERS** *just before charging over the hill at San Juan.*

my knees, a bullet having gone through his throat, cutting the carotid.

When O'Neill was shot, his troop, who were devoted to him, were for the moment at a loss whom to follow. One of their number, Henry Bardshar, a huge Arizona miner, immediately attached himself to me as my orderly, and from that moment he was closer to me, not only in the fight, but throughout the rest of the campaign, than any other man, not even excepting the color-sergeant, Wright.

Captain Mills was with me; gallant Shipp had already been killed. Mills was an invaluable aide, absolutely cool, absolutely unmoved or flurried in any way.

I sent messenger after messenger to try to find General Sumner or General Wood and get permission to advance, and was just about making up my mind that in the absence of orders I had better "march toward the guns," when Lieutenant-Colonel Dorst came riding up through the storm of bullets with the welcome command "to move forward and support the regulars in the assault on the hills in front." General Sumner had obtained authority to advance from Lieutenant Miley, who was representing General Shafter at the front, and was in the thick of the fire. The General at once ordered the first brigade to advance on the hills, and the second to support it. He himself was riding his horse along the lines, superintending the fight. Later I overheard a couple of my men talking together about him. What they said illustrates the value of a display of courage among the officers in hardening their soldiers; for their theme was how, as they were lying down under a fire which they could not return, and were in consequence feeling rather nervous, General

Sumner suddenly appeared on horseback, sauntering by quite unmoved; and, said one of the men, "That made us feel all right. If the General could stand it, we could."

The instant I received the order I sprang on my horse and then my "crowded hour" began. The guerillas had been shooting at us from the edges of the jungle and from their perches in the leafy trees, and as they used smokeless powder, it was almost impossible to see them, though a few of my men had from time to time responded. We had also suffered from the hill on our right front, which was held chiefly by guerillas, although there were also some Spanish regulars with them, for we found their dead. I formed my men in column of troops, each troop extended in open skirmishing order, the right resting on the wire fences which bordered the sunken lane. Captain Jenkins led the first squadron, his eyes literally dancing with joyous excitement.

## "The instant I received the order I sprang on my horse and then my 'crowded hour' began."

I started in the rear of the regiment, the position in which the colonel should theoretically stay. Captain Mills and Captain McCormick were both with me as aides; but I speedily had to send them off on special duty in getting the different bodies of men forward. I had intended to go into action on foot as at Las Guasimas, but the heat was so oppressive that I found I should be quite unable to run up and down the line and superintend matters unless I was mounted; and, moreover, when on horseback, I could see the men better and they could see me better.

A curious incident happened as I was getting the men started forward. Always when men have been lying down under cover for some time, and are required to advance, there is a little hesitation, each looking to see whether the others are going forward. As I rode down the line, calling to the troopers to go forward, and rasping brief directions to the captains and lieutenants, I came upon a man lying behind a little bush, and I ordered him to jump up. I do not think he understood that we were making a forward move, and he looked up at me for a moment with hesitation, and I again bade him rise, jeering him and saying: "Are you afraid to stand up when I am on horseback?" As I spoke, he suddenly fell forward on his face, a bullet having struck him and gone through him lengthwise. I suppose the bullet had been aimed at me; at any rate, I, who was on horseback in the open, was unhurt, and the man lying flat on the ground in the cover beside me was killed. There were several pairs of brothers with us; of the two Nortons one was killed; of the two McCurdys one was wounded.

I soon found that I could get that line, behind which I personally was, faster forward than the one immediately in front of it, with the result that the two rearmost lines of the regiment began to crowd together; so I rode through them both, the better to move on the one in front. This happened with every line in succession, until I found myself at the head of the regiment.

Both lieutenants of B Troop from Arizona had been exerting themselves greatly, and both were overcome by the heat; but Sergeants Campbell and Davidson took it forward in splendid shape. Some of the men from this troop and from the other Arizona troop (Bucky O'Neill's) joined me as a kind of fighting tail.

The Ninth Regiment was immediately in front of me, and the First on my left, and these went up Kettle Hill with my regiment. The Third, Sixth, and Tenth went partly up Kettle Hill (following the Rough Riders and the Ninth and First), and partly between that and the blockhouse hill, which the infantry were assailing. General Sumner in person gave the Tenth the order to charge the hills; and it went forward at a rapid gait. The three regiments went forward more or less intermingled, advancing steadily and keeping up a heavy fire. Up Kettle Hill Sergeant George Berry, of the Tenth, bore not only his own regimental colors but those of the Third, the color-sergeant of the Third having been shot down; he kept shouting: "Dress on the colors, boys, dress on the colors!" as he followed Captain Ayres, who was running

**THE ROUGH RIDERS AT KETTLE HILL, SANTIAGO, CUBA ON JULY 1, 1898** *by Mort Kunstler, 1984. The painting is in the Heritage Series collection of the National Guard.*

in advance of his men, shouting and waving his hat. The Tenth Cavalry lost a greater proportion of its officers than any other regiment in the battle—eleven out of twenty-two.

By the time I had come to the head of the regiment we ran into the left wing of the Ninth Regulars, and some of the First Regulars, who were lying down; that is, the troopers were lying down, while the officers were walking to and fro. The officers of the white and colored regiments alike took the greatest pride in seeing that the men more than did their duty; and the mortality among them was great.

I spoke to the captain in command of the rear platoons, saying that I had been ordered to support the regulars in the attack upon the hills, and that in my judgment we could not take these hills by firing at them, and that we must rush them. He answered that his orders were to keep his men lying where they were, and that he could not charge without orders. I asked where the Colonel was, and as he was not in sight, said, "Then I am the ranking officer here and I give the order to charge"—for I did not want to keep the men longer in the open suffering under a fire which they could not effectively return. Naturally the captain hesitated to obey this order when no word had been received from his own Colonel. So I said, "Then let my men through, sir," and rode on through the lines, followed by the grinning Rough Riders, whose attention had been completely taken off the Spanish bullets, partly by my dialogue with the regulars, and partly by the language I had been using to themselves as I got the lines forward, for I had been joking with some and swearing at others, as the exigencies of the case seemed to demand. When we started to go through, however, it proved too much for the regulars, and they jumped up and came along, their officers and troops mingling with mine, all being delighted at the chance. When I got to where the head of the left wing of the Ninth was lying, through the courtesy of Lieutenant Hartwick, two of whose colored troopers threw down the fence, I was enabled to get back into the lane, at the same time waving my hat, and giving the order to charge the hill on our right front. Out of my sight, over on the right, Captains McBlain and Taylor, of the Ninth, made up their minds independently to charge at just about this time; and at almost the same moment Colonels Carroll and Hamilton, who were off, I believe, to my left, where we could see neither them nor their men, gave the order to advance. But of all this I knew nothing at the time. The whole line, tired of waiting, and eager to close with the enemy, was straining to go forward; and it seems that different parts slipped the leash at almost the same moment. The First Cavalry came up the hill just behind, and partly mixed with my regiment and the Ninth. As already said, portions of the Third, Sixth, and Tenth followed, while the rest of the members of these three regiments kept more in touch with the infantry on our left.

THE ROUGH RIDERS *in the open fields at San Juan Hill, Santiago, Cuba, 1898.*

By this time we were all in the spirit of the thing and greatly excited by the charge, the men cheering and running forward between shots, while the delighted faces of the foremost officers, like Captain C. J. Stevens, of the Ninth, as they ran at the head of their troops, will always stay in my mind. As soon as I was in the line I galloped forward a few yards until I saw that the men were well started, and then galloped back to help Goodrich, who was in command of his troop, get his men across the road so as to attack the hill from that side. Captain Mills had already thrown three of the other troops of the regiment across this road for the same purpose. Wheeling around, I then again galloped toward the hill, passing the shouting, cheering, firing men, and went up the lane, splashing through a small stream; when I got abreast of the ranch buildings on the top of Kettle Hill, I turned and went up the slope. Being on horseback I was, of course, able to get ahead of the men on foot, excepting my orderly, Henry Bardshar, who had run ahead very fast in order to get better shots at the Spaniards, who were now running out of the ranch buildings. Sergeant Campbell and a number of the Arizona men, and Dudley Dean, among others, were very close behind. Stevens, with his platoon of the Ninth, was abreast of us; so were McNamee and Hartwick. Some forty yards from the top I ran into a wire fence and jumped off Little Texas, turning him loose. He had been scraped by a couple of bullets, one of which nicked my elbow, and I never expected to see him again. As I ran up to the hill, Bardshar stopped to shoot, and two Spaniards fell as he emptied his magazine. These were the only Spaniards I actually saw fall to aimed shots by any one of my men, with the exception of two guerillas in trees.

Almost immediately afterward the hill was covered by the troops, both Rough Riders and the colored troopers of the Ninth, and some men of the First. There was the usual confusion, and afterward there was much discussion as to exactly who had been on the hill first. The first guidons planted there were those of the three New Mexican troops, G, E, and F, of my regiment, under their Captains, Llewellen, Luna, and Muller, but on the extreme right of the hill, at the opposite end from where we struck it, Captains Taylor and McBlain and their men of the Ninth were first up. Each of the five captains was firm in the belief that his troop was first up. As for the individual men, each of whom honestly thought he was first on the summit, their name was legion. One Spaniard was captured in the buildings, another was shot as he tried to hide himself, and a few others were killed as they ran. ✶ ✶ ✶

**NO SOONER WERE WE ON THE CREST** than the Spaniards from the line of hills in our front, where they were strongly intrenched, opened a very heavy fire upon us with their rifles. They also opened upon us with one or two pieces of artillery, using time fuses which burned very accurately, the shells exploding right over our heads.

On the top of the hill was a huge iron kettle, or something of the kind, probably used for sugar refining. Several of our men took shelter behind this. We had a splendid view of the charge on the San Juan blockhouse to our left, where the infantry of Kent, led by Hawkins, were climbing the hill. Obviously the proper thing to do was to help them, and I got the men together and started them volley-firing against the Spaniards in the San Juan blockhouse and in the trenches around it. We could only see their heads; of course this was all we ever could see when we were firing at them in their trenches. Stevens was directing not only his own colored troopers, but a number of Rough Riders; for in a mêlée good soldiers are always prompt to recognize a good officer, and are eager to follow him.

We kept up a brisk fire for some five or ten minutes; meanwhile we were much cut up ourselves. Gallant Colonel Hamilton, than whom there was never a braver man, was killed, and equally gallant Colonel Carroll wounded. When near the summit Captain Mills had been shot through the head, the bullet destroying the sight of one eye permanently and of the other temporarily. He would not go back or let any man assist him, sitting down where he was and waiting until one of the men brought him word that the hill was stormed. Colonel Veile planted the standard of the First Cavalry on the hill, and General Sumner rode up. He was fighting his division in great form, and was always himself in the thick of the fire. As the men were much excited by the firing, they seemed to pay very little heed to their own losses.

Suddenly, above the cracking of the carbines, rose a peculiar drumming sound, and some of the men cried, "The Spanish machine-guns!" Listening, I made out that it came from the flat ground to the left, and jumped to my feet, smiting my hand on my thigh, and shouting aloud with exultation, "It's the Gatlings, men, our Gatlings!" Lieutenant Parker was bringing his four Gatlings into action, and shoving them nearer and nearer the front. Now and then the drumming ceased for a moment; then

it would resound again, always closer to San Juan hill, which Parker, like ourselves, was hammering to assist the infantry attack. Our men cheered lustily. We saw much of Parker after that, and there was never a more welcome sound than his Gatlings as they opened. It was the only sound which I ever heard my men cheer in battle.

The infantry got nearer and nearer the crest of the hill. At last we could see the Spaniards running from the rifle-pits as the Americans came on in their final rush. Then I stopped my men for fear they should injure their comrades, and called to them to charge the next line of trenches, on the hills in our front, from which we had been undergoing a good deal of punishment. Thinking that the men would all come, I jumped over the wire fence in front of us and started at the double; but, as a matter of fact, the troopers were so excited, what with shooting and being shot, and shouting and cheering, that

*The American troops employed the decisive use of* GATLING GUNS, *which had multiple barrels revolving around a central axis and were fired rapidly by turning a crank. This photograph of a Gatling was taken in another area of conflict, the Philippines, in 1899.*

they did not hear, or did not heed me; and after running about a hundred yards I found I had only five men along with me. Bullets were ripping the grass all around us, and one of the men, Clay Green, was mortally wounded; another, Winslow Clark, a Harvard man, was shot first in the leg and then through the body. He made not the slightest murmur, only asking me to put his water canteen where he could get at it, which I did; he ultimately recovered. There was no use going on with the remaining three men, and I bade them stay where they were while I went back and brought up the rest of the brigade. This was a decidedly cool request, for there was really no possible point in letting them stay there while I went back; but at the moment it seemed perfectly natural to me, and apparently so to them, for they cheerfully nodded, and sat down in the grass, firing back at the line of trenches from which the Spaniards were shooting at them. Meanwhile, I ran back, jumped over the wire fence, and went over the crest of the hill, filled with anger against the troopers, and especially those of my own regiment, for not having accompanied me. They, of course, were quite innocent of wrongdoing; and even while I taunted them bitterly for not having followed me, it was all I could do not to smile at the look of injury and surprise that came over their faces, while they cried out, "We didn't hear you, we didn't see you go, Colonel; lead on now, we'll sure follow you." I wanted the other regiments to come too, so I ran down to where General Sumner was and asked him if I might make the charge; and he told me to go and that he would see that the men followed. By this time everybody had his attention attracted, and when I leaped over the fence again, with Major Jenkins beside me, the men of the various regiments which were already on the hill came with a rush, and we started across the wide valley which lay between us and the Spanish intrenchments. Captain Dimmick, now in command of the Ninth, was bringing it forward; Captain McBlain had a number of Rough Riders mixed in with his troop, and led them all together; Captain Taylor had been severely wounded. The long-legged men like Greenway, Goodrich, sharpshooter

Proffit, and others, outstripped the rest of us, as we had a considerable distance to go. Long before we got near them the Spaniards ran, save a few here and there, who either surrendered or were shot down. When we reached the trenches we found them filled with dead bodies in the light blue and white uniform of the Spanish regular army. There were very few wounded. Most of the fallen had little holes in their heads from which their brains were oozing; for they were covered from the neck down by the trenches.

It was at this place that Major Wessels, of the Third Cavalry, was shot in the back of the head. It was a severe wound, but after having it bound up he again came to the front in command of his regiment. Among the men who were foremost was Lieutenant Milton F. Davis, of the First Cavalry. He had been joined by three men of the Seventy-first New York, who ran up, and, saluting, said, "Lieutenant, we want to go with you, our officers won't lead us." One of the brave fellows was soon afterward shot in the face. Lieutenant Davis's first sergeant, Clarence Gould, killed a Spanish soldier with his revolver, just as the Spaniard was aiming at one of my Rough Riders. At about the same time I also shot one. I was with Henry Bardshar, running up at the double, and two Spaniards leaped from the trenches and fired at us, not ten yards away. As they turned to run I closed in and fired twice, missing the first and killing the second. My revolver was from the sunken battleship *Maine*, and had been given me by my brother-in-law, Captain W. S. Cowles, of the Navy. At the time I did not know of Gould's exploit, and supposed my feat to be unique; and although Gould had killed his Spaniard in the trenches, not very far from me, I never learned of it until weeks after. It is astonishing what a limited area of vision and experience one has in the hurly-burly of a battle.

There was very great confusion at this time, the different regiments being completely intermingled—white regulars, colored regulars, and Rough Riders. General Sumner had kept a considerable force in reserve on Kettle Hill, under Major Jackson, of the Third Cavalry. We were

*The* **CHARGE OF THE ROUGH RIDERS AT SAN JUAN HILL** *by Frederic Remington, 1898. The painting is part of the collection at the Frederic Remington Art Museum in Ogdensburg, New York.*

still under a heavy fire and I got together a mixed lot of men and pushed on from the trenches and ranch-houses which we had just taken, driving the Spaniards through a line of palm trees, and over the crest of a chain of hills. When we reached these crests we found ourselves overlooking Santiago. Some of the men, including Jenkins, Greenway, and Goodrich, pushed on almost by themselves far ahead. Lieutenant Hugh Berkely, of the First, with a sergeant and two troopers, reached the extreme front. He was, at the time, ahead of everyone; the sergeant was killed and one trooper wounded; but the lieutenant and the remaining trooper stuck to their post for the rest of the afternoon until our line was gradually extended to include them.

While I was reforming the troops on the chain of hills, one of General Sumner's aides, Captain Robert Howze—as dashing and gallant an officer as there was in the whole gallant cavalry division, by the way—came up with orders to me to halt where I was, not advancing farther, but to hold the hill at all hazards. Howze had his horse, and I had some difficulty in making him take proper shelter; he stayed with us for quite a time, unable to make up his mind to leave the extreme front, and meanwhile jumping at the chance to render any service, of risk or otherwise, which the moment developed.

I now had under me all the fragments of the six cavalry regiments which were at the extreme front, being the highest officer left there, and I was in immediate command of them for the remainder of the afternoon and that night. The Ninth was over to the right, and the Thirteenth Infantry afterward came up beside it. The rest of Kent's infantry was to our left. Of the Tenth, Lieutenants Anderson, Muller, and Fleming reported to me; Anderson was slightly wounded, but he paid no heed to this. All three, like every other officer, had troopers of various regiments under them; such mixing was inevitable in making repeated charges through thick jungle; it was essentially a troop commanders', indeed, almost a squad leaders', fight. The Spaniards who had been holding the trenches and the line of hills, had fallen

THE VIEW FROM SAN JUAN HILL, *of the first hill and block-house captured on July 1, 1898.*

Bvtton-2014

back upon their supports and we were under a very heavy fire both from rifles and great guns. At the point where we were, the grass-covered hillcrest was gently rounded, giving poor cover, and I made my men lie down on the hither slope. ✳ ✳ ✳

ON THE HILL-SLOPE immediately around me I had a mixed force composed of members of most of the cavalry regiments, and a few infantrymen. There were about fifty of my Rough Riders with Lieutenants Goodrich and Carr. Among the rest were perhaps a score of colored infantrymen, but, as it happened, at this particular point without any of their officers. No troops could have behaved better than the colored soldiers had behaved so far; but they are, of course, peculiarly dependent upon their white officers. Occasionally they produce noncommissioned officers who can take the initiative and accept responsibility precisely like the best class of whites; but this cannot be expected normally, nor is it fair to expect it. With the colored troops there should always be some of their own officers; whereas, with the white regulars, as with my own Rough Riders, experience showed that the noncommissioned officers could usually carry on the fight by themselves if they were once started, no matter whether their officers were killed or not.

At this particular time it was trying for the men, as they were lying flat on their faces, very rarely responding to the bullets, shells, and shrapnel which swept over the hill-top, and which occasionally killed or wounded one of their number. Major Albert G. Forse, of the First Cavalry, a noted Indian fighter, was killed about this time. One of my best men, Sergeant Greenly, of Arizona, who was lying beside me, suddenly said, "Beg pardon, Colonel; but I've been hit in the leg." I asked, "Badly?" He said, "Yes, Colonel; quite badly." After one of his comrades had helped him fix up his leg with a first-aid-to-the-injured bandage, he limped off to the rear.

None of the white regulars or Rough Riders showed the slightest sign of weakening; but under the strain the colored infantrymen (who had none of their officers) began to get a little uneasy and to drift to the rear, either helping wounded men, or saying that they wished to find their own regiments. This I could not allow, as it was depleting my line, so I jumped up, and walking a few yards to the rear, drew my revolver, halted the retreating soldiers, and called out to them that I appreciated the gallantry with which they had fought and would be sorry to hurt them, but that I should shoot the first man who, on any pretence whatever, went to the rear. My own men had all sat up and were watching my movements with utmost interest; so was Captain Howze. I ended my statement to the colored soldiers by saying: "Now, I shall be very sorry to hurt you, and you don't know whether or not I will keep my word, but my men can tell you that I always do"; whereupon my cowpunchers, hunters, and miners solemnly nodded their heads and commented in chorus, exactly as if in a comic opera, "He always does; he always does!"

This was the end of the trouble, for the "smoked Yankees"—as the Spaniards called the colored soldiers—flashed their white teeth at one another, as they broke into broad grins, and I had no more trouble with them, they seeming to accept me as one of their own officers. The colored cavalrymen had already so accepted me; in return, the Rough Riders, although for the most part Southwesterners, who have a strong color prejudice, grew to accept them with hearty goodwill as comrades, and were entirely willing, in their own phrase, "to drink out of the same canteen." Where all the regular officers did so well, it is hard to draw any distinction; but in the cavalry division a peculiar meed of praise should be given to the officers of the Ninth and Tenth for their work, and under their leadership the colored troops did as well as any soldiers could possibly do.

In the course of the afternoon the Spaniards in our front made the only offensive movement which I saw them make during the entire campaign; for what were ordinarily called "attacks" upon our lines consisted merely of heavy firing from their trenches and from their skirmishers. In this case they did actually begin to make a forward movement, their cavalry coming up as well as the marines and reserve infantry, while their skirmishers, who were always bold, redoubled their activity. It could not be called a charge, and not only was it not pushed home, but it was stopped almost as soon as it began, our men immediately running forward to the crest of the hill with shouts of delight at seeing their enemies at last come into the open. A few seconds' firing stopped their advance and drove them into the cover of the trenches.

They kept up a very heavy fire for some time longer, and our men again lay down, only replying occasionally. Suddenly we heard on our right the peculiar drumming sound which had been so welcome in the morning, when the infantry were assailing the San Juan blockhouse. The Gatlings were up again! I started over to inquire, and found that Lieutenant Parker, not content with using his guns in support of the attacking forces, had thrust them forward to the extreme front of the fighting line, where he was handling them with great effect. From this time on, throughout the fighting, Parker's Gatlings were on the right of my regiment, and his men and mine fraternized in every way. He kept his pieces at the extreme front, using them on every occasion until the last Spanish shot was fired. Indeed, the dash and efficiency with which the Gatlings were handled by Parker was one of the most striking features of the campaign; he showed that a first-rate officer could use machineguns, on wheels, in battle and skirmish, in attacking and defending trenches, alongside of the best troops, and to their great advantage.

As night came on, the firing gradually died away. Before this happened, however, Captains Morton and Boughton, of the Third Cavalry, came over to tell me that a rumor had reached them to the effect that there had been some talk of retiring and that they wished to protest in the strongest manner. I had been watching them both, as they handled their troops with the cool confidence of the veteran regular officer, and had been congratulating myself that they were off toward the right flank, for as long as they were there, I knew I was perfectly safe in that direction. I had heard no rumor about retiring, and

I cordially agreed with them that it would be far worse than a blunder to abandon our position.

To attack the Spaniards by rushing across open ground, or through wire entanglements and low, almost impassable jungle, without the help of artillery, and to force unbroken infantry, fighting behind earthworks and armed with the best repeating weapons, supported by cannon, was one thing; to repel such an attack ourselves, or to fight our foes on anything like even terms in the open, was quite another thing. No possible number of Spaniards coming at us from in front could have driven us from our position, and there was not a man on the crest who did not eagerly and devoutly hope that our opponents would make the attempt, for it would surely have been followed, not merely by a repulse, but by our immediately taking the city. There was not an officer or a man on the firing-line, so far as I saw them, who did not feel this way.

As night fell, some of my men went back to the buildings in our rear and foraged through them, for we had now been fourteen hours charging and fighting without food. They came across what was evidently the Spanish officers' mess, where their dinner was still cooking, and they brought it to the front in high glee. It was evident that the Spanish officers were living well, however the Spanish rank and file were faring. There were three big iron pots, one filled with beef stew, one with boiled rice, and one with boiled peas; there was a big demi-john of rum (all along the trenches which the Spaniards held were empty wine and liquor bottles); there were a number of loaves of rice-bread; and there were even some small cans of preserves and a few salt fish. Of course, among so many men, the food, which was equally divided, did not give very much to each, but it freshened us all.

Soon after dark, General Wheeler, who in the afternoon had resumed command of the cavalry division, came to the front. A very few words with General Wheeler

*At a consultation at* GENERAL WHEELER'S HEADQUARTERS *in Cuba in 1898.*

**ROUGH RIDERS RECOMMENDED FOR PROMOTION** *for Gallantry in Action, photographed at Camp Wikoff, Montauk, New York. From left to right, back row: Maxwell Keyes, Frank Hayes, Woodbury Kane, Richard Cushing Day, and James Robb Church; front row: Robert Harry Munro Ferguson, David Marvin Goodrich (A.B. 1898), Frank Frantz, Alexander O. Brodie, Theodore Roosevelt, John Campbell Greenway, and Samuel Greenwald.*

reassured us about retiring. He had been through too much heavy fighting in the Civil War to regard the present fight as very serious, and he told us not to be under any apprehension, for he had sent word that there was no need whatever of retiring, and was sure we would stay where we were until the chance came to advance. He was second in command; and to him more than to any other one man was due the prompt abandonment of the proposal to fall back—a proposal which, if adopted, would have meant shame and disaster.

Shortly afterward General Wheeler sent us orders to intrench. The men of the different regiments were now getting in place again and sifting themselves out. All of our troops who had been kept at Kettle Hill came forward and rejoined us after nightfall. During the afternoon Greenway, apparently not having enough to do in the fighting, had taken advantage of a lull to explore the buildings himself, and had found a number of Spanish intrenching tools, picks, and shovels, and these we used in digging trenches along our line. The men were very tired indeed, but they went cheerfully to work, all the officers doing their part.

Crockett, the ex-Revenue officer from Georgia, was a slight man, not physically very strong. He came to me and told me he didn't think he would be much use in digging, but that he had found a lot of Spanish coffee and would spend his time making coffee for the men, if I approved. I did approve very heartily, and Crockett officiated as cook for the next three or four hours until the trench was dug, his coffee being much appreciated by all of us.

So many acts of gallantry were performed during the day that it is quite impossible to notice them all, and it seems unjust to single out any; yet I shall mention a few, which it must always be remembered are to stand, not as exceptions, but as instances of what very many men did. It happened that I saw these myself. There were innumerable others, which either were not seen at all, or were seen only by officers who happened not to mention them; and, of course, I know chiefly those that happened in my own regiment.

Captain Llewellen was a large, heavy man, who had a grown-up son in the ranks. On the march he had frequently carried the load of some man who weakened, and he was not feeling well on the morning of the fight. Nevertheless, he kept at the head of his troop all day. In the charging and rushing, he not only became very much exhausted, but finally fell, wrenching himself terribly, and though he remained with us all night, he was so sick by morning that we had to take him behind the hill into an improvised hospital. Lieutenant Day, after handling his troop with equal gallantry and efficiency, was shot, on the summit of Kettle Hill. He was hit in the arm and was forced to go to the rear, but he would not return to the States, and rejoined us at the front long before his wound was healed. Lieutenant Leahy was also wounded, not far from him. Thirteen of the men were wounded and yet kept on fighting until the end of the day, and in some cases never went to the rear at all, even to have their wounds dressed. They were Corporals Waller and Fortescue and Trooper McKinley of Troop E; Corporal Roades of Troop D; Troopers Albertson, Winter, McGregor, and Ray Clark of Troop F; Troopers Bugbee, Jackson, and Waller of Troop A; Trumpeter McDonald of Troop L; Sergeant Hughes of Troop B; and Trooper Gievers of Troop G. One of the Wallers was a cowpuncher from New Mexico, the other the champion Yale high-jumper. The first was shot through the left arm so as to paralyze the fingers, but he continued in battle, pointing his rifle over the wounded arm as though it had been a rest. The other Waller, and Bugbee, were hit in the head, the bullets merely inflicting scalp wounds. Neither of them paid any heed to the wounds except that after nightfall each had his head done up in a bandage. Fortescue I was at times using as an extra orderly. I noticed he limped, but supposed that his foot was skinned. It proved, however, that he had been struck in the foot, though not very seriously, by a bullet, and I never knew what was the matter until the next day I saw him making wry faces as he drew off his bloody boot, which was stuck fast to the foot. Trooper Rowland again distinguished himself by his fearlessness.

For gallantry on the field of action Sergeants Dame, Ferguson, Tiffany, Greenwald, and, later on, McIlhenny, were promoted to second lieutenancies, as Sergeant Hayes had already been. Lieutenant Carr, who commanded his troop, and behaved with great gallantry throughout the day, was shot and severely wounded at nightfall. He was the son of a Confederate officer; his was the fifth generation which, from father to son, had fought in every war of the United States. Among the men whom I noticed as leading in the charges and always being nearest the enemy, were the Pawnee, Pollock, Simpson of Texas, and Dudley Dean. Jenkins was made major, Woodbury Kane, Day, and Frantz captains, and Greenway and Goodrich first lieutenants, for gallantry in action, and for the efficiency with which the first had handled his squadron, and the other five their troops—for each of them, owing to some accident to his superior, found himself in command of his troop.

Dr. Church had worked quite as hard as any man at the front in caring for the wounded; as had Chaplain Brown. Lieutenant Keyes, who acted as adjutant, did so well that he was given the position permanently. Lieutenant Coleman similarly won the position of quartermaster.

We finished digging the trench soon after midnight, and then the wornout men laid down in rows on their rifles and dropped heavily to sleep. About one in ten of them had blankets taken from the Spaniards. Henry Bardshar, my orderly, had procured one for me. He, Goodrich, and I slept together. If the men without blankets had not been so tired that they fell asleep anyhow, they would have been very cold, for, of course, we were all drenched with sweat, and above the waist had on nothing but our flannel shirts, while the night was cool, with a heavy dew.

Before anyone had time to wake from the cold, however, we were all awakened by the Spaniards, whose skirmishers suddenly opened fire on us. Of course, we could not tell whether or not this was the forerunner of a heavy attack, for our Cossack posts were responding briskly. It was about three o'clock in the morning, at which time men's courage is said to be at the lowest ebb; but the cavalry division was certainly free from any weakness in that direction. At the alarm everybody jumped to his feet and the stiff, shivering, haggard men, their eyes only half-opened, all clutched their rifles and ran forward to the trench on the crest of the hill. ✶ ✶ ✶

THE SECOND BRIGADE LOST more heavily than the First; but neither its brigade commander nor any of its regimental commanders were touched, while the commander of the First Brigade and two of its three regimental commanders had been killed or wounded.

In this fight our regiment had numbered four hundred ninety men, as, in addition to the killed and wounded of the first fight, some had had to go to the hospital for sickness and some had been left behind with the baggage, or were detailed on other duty. Eighty-nine were killed and wounded: the heaviest loss suffered by any regiment in the cavalry division. The Spaniards made a stiff fight, standing firm until we charged home. They fought much more stubbornly than at Las Guasimas. We ought to have expected this, for they have always done well in holding intrenchments. On this day they showed themselves to be brave foes, worthy of honor for their gallantry.

In the attack on the San Juan hills our forces numbered about 6,600. There were about 4,500 Spaniards against us. Our total loss in killed and wounded was 1,071. Of the cavalry division there were, all told, some 2,300 officers and men, of whom 375 were killed and wounded. In the division over a fourth of the officers were killed or wounded, their loss being relatively half as great again as that of the enlisted men—which was as it should be.

I think we suffered more heavily than the Spaniards did in killed and wounded (though we also captured some scores of prisoners). It would have been very extraordinary if the reverse was the case, for we did the charging; and to carry earthworks on foot with dismounted cavalry, when these earthworks are held by unbroken infantry armed with the best modern rifles, is a serious task.

# In the Trenches

When the shrapnel burst among us on the hillside we made up our minds that we had better settle down to solid siege work. All of the men who were not in the trenches I took off to the right, back of the Gatling guns, where there was a valley, and dispersed them by troops in sheltered parts. It took us an hour or two's experimenting to find out exactly what spots were free from danger, because some of the Spanish sharpshooters were in trees in our front, where we could not possibly place them from the trenches; and these were able to reach little hollows and depressions where the men were entirely safe from the Spanish artillery and from their trench-fire. Moreover, in one hollow, which we thought safe, the Spaniards succeeded in dropping a shell, a fragment of which went through the head of one of my men, who, astonishing to say, lived, although unconscious, for two hours afterward. Finally, I got all eight troops settled, and the men promptly proceeded to make themselves as much at home as possible. For the next twenty-four hours, however, the amount of comfort was small, as in the way of protection and covering we only had what blankets, raincoats, and hammocks we took from the dead Spaniards. Ammunition, which was, of course, the most vital need, was brought up in abundance; but very little food reached us. That afternoon we had just enough to allow each man for his supper two hardtacks, and one hardtack extra for every four men.

During the first night we had dug trenches sufficient in length and depth to shelter our men and insure safety against attack, but we had not put in any traverses or approaches, nor had we arranged the trenches at all points in the best places for offensive work; for we were working at night on ground which we had but partially explored. Later on an engineer officer stated that he did not think our work had been scientific; and I assured him that I did not doubt that he was right, for I had never before seen a trench, excepting those we captured from the Spaniards, or heard of a traverse, save as I

SOLDIERS TAKING COVER *in the trenches before Santiago.*

vaguely remembered reading about them in books. For such work as we were engaged in, however, the problem of intrenchment was comparatively simple, and the work we did proved entirely adequate. No man in my regiment was ever hit in the trenches or going in or out of them. ✳ ✳ ✳

**WHEN THE HARDTACK CAME UP** that afternoon I felt much sympathy for the hungry unfortunates in the trenches and hated to condemn them to six hours more without food; but I did not know how to get food into them. Little McGinty, the bronco buster, volunteered to make the attempt, and I gave him permission. He simply took a case of hardtack in his arms and darted toward the trenches. The distance was but short, and though there was an outburst of fire, he was actually missed. One bullet, however, passed through the case of hardtack just before he disappeared with it into the trench.

A trooper named Shanafelt repeated the feat, later, with a pail of coffee. Another trooper, George King, spent a leisure hour in the rear making soup out of some rice and other stuff he found in a Spanish house; he brought some of it to General Wood, Jack Greenway, and myself, and nothing could have tasted more delicious.

At this time our army in the trenches numbered about eleven thousand men; and the Spaniards in Santiago about nine thousand, their reinforcements having just arrived. Nobody on the firing-line, whatever was the case in the rear, felt the slightest uneasiness as to the Spaniards being able to break out; but there were plenty who doubted the advisability of trying to rush the heavy earthworks and wire defenses in our front.

All day long the firing continued—musketry and cannon. Our artillery gave up the attempt to fight on the firing line, and was withdrawn well to the rear out of range of the Spanish rifles; so far as we could see, it accomplished very little. The dynamite gun was brought up to the right of the regimental line. It was more effective than the regular artillery because it was fired with smokeless powder, and as it was used like a mortar from behind the hill, it did not betray its presence, and those firing it suffered no loss. Every few shots it got out of order, and the Rough Rider machinists and those furnished by Lieutenant Parker—whom we by this time began to consider as an exceedingly valuable member of our own regiment—would spend an hour or two in setting it right. Sergeant Borrowe had charge of it and handled it well. With him was Sergeant Guitilias, a gallant old fellow, a veteran of the Civil War, whose duties were properly those of standard-bearer, he having charge of the yellow cavalry standard of the regiment; but in the Cuban campaign he was given the more active work of helping run the dynamite gun. The shots from the dynamite gun made a terrific explosion, but they did not seem to go accurately. Once one of them struck a Spanish trench and wrecked part of it. On another occasion one struck a big building, from which there promptly swarmed both Spanish cavalry and infantry, on whom the Colt automatic guns played with good effect, during the minute that elapsed before they could get other cover.

These Colt automatic guns were not, on the whole, very successful. The gun detail was under the charge of Sergeant (afterward Lieutenant) Tiffany, assisted by some of our best men, like Stevens, Crowninshield, Bradley, Smith, and Herrig. The guns were mounted on tripods. They were too heavy for men to carry any distance and we could not always get mules. They would have been more effective if mounted on wheels, as the Gatlings were. Moreover, they proved more delicate than the Gatlings, and very readily got out of order. A further and serious disadvantage was that they did not use the Krag ammunition, as the Gatlings did, but the Mauser ammunition. The Spanish cartridges which we captured came in quite handily for this reason. Parker took the same fatherly interest in these two Colts that he did in the dynamite gun, and finally I put all three and their men under his immediate care, so that he had a battery of seven guns. ✶ ✶ ✶

**AFTER THE BATTLE OF SAN JUAN** my men had really become veterans; they and I understood each other perfectly, and trusted each other implicitly; they knew I would share every hardship and danger with them, would do everything in my power to see that they were fed, and so far as might be, sheltered and spared; and in return I knew that they would endure every kind of hardship and fatigue without a murmur and face every danger with entire fearlessness. I felt utter confidence in them, and would have been more than willing to put them to any task which any crack regiment of the world, at home or abroad, could perform. They were natural fighters, men of great intelligence, great courage, great hardihood, and physical prowess; and I could draw on these qualities and upon their spirit of ready, soldierly obedience to make up for any deficiencies in the technique of the trade which they had temporarily adopted. It must be remembered that they were already good individual fighters, skilled in the use of the horse and the rifle, so that there was no need of putting them through the kind of training in which the ordinary raw recruit must spend his first year or two.

> "After the battle of San Juan my men had really become veterans; they and I understood each other perfectly, and trusted each other implicitly."

On July 2nd, as the day wore on, the fight, though raging fitfully at intervals, gradually died away. The Spanish guerillas were causing us much trouble. They showed great courage, exactly as did their soldiers who were defending the trenches. In fact, the Spaniards throughout showed precisely the qualities they did early in the century, when, as every student will remember, their fleets were a helpless prey to the English warships, and their armies utterly unable to stand in the open against those of Napoleon's marshals, while on the other hand their guerillas performed marvelous feats, and their defence of intrenchments and walled towns, as at Saragossa and Gerona, were the wonder of the civilized world.

In our front their sharpshooters crept up before dawn and either lay in the thick jungle or climbed into

THE AFRICAN-AMERICAN TWENTY-THIRD COLORED INFANTRY *in the San Juan trenches, under severe fire from the enemy, July 2, 1898.*

some tree with dense foliage. In these places it proved almost impossible to place them, as they kept cover very carefully, and their smokeless powder betrayed not the slightest sign of their whereabouts. They caused us a great deal of annoyance and some little loss, and though our own sharpshooters were continually taking shots at the places where they supposed them to be, and though occasionally we would play a Gatling or a Colt all through the top of a suspicious tree, I but twice saw Spaniards brought down out of their perches from in front of our lines—on each occasion the fall of the Spaniard being hailed with loud cheers by our men.

These sharpshooters in our front did perfectly legitimate work, and were entitled to all credit for their courage and skill. It was different with the guerillas in our rear. Quite a number of these had been posted in trees at the time of the San Juan fight. They were using, not Mausers, but Remingtons, which shot smokeless powder and a brass-coated bullet. It was one of these bullets which had hit Winslow Clark by my side on Kettle Hill; and though for long-range fighting the Remingtons were, of course, nothing like as good as the Mausers, they were equally serviceable for short-range bush work, as they used smokeless powder. When our troops advanced and the Spaniards in the trenches and in reserve behind the hill fled, the guerillas in the trees had no time to get away and in consequence were left in the rear of our lines. As we found out from the prisoners we took, the Spanish officers had been careful to instill into the minds of their soldiers the belief that the Americans never granted quarter, and I suppose it was in consequence of this that the guerillas did not surrender; for we found that the Spaniards were anxious enough to surrender as soon as they became convinced that we would treat them mercifully. At any rate, these guerillas kept up in their trees and showed not only courage but wanton cruelty and barbarity. At times they fired upon armed men in bodies, but they much preferred for their victims the unarmed attendants, the doctors, the chaplains, the hospital stewards. They fired at the men who were bearing off the wounded in litters;

they fired at the doctors who came to the front, and at the chaplains who started to hold burial service; the conspicuous Red Cross brassard worn by all of these noncombatants, instead of serving as a protection, seemed to make them the special objects of the guerilla fire. So annoying did they become that I sent out that afternoon and next morning a detail of picked sharpshooters to hunt them out, choosing, of course, first-class woodsmen and mountain men who were also good shots. My sharpshooters felt very vindictively toward these guerillas and showed them no quarter. They started systematically to hunt them, and showed themselves much superior at the guerillas' own game, killing eleven, while not one of my men was scratched. Two of the men who did conspicuously good service in this work were Troopers Goodwin and Proffit, both of Arizona, but one by birth a Californian and the other a North Carolinian. Goodwin was a

**ROUGH RIDERS GUIDON**, *1898. The white "1" on the red indicates the 1st U.S. Volunteer Calvary. The red "L" on the white indicates it is the L Troop. This guidon was carried in all the engagements in Cuba, 1898, and was given to the widow of Captain Allyn Capron.*

natural shot, not only with the rifle and revolver, but with the sling. Proffit might have stood as a type of the mountaineers described by John Fox and Miss Murfree. He was a tall, sinewy, handsome man of remarkable strength, an excellent shot and a thoroughly good soldier. His father had been a Confederate officer, rising from the ranks, and if the war had lasted long enough the son would have risen in the same manner. As it was, I should have been glad to have given him a commission, exactly as I should have been glad to have given a number of others in the regiment commissions, if I had only had them. Proffit was a saturnine, reserved man, who afterward fell very sick with the fever, and who, as a reward for his soldierly good conduct, was often granted unusual privileges; but he took the fever and the privileges with the same iron indifference, never grumbling, and never expressing satisfaction. ✶ ✶ ✶

THAT NIGHT WE SPENT in perfecting the trenches and arranging entrances to them, doing about as much work as we had the preceding night. Greenway and Goodrich, from their energy, eagerness to do every duty, and great physical strength, were peculiarly useful in this work; as, indeed, they were in all work. They had been up practically the entire preceding night, but they were too good men for me to spare them, nor did they wish to be spared; and I kept them up all this night too. Goodrich had also been on guard as officer of the day the night we were at El Paso, so that it turned out that he spent nearly four days and three nights with practically hardly any sleep at all.

Next morning, at daybreak, the firing began again. This day, the 3rd, we suffered nothing, save having one man wounded by a sharpshooter, and, thanks to the approaches to the trenches, we were able to relieve the guards without any difficulty. The Spanish sharpshooters in the trees and jungle nearby, however, annoyed us very much, and I made preparations to fix them next day. With this end in view I chose out some twenty first-class men, in many instances the same that I had sent after the guerillas, and arranged that each should take his canteen and a little food. They were to slip into the jungle between us and the Spanish lines before dawn next morning, and there to spend the day, getting as close to the Spanish lines as possible, moving about with great stealth, and picking off any hostile sharpshooter, as well as any soldier who exposed himself in the trenches. I had plenty of men who possessed a training in woodcraft that fitted them for this work; and as soon as the rumor got abroad what I was planning, volunteers thronged to me. Daniels and Love were two of the men always to the front in any enterprise of this nature; so were Wadsworth, the two Bulls, Fortescue, and Cowdin. But I could not begin to name all the troopers who so eagerly craved the chance to win honor out of hazard and danger.

Among them was good, solemn Fred Herrig, the Alsatian. I knew Fred's patience and skill as a hunter from the trips we had taken together after deer and mountain sheep through the Bad Lands of the Little Missouri. He still spoke English with what might be called Alsatian variations—he always spoke of the gun detail as the "góndêtle," with the accent on the first syllable—and he expressed a wish to be allowed "a holiday from the gondetle to go after dem gorrillas." I told him he could have the holiday, but to his great disappointment the truce came first, and then Fred asked that, inasmuch as the "gorrillas" were now forbidden game, he might be allowed to go after guinea-hens instead.

Even after the truce, however, some of my sharpshooters had occupation, for two guerillas in our rear took occasional shots at the men who were bathing in a pond, until one of our men spied them, when they were both speedily brought down. One of my riflemen who did best at this kind of work, by the way, got into trouble because of it. He was much inflated by my commendation of him, and when he went back to his troop he declined to obey the first Sergeant's orders on the ground that he was "the Colonel's sharpshooter." The Lieutenant in command, being somewhat puzzled, brought him to me, and I had to explain that if the offence, disobedience of orders

A VIEW OF SAN JUAN HILL *and block-house showing the camp of the U.S. forces, 1898.*

in face of the enemy, was repeated he might incur the death penalty; whereat he looked very crestfallen. That afternoon he got permission, like Fred Herrig, to go after guinea-hens, which were found wild in some numbers round about; and he sent me the only one he got as a peace offering. The few guinea-hens thus procured were all used for the sick.

Dr. Church had established a little field hospital under the shoulder of the hill in our rear. He was himself very sick and had almost nothing in the way of medicine or supplies or apparatus of any kind, but the condition of the wounded in the big field hospitals in the rear was so horrible, from the lack of attendants as well as of medicines, that we kept all the men we possibly could at the front. Some of them had now begun to come down with fever. They were all very patient, but it was pitiful to see the sick and wounded soldiers lying on their blankets,

if they had any, and if not then simply in the mud, with nothing to eat but hardtack and pork, which of course they could not touch when their fever got high, and with no chance to get more than the rudest attention. Among the very sick here was gallant Captain Llewellen. I feared he was going to die. We finally had to send him to one of the big hospitals in the rear. Doctors Brewer and Fuller of the Tenth had been unwearying in attending to the wounded, including many of those of my regiment.

At twelve o'clock we were notified to stop firing and a flag of truce was sent in to demand the surrender of the city. The negotiations gave us a breathing spell.

That afternoon I arranged to get our baggage up, sending back strong details of men to carry up their own goods, and, as usual, impressing into the service a kind of improvised pack-train consisting of the officers' horses, of two or three captured Spanish cavalry horses, two or three mules which had been shot and abandoned and which our men had taken and cured, and two or three Cuban ponies. Hitherto we had simply been sleeping by the trenches or immediately in their rear, with nothing in the way of shelter and only one blanket to every three or four men. Fortunately there had been little rain. We now got up the shelter tents of the men and some flies for the hospital and for the officers; and my personal baggage appeared. I celebrated its advent by a thorough wash and shave.

Later, I twice snatched a few hours to go to the rear and visit such of my men as I could find in the hospitals. Their patience was extraordinary. Kenneth Robinson, a gallant young trooper, though himself severely (I supposed at the time mortally) wounded, was noteworthy for the way in which he tended those among the wounded who were even more helpless, and the cheery courage with which he kept up their spirits. Gievers, who was shot through the hips, rejoined us at the front in a fortnight. Captain Day was hardly longer away. Jack Hammer, who, with poor Race Smith, a gallant Texas lad who was mortally hurt beside me on the summit of the hill, had been on kitchen detail, was wounded and sent to the rear; he was ordered to go to the United States, but he heard that we were to assault Santiago, so he struggled out to rejoin us, and thereafter stayed at the front. Cosby, badly wounded, made his way down to the seacoast in three days, unassisted.

With all volunteer troops, and I am inclined to think with regulars, too, in time of trial, the best work can be got out of the men only if the officers endure the same hardships and face the same risks. In my regiment, as in the whole cavalry division, the proportion of loss in killed and wounded was considerably greater among the officers than among the troopers, and this was exactly as it should be. Moreover, when we got down to hard pan, we all, officers and men, fared exactly alike as regards both shelter and food. This prevented any grumbling. When the troopers saw that the officers had nothing but hardtack, there was not a man in the regiment who would

not have been ashamed to grumble at faring no worse, and when all alike slept out in the open, in the rear of the trenches, and when the men always saw the field officers up at night, during the digging of the trenches, and going the rounds of the outposts, they would not tolerate, in any of their number, either complaint or shirking work. When things got easier I put up my tent and lived a little apart, for it is a mistake for an officer ever to grow too familiar with his men, no matter how good they are; and it is of course the greatest possible mistake to seek popularity either by showing weakness or by mollycoddling the men. They will never respect a commander who does not enforce discipline, who does not know his duty, and who is not willing both himself to encounter and to make them encounter every species of danger and hardship

COLONEL ROOSEVELT VISITING COLONEL TURNER, *of the First Illinois Regiment, U.S.V., Cuba.*

when necessary. The soldiers who do not feel this way are not worthy of the name and should be handled with iron severity until they become fighting men and not shams. In return the officer should carefully look after his men, should see that they are well fed and well sheltered, and that, no matter how much they may grumble, they keep the camp thoroughly policed.

After the cessation of the three days' fighting we began to get our rations regularly and had plenty of hardtack and salt pork, and usually about half the ordinary amount of sugar and coffee. It was not a very good ration for the tropics, however, and was of very little use indeed to the sick and half sick. On two or three occasions during the siege I got my improvised pack-train together and either took or sent it down to the seacoast for beans, canned tomatoes, and the like. We got these either from the transports which were still landing stores on the beach or from the Red Cross. If I did not go myself I sent some man who had shown that he was a driving, energetic, tactful fellow, who would somehow get what we wanted. Chaplain Brown developed great capacity in this line, and so did one of the troopers named Knoblauch, he who had dived after the rifles that had sunk off the pier at Daiquiri. The supplies of food we got in this way had a very beneficial effect, not only upon the men's health, but upon their spirits. To the Red Cross and similar charitable organizations we owe a great deal. We also owed much to Colonel Weston of the Commissary Department, who always helped us and never let himself be hindered by red tape; thus he always let me violate the absurd regulation which forbade me, even in war time, to purchase food for my men from the stores, although letting me purchase for the officers. I, of course, paid no heed to the regulation when by violating it I could get beans, canned tomatoes, or tobacco. Sometimes I used my own money, sometimes what was given me by Woody Kane, or what was sent me by my brother-in-law, Douglas Robinson, or by the other Red Cross people in New York. My regiment did not fare very well; but I think it fared better than any other. Of course no one would have minded in the least such hard-

ships as we endured had there been any need of enduring them; but there was none. System and sufficiency of transportation were all that were needed. ✶ ✶ ✶

**I WAS VERY MUCH TOUCHED** by the devotion my men showed to me. After they had once become convinced that I would share their hardships, they made it a point that I should not suffer any hardships at all; and I really had an extremely easy time. Whether I had any food or not myself made no difference, as there were sure to be certain troopers, and, indeed, certain troop messes, on the lookout for me. If they had any beans they would send me over a cupful, or I would suddenly receive a present of doughnuts from some ex-roundup cook who had succeeded in obtaining a little flour and sugar, and if a man shot a guinea-hen it was all I could do to make him keep half of it for himself. Wright, the color sergeant, and Henry Bardshar, my orderly, always pitched and struck my tent and built me a bunk of bamboo poles, whenever we changed camp. So I personally endured very little discomfort; for, of course, no one minded the two or three days preceding or following each fight, when we all had to get along as best we could. Indeed, as long as we were under fire or in the immediate presence of the enemy, and I had plenty to do, there was nothing of which I could legitimately complain; and what I really did regard as hardships, my men did not object to—for later on, when we had some leisure, I would have given much for complete solitude and some good books.

Whether there was a truce, or whether, as sometimes happened, we were notified that there was no truce but merely a further cessation of hostilities by tacit agreement, or whether the fight was on, we kept equally vigilant watch, especially at night. In the trenches every fourth man kept awake, the others sleeping beside or behind him on their rifles; and the Cossack posts and pickets were pushed out in advance beyond the edge of the jungle. At least once a night at some irregular hour I tried to visit every part of our line, especially if it was dark and rainy, although sometimes, when the lines were

THEODORE ROOSEVELT *with his Rough Riders.*

in charge of some officer like Wilcox or Kane, Greenway or Goodrich, I became lazy, took off my boots, and slept all night through. Sometimes at night I went not only along the lines of our own brigade, but of the brigades adjoining. It was a matter of pride, not only with me, but with all our men, that the lines occupied by the Rough Riders should be at least as vigilantly guarded as the lines of any regular regiment. ✳ ✳ ✳

IF THE CITY [OF SANTIAGO] could be taken without direct assault on the intrenchments and wire entanglements, we earnestly hoped it would be, for such an assault meant, as we knew by past experience, the loss of a quarter of the attacking regiments (and we were bound that the Rough Riders should be one of these attacking regiments, if the attack had to be made). There was, of course, nobody who would not rather have assaulted than have run the risk of failure; but we

hoped the city would fall without need arising for us to suffer the great loss of life which a further assault would have entailed. ✳ ✳ ✳

THE WEEK OF NON-FIGHTING was not all a period of truce; part of the time was passed under a kind of nondescript arrangement, when we were told not to attack ourselves, but to be ready at any moment to repulse an attack and to make preparations for meeting it. During these times I busied myself in putting our trenches into first-rate shape and in building bomb-proofs and traverses. One night I got a detail of sixty men from the First, Ninth, and Tenth, whose officers always helped us in every way, and with these, and with sixty of my own men, I dug a long, zigzag trench in advance of the salient of my line out to a knoll well in front, from which we could command the Spanish trenches and block-houses immediately ahead of us. On this knoll we made a kind of bastion consisting of a deep, semicircular trench with sandbags arranged along the edge so as to constitute a wall with loopholes. Of course, when I came to dig this trench, I kept both Greenway and Goodrich supervising the work all night, and equally of course I got Parker and Stevens to help me. By employing as many men as we did we were able to get the work so far advanced as to provide against interruption before the moon rose, which was about midnight. Our pickets were thrown far out in the jungle, to keep back the Spanish pickets and prevent any interference with the diggers. The men seemed to think the work rather good fun than otherwise, the possibility of a brush with the Spaniards lending a zest that prevented its growing monotonous.

Parker had taken two of his Gatlings, removed the wheels, and mounted them in the trenches; also mounting the two automatic Colts where he deemed they could do best service. With the completion of the trenches, bomb-proofs, and traverses, and the mounting of these guns, the fortifications of the hill assumed quite a respectable character, and the Gatling men christened it Fort Roosevelt, by which name it afterward went. ✳ ✳ ✳

THE BATTLE OF SAN JUAN
RIDGE, CUBA, 1898.

TROOPS IN TRENCHES *waving hats when Santiago surrendered, San Juan, Cuba, 1898.*

SHORTLY AFTER MIDDAY on the 10th fighting began again, but it soon became evident that the Spaniards did not have much heart in it. The American field artillery was now under the command of General Randolph, and he fought it effectively. A mortar battery had also been established, though with an utterly inadequate supply of ammunition, and this rendered some service. Almost the only Rough Riders who had a chance to do much firing were the men with the Colt automatic guns, and the twenty picked sharpshooters, who were placed in the newly dug little fort out at the extreme front. Parker had a splendid time with the Gatlings and the Colts. With these machine guns he completely silenced the battery in front of us. This battery had caused us a good deal of trouble at first, as we could not place it. It was immediately in front of the hospital, from which many Red Cross flags were flying, one of them floating just above this battery, from where we looked at it. In consequence, for some time, we did not know it was a hostile battery at all, as, like all the other Spanish batteries, it was using smokeless powder. It was only by the aid of powerful glasses that we finally discovered its real nature. The Gatlings and Colts then actually put it out of action, silencing the big guns and the two field-pieces. Furthermore, the machine guns and our sharpshooters together did good work in supplementing the effects of the dynamite gun; for when a shell from the latter struck near a Spanish trench, or a building in which there were Spanish troops, the shock was seemingly so great that the Spaniards almost always showed themselves, and gave our men a chance to do some execution.

As the evening of the 10th came on, the men began to make their coffee in sheltered places. By this time they knew how to take care of themselves so well that not a man was touched by the Spaniards during the second bombardment. While I was lying with the officers just outside one of the bomb-proofs I saw a New Mexican trooper named Morrison making his coffee under the protection of a traverse high up on the hill. Morrison was originally a Baptist preacher who had joined the

THE SANTIAGO SURRENDER TREE *where the Spanish surrendered in 1898.*

regiment purely from a sense of duty, leaving his wife and children, and had shown himself to be an excellent soldier. He had evidently exactly calculated the danger zone, and found that by getting close to the traverse he could sit up erect and make ready his supper without being cramped. I watched him solemnly pounding the coffee with the butt end of his revolver, and then boiling the water and frying his bacon, just as if he had been in the lee of the roundup wagon somewhere out on the plains.

By noon of next day, the 11th, my regiment with one of the Gatlings was shifted over to the right to guard the Caney road. We did no fighting in our new position, for the last straggling shot had been fired by the time we got there. That evening there came up the worst storm we had had, and by midnight my tent blew over. I had for the first time in a fortnight undressed myself completely, and I felt fully punished for my love of luxury when I jumped out into the driving downpour of tropic rain, and groped blindly in the darkness for my clothes as they lay in the liquid mud. It was Kane's night on guard, and I knew the wretched Woody would be out along the line and taking care of the pickets, no matter what the storm might be; and so I basely made my way to the kitchen tent, where good Holderman, the Cherokee, wrapped me in dry blankets, and put me to sleep on a table which he had just procured from an abandoned Spanish house.

On the 17th the city formally surrendered and our regiment, like the rest of the army, was drawn up on the trenches. When the American flag was hoisted the trumpets blared and the men cheered, and we knew that the fighting part of our work was over. ✴ ✴ ✴

ON THE MORNING OF THE 3RD the Spaniards had sent out of Santiago many thousands of women, children, and other non-combatants, most of them belonging to the poorer classes, but among them not a few of the best families. These wretched creatures took very little with them. They came through our lines and for the most part went to El Caney in our rear, where we had to feed them and protect them from the Cubans. As we had barely enough food for our own men the rations of the refugees were scanty indeed and their sufferings great. Long before the surrender they had begun to come to

> "When the American flag was hoisted the trumpets blared and the men cheered, and we knew that the fighting part of our work was over."

our lines to ask for provisions, and my men gave them a good deal out of their own scanty stores, until I had positively to forbid it and to insist that the refugees should go to headquarters; as, however hard and merciless it seemed, I was in duty bound to keep my own regiment at the highest pitch of fighting efficiency.

As soon as the surrender was assured the refugees came streaming back in an endless squalid procession down the Caney road to Santiago. My troopers, for all their roughness and their ferocity in fight, were rather tenderhearted than otherwise, and they helped the poor creatures, especially the women and children, in every way, giving them food and even carrying the children and the burdens borne by the women. I saw one man, Happy Jack, spend the entire day in walking to and fro for about a quarter of a mile on both sides of our lines along the road, carrying the bundles for a series of poor old women, or else carrying young children. Finally the doctor warned us that we must not touch the bundles of the refugees for fear of infection, as disease had broken out and was rife among them. Accordingly I had to put a stop to these acts of kindness on the part of my men; against which action Happy Jack respectfully but strongly protested upon the unexpected ground that "the Almighty would never let a man catch a disease while he was doing a good action." I did not venture to take so advanced a theological stand.

THE AMERICAN FLAG *on San Juan Heights after the Spanish surrender, 1898.*

# The Return Home

Two or three days after the surrender the cavalry division was marched back to the foothills west of El Caney, and there went into camp, together with the artillery. It was a most beautiful spot beside a stream of clear water, but it was not healthy. In fact no ground in the neighborhood was healthy. For the tropics the climate was not bad, and I have no question but that a man who was able to take good care of himself could live there all the year round with comparative impunity; but the case was entirely different with an army which was obliged to suffer great exposure, and to live under conditions which almost insured being attacked by the severe malarial fever of the country. My own men were already suffering badly from fever, and they got worse rather than better in the new camp. The same was true of the other regiments in the cavalry division. A curious feature was that the colored troops seemed to suffer as heavily as the white. From week to week there were slight relative changes, but on the average all the six cavalry regiments, the Rough Riders, the white regulars, and the colored regulars seemed to suffer about alike, and we were all very much weakened; about as much as the regular infantry, although naturally not as much as the volunteer infantry.

Yet even under such circumstances adventurous spirits managed to make their way out to us. In the fortnight following the last bombardment of the city I enlisted no less than nine such recruits, six being from Harvard, Yale, or Princeton; and Bull, the former Harvard oar, who had been back to the States crippled after the first fight, actually got back to us as a stowaway on one of the transports, bound to share the luck of the regiment, even if it meant yellow fever.

There were but twelve ambulances with the army, and these were quite inadequate for their work; but the conditions in the large field hospitals were so bad, that

WOUNDED U.S. TROOPS *in a hospital in Santiago, Cuba, 1898.*

as long as possible we kept all of our sick men in the regimental hospital at the front. Dr. Church did splendid work, although he himself was suffering much more than half the time from fever. Several of the men from the ranks did equally well, especially a young doctor from New York, Harry Thorpe, who had enlisted as a trooper, but who was now made acting assistant-surgeon. It was with the greatest difficulty that Church and Thorpe were able to get proper medicine for the sick, and it was almost the last day of our stay before we were able to get cots for them. Up to that time they lay on the ground. No food was issued suitable for them, or for the half-sick men who were not on the doctor's list; the two classes by this time included the bulk of the command. Occasionally we got hold of a wagon or of some Cuban carts, and at other times I used my improvised pack-train (the animals of which, however, were continually being taken away from us by our superiors) and went or sent back to the seacoast at Siboney or into Santiago itself to get rice, flour, cornmeal, oatmeal, condensed milk, potatoes, and canned vegetables. The rice I bought in Santiago; the best of the other stuff I got from the Red Cross through Mr. George Kennan and Miss Clara Barton and Dr. Lesser; but some of it I got from our own transports. Colonel Weston, the Commissary-General, as always, rendered us every service in his power. This additional and varied food was of the utmost service, not merely to the sick but in preventing the well from becoming sick. Throughout the campaign the Division Inspector-General, Lieutenant-Colonel Garlington, and Lieutenants West and Dickman, the acting division quartermaster and commissary, had done everything in their power to keep us supplied with food; but where there were so few mules and wagons even such able and zealous officers could not do the impossible.

We had the camp policed thoroughly, and I made the men build little bunks of poles to sleep on. By July

23rd, when we had been ashore a month, we were able to get fresh meat, and from that time on we fared well; but the men were already sickening. The chief trouble was the malarial fever, which was recurrent. For a few days the man would be very sick indeed; then he would partially recover, and be able to go back to work; but after a little time he would be again struck down. Every officer other than myself except one was down with sickness at one time or another. Even Greenway and Goodrich succumbed to the fever and were knocked out for a few days. Very few of the men indeed retained their strength and energy, and though the percentage actually on the sick list never got over twenty, there were less than fifty per cent who were fit for any kind of work. All the clothes were in rags; even the officers had neither socks nor underwear. The lithe college athletes had lost their spring; the tall, gaunt hunters and cowpunchers lounged listlessly in their dog-tents, which were steaming morasses during the torrential rains, and then ovens when the sun blazed down; but there were no complaints.

Through some blunder our march from the intrenchments to the camp on the foothills, after the surrender, was made during the heat of the day; and though it was only some five miles or thereabouts, very nearly half the men of the cavalry division dropped out. Captain Llewellen had come back, and led his troop on the march. He carried a pick and shovel for one of his sick men, and after we reached camp walked back with a mule to get another trooper who had fallen out from heat exhaustion. The result was that the captain himself went down and became exceedingly sick. We at last succeeded in sending him to the States. I never thought he would live, but he did, and when I met him again at Montauk Point he had practically entirely recovered. My orderly, Henry Bardshar, was struck down, and though he ultimately recovered, he was a mere skeleton, having lost over eighty pounds.

Yellow fever also broke out in the rear, chiefly among the Cubans. It never became epidemic, but it caused a perfect panic among some of our own doctors, and especially in the minds of one or two generals and of the home authorities. We found that whenever we sent a man to the rear he was decreed to have yellow fever, whereas, if we kept him at the front, it always turned out that he had malarial fever, and after a few days he was back at work again. I doubt if there were ever more than a dozen genuine cases of yellow fever in the whole cavalry division; but the authorities at Washington, misled by the reports they received from one or two of their military and medical advisers at the front, became panic-struck, and under the influence of their fears hesitated to bring the army home, lest it might import yellow fever into the United States. Their panic was absolutely groundless, as shown by the fact that when brought home not a single case of yellow fever developed upon American soil. Our real foe was not the yellow fever at all, but malarial fever, which was not infectious, but which was certain, if the troops were left throughout the summer in Cuba, to destroy them, either killing them outright, or weakening them so that they would have fallen victims to any disease that attacked them.

However, for a time our prospects were gloomy, as the Washington authorities seemed determined that we should stay in Cuba. They unfortunately knew nothing of the country nor of the circumstances of the army, and the plans that were from time to time formulated in the Department (and even by an occasional general or surgeon at the front) for the management of the army would have been comic if they had not possessed such tragic possibilities. Thus, at one period it was proposed that we should shift camp every two or three days. Now, our transportation, as I have pointed out before, was utterly inadequate. In theory, under the regulations of the War Department, each regiment should have had at least twenty-five wagons. As a matter of fact our regiment often had none, sometimes one, rarely two, and never three; yet it was better off than any other in the cavalry division. In consequence it was impossible to carry much of anything save what the men had on their backs, and half of the men were too weak to walk three miles with their packs. Whenever we shifted camp the exertion among the half-sick caused our sick-roll to double next morning, and it took at least three days, even when the shift was for but a short distance, before we were able to bring up the officers' luggage, the hospital spare food, the ammunition, etc. Meanwhile the officers slept wherever they could, and those men who had not been able to carry their own bedding, slept as the officers did. In the weak condition of the men the labor of pitching camp was severe and told heavily upon them. In short, the scheme of continually shifting camp was impossible of fulfillment. It would merely have resulted in the early destruction of the army.

Again, it was proposed that we should go up the mountains and make our camps there. The palm and the bamboo grew to the summits of the mountains, and the soil along their sides was deep and soft, while the rains were very heavy, much more so than immediately on the coast—every mile or two inland bringing with it a great increase in the rainfall. We could, with much difficulty, have got our regiments up the mountains, but not half the men could have got up with their belongings; and once there it would have been an impossibility to feed them. It was all that could be done, with the limited number of wagons and mule-trains on hand, to feed the men in the existing camps, for the travel and the rain gradually rendered each road in succession wholly impassable. To have gone up the mountains would have meant early starvation.

**ROUGH RIDERS AND INFANTRYMEN** *listening to a sermon delivered by Chaplain Henry A. Brown. Standing beside the tree in the background are, right to left: Theodore Roosevelt, Leonard Wood, Joseph Wheeler, Major Drum, Alexander O. Brodie, and other officers.*

The third plan of the Department was even more objectionable than either of the others. There was, some twenty-five miles in the interior, what was called a high interior plateau, and at one period we were informed that we were to be marched thither. As a matter of fact, this so-called high plateau was the sugarcane country, where, during the summer, the rainfall was prodigious. It was a rich, deep soil, covered with a rank tropic growth, the guinea-grass being higher than the head of a man on horseback. It was a perfect hotbed of malaria, and there was no dry ground whatever in which to camp. To have sent the troops there would have been simple butchery.

Under these circumstances the alternative to leaving the country altogether was to stay where we were, with the hope that half the men would live through to the cool season. We did everything possible to keep up the spirits of the men, but it was exceedingly difficult because there was nothing for them to do. They were weak and languid, and in the wet heat they had lost energy, so that it was not possible for them to indulge in sports or pastimes. There were exceptions; but the average man who went off to shoot guinea-hens or tried some vigorous game always felt much the worse for his exertions. Once or twice I took some of my comrades with me, and climbed up one or another of the surrounding mountains, but the result generally was that half of the party were down with some kind of sickness next day. It was impossible to take heavy exercise in the heat of the day; the evening usually saw a rainstorm which made the country a quagmire; and in the early morning the drenching dew and wet, slimy soil made walking but little pleasure. Chaplain Brown held service every Sunday under a low tree outside my tent; and we always had a congregation of a few score troopers, lying or sitting round, their strong hard faces turned toward the preacher. I let a few of the men visit Santiago, but the long walk in and out was very tiring,

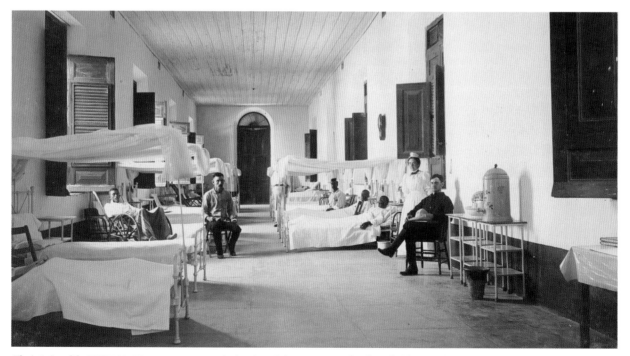

*The interior of the* GENERAL MILITARY HOSPITAL *in Santiago, Cuba, 1898. Even after the end of the war, the casualty numbers continued to rise due to disease, prompting Roosevelt and the other officers to arrange for speedy transport of the troops back to the United States.*

and, moreover, wise restrictions had been put as to either officers or men coming in. * * *

WE SHOULD PROBABLY HAVE SPENT the summer in our sick camps, losing half the men and hopelessly shattering the health of the remainder, if General Shafter had not summoned a council of officers, hoping by united action of a more or less public character to wake up the Washington authorities to the actual condition of things. As all the Spanish forces in the province of Santiago had surrendered, and as so-called immune regiments were coming to garrison the conquered territory, there was literally not one thing of any kind whatsoever for the army to do, and no purpose to serve by keeping it at Santiago. We did not suppose that peace was at hand, being ignorant of the negotiations. We were anxious to take part in the Porto Rico campaign, and would have been more than willing to suffer any amount of sickness, if by so doing we could get into action. But if we were not to take part in the Porto Rico campaign, then we knew it was absolutely indispensable to get our commands north immediately, if they were to be in trim for the great campaign against Havana, which would surely be the main event of the winter if peace were not declared in advance.

Our army included the great majority of the regulars, and was, therefore, the flower of the American force. It was on every account imperative to keep it in good trim; and to keep it in Santiago meant its entirely purposeless destruction. As soon as the surrender was an accomplished fact, the taking away of the army to the north should have begun.

Every officer, from the highest to the lowest, especially among the regulars, realized all of this, and about the last day of July, General Shafter called a conference, in the palace, of all the division and brigade commanders. By this time, owing to Wood's having been made governor-general, I was in command of my brigade, so I went to the conference too, riding in with Generals Sumner and Wheeler, who were the other representatives of the cav-alry division. Besides the line officers all the chief medical officers were present at the conference. The telegrams from the secretary stating the position of himself and the surgeon-general were read, and then almost every line and medical officer present expressed his views in turn. They were almost all regulars and had been brought up to lifelong habits of obedience without protest. They were ready to obey still, but they felt, quite rightly, that it was their duty to protest rather than to see the flower of the United States forces destroyed as the culminating act of a campaign in which the blunders that had been committed had been retrieved only by the valor and splendid soldierly qualities of the officers and enlisted men of the infantry and dismounted cavalry. There was not a dissenting voice; for there could not be. There was but one side to the question. To talk of continually shifting camp or of moving up the mountains or of moving into the interior was idle, for not one of the plans could be carried out with our utterly insufficient transportation, and at that season and in that climate they would merely have resulted in aggravating the sickliness of the soldiers. It was deemed best to make some record of our opinion, in the shape of a letter or report, which would show that to keep the army in Santiago meant its absolute and objectless ruin, and that it should at once be recalled. At first there was naturally some hesitation on the part of the regular officers to take the initiative, for their entire future career might be sacrificed. So I wrote a letter to General Shafter, reading over the rough draft to the various Generals and adopting their corrections. Before I had finished making these corrections it was determined that we should send a circular letter on behalf of all of us to General Shafter, and when I returned from presenting him mine, I found this circular letter already prepared and we all of us signed it. Both letters were made public. The result was immediate. Within three days the army was ordered to be ready to sail for home.

As soon as it was known that we were to sail for home the spirits of the men changed for the better. In my regiment the officers began to plan methods of drilling the men on horseback, so as to fit them for use against the Spanish cavalry, if we should go against Havana in December. We had, all of us, eyed the captured Spanish cavalry with particular interest. The men were small, and the horses, though well trained and well built, were diminutive ponies, very much smaller than cow ponies. We were certain that if we ever got a chance to try shock tactics against them they would go down like nine-pins, provided only that our men could be trained to charge in any kind of line, and we made up our minds to devote our time to this. Dismounted work with the rifle we already felt thoroughly competent to perform. ✶ ✶ ✶

**ON AUGUST 6TH** we were ordered to embark, and next morning we sailed on the transport Miami. General Wheeler was with us and a squadron of the Third Cavalry under Major Jackson. The General put the policing and management of the ship into my hands, and I had great aid from Captain McCormick, who had been acting with me as adjutant-general of the brigade. I had profited by my experience coming down, and as Dr. Church knew his work well, although he was very sick, we kept the ship in such good sanitary condition, that we were one of the very few organizations allowed to land at Montauk immediately upon our arrival.

Soon after leaving port the captain of the ship notified me that his stokers and engineers were insubordinate and drunken, due, he thought, to liquor which my men had given them. I at once started a search of the ship, explaining to the men that they could not keep the liquor; that if they surrendered whatever they had to me I should return it to them when we went ashore; and that meanwhile I would allow the sick to drink when they really needed it; but that if they did not give the liquor to me of their own accord I would throw it overboard. About seventy flasks and bottles were handed to me, and I found and threw overboard about twenty. This at once put a stop to all drunkenness. The stokers and engineers were sullen and half mutinous, so I sent a detail of my men down to watch them and see that they did their work under the orders of the chief engineer; and we reduced them to obedience in short order. I could easily have drawn from the regiment sufficient skilled men to fill every position in the entire ship's crew, from captain to stoker. ✶ ✶ ✶

**BY CARE AND DILIGENCE** we succeeded in preventing any serious sickness. One man died, however. He had been suffering from dysentery ever since we landed, owing purely to his own fault, for on the very first night ashore he obtained a lot of fiery liquor from some of the Cubans, got very drunk, and had to march next day through the hot sun before he was entirely sober. He never recovered, and was useless from that time on. On board ship he died, and we gave him sea burial. Wrapped in a hammock, he was placed opposite a port, and the American flag thrown over him. The engine was stilled, and the great ship rocked on the waves unshaken by the screw, while the war-worn troopers clustered around with bare heads, to listen to Chaplain Brown read the funeral service, and to the band of the Third Cavalry as it played the funeral dirge. Then the port was knocked free, the flag withdrawn, and the shotted hammock plunged heavily over the side, rushing down through the dark water to lie, till the Judgment Day, in the ooze that holds the timbers of so many gallant ships, and the bones of so many fearless adventurers.

We were favored by good weather during our nine days' voyage, and much of the time when there was little to do we simply sat together and talked, each man contributing from the fund of his own experiences. Voyages around Cape Horn, yacht races for the America's cup, experiences on football teams which are famous in the annals of college sport; more serious feats of desperate prowess in Indian fighting and in breaking up gangs of white outlaws; adventures in hunting big game, in breaking wild horses, in tending great herds of cattle, and in wandering winter and summer among the mountains and across the lonely plains—the men who told the tales could draw upon countless memories such as these of the things they had done and the things they had seen others do. Sometimes General Wheeler joined us and told us about the great war, compared with which ours was such a small war—far-reaching in their importance though its effects were destined to be. When we had become convinced that we would escape an epidemic of sickness the homeward voyage became very pleasant.

> "We were favored by good weather during our nine days' voyage, and much of the time when there was little to do we simply sat together and talked, each man contributing from the fund of his own experiences."

On the eve of leaving Santiago I had received from Mr. Laffan of the Sun, a cable with the single word "Peace," and we speculated much on this, as the clumsy transport steamed slowly northward across the trade wind and then into the Gulf Stream. At last we sighted the low,

sandy bluffs of the Long Island coast, and late on the afternoon of the 14th we steamed through the still waters of the Sound and cast anchor off Montauk. A gunboat of the Mosquito fleet came out to greet us and to inform us that peace negotiations had begun.

Next morning we were marched on shore. Many of the men were very sick indeed. Of the three or four who had been closest to me among the enlisted men, Color-Sergeant Wright was the only one in good health. Henry Bardshar was a wreck, literally at death's door. I was myself in first-class health, all the better for having lost twenty pounds. Faithful Marshall, my colored body-servant, was so sick as to be nearly helpless.

Bob Wrenn nearly died. He had joined us very late and we could not get him a Krag carbine; so I had given him my Winchester, which carried the government cartridge; and when he was mustered out he carried it home in triumph, to the envy of his fellows, who themselves had to surrender their beloved rifles.

For the first few days there was great confusion and some want even after we got to Montauk. The men in

**THEODORE ROOSEVELT AND THE ROUGH RIDERS** *at Camp Wikoff, Montauk, New York, 1898.*

A BASEBALL GAME *featuring the Rough Riders vs. the 2nd Cavalry at Camp Wikoff.*

hospitals suffered from lack of almost everything, even cots. But after these few days we were very well cared for and had abundance of all we needed, except that on several occasions there was a shortage of food for the horses, which I should have regarded as even more serious than a shortage for the men, had it not been that we were about to be disbanded. The men lived high, with milk, eggs, oranges, and any amount of tobacco, the lack of which during portions of the Cuban campaign had been felt as seriously as any lack of food. One of the distressing features of the malarial fever which had been ravaging the troops was that it was recurrent and persistent. Some of my men died after reaching home, and many were very

sick. We owed much to the kindness not only of the New York hospitals and the Red Cross and kindred societies, but of individuals, notably Mr. Bayard Cutting and Mrs. Armitage, who took many of our men to their beautiful Long Island homes.

On the whole, however, the month we spent at Montauk before we disbanded was very pleasant. It was good to meet the rest of the regiment. They all felt dreadfully at not having been in Cuba. It was a sore trial to men who had given up much to go to the war, and who rebelled at nothing in the way of hardship or suffering, but who did bitterly feel the fact that their sacrifices seemed to have been useless. Of course those who stayed had done their duty precisely as did those who went, for the question of glory was not to be considered in comparison to the faithful performance of whatever was ordered; and no distinction of any kind was allowed in the regiment between those whose good fortune it had been to go and those whose harder fate it had been to remain. Nevertheless the latter could not be entirely comforted.

The regiment had three mascots; the two most characteristic—a young mountain lion brought by the Arizona troops, and a war eagle brought by the New Mexicans—we had been forced to leave behind in Tampa. The third, a rather disreputable but exceedingly knowing little dog named Cuba, had accompanied us through all the vicissitudes of the campaign. The mountain lion, Josephine, possessed an infernal temper; whereas both Cuba and the eagle, which have been named in my honor, were extremely good-humored. Josephine was kept tied up. She sometimes escaped. One cool night in early September she wandered off and, entering the tent of a Third Cavalry man, got into bed with him; whereupon he fled into the darkness with yells, much more unnerved than he would have been by the arrival of any number of Spaniards. The eagle was let loose and not only walked at will up and down the company streets, but also at times flew wherever he wished. He was a young bird, having been taken out of his nest when a fledgling. Josephine hated him and was always trying to make a meal of him, especially when we endeavored to take their photographs together. The eagle, though good-natured, was an entirely competent individual and ready at any moment to beat Josephine off. Cuba was also oppressed at times by Josephine, and was of course no match for her, but was frequently able to overawe by simple decision of character.

In addition to the animal mascots, we had two or three small boys who had also been adopted by the regiment. One, from Tennessee, was named Dabney Royster. When we embarked at Tampa he smuggled himself on board the transport with a 22-calibre rifle and three boxes of cartridges, and wept bitterly when sent ashore. The squadron which remained behind adopted him, got

him a little Rough Rider's uniform, and made him practically one of the regiment.

The men who had remained at Tampa, like ourselves, had suffered much from fever, and the horses were in bad shape. So many of the men were sick that none of the regiments began to drill for some time after reaching Montauk. There was a great deal of paperwork to be done; but as I still had charge of the brigade only a little of it fell on my shoulders. Of this I was sincerely glad, for I knew as little of the paperwork as my men had originally known of drill. We had all of us learned how to fight and march; but the exact limits of our rights and duties in other respects were not very clearly defined in our minds; and as for myself, as I had not had the time to learn exactly what they were, I had assumed a large authority in giving rewards and punishments. In particular I had looked on court-martials much as Peter Bell looked on primroses—they were court-martials and nothing more, whether resting on the authority of a lieutenant-colonel or of a major-general. The mustering-out officer, a thorough soldier, found to his horror that I had used the widest discretion both in imposing heavy sentences which I had no power to impose on men who shirked their duties, and, where men atoned for misconduct by marked gallantry, in blandly remitting sentences approved by my chief of division. However, I had done substantial, even though somewhat rude and irregular, justice—and no harm could result, as we were just about to be mustered out.

My chief duties were to see that the camps of the three regiments were thoroughly policed and kept in first-class sanitary condition. This took up some time, of course, and there were other matters in connection with the mustering out which had to be attended to; but I could always get two or three hours a day free from work. Then I would summon a number of the officers, Kane, Greenway, Goodrich, Church, Ferguson, McIlhenny, Frantz, Ballard and others, and we would gallop down to the beach and bathe in the surf, or else go for long rides over the beautiful rolling plains, thickly studded with pools which were white with water-lilies. Sometimes I went off alone with my orderly, young Gordon Johnston, one of the best men in the regiment; he was a nephew of the Governor of Alabama, and when at Princeton had played on the eleven. We had plenty of horses, and these rides were most enjoyable. Galloping over the open, rolling country, through the cool fall evenings, made us feel as if we were out on the great Western plains and might at any moment start deer from the brush, or see antelope stand and gaze, far away, or rouse a band of mighty elk and hear their horns clatter as they fled. ✳ ✳ ✳

**ONE SUNDAY** before the regiment disbanded I supplemented Chaplain Brown's address to the men by a short sermon of a rather hortatory character. I told them how proud I was of them, but warned them not to think that they could now go back and rest on their laurels, bidding them remember that though for ten days or so the world would be willing to treat them as heroes, yet after that time they would find they had to get down to hard work just like everyone else, unless they were willing to be regarded as worthless do-nothings. They took the sermon in good part, and I hope that some of them profited by it. At any rate, they repaid me by a very much more tangible expression of affection. One afternoon, to my genuine surprise, I was asked out of my tent by Lieutenant-Colonel Brodie (the gallant old boy had rejoined us), and found the whole regiment formed in hollow square, with the officers and color-sergeant in the middle. When I went in, one of the troopers came forward and on behalf of the regiment presented me with Remington's fine bronze, The Bronco-buster. There could have been no more appropriate gift from such a regiment, and I was not only pleased with it, but very deeply touched with the feeling which made them join in giving it. Afterward they all filed past and I shook the hands of each to say good-by.

Most of them looked upon the bronze with the critical eyes of professionals. I doubt if there was any regiment in the world which contained so large a number of men

SERGEANT THOMAS DARNELL *giving a horse-breaking demonstration on the Third Cavalry Bucker, Camp Wikoff, Montauk, New York, 1898.*

able to ride the wildest and most dangerous horses. One day while at Montauk Point some of the troopers of the Third Cavalry were getting ready for mounted drill when one of their horses escaped, having thrown his rider. This attracted the attention of some of our men and they strolled around to see the trooper remount. He was instantly thrown again, the horse, a huge, vicious sorrel, being one of the worst buckers I ever saw; and none of his comrades were willing to ride the animal. Our men, of course, jeered and mocked at them, and in response were dared to ride the horse themselves. The challenge was instantly accepted, the only question being as to which of a dozen noted bronco-busters who were in the ranks should undertake the task. They finally settled on a man named Darnell. It was agreed that the experiment should take place next day when the horse would be fresh, and accordingly next day the majority of both regiments turned out on a big open flat in front of my tent—brigade headquarters. The result was that, after as fine a bit of rough riding as one would care to see, in which one scarcely knew whether most to wonder at the extraordinary viciousness and agile strength of the horse or at the horsemanship and courage of the rider, Darnell came off victorious, his seat never having been shaken. After this almost every day we had exhibitions of bronco-busting, in which all the crack riders of the regiment vied with one another, riding not only all of our own bad horses but any horse which was deemed bad in any of the other regiments. Darnell, McGinty, Wood, Smoky Moore, and a score of others took part in these exhibitions, which included not merely feats in mastering vicious horses, but also feats of broken horses which the riders had trained to lie down at command, and upon which they could mount while at full speed.

Toward the end of the time we also had mounted drill on two or three occasions; and when the President visited the camp we turned out mounted to receive him as did the rest of the cavalry. The last night before we were mustered out was spent in noisy, but entirely harmless hilarity, which I ignored. Every form of celebration took place in the ranks. A former Populist candidate for attorney-general in Colorado delivered a fervent oration in favor of free silver; a number of the college boys sang; but most of the men gave vent to their feelings by improvised dances. In these the Indians took the lead, pure bloods and half-breeds alike, the cowboys and miners cheerfully joining in and forming part of the howling, grunting rings, that went bounding around the great fires they had kindled.

Next morning Sergeant Wright took down the colors, and Sergeant Guitilias the standard, for the last time; the horses, the rifles, and the rest of the regimental property had been turned in; officers and men shook hands and said good-by to one another, and then they scattered to their homes in the North and the South, the few going back to the great cities of the East, the many turning

ROOSEVELT'S FAREWELL *to the Rough Riders at Camp Wikoff, Montauk, New York, 1898.*

again toward the plains, the mountains, and the deserts of the West and the strange Southwest. This was on September 15th, the day which marked the close of the four months' life of a regiment of as gallant fighters as ever wore the United States uniform. ✳ ✳ ✳

THE REGIMENT WAS a wholly exceptional volunteer organization, and its career cannot be taken as in any way a justification for the belief that the average volunteer regiment approaches the average regular regiment in point of efficiency until it has had many months of active service. In the first place, though the regular regiments may differ markedly among themselves, yet the range of variation among them is nothing like so wide as that among volunteer regiments, where at first there is no common standard at all; the very best being, perhaps, up to the level of the regulars (as has recently been shown at Manila), while the very worst are no better than mobs, and the great bulk come in between. The average regular regiment is superior to the average volunteer regiment in the physique of the enlisted men, who have been very carefully selected, who have been trained to life in the open, and who know how to cook and take care of themselves generally.

Now, in all these respects, and in others like them, the Rough Riders were the equals of the regulars. They were hardy, self-reliant, accustomed to shift for themselves in the open under very adverse circumstances. The two all-important qualifications for a cavalryman, are riding and shooting—the modern cavalryman being so often used dismounted, as an infantryman. The average recruit requires a couple of years before he becomes proficient in horsemanship and marksmanship; but my men were already good shots and first-class riders when they came into the regiment. The difference as regards officers and noncommissioned officers, between regulars and volunteers, is usually very great; but in my regiment (keeping in view the material we had to handle), it was easy to develop noncommissioned officers out of men who had been round-up foremen, ranch foremen, mining bosses,

and the like. These men were intelligent and resolute; they knew they had a great deal to learn, and they set to work to learn it; while they were already accustomed to managing considerable interests, to obeying orders, and to taking care of others as well as themselves.

As for the officers, the great point in our favor was the anxiety they showed to learn from those among their number who, like Capron, had already served in the regular army; and the fact that we had chosen a regular army man as Colonel. If a volunteer organization consists of good material, and is eager to learn, it can readily do so if it has one or two first-class regular officers to teach it. Moreover, most of our captains and lieutenants were men who had seen much of wild life, who were accustomed to handling and commanding other men, and who had usually already been under fire as sheriffs, marshals, and the like. As for the second in command, myself, I had served three years as captain in the National Guard; I had been deputy sheriff in the cow country, where the position was not a sinecure; I was accustomed to big game hunting and to work on a cow ranch, so that I was thoroughly familiar with the use both of horse and rifle, and knew how to handle cowboys, hunters, and miners; finally, I had studied much in the literature of war, and especially the literature of the great modern wars, like our own Civil War, the Franco–German War, the Turco–Russian War; and I was especially familiar with the deeds, the successes and failures alike, of the frontier horse riflemen who had fought at King's Mountain and the Thames, and on the Mexican border. Finally, and most important of all, officers and men alike were eager for fighting, and resolute to do well and behave properly, to encounter hardship and privation, and the irksome monotony of camp routine, without grumbling or complaining; they had counted the cost before they went in, and were delighted to pay the penalties inevitably attendant upon the career of a fighting regiment; and from the moment when the regiment began to gather, the higher officers kept instilling

COLOR-SERGEANT ALBERT P. WRIGHT *with the battle flag used by the Rough Riders in Cuba at Camp Wikoff, 1898.*

**ROUGH RIDER OFFICERS** *in San Antonio, Texas, 1898. From left to right, front row: Jacob Schweizer, Henry B. Hersey, Alexander O. Brodie, Leonard Wood, Theodore Roosevelt, George M. Dunn, and Thomas W. Hall; second row: Joseph A. Carr, Hal Sayre, James H. McClintock, Robert S. Patterson, Joseph L. B. Alexander, Ode C. Nichols, Robert B. Huston, Maximiliano Luna, Robert H. Bruce, Horace W. Weakley, Frederick Muller, William Elkins Griffin, and George Curry; third row: David M. Goodrich, Frederick W. Wientge, George B. Wilcox, John C. Greenway, William O. O'Neill, Frank Frantz, Charles L. Ballard, William H. Kelly, Allyn L. Capron, and Maxwell Keyes; back row: Schuyler A. McGinnis, Horace K. Devereaux, William H. H. Llewellyn, Woodbury Kane, John Wesley Green, James Robb Church, Richard Cushing Day, Ernest Eddy Haskell, David J. Leahy, and Thomas H. Rymning; with the mountain lion mascot, Josephine, in the foreground.*

**MONUMENT TO THE 266 SAILORS OF THE BATTLESHIP MAINE** *at the National Cemetery, in Arlington, Virginia, constructed of the salvaged mast from the wreck.*

into those under them the spirit of eagerness for action and of stern determination to grasp at death rather than forfeit honor.

The self-reliant spirit of the men was well shown after they left the regiment. Of course, there were a few weaklings among them; and there were others, entirely brave and normally self-sufficient, who, from wounds or fevers, were so reduced that they had to apply for aid—or at least, who deserved aid, even though they often could only be persuaded with the greatest difficulty to accept it. The widows and orphans had to be taken care of. There were a few light-hearted individuals, who were entirely ready to fight in time of war, but in time of peace felt that somebody ought to take care of them; and there were others who, never having seen any aggregation of buildings larger than an ordinary cow-town, fell a victim to the fascinations of New York. But, as a whole, they scattered out to their homes on the disbandment of the regiment; gaunter than when they had enlisted, sometimes weakened by fever or wounds, but just as full as ever of sullen, sturdy capacity for self-help; scorning to ask for aid, save what was entirely legitimate in the way of one comrade giving help to another. A number of the examining surgeons, at the muster-out, spoke to me with admiration of the contrast offered by our regiment to so many others, in the fact that our men always belittled their own bodily injuries and sufferings; so that whereas the surgeons ordinarily had to be on the lookout lest a man who was not really disabled should claim to be so, in our case they had to adopt exactly the opposite attitude and guard the future interests of the men, by insisting upon putting upon their certificates of discharge whatever disease they had contracted or wound they had received in line of duty. Major J. H. Calef, who had more than any other one man to do with seeing to the proper discharge papers of our men, and who took a most generous interest in them, wrote me as follows: "I also wish to bring to your notice the fortitude displayed by the men of your regiment, who have come before me to be mustered out of service, in making their personal declarations as to their physical conditions. Men who bore on their faces and in their forms the traces of long days of illness, indicating wrecked constitutions, declared that nothing was the matter with them, at the same time disclaiming any intention of applying for a pension. It was exceptionally heroic."

When we were mustered out, many of the men had lost their jobs, and were too weak to go to work at once, while there were helpless dependents of the dead to care for. Certain of my friends, August Belmont, Stanley and Richard Mortimer, Major Austin Wadsworth—himself fresh from the Manila campaign—Belmont Tiffany, and others, gave me sums of money to be used for helping these men. In some instances, by the exercise of a good deal of tact and by treating the gift as a memorial of poor young Lieutenant Tiffany, we got the men to accept something; and, of course, there were a number who, quite rightly, made no difficulty about accepting. But most of the men would accept no help whatever. In the first chapter, I spoke of a lady, a teacher in an academy in the Indian Territory, three or four of whose pupils had come into my regiment, and who had sent with them a letter of introduction to me. When the regiment disbanded, I wrote to her to ask if she could not use a little money among the Rough Riders, white, Indian, and half-breed, that she might personally know. I did not hear from her for some time, and then she wrote as follows:

*Muscogee, Ind. Ter., December 19, 1898*
*My Dear Colonel Roosevelt: I did not at once reply to your letter of September 23rd, because I waited for a time to see if there should be need among any of our Rough Riders of the money you so kindly offered. Some of the boys are poor, and in one or two cases they seemed to me really needy, but they all said no. More than once I saw the tears come to their eyes, at thought of your care for them, as I told them of your letter. Did you hear any echoes of our Indian war-whoops over your election? They were pretty loud. I was particularly exultant, because my father*

*was a New Yorker and I was educated in New York, even if I was born here. So far as I can learn, the boys are taking up the dropped threads of their lives, as though they had never been away. Our two Rough Rider students, Meagher and Gilmore, are doing well in their college work.*

*I am sorry to tell you of the death of one of your most devoted troopers, Bert Holderman, who was here serving on the Grand Jury. He was stricken with meningitis in the jury-room, and died after three days of delirium. His father, who was twice wounded, four times taken prisoner, and fought in thirty-two battles of the Civil War, now old and feeble, survives him, and it was indeed pathetic to see his grief. Bert's mother, who is a Cherokee, was raised in my grandfather's family. The words of commendation which you wrote upon Bert's discharge are the greatest comfort to his friends. They wanted you to know of his death, because he loved you so.*

*I am planning to entertain all the Rough Riders in this vicinity some evening during my holiday vacation. I mean to have no other guests, but only give them an opportunity for reminiscences. I regret that Bert's death makes one less. I had hoped to have them sooner, but our struggling young college salaries are necessarily small and duties arduous. I make a home for my widowed mother and an adopted Indian daughter, who is in school; and as I do the cooking for a family of five, I have found it impossible to do many things I would like to.*

*Pardon me for burdening you with these details, but I suppose I am like your boys, who say, "The Colonel was always as ready to listen to a private as to a major-general."*

*Wishing you and yours the very best gifts the season can bring, I am,*

*Very truly yours, Alice M. Robertson.*

Is it any wonder that I loved my regiment?

**MONUMENT TO THE 71ST REGIMENT** *in San Juan Heights, Cuba, after 1898.*

**THE 71ST REGIMENT** *marching up Broadway on their arrival from Cuba in 1898, at the close of the Spanish–American War, 1898.*

# Appendix

The following is the report of the Associated Press correspondent of the "round-robin" incident. It is literally true in every detail. I was present when he was handed both letters; he was present while they were being written. —TR

SANTIAGO DE CUBA, August 3rd (delayed in transmission). Summoned by Major-General Shafter, a meeting was held here this morning at headquarters, and in the presence of every commanding and medical officer of the Fifth Army Corps, General Shafter read a cable message from Secretary Alger, ordering him, on the recommendation of Surgeon-General Sternberg, to move the army into the interior, to San Luis, where it is healthier.

As a result of the conference General Shafter will insist upon the immediate withdrawal of the army North.

As an explanation of the situation the following letter from Colonel Theodore Roosevelt, commanding the First Cavalry, to General Shafter, was handed by the latter to the correspondent of the Associated Press for publication:

*Major-General Shafter.*

*Sir: In a meeting of the general and medical officers called by you at the Palace this morning we were all, as you know, unanimous in our views of what should be done with the army. To keep us here, in the opinion of every officer commanding a division or a brigade, will simply involve the destruction of thousands. There is no possible reason for not shipping practically the entire command North at once.*

*Yellow-fever cases are very few in the cavalry division, where I command one of the two brigades, and not one true case of yellow fever has occurred in this division, except among the men sent to the hospital at Siboney, where they have, I believe, contracted it.*

*But in this division there have been one thousand five hundred cases of malarial fever. Hardly a*

*man has yet died from it, but the whole command is so weakened and shattered as to be ripe for dying like rotten sheep, when a real yellow-fever epidemic instead of a fake epidemic, like the present one, strikes us, as it is bound to do if we stay here at the height of the sickness season, August and the beginning of September. Quarantine against malarial fever is much like quarantining against the toothache.*

*All of us are certain that as soon as the authorities at Washington fully appreciate the condition of the army, we shall be sent home. If we are kept here it will in all human possibility mean an appalling disaster, for the surgeons here estimate that over half the army, if kept here during the sickly season, will die.*

*This is not only terrible from the standpoint of the individual lives lost, but it means ruin from the standpoint of military efficiency of the flower of the American army, for the great bulk of the regulars are here with you. The sick list, large though it is, exceeding four thousand, affords but a faint index of the debilitation of the army. Not twenty per cent are fit for active work.*

*Six weeks on the North Maine coast, for instance, or elsewhere where the yellow-fever germ cannot possibly propagate, would make us all as fit as fighting-cocks, as able as we are eager to take a leading part in the great campaign against Havana in the fall, even if we are not allowed to try Puerto Rico.*

*We can be moved North, if moved at once, with absolute safety to the country, although, of course, it would have been infinitely better if we had been moved North or to Puerto Rico two weeks ago. If there were any object in keeping us here, we would face yellow fever with as much indifference as we faced bullets. But there is no object.*

*The four immune regiments ordered here are sufficient to garrison the city and surrounding towns, and there is absolutely nothing for us to do here, and there has not been since the city surrendered. It is impossible to move into the interior. Every shifting of camp doubles the sick-rate in our present weakened condition, and, anyhow, the interior is rather worse than the coast, as I have found by actual reconnaissance. Our present camps are as healthy as any camps at this end of the island can be.*

*I write only because I cannot see our men, who have fought so bravely and who have endured extreme hardship and danger so uncomplainingly, go to destruction without striving so far as lies in me to avert a doom as fearful as it is unnecessary and undeserved.*

*Yours respectfully,*
*Theodore Roosevelt, Colonel Commanding*
*Second Cavalry Brigade*

After Colonel Roosevelt had taken the initiative, all the American general officers united in a "round robin" addressed to General Shafter. It reads:

*We, the undersigned officers commanding the various brigades, divisions, etc., of the Army of Occupation in Cuba, are of the unanimous opinion that this army should be at once taken out of the island of Cuba and sent to some point on the northern seacoast of the United States; that can be done without danger to the people of the United States; that yellow fever in the army at present is not epidemic; that there are only a few sporadic cases; but that the army is disabled by malarial fever to the extent that its efficiency is destroyed, and that it is in a condition to be practically entirely destroyed by an epidemic of yellow fever, which is sure to come in the near future.*

*We know from the reports of competent officers and from personal observations that the army is unable to move into the interior, and that there are no facilities for such a move if attempted, and that it could not be attempted until too late. Moreover, the best medical authorities of the island say that with our present equipment we could not live in the interior during the*

*rainy season without losses from malarial fever, which is almost as deadly as yellow fever.*

*This army must be moved at once, or perish. As the army can be safely moved now, the persons responsible for preventing such a move will be responsible for the unnecessary loss of many thousands of lives.*

*Our opinions are the result of careful personal observation, and they are also based on the unanimous opinion of our medical officers with the army, who understand the situation absolutely.*

*J. Ford Kent, Major-General Volunteers*
*Commanding First Division, Fifth Corps*

*J. C. Bates, Major-General Volunteers*
*Commanding Provisional Division*

*Adna R. Chaffee, Major-General Commanding*
*Third Brigade, Second Division*

*Samuel S. Sumner, Brigadier-General*
*Volunteers Commanding First Brigade, Cavalry*

*Will Ludlow, Brigadier-General Volunteers*
*Commanding First Brigade, Second Division*

*Adelbert Ames, Brigadier-General Volunteers*
*Commanding Third Brigade, First Division*

*Leonard Wood, Brigadier-General Volunteers*
*Commanding the City of Santiago*

*Theodore Roosevelt, Colonel Commanding*
*Second Cavalry Brigade*

Major M. W. Wood, the chief surgeon of the First Division, said: "The army must be moved North," adding, with emphasis, "or it will be unable to move itself."

General Ames has sent the following cable message to Washington:

*Charles H. Allen, Assistant Secretary of the Navy:*
*This army is incapable, because of sickness, of marching anywhere except to the transports. If it is ever to return to the United States it must do so at once.*

*Survivors of the* 1ST U.S. CAVALRY REGIMENT (ROUGH RIDERS) *at the 50th anniversary celebration of the Roosevelt's Rough Riders' Association in Prescott, Arizona, June 24–25, 1948.*

# 5.

# NEW BATTLEFIELDS

BEFORE ROOSEVELT'S MILITARY UNIFORM could be cleaned and stored, he was on to his next big adventure: becoming Governor of the State of New York. The returning war hero was nominated at the Republican State Convention on September 27, 1898, and immediately embarked on a whistle-stop campaign around the state. He defeated his Democratic opponent, Augustus van Wyck, by some 18,000 votes in the November election and began the year 1899 occupying the highest office of his home state.

Roosevelt would soon experience the realities of machine politics as he never had before—and find his new "battlefield" as treacherous in its own way as the hills of Cuba had been. Beginning his term by working with state Republican party boss Thomas Platt on appointments, he soon ran afoul of Platt and his crew when they found themselves at loggerheads over such issues as taxation of corporate transit and utility franchises. Platt's machine was dedicated to the protection of big-business interests, but Roosevelt would have none of it—and in his characteristically incisive fashion, he set about reversing the stranglehold of wealthy special interests on the state's budget and legislature.

Working as if he knew his time in power was limited, Roosevelt got a strong version of his franchise tax bill through, as well as passing legislation designed to improve sweatshop conditions, strengthen factory inspections, and limit the working hours of women and children. In the

*overleaf:* **THE REPUBLICAN CONVENTION OF 1900** *in Philadelphia, Pennsylvania. Theodore Roosevelt is seated, fourth man from the left. Thomas Collier Platt is on his left, and Benjamin B. (Barker) Odell is behind Platt in the light suit.*

*opposite:* **THEODORE ROOSEVELT'S OFFICIAL PRESIDENTIAL PORTRAIT,** *painted by John Singer Sargent in 1903, is currently located in the White House.*

*left:* **A 1904 CAMPAIGN POSTER** *for Republican incumbent Roosevelt.*

midst of it all, he managed to take a break in order to travel to a Rough Riders reunion in Las Vegas, New Mexico, where he was greeted by throngs of cheering fans.

*The Rough Riders*, his rousing chronicle of his experiences in Cuba, came out that summer, as Roosevelt continued to hammer away at Platt's machine. Undoubtedly, Platt would have done anything to get Roosevelt out of power—and out of New York. Soon, his prayers were answered. McKinley's Vice President, Garret Hobart, died on November 21, and there was immediate talk in Washington of Roosevelt as a potential replacement. At the center of the conversation was— Thomas Platt.

Although McKinley's own top ally, Senator Mark Hanna, feared him as a maverick, Roosevelt officially joined the ticket at the Republican convention in June 1900 and immediately made himself useful, traveling 21,000 miles over 24 states, making hundreds of speeches on behalf of the ticket. (For his part, McKinley sat out the campaign at home, in Canton, Ohio.) The result was a landslide: McKinley defeated William Jennings Bryan yet again, this time by 860,000 votes.

But if ever there was a role Roosevelt was *unsuited* for, it was Vice President. It must have felt like a vacation compared to his stint as New York Governor. He spent the spring and summer of 1901 at Sagamore Hill with few official responsibilities—and even considered returning to the study of law he'd abandoned 20 years earlier to run his first political race. One thing of note did come out of his Vice Presidency, however. On September 2, 1901, Roosevelt delivered a speech at the Minnesota State Fair in which he first used the phrase that would forever be associated with him: "Speak softly and carry a big stick, and you will go far."

Each time Roosevelt found himself second-in-command, it was only a matter of time before the driver's seat was his. The Presidency was no different, but this time the circumstances of his ascension were tragic. While visiting the Pan-American Exposition in Buffalo on September 6, 1901, President McKinley was shot twice by an anarchist named Leon Czolgosz. On September 13, as Roosevelt was coming down from a climb to the summit of Mount Marcy, a park ranger accosted him with a telegram informing him that McKinley was near death. By the time he and his family reached Buffalo, the President was gone. Roosevelt was sworn in on that day, and promised to keep the country on an even keel while

MCKINLEY-ROOSEVELT CAMPAIGN RIBBON, *1900*.

*opposite:* **THEODORE ROOSEVELT** *addressing a crowd in Hastings, Nebraska, while on the campaign trail for the McKinley-Roosevelt ticket during the 1900 election.*

# THE HISTORY OF A NICKNAME

To his dismay, the nickname "Teddy" adhered tenaciously to Roosevelt, in the press, in common parlance, and down through history. It is almost certain that it was given him by his first wife, Alice (who must have thought it an improvement on his childhood nickname, "Teedie"), but over the years, other stories have have attached themselves to the nickname's origin. According to one version, disseminated widely as the subject of a 1902 political cartoon, while on a hunting trip in Mississippi, Roosevelt refused to shoot a bear cub tied to a tree, inspiring the term "Teddy Bear." An alternate version describes Roosevelt ordering the mercy killing of a wounded black bear. In any case, after the cartoon appeared, Roosevelt was approached by a toy maker who asked his permission to manufacture a "teddy bear"—and surprisingly, the President agreed. From then on, Roosevelt's name and image have been inextricably linked to the huggable creatures.

*top:* A cartoon called "DRAWING THE LINE IN MISSISSIPPI" *drawn by Clifford Berryman which shows Roosevelt refusing to kill a captured bear in Mississippi in 1902.*

*bottom:* THE ORIGINAL TEDDY BEAR, *made in 1903 by Morris & Rose Michtom.*

continuing to promote McKinley's policies.

Roosevelt tackled the Presidency with guns blazing. In his first official address to Congress on December 3, he called for the creation of a Department of Commerce and Labor, the regulation of large corporations, forest conservation, federal irrigation of western lands, and the expansion of the Navy.

Through attrition, McKinley's Cabinet was replaced with Roosevelt's own appointees. On March 10, 1902, the Department of Justice filed an anti-trust suit against the Northern Securities Company (a holding company that controlled the three major railroads in the Northeast), sounding the first salvo in the aggressive "trust-busting" initiative that would characterize Roosevelt's presidency. Keep in mind that the Republicans had unequivocally been the big-business party, and you might get a sense of how astonishing it was that, over the course of seven years, Roosevelt "trust-busted" 44 major corporations, somehow prevailing against his own conservative Republican congress.

At the same time that he was assailing the monoliths of industry and an increasingly unionized workforce, Roosevelt was laboring hard to preserve and protect his beloved American wilderness. On May 22, 1902, he signed a bill establishing Crater Lake National Park in Oregon, and over the course of his time in office, he would have a bigger impact on land preservation than any President in U.S. history.

**BRONCO BUSTING IN THE WEST**
"Amuses us and don't hurt the hoss"

THEODORE ROOSEVELT TRIED TO CURB *the power of large corporations and was called a "trust buster." This 1903 cartoon depicts Roosevelt with Uncle Sam busting a bronco labeled "Trusts."*

But it wasn't all "My Country 'Tis of Thee"; President Roosevelt found himself faced with foreign challenges as well as domestic ones. American troops were fighting in the Philippines (and by all reports committing unforgiveable atrocities) while U.S. administration of Cuba was coming to an end. Congress approved a plan to build a canal through the isthmus of Panama and authorized negotiations with Colombia in order to pave the way for it. And at the end of 1902, Britain and Germany set up a naval blockade of Venezuela in an effort to get its government to pay its foreign debt. Worried that this would provide Germany a foothold in Latin America, Roosevelt sent additional troops to the Caribbean and extracted an agreement from Germany that it would end the blockade and agree to international arbitration on the matter.

Between April 1 and June 5 of 1903, Roosevelt somehow managed

to visit 25 states and travel 14,000 miles, highlighted by camping trips in Yellowstone National Park with nature writer John Burroughs and in Yosemite National Park with the legendary John Muir. Upon his return to Washington, he faced rebellion in Panama. Ultimately, the United States guaranteed Panama its independence—and deposited 10 million dollars into its coffers along with the promise of an ongoing annuity—in return for American sovereignty over the canal zone.

On June 23, 1904, Roosevelt accepted his party's nomination for President, selecting Senator Charles Fairbanks of Indiana as his running mate. A few weeks later, the Democrats nominated Alton B. Parker, a New York judge, as their candidate. Following the (arguably wise) protocol of the time, Roosevelt did not actively campaign. No matter—he won in a landslide, capturing 336 electoral votes to Parker's 140, and 56 percent of the popular vote.

On election night, Roosevelt declared that after this term, he would not seek re-election. The already freewheeling President was now completely unleashed.

**PRESIDENT ROOSEVELT AND PARTY,** *Inspiration Point, Yosemite Valley, California, c. 1903. During Roosevelt's three-day tour of the wilderness, naturalist (and guide) John Muir engaged Roosevelt in several discussions regarding the importance of land conservation and the need to preserve certain areas as national parks.*

IN THE FOLLOWING speeches, essays, letters, and excerpts from his autobiography, Roosevelt moves from newly minted Governor to duly elected President, fomenting change on a seemingly daily basis. In sheer range and number of his accomplishments, it was the most fertile five-year period of his (and possibly any American leader's) career.

# The New York Governorship

It was Mr. Quigg who called on me at Montauk Point to sound me about the Governorship; Mr. Platt being by no means enthusiastic over Mr. Quigg's mission, largely because he disapproved of the Spanish War and of my part in bringing it about. Mr. Quigg saw me in my tent, in which he spent a couple of hours with me, my brother-in-law, Douglas Robinson, being also present. Quigg spoke very frankly to me, stating that he earnestly desired to see me nominated and believed that the great body of Republican voters in the State so desired, but that the organization and the State Convention would finally do what Senator Platt desired. He said that county leaders were already coming to Senator Platt, hinting at a close election, expressing doubt of Governor Black's availability for reelection, and asking why it would not be a good thing to nominate me; that now that I had returned to the United States this would go on more and more all the time, and that he (Quigg) did not wish that these men should be discouraged and be sent back to their localities to suppress a rising sentiment in my favor. For this reason he said that he wanted from me a plain statement as to whether or not I wanted the nomination, and as to what would be my attitude toward the organization in the event of my nomination and election, whether or not I would "make war" on Mr. Platt and his friends, or whether I would confer with them and with the organization leaders generally, and give fair consideration to their point of view as to party policy and public interest.

He said he had not come to make me any offer of the nomination, and had no authority to do so, nor to get any pledges or promises. He simply wanted a frank definition of my attitude towards existing party conditions.

To this I replied that I should like to be nominated, and if nominated would promise to throw myself into the campaign with all possible energy. I said that I should not make war on Mr. Platt or anybody else if war could be avoided; that what I wanted was to be Governor and not a faction leader; that I certainly would confer with the organization men, as with everybody else who seemed to me to have knowledge of and interest in public affairs, and that as to Mr. Platt and the organization leaders, I would do so in the sincere hope that there might always result harmony of opinion and purpose ; but that while I would try to get on well with the organization, the organization must with equal sincerity strive to do what I regarded as essential for the public good; and that in every case, after full consideration of what everybody had to say who might possess real knowledge of the matter, I should have to act finally as my own judgment and conscience dictated and administer the State government as I thought it ought to be administered. Quigg said that this was precisely what he supposed I would say, that it was all anybody could expect, and that he would state it to Senator Platt precisely as I had put it to him, which he accordingly did; and, throughout my term as Governor, Quigg lived loyally up to our understanding.

# INAUGURAL ADDRESS OF THEODORE ROOSEVELT, GOVERNOR

January 2, 1899

**ON MONDAY, JANUARY 2, 1899,** Theodore Roosevelt was sworn in as Governor of the State of New York, beginning his term with a call for unity, "common sense, honesty, and courage." Even as he took office, he stated that he would never put his party's interests above those of the people—a promise he would endeavor quite vigorously to keep, to the dismay of some of his cohorts.

THEODORE ROOSEVELT, *Governor of New York, c. 1900.*

I appreciate very deeply all you say, and the spirit that prompts you to say it. We have the same ends in view; we are striving to accomplish the same results; each of us, according to the light that is in him, is seeking to advance the welfare of the people.

A very heavy responsibility rests upon the Governor of New York State, a State of seven millions of inhabitants, of great wealth, of widely varied industries and with a population singularly diversified, not merely in occupation, but in race origin, in habits of life and in ways of thought. It is not an easy task so to frame our laws that justice may be done to all alike in such a population, so many of whom have interests that seem entirely antagonistic. But upon the great and fundamental issues of good government there must always be a unity of interest among all persons who wish well to the commonwealth.

There is much less need of genius or of any special brilliancy in the administration of our government than there is need of such homely virtues and qualities as common sense, honesty and courage. There are very many difficult problems to face, some of which are as old as government itself, while others have sprung into being in consequence of the growing complexity and steadily increasing tension of our social life for the last two generations. It is not given to any man, or to any set of men, to see with absolutely clear vision into the future. All that can be done is to face the facts as we find them, to meet each difficulty in practical fashion and to strive steadily for the betterment both of our civic and our social conditions.

We must realize on the one hand, that we can do little if we do not set ourselves a high ideal, and, on the other, that we will fail in accomplishing even this little if we do not work through practical methods and with a readiness to face life as it is, and not as we think it ought to be. Under no form of government is it so necessary thus to combine efficiency and morality, high principle and rough common sense, justice and the sturdiest physical and moral courage, as in a republic. It is absolutely impossible for a republic long to endure if it becomes either corrupt or cowardly; if its public men, no less than its private men, lose the indispensable virtue of honesty, if its leaders of thought become visionary doctrinaires, or if it shows a lack of courage in dealing With the many grave problems which it must surely face, both at home and abroad, as it strives to work out the destiny meet for a mighty nation.

It is only through the party system that free governments are now successfully carried on, and yet we must keep ever vividly before us that the usefulness of a party is strictly limited by its usefulness to the State, and that in the long run, he serves his party best who most helps to make it instantly responsive to every need of the people and to the highest demands of that spirit which tends to drive us onward and upward.

It shall be my purpose, so far as I am given strength, to administer my office with an eye single to the welfare of all the people of this great commonwealth.

# A MAN OF LETTERS

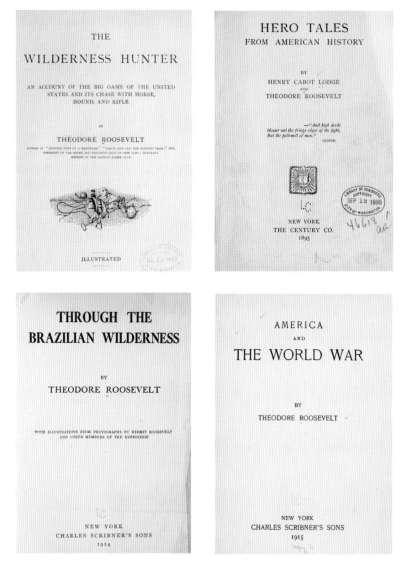

THE

## WILDERNESS HUNTER

AN ACCOUNT OF THE BIG GAME OF THE UNITED
STATES AND ITS CHASE WITH HORSE,
HOUND, AND RIFLE

BY

THEODORE ROOSEVELT

ILLUSTRATED

HERO TALES
FROM AMERICAN HISTORY

BY

HENRY CABOT LODGE
AND
THEODORE ROOSEVELT

—"And high deeds
Haunt not the fringy edges of the fight,
But the pell-mell of men."
CLOUGH

NEW YORK
THE CENTURY CO.
1895

THROUGH THE
BRAZILIAN WILDERNESS

BY

THEODORE ROOSEVELT

WITH ILLUSTRATIONS FROM PHOTOGRAPHS BY KERMIT ROOSEVELT
AND OTHER MEMBERS OF THE EXPEDITION

NEW YORK
CHARLES SCRIBNER'S SONS
1914

AMERICA
AND
THE WORLD WAR

BY

THEODORE ROOSEVELT

NEW YORK
CHARLES SCRIBNER'S SONS
1915

**TITLE PAGES FROM**
*four of Roosevelt's*
*published books.*

Whatever else he was involved in, Roosevelt remained a voracious reader and prolific author all his life. In addition to many articles, speeches, monographs, and a thesis, he published 30 books in the course of his momentous career (as well as sending a reported 150,000 letters). The range, depth, and diversity of subject matter form a testament to his remarkably fertile mind. Clearly, Roosevelt led a "strenuous life" intellectually as well as physically.

1889 * *The Winning of the West, Vol. 1*

1889 * *The Winning of the West, Vol. 2*

1891 * *History of the City of New York*

1893 * *The Wilderness Hunter*

1894 * *The Winning of the West, Vol. 3*

1895 * *Hero Tales From American History* (with Henry Cabot Lodge)

1896 * *The Winning of the West, Vol. 4*

1897 * *American Ideals*

1899 * *The Rough Riders*

1900 * *Oliver Cromwell*

1900 * *The Strenuous Life*

1905 * *Outdoor Pastimes of an American Hunter*

1910 * *African Game Trails*

1911 * *Realizable Ideals*

1912 * *The Conservation of Womanhood and Children*

1913 * *An Autobiography*

1913 * *History as Literature*

1914 * *Life Histories of African Game Animals* (with Edmund Heller)

1914 * *Through the Brazilian Wilderness*

1915 * *America and the World War*

1916 * *Fear God and Take Your Own Part*

1916 * *A Book Lover's Holiday in the Open*

1917 * *The Foes of Our Own Household*

1918 * *The Great Adventure: Present Day Studies in American Nationalism*

# GOVERNOR ROOSEVELT SPEECH
## URGING FIRM ACTION TO THE COMMODORE OF THE NAVY
New York, New York, February 3, 1899

**WHILE HE TOOK HIS WORK AS GOVERNOR** extremely seriously, Roosevelt, so recently back from his triumphant tour of duty in Cuba, was still preoccupied with international affairs. No sooner had the peace treaty with Spain been signed (Spain ceding Puerto Rico, Guam, and the Philippines and renouncing all claims to Cuba) than insurrection against American rule began in the Philippines. He here urges the Commodore of the Navy to "see that the triumph is not made void" by taking a firm stand in the Philippines. It's safe to say that no other New York Governor has made such a speech.

Commodore Philip: It is peculiarly pleasant to me to present you with this sword, for one of my last official acts, as assistant secretary of the navy, was to break through regulations in order to give you the chance to have the turrets of the *Texas* so geared that her great guns could be used to the best possible advantage; and the sequel showed how well it was for the service, that you should be given the opportunity to get the utmost service from the mighty war-engine intrusted to your care.

When a commander-in-chief, afloat or ashore, has done the best possible with his forces, then rightly the chief credit belongs to him, and wise and patriotic students of the Santiago sea-campaign gladly pay their homage first to Admiral Sampson. It was Admiral Sampson who initiated and carried on the extraordinary blockade, letting up even less by night than by day, that will stand as the example for all similar blockades in the future. It was owing to the closeness and admirable management of the system of night blockades which he introduced, that Cervera's fleet was forced to come out by daylight. In other words, it was the success of his system which insured to the splendid sea-captains, under him, the chance to show their prowess to the utmost possible advantage. But the actual fight, although Admiral Sampson was present and in command, was a captains' fight, and in this actual fighting, each captain did his work according to his own best judgment.

You, sir, by your conduct, alike during and after the fight; by your courage, by your professional skill and by your humanity, reflected honor upon the service to which you belong, upon the State in which you were born, and upon the mighty nation on the roll of whose worthies you that day wrote your name with your sword. I give utterance to the sentiment of all New York State—a sentiment from which no man in the Commonwealth will dissent when I ask you to take this sword as a token of the high esteem in which we hold you and of our grateful acknowledgment of your having done a deed which has added to the long honor-roll in which all Americans take lasting price.

You and your comrades at Manila and Santiago did their part well, and more than well. Sailor and soldier, on sea and on land, have bought with their valor, their judgment, their skill, and their blood, a wonderful triumph for America. It now rests with our statesmen to see that the triumph is not made void, in whole or in part. By your sword you won from a war glorious peace. It is for the statesmen at Washington to see that the treaty which concludes the peace is ratified. Cold indeed are the hearts of those Americans who shrink both from war and peace, when the war and peace alike are for the honor and the interest of America. To refuse to ratify the treaty would be a crime not only against America but against civilization. We cannot with honor shrink from completing the work we have begun. To leave the task half done whether in the East or the West Indies would be to make the matter worse than if we had never entered upon it. We have driven out a corrupt medieval tyranny. In Cuba and Porto Rico we are already striving to introduce orderly liberty. We shall be branded with the steel of clinging shame if we leave the Philippines to fall into a welter of bloody anarchy, instead of taking hold of them and governing them with righteousness and justice, in the interests of their own people even more than in the interests of ours. All honor to you and your comrades, to the generals and admirals, the captains and the men of might who showed such courage on the high seas and in the tropic islands of the sea! All shame to us if the statesmen flinch where the soldiers have borne themselves so well, if they fail to ratify the treaty which has been bought by such daring and such suffering, and which will fittingly crown the most righteous war the present generation has seen!

# THE STRENUOUS LIFE

Hamilton Club, Chicago, Illinois
April 10, 1899

**EVEN WHILE TICKING OFF** an ambitious list of reforms within the
state he had sworn to govern, Roosevelt was not one to squander his
national celebrity. He took time out to travel, greet the public he'd captivated as a Rough Rider, and expound upon subjects dear to him. At a
distinguished Republican social club in Chicago, he espoused "the doctrine
of the strenuous life" for each individual and for the nation as a whole,
using his own life as an example. And who was more qualified to preach
such a gospel?

In speaking to you, men of the greatest city of the West, men of the State which
gave to the country Lincoln and Grant, men who preëminently and distinctly
embody all that is most American in the American character, I wish to preach,
not the doctrine of ignoble ease, but the doctrine of the strenuous life, the life of
toil and effort, of labor and strife; to preach that highest form of success which
comes, not to the man who desires mere easy peace, but to the man who does
not shrink from danger, from hardship, or from bitter toil, and who out of these
wins the splendid ultimate triumph.

A life of slothful ease, a life of that peace which springs merely from lack either
of desire or of power to strive after great things, is as little worthy of a nation as
of an individual. I ask only that what every self-respecting American demands
from himself and from his sons shall be demanded of the American nation as a
whole. Who among you would teach your boys that ease, that peace, is to be the
first consideration in their eyes—to be the ultimate goal after which they strive?
You men of Chicago have made this city great, you men of Illinois have done
your share, and more than your share, in making America great, because you
neither preach nor practise such a doctrine. You work yourselves, and you bring
up your sons to work. If you are rich and are worth your salt, you will teach your
sons that though they may have leisure, it is not to be spent in idleness; for
wisely used leisure merely means that those who possess it, being free from the
necessity of working for their livelihood, are all the more bound to carry on
some kind of non-remunerative work in science, in letters, in art, in exploration,
in historical research—work of the type we most need in this country, the
successful carrying out of which reflects most honor upon the nation. We do not
admire the man of timid peace. We admire the man who embodies victorious
effort; the man who never wrongs his neighbor, who is prompt to help a friend,

but who has those virile qualities necessary to win in the stern strife of actual life. It is hard to fail, but it is worse never to have tried to succeed. In this life we get nothing save by effort. Freedom from effort in the present merely means that there has been stored up effort in the past. A man can be freed from the necessity of work only by the fact that he or his fathers before him have worked to good purpose. If the freedom thus purchased is used aright, and the man still does actual work, though of a different kind, whether as a writer or a general, whether in the field of politics or in the field of exploration and adventure, he shows he deserves his good fortune. But if he treats this period of freedom from the need of actual labor as a period, not of preparation, but of mere enjoyment, even though perhaps not of vicious enjoyment, he shows that he is simply a cumberer of the earth's surface, and he surely unfits himself to hold his own with his fellows if the need to do so should again arise. A mere life of ease is not in the end a very satisfactory life, and, above all, it is a life which ultimately unfits those who follow it for serious work in the world.

In the last analysis a healthy state can exist only when the men and women who make it up lead clean, vigorous, healthy lives; when the children are so trained that they shall endeavor, not to shirk difficulties, but to overcome them; not to seek ease, but to know how to wrest triumph from toil and risk. The man must be glad to do a man's work, to dare and endure and to labor; to keep himself, and to keep those dependent upon him. The woman must be the housewife, the helpmeet of the homemaker, the wise and fearless mother of many healthy children. In one of Daudet's powerful and melancholy books he speaks of "the fear of maternity, the haunting terror of the young wife of the present day." When such words can be truthfully written of a nation, that nation is rotten to the heart's core. When men fear work or fear righteous war, when women fear motherhood, they tremble on the brink of doom; and well it is that they should vanish from the earth, where they are fit subjects for the scorn of all men and women who are themselves strong and brave and high-minded.

As it is with the individual, so it is with the nation. It is a base untruth to say that happy is the nation that has no history. Thrice happy is the nation that has a glorious history. Far better it is to dare mighty things, to win glorious triumphs, even though checkered by failure, than to take rank with those poor spirits who neither enjoy much nor suffer much, because they live in the gray twilight that knows not victory nor defeat. If in 1861 the men who loved the Union had believed that peace was the end of all things, and war and strife the worst of all things, and had acted up to their belief, we would have saved hundreds of thousands of lives, we would have saved hundreds of millions of dollars. Moreover, besides saving all the blood and treasure we then lavished, we would have prevented the heartbreak of many women, the dissolution of many homes, and we would have spared the country those months of gloom and shame when it seemed as if our armies marched only to defeat. We could have avoided all this suffering simply by shrinking from strife. And if we had thus avoided it, we would have shown that we were weaklings, and that we were unfit to stand among the great nations of the earth. Thank God for the iron in the blood of our fathers, the men who upheld the wisdom of Lincoln, and bore sword or rifle in the armies of Grant! Let us, the children of the men who proved themselves equal to the mighty days, let us, the children of the men who carried the great Civil War to a triumphant conclusion, praise the God of our fathers that the ignoble counsels of peace were rejected; that the suffering and loss, the blackness of sorrow and despair, were unflinchingly faced, and the years of strife endured; for in the end the slave was freed, the Union restored, and the mighty American republic placed once more as a helmeted queen among nations.

We of this generation do not have to face a task such as that our fathers faced, but we have our tasks, and woe to us if we fail to perform them! We cannot, if we would, play the part of China, and be content to rot by inches in ignoble ease within our borders, taking no interest in what goes on beyond them, sunk in a scrambling commercialism; heedless of the higher life, the life of aspiration, of toil and risk, busying ourselves only with the wants of our bodies for the day, until suddenly we should find, beyond a shadow of question, what China has already found, that in this world the nation that has trained itself to a career of unwarlike and isolated ease is bound, in the end, to go down before other nations which have not lost the manly and adventurous qualities. If we are to be a really great people, we must strive in good faith to play a great part in the world. We cannot avoid meeting great issues. All that we can determine for ourselves is whether we shall meet them well or ill. In 1898 we could not help being brought face to face with the problem of war with Spain. All we could decide was whether we should shrink like cowards from the contest, or enter into it as beseemed a brave and high-spirited people; and, once in, whether failure or success should crown our banners. So it is now. We cannot avoid the responsibilities that confront us in Hawaii, Cuba, Porto Rico, and the Philippines. All we can decide is whether we shall meet them in a way that will redound to the national credit, or whether we shall make of our dealings with these new problems a dark and shameful page in our history. To refuse to deal with them at all merely amounts to dealing with them badly. We have a given problem to solve. If we undertake the solution, there is, of course, always danger that we may not solve it aright; but to refuse to undertake the solution simply renders it certain that we cannot possibly solve it aright. The timid man, the lazy man, the man who distrusts his country, the over-civilized man, who has lost the great fighting, masterful virtues, the ignorant man, and the man of dull mind, whose soul is incapable of feeling the mighty lift that thrills "stern men with empires in their brains"—all these, of course, shrink from seeing the nation undertake its new duties; shrink from seeing us build a navy and an army adequate to our needs; shrink from seeing us do our share of the world's work, by bringing order out of chaos in the great, fair tropic islands from which the valor of our soldiers and sailors has driven the Spanish flag. These are the men who fear the strenuous life, who fear the only national life which is really worth leading. They believe in that cloistered life which saps the hardy virtues in a nation, as it saps them in the individual; or else they are wedded to that base spirit of gain and greed which recognizes in commercialism the be-all and end-all of national life, instead of realizing that, though an indispensable element, it is, after all, but one of the many elements that go to make up true national greatness. No country can long endure if its foundations are not laid deep in the material prosperity which comes from thrift, from business energy and enterprise, from hard, unsparing effort in the fields of industrial activity; but neither was any nation ever yet truly great if it relied upon material prosperity alone. All honor must be paid to the architects of our material prosperity, to the great captains of industry who have built our factories and our railroads, to the strong men who toil for wealth with brain or hand; for great is the debt of the nation to these and their kind. But our debt is yet greater to the men whose highest type is to be found in a statesman like Lincoln, a soldier like Grant. They showed by their lives that they recognized the law of work, the law of strife; they toiled to win a competence for themselves and those dependent upon them; but they recognized that there were yet other and even loftier duties—duties to the nation and duties to the race.

We cannot sit huddled within our own borders and avow ourselves merely an assemblage of well-to-do hucksters who care nothing for what happens beyond. Such a policy would defeat even its own end; for as the nations grow to have ever wider and wider interests, and are brought into closer and closer contact, if we are to hold our own in the struggle for naval and commercial supremacy, we must build up our power without our own borders. We must build the isthmian canal, and we must grasp the points of vantage which will enable us to have our say in deciding the destiny of the oceans of the East and the West.

So much for the commercial side. From the standpoint of international honor the argument is even stronger. The guns that thundered off Manila and Santiago left us echoes of glory, but they also left us a legacy of duty. If we drove out a medieval tyranny only to make room for savage anarchy, we had better not have begun the task at all. It is worse than idle to say that we have no duty to perform, and can leave to their fates the islands we have conquered. Such a course would be the course of infamy. It would be followed at once by utter chaos in the wretched islands themselves. Some stronger, manlier power would have to step in and do the work, and we would have shown ourselves weaklings, unable to carry to successful completion the labors that great and high-spirited nations are eager to undertake.

The work must be done; we cannot escape our responsibility; and if we are worth our salt, we shall be glad of the chance to do the work—glad of the chance to show ourselves equal to one of the great tasks set modern civilization. But let us not deceive ourselves as to the importance of the task. Let us not be misled by vainglory into underestimating the strain it will put on our powers. Above all, let us, as we value our own self-respect, face the responsibilities with proper seriousness, courage, and high resolve. We must demand the highest order of integrity and ability in our public men who are to grapple with these new problems. We must hold to a rigid accountability those public servants who show unfaithfulness to the interests of the nation or inability to rise to the high level of the new demands upon our strength and our resources.

Of course we must remember not to judge any public servant by any one act, and especially should we beware of attacking the men who are merely the occasions and not the causes of disaster. Let me illustrate what I mean by the army and the navy. If twenty years ago we had gone to war, we should have found the navy as absolutely unprepared as the army. At that time our ships could not have encountered with success the fleets of Spain any more than nowadays we can put untrained soldiers, no matter how brave, who are armed with archaic black-powder weapons, against well-drilled regulars armed with the highest type of modern repeating rifle. But in the early eighties the attention of the nation became directed to our naval needs. Congress most wisely made a series of appropriations to build up a new navy, and under a succession of able and patriotic secretaries, of both political parties, the navy was gradually built up, until its material became equal to its splendid personnel, with the result that in the summer of 1898 it leaped to its

*An* ADVERTISEMENT FOR AN ADDRESS *to be given by Theodore Roosevelt, "The Hero of Santiago," in Waverly, New York, October 6, 1899.*

proper place as one of the most brilliant and formidable fighting navies in the entire world. We rightly pay all honor to the men controlling the navy at the time it won these great deeds, honor to Secretary Long and Admiral Dewey, to the captains who handled the ships in action, to the daring lieutenants who braved death in the smaller craft, and to the heads of bureaus at Washington who saw that the ships were so commanded, so armed, so equipped, so well engined, as to insure the best results. But let us also keep ever in mind that all of this would not have availed if it had not been for the wisdom of the men who during the preceding fifteen years had built up the navy. Keep in mind the secretaries of the navy during those years; keep in mind the senators and congressmen who by their votes gave the money necessary to build and to armor the ships, to construct the great guns, and to train the crews; remember also those who actually did build the ships, the armor, and the guns; and remember the admirals and captains who handled battle-ship, cruiser, and torpedo-boat on the high seas, alone and in squadrons, developing the seamanship, the gunnery, and the power of acting together, which their successors utilized so gloriously at Manila and off Santiago. And, gentlemen, remember the converse, too. Remember that justice has two sides. Be just to those who built up the navy, and, for the sake of the future of the country, keep in mind those who opposed its building up. Read the "Congressional Record." Find out the senators and congressmen who opposed the grants for building the new ships; who opposed the purchase of armor, without which the ships were worthless; who opposed any adequate maintenance for the Navy Department, and strove to cut down the number of men necessary to man our fleets. The men who did these things were one and all working to bring disaster on the country. They have no share in the glory of Manila, in the honor of Santiago. They have no cause to feel proud of the valor of our sea-captains, of the renown of our flag. Their motives may or may not have been good, but their acts were heavily fraught with evil. They did ill for the national honor, and we won in spite of their sinister opposition.

Now, apply all this to our public men of to-day. Our army has never been built up as it should be built up. I shall not discuss with an audience like this the puerile suggestion that a nation of seventy millions of freemen is in danger of losing its liberties from the existence of an army of one hundred thousand men, three fourths of whom will be employed in certain foreign islands, in certain coast fortresses, and on Indian reservations. No man of good sense and stout heart can take such a proposition seriously. If we are such weaklings as the proposition implies, then we are unworthy of freedom in any event. To no body of men in the United States is the country so much indebted as to the splendid officers and enlisted men of the regular army and navy. There is no body from which the country has less to fear, and none of which it should be prouder, none which it should be more anxious to upbuild.

Our army needs complete reorganization,—not merely enlarging,—and the reorganization can only come as the result of legislation. A proper general staff should be established, and the positions of ordnance, commissary, and quartermaster officers should be filled by detail from the line. Above all, the army must be given the chance to exercise in large bodies. Never again should we see, as we saw in the Spanish war, major-generals in command of divisions who had never before commanded three companies together in the field. Yet, incredible to relate, Congress has shown a queer inability to learn some of the lessons of the war. There were large bodies of men in both branches who opposed the declaration of war, who opposed the ratification of peace, who opposed the upbuilding of the army, and who even opposed the purchase of armor at a reasonable price for the battle-ships and cruisers, thereby putting an absolute stop to the building of any new fighting-ships for the navy. If, during the years to come, any disaster should befall our arms, afloat or ashore, and thereby any shame come to the United States, remember that the blame will lie upon the men whose names appear upon the roll-calls of Congress on the wrong side of these great questions. On them will lie the burden of any loss of our soldiers and sailors, of any dishonor to the flag; and upon you and the people of this country will lie the blame if you do not repudiate, in no unmistakable way, what these men have done. The blame will not rest upon the untrained commander of untried troops, upon the civil officers of a department the organization of which has been left utterly inadequate, or upon the admiral with an insufficient number of ships; but upon the public men who have so lamentably failed in forethought as to refuse to remedy these evils long in advance, and upon the nation that stands behind those public men.

So, at the present hour, no small share of the responsibility for the blood shed in the Philippines, the blood of our brothers, and the blood of their wild and ignorant foes, lies at the thresholds of those who so long delayed the adoption of the treaty of peace, and of those who by their worse than foolish words deliberately invited a savage people to plunge into a war fraught with sure disaster for them—a war, too, in which our own brave men who follow the flag must pay with their blood for the silly, mock humanitarianism of the prattlers who sit at home in peace.

The army and the navy are the sword and the shield which this nation must carry if she is to do her duty among the nations of the earth—if she is not to stand merely as the China of the western hemisphere. Our proper conduct toward the tropic islands we have wrested from Spain is merely the form which our duty has taken at the moment. Of course we are bound to handle the affairs of our own household well. We must see that there is civic honesty, civic cleanliness, civic good sense in our home administration of city, State, and nation. We must strive for honesty in office, for honesty toward the creditors of the nation and of the individual; for the widest freedom of individual initiative where possible, and for the wisest control of individual initiative where it is hostile to the welfare of the many. But because we set our own household in order we are not thereby excused from playing our part in the great affairs of the world. A man's first duty is to his own home, but he is not thereby excused from doing his duty to the State; for if he fails in this second duty it is under the penalty of ceasing to be a freeman. In the same way, while a nation's first duty is within its own borders, it is not thereby absolved from facing its duties in the world as a whole; and if it refuses to do so, it merely forfeits its right to struggle for a place among the peoples that shape the destiny of mankind.

In the West Indies and the Philippines alike we are confronted by most difficult problems. It is cowardly to shrink from solving them in the proper way; for solved they must be, if not by us, then by some stronger and more manful race. If we are too weak, too selfish, or too foolish to solve them, some bolder and abler people must undertake the solution. Personally, I am far too firm a believer in the greatness of my country and the power of my countrymen to admit for one moment that we shall ever be driven to the ignoble alternative.

*The February 4, 1899,* COVER OF JUDGE MAGAZINE *featured an illustration of President McKinley swatting at "mosquitos" (insurgents) in the Philippines.*

HIT HIM HARD!

PRESIDENT McKINLEY—"Mosquitoes seem to be worse here in the Philippines than they were in Cuba."

During Roosevelt's first (partial) term as president, he invited the prominent African American Booker T. Washington to a family dinner at the White House, stirring up a firestorm in the South over what was perceived to be a dangerous move toward social equality.

Roosevelt's record on matters of race and immigration is, in a word, complex. Shortly after the Washington incident, he wrote in a letter to Albion Tourgee, a diplomat and expert on the Civil War, " . . . as things have turned out, I am very glad that I asked [Washington to dinner], for the clamor aroused by the act makes me feel as if the act was necessary." Yet, he added, "I have not been able to think out any solution of the terrible problem offered by the presence of the Negro on the continent, but of one thing I am sure, and that is that inasmuch as he is here and can neither be killed nor driven away, the only wise and honorable and Christian thing to do is to treat each black man and each white man strictly on his merits as a man, giving him no more and no less than he shows himself worthy to have."

A true adherent to meritocracy, Roosevelt went on to appoint many African Americans to federal office. (He was also the first President to appoint a Jew, Oscar S. Straus, to a Cabinet position.) By the same token, he had earlier been forced to retract meretricious statements about the performance of African-American troops at the battle of San Juan Hill.

As for immigrants, Roosevelt tolerated them only in so far as they were willing to surrender any vestige of their original identities and become fully and wholeheartedly American. And on the subject of Native Americans, Roosevelt famously (and ungrammatically) stated, "I don't go so far as to think that the only good Indians are dead Indians, but I believe nine out of ten are, and I shouldn't like to inquire too closely into the case of the tenth." (In all fairness, his views on this softened in later years.)

"EQUALITY" ILLUSTRATION
*depicting Booker T. Washington dining at the White House with Theodore Roosevelt in 1901, by C. H. Thomas and P. H. Lacey, 1903.*

The problems are different for the different islands. Porto Rico is not large enough to stand alone. We must govern it wisely and well, primarily in the interest of its own people. Cuba is, in my judgment, entitled ultimately to settle for itself whether it shall be an independent state or an integral portion of the mightiest of republics. But until order and stable liberty are secured, we must remain in the island to insure them, and infinite tact, judgment, moderation, and courage must be shown by our military and civil representatives in keeping the island pacified, in relentlessly stamping out brigandage, in protecting all alike, and yet in showing proper recognition to the men who have fought for Cuban liberty. The Philippines offer a yet graver problem. Their population includes half-caste and native Christians, warlike Moslems, and wild pagans. Many of their people are utterly unfit for self-government, and show no signs of becoming fit. Others may in time become fit but at present can only take part in self-government under a wise supervision, at once firm and beneficent. We have driven Spanish tyranny from the islands. If we now let it be replaced by savage anarchy, our work has been for harm and not for good. I have scant patience with those who fear to undertake the task of governing the Philippines, and who openly avow that they do fear to undertake it, or that they shrink from it because of the expense and trouble; but I have even scanter patience with those who make a pretense of humanitarianism to hide and cover their timidity, and who cant about "liberty" and the "consent of the governed," in order to excuse themselves for their unwillingness to play the part of men. Their doctrines, if carried out, would make it incumbent upon us to leave the Apaches of Arizona to work out their own salvation, and to decline to interfere in a single Indian reservation. Their doctrines condemn your forefathers and mine for ever having settled in these United States.

England's rule in India and Egypt has been of great benefit to England, for it has trained up generations of men accustomed to look at the larger and loftier side of public life. It has been of even greater benefit to India and Egypt. And finally, and most of all, it has advanced the cause of civilization. So, if we do our duty aright in the Philippines, we will add to that national renown which is the highest and finest part of national life, will greatly benefit the people of the Philippine Islands, and, above all, we will play our part well in the great work of uplifting mankind. But to do this work, keep ever in mind that we must show in a very high degree the qualities of courage, of honesty, and of good judgment. Resistance must be stamped out. The first and all-important work to be done is to establish the supremacy of our flag. We must put down armed resistance before we can accomplish anything else, and there should be no parleying, no faltering, in dealing with our foe. As for those in our own country who encourage the foe, we can afford contemptuously to disregard them; but it must be remembered that their utterances are not saved from being treasonable merely by the fact that they are despicable.

When once we have put down armed resistance, when once our rule is acknowledged, then an even more difficult task will begin, for then we must see to it that the islands are administered with absolute honesty and with good judgment. If we let the public service of the islands be turned into the prey of the spoils politician, we shall have begun to tread the path which Spain trod to her own destruction. We must send out there only good and able men, chosen for their fitness, and not because of their partizan service, and these men must not only administer impartial justice to the natives and serve their own government with honesty and fidelity, but must show the utmost tact and firmness, remembering that, with such people as those with whom we are to deal, weakness is the greatest of crimes, and that next to weakness comes lack of consideration for their principles and prejudices.

I preach to you, then, my countrymen, that our country calls not for the life of ease but for the life of strenuous endeavor. The twentieth century looms before us big with the fate of many nations. If we stand idly by, if we seek merely swollen, slothful ease and ignoble peace, if we shrink from the hard contests where men must win at hazard of their lives and at the risk of all they hold dear, then the bolder and stronger peoples will pass us by, and will win for themselves the domination of the world. Let us therefore boldly face the life of strife, resolute to do our duty well and manfully; resolute to uphold righteousness by deed and by word; resolute to be both honest and brave, to serve high ideals, yet to use practical methods. Above all, let us shrink from no strife, moral or physical, within or without the nation, provided we are certain that the strife is justified, for it is only through strife, through hard and dangerous endeavor, that we shall ultimately win the goal of true national greatness.

# EXPANSION AND PEACE

## PUBLISHED IN THE "INDEPENDENT"
## DECEMBER 21, 1899

**WHILE MANY WERE TALKING** of the cost of war in the Pacific, Roosevelt held firm in his belief that the cost of *peace* could be far higher. In this article (slightly abridged here), he makes the case that peace among civilized nations can only be safeguarded by vanquishing "barbarism" wherever it rears its head. "Every expansion of a great civilized power means a victory for law, order, and righteousness," he states unequivocally. If Roosevelt entertained any personal doubts about his unalloyed imperialism, he never betrayed them.

*It was the gentlest of our poets who wrote:*
*"Be bolde! Be bolde! and everywhere, Be bolde";*
*Be not too bold! Yet better the excess*
*Than the defect; better the more than less.*

Longfellow's love of peace was profound; but he was a man, and a wise man, and he knew that cowardice does not promote peace, and that even the great evil of war may be a less evil than cringing to iniquity. ✳ ✳ ✳

Peace is a great good; and doubly harmful, therefore, is the attitude of those who advocate it in terms that would make it synonymous with selfish and cowardly shrinking from warring against the existence of evil. The wisest and most far-seeing champions of peace will ever remember that, in the first place, to be good it must be righteous, for unrighteous and cowardly peace may be worse than any war; and, in the second place, that it can often be obtained only at the cost of war. ✳ ✳ ✳

Wars between civilized communities are very dreadful, and as nations grow more and more civilized we have every reason, not merely to hope, but to believe that they will grow rarer and rarer. Even with civilized peoples, as was shown by our own experience in 1861, it may be necessary at last to draw the sword rather than to submit to wrong-doing. But a very marked feature in the world-history of the present century has been the growing infrequency of wars between great civilized nations. The Peace Conference at The Hague is but one of the signs of this growth. I am among those who believe that much was accomplished at that conference, and I am proud of the leading position taken in the conference by our delegates. Incidentally I may mention that the testimony is unanimous that they were able to take this leading position chiefly because we had just emerged victorious from our most righteous war with Spain. Scant attention is paid to the weakling or the coward who babbles of peace; but due heed is given to the strong man with sword girt on thigh who preaches peace, not from ignoble motives, not from fear or distrust of his own powers, but from a deep sense of moral obligation.

The growth of peacefulness between nations, however, has been confined strictly to those that are civilized. It can only come when both parties to a possible quarrel feel the same spirit. With a barbarous nation peace is the exceptional

THE WORLD'S CONSTABLE.

*This* **POLITICAL CARTOON** *from the January 3, 1905, issue of* Judge *presents Roosevelt as "The World's Constable."*

condition. On the border between civilization and barbarism war is generally normal because it must be under the conditions of barbarism. Whether the barbarian be the Red Indian on the frontier of the United States, the Afghan on the border of British India, or the Turkoman who confronts the Siberian Cossack, the result is the same. In the long run civilized man finds he can keep the peace only by subduing his barbarian neighbor; for the barbarian will yield only to force, save in instances so exceptional that they may be disregarded. Back of the force must come fair dealing, if the peace is to be permanent. But without force fair dealing usually amounts to nothing. In our history we have had more trouble from the Indian tribes whom we pampered

and petted than from those we wronged; and this has been true in Siberia, Hindustan, and Africa.

Every expansion of civilization makes for peace. In other words, every expansion of a great civilized power means a victory for law, order, and righteousness. This has been the case in every instance of expansion during the present century, whether the expanding power were France or England, Russia or America. In every instance the expansion has been of benefit, not so much to the power nominally benefited, as to the whole world. In every instance the result proved that the expanding power was doing a duty to civilization far greater and more important than could have been done by any stationary power. Take the case of France and Algiers. During the early decades of the present century piracy of the most dreadful description was rife on the Mediterranean, and thousands of civilized men were yearly dragged into slavery by the Moorish pirates. A degrading peace was purchased by the civilized powers by the payment of tribute. Our own country was one among the tributary nations which thus paid blood-money to the Moslem bandits of the sea. We fought occasional battles with them; and so, on a larger scale, did the English. But peace did not follow, because the country was not occupied. Our last payment was made in 1830, and the reason it was the last was because in that year the French conquest of Algiers began. Foolish sentimentalists, like those who wrote little poems in favor of the Mahdists against the English, and who now write little essays in favor of Aguinaldo against the Americans, celebrated the Algerian freebooters as heroes who were striving for liberty against the invading French. But the French continued to do their work; France expanded over Algiers, and the result was that piracy on the Mediterranean came to an end, and Algiers has thriven as never before in its history. On an even larger scale the same thing is true of England and the Sudan. The expansion of England throughout the Nile valley has been an incalculable gain for civilization. Any one who reads the writings of the Austrian priests and laymen who were prisoners in the Sudan under the Mahdi will realize that when England crushed him and conquered the Sudan she conferred a priceless boon upon humanity and made the civilized world her debtor. Again, the same thing is true of the Russian advance in Asia. As in the Sudan the English conquest is followed by peace, and the endless massacres of the Mahdi are stopped forever, so the Russian conquest of the khanates of central Asia meant the cessation of the barbarous warfare under which Asian civilization had steadily withered away since the days of Jenghiz Khan, and the substitution in its place of the reign of peace and order. All civilization has been the gainer by the Russian advance, as it was the gainer by the advance of France in North Africa; as it has been the gainer by the advance of England in both Asia and Africa,

THEODORE ROOSEVELT *in the Executive Office of the White House, c. 1903. The room is now called the Roosevelt Room.*

both Canada and Australia. Above all, there has been the greatest possible gain in peace. The rule of law and of order has succeeded to the rule of barbarous and bloody violence. Until the great civilized nations stepped in there was no chance for anything but such bloody violence.

So it has been in the history of our own country. Of course our whole national history has been one of expansion. Under Washington and Adams we expanded westward to the Mississippi; under Jefferson we expanded across the continent to the mouth of the Columbia; under Monroe we expanded into Florida; and then into Texas and California; and finally, largely through the instrumentality of Seward, into Alaska; while under every administration the process of expansion in the great plains and the Rockies has continued with growing rapidity. While we had a frontier the chief feature of frontier life was the endless war between the settlers and the red men. Sometimes the immediate occasion for the war was to be found in the conduct of the whites and sometimes in that of the reds, but the ultimate cause was simply that we were in contact with a country held by savages or half-savages. Where we abut on Canada there is no danger of war, nor is there any danger where we abut on the well-settled regions of Mexico. But elsewhere war had to continue until we expanded over the country. Then it was succeeded at once by a peace which has remained unbroken to the present day. In North America, as elsewhere throughout the entire world, the expansion of a civilized nation has invariably meant the growth of the area in which peace is normal throughout the world.

The same will be true of the Philippines. If the men who have counseled national degradation, national dishonor, by urging us to leave the Philippines and put the Aguinaldan oligarchy in control of those islands, could have their way, we should merely turn them over to rapine and bloodshed until some stronger, manlier power stepped in to do the task we had shown ourselves fearful of performing. But, as it is, this country will keep the islands and will establish therein a stable and orderly government, so that one more fair spot of the world's surface shall have been snatched from the forces of darkness. Fundamentally the cause of expansion is the cause of peace. ✳ ✳ ✳

It is only the warlike power of a civilized people that can give peace to the world. The Arab wrecked the civilization of the Mediterranean coasts, the Turk wrecked the civilization of southeastern Europe, and the Tatar desolated from China to Russia and to Persia, setting back the progress of the world for centuries, solely because the civilized nations opposed to them had lost the great fighting qualities, and, in becoming overpeaceful, had lost the power of keeping peace with a strong hand. Their passing away marked the beginning of a period of chaotic barbarian warfare. Those whose memories are not so short as to have forgotten the defeat of the Greeks by the Turks, of the Italians by the Abyssinians, and the feeble campaigns waged by Spain against feeble Morocco, must realize that at the present moment the Mediterranean coasts would be overrun either by the Turks or by the Sudan Mahdists if these warlike barbarians had only to fear those southern European powers which have lost the fighting edge. Such a barbarian conquest would mean endless war; and the fact that nowadays the reverse takes place, and that the barbarians recede or are conquered, with the attendant fact that peace follows their retrogression or conquest, is due solely to the power of the mighty civilized races which have not lost the fighting instinct, and which by their expansion are gradually bringing peace into the red wastes where the barbarian peoples of the world hold sway.

# PROMISE AND PERFORMANCE

PUBLISHED IN THE "OUTLOOK"
JULY 28, 1900

**THE CONTEMPORARY RESONANCE** in this passionate article, published just weeks after he received the nomination to run as McKinley's Vice-Presidential candidate, is uncanny—and its vehemence was surely fueled by his experiences as Assemblyman and Commissioner as well as Governor. He excoriates Machiavellian political maneuvering as the height of cynicism, a corrosive force upon the leadership and the governed alike. And, as always, Roosevelt spreads the responsibility for good government to the electorate—to individuals—as well as those they vote into office. In other words (and it is as true today), we get the government we deserve.

It is customary to express wonder and horror at the cynical baseness of the doctrines of Machiavelli. Both the wonder and the horror are justified—though it would perhaps be wiser to keep them for the society which the Italian described rather than for the describer himself—but it is somewhat astonishing that there should be so little insistence upon the fact that Machiavelli rests his whole system upon his contemptuous belief in the folly and low civic morality of the multitude, and their demand for fine promises and their indifference to performance. Thus he says: "It is necessary to be a great deceiver and hypocrite; for men are so simple and yield so readily to the wants of the moment that he who will trick shall always find another who will suffer himself to be tricked. . . . Therefore a ruler must take great care that no word shall slip from his mouth that shall not be full of piety, trust, humanity, religion, and simple faith, and he must appear to eye and ear all compact of these, . . . because the vulgar are always caught by appearance and by the event, and in this world there are none but the vulgar."

THEODORE ROOSEVELT *on the day he was notified of his nomination for Vice President, Oyster Bay, New York, July 12, 1900.*

It therefore appears that Machiavelli's system is predicated partly on the entire indifference to performance of promise by the prince and partly upon a greedy demand for impossible promises among the people. The infamy of the conduct championed by Machiavelli as proper for public men is usually what rivets the attention, but the folly which alone makes such infamy possible is quite as well worthy of study. Hypocrisy is a peculiarly revolting vice alike in public and private life; and in public life—at least in high position—it can only be practised on a large scale for any length of time in those places where the people in mass really warrant Machiavelli's description, and are content with a complete divorce between promise and performance.

It would be difficult to say which is the surest way of bringing about such a complete divorce: on the one hand, the tolerance in a public man of the non-performance of promises which can be kept; or, on the other hand, the insistence by the public upon promises which they either know or ought to know cannot be kept. When in a public speech or in a party platform a policy is outlined which it is known cannot or will not be pursued, the fact is a reflection not

A 1900 CAMPAIGN POSTER *supporting the Republican candidate for President, William McKinley, and his running mate, Theodore Roosevelt.*

only upon the speaker and the platform-maker, but upon the public feeling to which they appeal. When a section of the people demand from a candidate promises which he cannot believe that he will be able to fulfill, and, on his refusal, support some man who cheerfully guarantees an immediate millennium, why, under such circumstances the people are striving to bring about in America some of the conditions of public life which produced the profligacy and tyranny of medieval Italy. Such conduct means that the capacity for self-government has atrophied; and the hard-headed common sense with which the American people, as a whole, refuse to sanction such conduct is the best possible proof and guarantee of their capacity to perform the high and difficult task of administering the greatest republic upon which the sun has ever shown.

There are always politicians willing, on the one hand, to promise everything to the people, and, on the other, to perform everything for the machine or the boss, with chuckling delight in the success of their efforts to hoodwink the former and serve the latter. Now, not only should such politicians be regarded as infamous, but the people who are hoodwinked by them should share the blame.

The man who is taken in by, or demands, impossible promises is not much less culpable than the politician who deliberately makes such promises and then breaks faith. Thus when any public man says that he "will never compromise under any conditions," he is certain to receive the applause of a few emotional people who do not think correctly, and the one fact about him that can be instantly asserted as true beyond peradventure is that, if he is a serious personage at all, he is deliberately lying, while it is only less certain that he will be guilty of base and dishonorable compromise when the opportunity arises. "Compromise" is so often used in a bad sense that it is difficult to remember that properly it merely describes the process of reaching an agreement. Naturally there are certain subjects on which no man can compromise. For instance, there must be no compromise under any circumstances with official corruption, and of course no man should hesitate to say as much. Again, an honest politician is entirely justified in promising on the stump that he will make no compromise on any question of right and wrong. This promise he can and ought to make good. But when questions of policy arise—and most questions, from the tariff to municipal ownership of public utilities and the franchise tax, are primarily questions of policy—he will have to come to some kind of working agreement with his fellows, and if he says that he will not, he either deliberately utters what he knows to be false, or else he insures for himself the humiliation of being forced to break his word. No decent politician need compromise in any way save as Washington and Lincoln did. He need not go nearly as far as Hamilton, Jefferson, and Jackson went; but some distance he must go if he expects to accomplish anything. . . .

Wise legislation and upright administration can undoubtedly work very great good to a community, and, above all, can give to each individual the chance to do the best work for himself. But ultimately the individual's own faculties must form the chief factor in working out his own salvation. In the last analysis it is the thrift, energy, self-mastery, and business intelligence of each man which have most to do with deciding whether he rises or falls. It is easy enough to devise a scheme of government which shall absolutely nullify all these qualities and insure failure to everybody, whether he deserves success or not. But the best scheme of government can do little more than provide against injustice, and then let the individual rise or fall on his own merits. Of course something can be done by the State acting in its collective capacity, and in certain instances such action may be necessary to remedy real wrong. Gross misconduct of individuals or corporations may make it necessary for the State or some of its subdivisions to assume the charge of what are called public utilities. But when all that can be done in this way has been done, when every individual has been saved so far as the State can save him from the tyranny of any other man or body of men, the individual's own qualities of body and mind, his own strength of heart and hand, will remain the determining conditions in his career. The people who trust to or exact promises that, if a certain political leader is followed or a certain public policy adopted, this great truth will cease to operate, are not merely leaning on a broken reed, but are working for their own undoing.

So much for the men who by their demands for the impossible encourage the promise of the impossible, whether in the domain of economic legislation or of legislation which has for its object the promotion of morality. The other side is that no man should be held excusable if he does not perform what he promises, unless for the best and most sufficient reason. This should be especially true of every politician. It shows a thoroughly unhealthy state of mind when the public pardons with a laugh failure to keep a distinct pledge, on the ground that a politician cannot be expected to confine himself to the truth when on the stump or the platform. A man should no more be excused for lying on the stump than for lying off the stump. Of course matters may so change that it may be impossible for him, or highly inadvisable for the country, that he should try to do what he in good faith said he was going to do. But the necessity for the change should be made very evident, and it should be well understood that such a case is the exception and not the rule. As a rule, and speaking with due regard to the exceptions, it should be taken as axiomatic that when a man in public life pledges himself to a certain course of action he shall as a matter of course do what he said he would do, and shall not be held to have acted honorably if he does otherwise. . . .

We cannot trust the mere doctrinaire; we cannot trust the mere closet reformer, nor yet his acrid brother who himself does nothing, but who rails at those who endure the heat and burden of the day. Yet we can trust still less those base beings who treat politics only as a game out of which to wring a soiled livelihood, and in whose vocabulary the word "practical" has come to be a synonym for whatever is mean and corrupt. A man is worthless unless he has in him a lofty devotion to an ideal, and he is worthless also unless he strives to realize this ideal by practical

INAUGURATION OF PRESIDENT MCKINLEY, *in Washington, D.C., March 4, 1901.*

methods. He must promise, both to himself and to others, only what he can perform; but what really can be performed he must promise, and such promise he must at all hazards make good.

The problems that confront us in this age are, after all, in their essence the same as those that have always confronted free peoples striving to secure and to keep free government. No political philosopher of the present day can put the case more clearly than it was put by the wonderful old Greeks. Says Aristotle: "Two principles have to be kept in view: what is possible, what is becoming; at these every man ought to aim." Plato expresses precisely the same idea: "Those who are not schooled and practised in truth [who are not honest and upright men] can never manage aright the government, nor yet can those who spend their lives as closet philosophers; because the former have no high purpose to guide their actions, while the latter keep aloof from public life, having the idea that even while yet living they have been translated to the Islands of the Blest. . . . [Men must] both contemplate the good and try actually to achieve it. Thus the state will be settled as a reality, and not as a dream, like most of those inhabited by persons fighting about shadows."

AFTER SERVING ONLY SIX MONTHS as Vice President, Roosevelt found himself promoted to President following McKinley's assassination on September 6, 1901. In these excerpts from his autobiography, Roosevelt gives a rather dispassionate account of McKinley's death and his own ascendancy. Whether or not he was feeling grief, apprehension, or any combination of discomfiting feelings at the time, we'll never know. Rather than reveal what was in his heart, Roosevelt chose to reinforce the notion that a "fit" man—a leader—can rise to any challenge.

## The Presidency; Making an Old Party Progressive

On September 6, 1901, President McKinley was shot by an Anarchist in the city of Buffalo. I went to Buffalo at once. The President's condition seemed to be improving, and after a day or two we were told that he was practically out of danger. I then joined my family, who were in the Adirondacks, near the foot of Mount Tahawus. A day or two afterwards we took a long tramp through the forest, and in the afternoon I climbed Mount Tahawus. After reaching the top I had descended a few hundred feet to a shelf of land where there was a little lake, when I saw a guide coming out of the woods on our trail from below. I felt at once that he had bad news, and, sure enough, he handed me a telegram saying that the President's condition was much worse and that I must

The LAST PHOTO TAKEN OF PRESIDENT MCKINLEY *(center), with John G. Milburn (left) and George B. Cortelyou (right), in Buffalo, New York, on his way to the Temple of Music, where he was fatally wounded on September 6, 1901.*

LEON FRANK CZOLGOSZ SHOOTS PRESIDENT MCKINLEY *with a concealed revolver in this engraving by T. Dart Walker, c. 1901.*

POLICE MUG SHOT OF LEON F. CZOLGOSZ, *the assassin of President McKinley, who was found guilty and eventually electrocuted on October 29, 1901.*

come to Buffalo immediately. It was late in the afternoon, and darkness had fallen by the time I reached the clubhouse where we were staying. It was some time afterwards before I could get a wagon to drive me out to the nearest railway station, North Creek, some forty or fifty miles distant. The roads were the ordinary wilderness roads and the night was dark. But we changed horses two or three times—when I say "we" I mean the driver and I, as there was no one else with us—and reached the station just at dawn, to learn from Mr. Loeb, who had a special train waiting, that the President was dead. That evening I took the oath of office, in the house of Ansley Wilcox, at Buffalo.

On three previous occasions the Vice President had succeeded to the Presidency on the death of the President.

In each case there had been a reversal of party policy, and a nearly immediate and nearly complete change in the personnel of the higher offices, especially the Cabinet. I had never felt that this was wise from any standpoint. If a man is fit to be President, he will speedily so impress himself in the office that the policies pursued will be his anyhow, and he will not have to bother as to whether he is changing them or not; while as regards the offices under him, the important thing for him is that his subordinates shall make a success in handling their several departments. The subordinate is sure to desire to make a success of his department for his own sake, and if he is a fit man, whose views on public policy are sound, and whose abilities entitle him to his position, he will do excellently under almost any chief with the same purposes.

# HOLIDAYS IN THE WHITE HOUSE

**ROOSEVELT'S SECOND CHILD** and oldest son, Kermit, was thirteen and attending Groton when his father sent him this newsy holiday missive.

*White House, Nov. 28, 1902.*

DARLING KERMIT:
Yesterday was Thanksgiving, and we all went out riding, looking as we started a good deal like the Cumberbach family. Archie on his beloved pony, and Ethel on Yagenka went off with Mr. Proctor to the hunt. Mother rode Jocko Root, Ted a first-class cavalry horse, I rode Renown, and with us went Senator Lodge, Uncle Douglas, Cousin John Elliott, Mr. Bob Fergie, and General Wood. We had a three hours' scamper which was really great fun.

Yesterday I met Bozie for the first time since he came to Washington, and he almost wiggled himself into a fit, he was so overjoyed at renewing acquaintance. To see Jack and Tom Quartz play together is as amusing as it can be. We have never had a more cunning kitten than Tom Quartz. I have just had to descend with severity upon Quentin because he put the unfortunate Tom into the bathtub and then turned on the water. He didn't really mean harm.

Last evening, besides our own entire family party, all the Lodges, and their connections, came to dinner. We dined in the new State Dining-room and we drank the health of you and all the rest of both families that were absent. After dinner we cleared away the table and danced. Mother looked just as pretty as a picture and I had a lovely waltz with her. Mrs. Lodge and I danced the Virginia Reel. ✳ ✳ ✳

**KERMIT ROOSEVELT AND JACK,** *the dog, c. 1902.*

**MRS. THEODORE ROOSEVELT** *at home in the White House, Washington, D.C., c. 1903.*

**IT'S SAID THAT ROOSEVELT WROTE** some 150,000 letters in his lifetime, and it is charming to find that a number of them were to the children of his colleagues. He sent this holiday thank-you note to young James A. Garfield, son of his Secretary of the Interior and grandson of the twentieth U.S. President.

*White House, Dec. 26, 1902.*

JIMMIKINS:

Among all the presents I got I don't think there was one I appreciated more than yours; for I was brought up to admire and respect your grandfather, and I have a very great fondness and esteem for your father. It always seems to me as if you children were being brought up the way that mine are. Yesterday Archie got among his presents a small rifle from me and a pair of riding-boots from his mother. He won't be able to use the rifle until next summer, but he has gone off very happy in the riding boots for a ride on the calico pony Algonquin, the one you rode the other day. Yesterday morning at a quarter of seven all the children were up and dressed and began to hammer at the door of their mother's and my room, in which their six stockings, all bulging out with queer angles and rotundities, were hanging from the fireplace. So their mother and I got up, shut the window, lit the fire, taking down the stockings, of course, put on our wrappers and prepared to admit the children. But first there was a surprise for me, also for their good mother, for Archie had a little Christmas tree of his own which he had rigged up with the help of

*POLICE "ROLL CALL INSPECTION" at the White House, with Archie and Quentin in the line, 1902.*

one of the carpenters in a big closet; and we all had to look at the tree and each of us got a present off of it. There was also one present each for Jack the dog, Tom Quartz the kitten, and Algonquin the pony, whom Archie would no more think of neglecting than I would neglect his brothers and sisters. Then all the children came into our bed and there they opened their stockings. Afterwards we got dressed and took breakfast, and then all went into the library, where each child had a table set for his bigger presents. Quentin had a perfectly delightful electric railroad, which had been rigged up for him by one of his friends, the White House electrician, who has been very good to all the children. Then Ted and I, with General Wood and Mr. Bob Ferguson, who was a lieutenant in my regiment, went for a three hours' ride; and all of us, including all the children, took lunch at the house with the children's aunt, Mrs. Captain Cowles—Archie and Quentin having their lunch at a little table with their cousin Sheffield. Late in the afternoon I played at single stick with General Wood and Mr. Ferguson. I am going to get your father to come on and try it soon. We have to try to hit as light as possible, but sometimes we hit hard, and to-day I have a bump over one eye and a swollen wrist. Then all our family and kinsfolk and Senator and Mrs. Lodge's family and kinsfolk had our Christmas dinner at the White House, and afterwards danced in the East Room, closing up with the Virginia Reel.

QUENTIN ON HIS CALICO PONY, ALGONQUIN, *June 17, 1902. Quentin once took his pony into the White House and up the elevator to cheer up his brother Archie, who was sick.*

THE FOLLOWING EXCERPTS from Roosevelt's autobiography reveal his more tranquil and contemplative side: his love of nature and the National Parks he helped safeguard, the strength he derived from his beloved Sagamore Hill, and his high regard for the great books of the world. It is interesting to remember that the camping trips he mentions here, taken in the company of famed naturalists John Burroughs and John Muir, occurred in 1903, while he was shouldering the responsibilities an eventful Presidency.

# Outdoors and Indoors

There are men who love out-of-doors who yet never open a book; and other men who love books but to whom the great book of nature is a sealed volume, and the lines written therein blurred and illegible. Nevertheless among those men whom I have known the love of books and the love of outdoors, in their highest expressions, have usually gone hand in hand. It is an affectation for the man who is praising outdoors to sneer at books. Usually the keenest appreciation of what is seen in nature is to be found in those who have also profited by the hoarded and recorded wisdom of their fellow-men. Love of outdoor life, love of simple and hardy pastimes, can be gratified by men and women who do not possess large means, and who work hard; and so can love of good books—not of good bindings and of first editions, excellent enough in their way but sheer luxuries—I mean love of reading books, owning them if possible of course, but, if that is not possible, getting them from a circulating library. * * *

ONE APRIL I went to Yellowstone Park, when the snow was still very deep, and I took John Burroughs with me. I wished to show him the big game of the Park, the wild creatures that have become so astonishingly tame and tolerant of human presence. In the Yellowstone the animals seem always to behave as one wishes them to! It is always possible to see the sheep and deer and antelope, and also the great herds of elk, which are shyer than the smaller beasts. In April we found the elk weak after the short commons and hard living of winter. Once without much difficulty I regularly rounded up a big band of them, so that John Burroughs could look at them. I do not think, however, that he cared to see them as much as I did. The birds interested him more, especially a tiny owl the size of a robin which we saw perched on the top of a tree in mid-afternoon entirely uninfluenced by the sun and making a queer noise like a cork being pulled from a bottle. I was rather ashamed to find how much better his eyes were than mine in seeing the birds and grasping their differences. * * *

PRESIDENT ROOSEVELT (fourth from the right) and naturalist John Burroughs at Yellowstone Park, along with other men including Yellowstone's superintendent, John Pitcher, c. 1903.

WHEN I FIRST VISITED CALIFORNIA, it was my good fortune to see the "big trees," the Sequoias, and then to travel down into the Yosemite, with John Muir. Of course of all people in the world he was the one with whom it was best worth while thus to see the Yosemite. He told me that when Emerson came to California he tried to get him to come out and camp with him, for that was the only way in which to see at their best the majesty and charm of the Sierras. But at the time Emerson was getting old and could not go. John Muir met me with a couple of packers and two mules to carry our tent, bedding, and food for a three days' trip. The first night was clear, and we lay down in the darkening aisles of the great Sequoia grove. The majestic trunks, beautiful in color and in symmetry, rose round us like the pillars of a mightier cathedral than ever was conceived even by the fervor of the Middle Ages. Hermit thrushes sang beautifully in the evening, and again, with a burst of wonderful music, at dawn. I was interested and a little surprised to find that, unlike John Burroughs, John Muir cared little for birds or bird songs, and knew little about them. The hermit-thrushes meant nothing to him, the trees and the

THEODORE ROOSEVELT *and* JOHN MUIR *on Glacier Point, Yosemite Valley, California, 1903.*

flowers and the cliffs everything. The only birds he noticed or cared for were some that were very conspicuous, such as the water-ousels—always particular favorites of mine too. The second night we camped in a snow-storm, on the edge of the cañon walls, under the spreading limbs of a grove of mighty silver fir; and next day we went down into the wonderland of the valley itself. I shall always be glad that I was in the Yosemite with John Muir and in the Yellowstone with John Burroughs. ✳ ✳ ✳

AT SAGAMORE HILL we love a great many things—birds and trees and books, and all things beautiful, and horses and rifles and children and hard work and the joy of life. We have great fireplaces, and in them the logs roar and crackle during the long winter evenings. The big piazza is for the hot, still afternoons of summer. As in every house, there are things that appeal to the house-holder because of their associations, but which would not mean much to others. Naturally, any man who has been President, and filled other positions, accumulates such things, with scant regard to his own personal merits. Perhaps our most cherished possessions are a Remington bronze, "The Bronco Buster," given me by my men when the regiment was mustered out, and a big Tiffany silver vase given to Mrs. Roosevelt by the enlisted men of the battleship *Louisiana* after we returned from a cruise on her to Panama. It was a real surprise gift, presented to her in the White House, on behalf of the whole crew, by four as strapping man-of-war's-men as ever swung a turret or pointed a twelve-inch gun. The enlisted men of the army I already knew well—of course I knew well the officers of both army and navy. But the enlisted men of the navy I only grew to know well when I was President. On the *Louisiana* Mrs. Roosevelt and I once dined at the chief petty officers' mess, and on another battleship, the *Missouri* (when I was in company with Admiral Evans and Captain Cowles), and again on the *Sylph* and on the *Mayflower*, we also dined as guests of the crew. When we finished our trip on the *Louisiana* I made a short speech to the assembled crew, and at its close one of the petty

*Frederick Remington was asked to illustrate an article by Theodore Roosevelt in* Harper's Weekly *(April 30, 1892) which became the inspiration for this famous sculpture* "THE BRONCO BUSTER." *An original cast resides in the Oval Office of the White House.*

officers, the very picture of what a man-of-war's-man should look like, proposed three cheers for me in terms that struck me as curiously illustrative of America at her best; he said, "Now then, men, three cheers for Theodore Roosevelt, the typical American citizen!" That was the way in which they thought of the American President—and a very good way, too. It was an expression that would have come naturally only to men in whom the American principles of government and life were ingrained, just as they were ingrained in the men of my regiment. I need scarcely add, but I will add for the benefit of those who do not know, that this attitude of self-respecting identification of interest and purpose is not only com-patible with but can only exist when there is fine and real discipline, as thorough and genuine as the discipline that has always obtained in the most formidable fighting fleets and armies. The discipline and the mutual respect are complementary, not antagonistic. . . . ✳ ✳ ✳

> "'Now then, men, three cheers for Theodore Roosevelt, the typical American citizen!' That was the way in which they thought of the American President—and a very good way, too."

NOW AND THEN I am asked as to "what books a statesman should read," and my answer is, poetry and novels—including short stories under the head of novels. I don't mean that he should read only novels and modern poetry. If he cannot also enjoy the Hebrew prophets and the Greek dramatists, he should be sorry. He ought to read interesting books on history and government, and books of science and philosophy; and really good books on these subjects are as enthralling as any fiction ever written in prose or verse. Gibbon and Macaulay, Herodotus, Thucydides and Tacitus, the Heimskringla, Froissart, Joinville and Villehardouin, Parkman and Mahan, Mommsen and Ranke—why! there are scores and scores of solid histories, the best in the world, which are as absorbing as the best of all the novels, and of as permanent value. The same thing is true of Darwin and Huxley and Carlyle and Emerson, and parts of Kant, and of volumes like Sutherland's "Growth of the Moral Instinct," or Acton's Essays and Lounsbury's studies— here again I am not trying to class books together, or measure one by another, or enumerate one in a thousand of those worth reading, but just to indicate that any man or woman of some intelligence and some cultivation can in some line or other of serious thought, scientific or historical or philosophical or economic or governmental, find any number of books which are charming to read, and which in addition give that for which his or her soul

hungers. I do not for a minute mean that the statesman ought not to read a great many different books of this character, just as every one else should read them. But, in the final event, the statesman, and the publicist, and the reformer, and the agitator for new things, and the upholder of what is good in old things, all need more than anything else to know human nature, to know the needs of the human soul; and they will find this nature and these needs set forth as nowhere else by the great imaginative writers, whether of prose or of poetry.

THEODORE ROOSEVELT *in the library at Sagamore Hill, c. 1895.*

*overleaf:* THEODORE ROOSEVELT *(fourth from left),* JOHN MUIR *(to Theodore Roosevelt's right) and others standing in front of a redwood tree called the "Grizley Giant," California, c. 1903.*

# WESTWARD BOUND

**IN MARCH 1903,** Roosevelt created the first national wildlife refuge, and would go on to establish 54 more over the course of his Presidency. On April 1 of that year, he embarked on the epic western trip that included his famous visits with the two Johns—Burroughs and Muir. These letters are among the many he sent from that trip, before returning to the White House in June.

JOHN MUIR AND JOHN BURROUGHS *standing in the snow, photographed by Edward S. Curtis, c. 1899.*

*Del Monte, Cal., May 10, 1903.*

DARLING ETHEL:

I have thought it very good of you to write me so much. Of course I am feeling rather fagged, and the next four days, which will include San Francisco, will be tiresome; but I am very well. This is a beautiful hotel in which we are spending Sunday, with gardens and a long seventeen-mile drive beside the beach and the rocks and among the pines and cypresses. I went on horseback. My horse was a little beauty, spirited, swift, sure-footed and enduring. As is usually the case here they had a great deal of silver on the bridle and headstall, and much carving on the saddle.

We had some splendid gallops. By the way, tell mother that everywhere out here, from the Mississippi to the Pacific, I have seen most of the girls riding astride, and most of the grown-up women. I must say I think it very much better for the horses' backs. I think by the time that you are an old lady the side-saddle will almost have vanished—I am sure I hope so. I have forgotten whether you like the side-saddle or not.

*opposite:* **THE LOWER GORGE** *of the Grand Canyon, Arizona, by Thomas Moran, 1910.*

GRAND CANYON NATIONAL PARK, *view from the canyon rim near the Grand View Hotel. August 28, 1905, by R. Arnold*

It was very interesting going through New Mexico and seeing the strange old civilization of the desert, and next day the Grand Canyon of Arizona, wonderful and beautiful beyond description. I could have sat and looked at it for days.

It is a tremendous chasm, a mile deep and several miles wide, the cliffs carved into battlements, amphitheatres, towers and pinnacles, and the coloring wonderful, red and yellow and gray and green. Then we went through the desert, passed across the Sierras and came into this semi-tropical country of southern California, with palms and orange groves and olive orchards and immense quantities of flowers. ✶ ✶ ✶

*Del Monte, Cal., May 10, 1903.*

BLESSED ARCHIE:

I think it was very cunning for you and Quentin to write me that letter together. I wish you could have been with me to-day on Algonquin, for we had a perfectly lovely ride. Dr. Rixey and I were on two very handsome horses, with Mexican saddles and bridles; the reins of very slender leather with silver rings. The road led through pine and cypress forests and along the beach. The surf was beating on the rocks in one place and right between two of the rocks where I really did not see how anything could swim a seal appeared and stood up on his tail half out of the foaming water and flapped his flippers, and was as much at home as anything could be. Beautiful gulls flew close to us all around, and cormorants swam along the breakers or walked along the beach.

I have a number of treasures to divide among you children when I get back. One of the treasures is Bill the Lizard. He is a little live lizard, called a horned frog, very cunning, who lives in a small box. The little badger, Josh, is very well and eats milk and potatoes. We took him out and gave him a run in the sand to-day. So far he seems as friendly as possible. When he feels hungry he squeals and the colored porters insist that he says "Du-la-ny, Du-la-ny," because Dulany is very good to him and takes care of him.

ARCHIE ROOSEVELT, *c. 1903.*

# MERITS OF MILITARY
# AND CIVIL LIFE

**LIKE HIS OWN FATHER,** who had carefully advised him from an early age on the pros and cons of various career options, Roosevelt attempted to help his children determine their paths in life without telling them what to do. In this letter, written during his first partial term as President, he offers his oldest son some measured advice on the subject of entering West Point or Annapolis and embarking on a career in the military.

*White House, Jan. 21, 1904.*

DEAR TED:

This will be a long business letter. I sent to you the examination papers for West Point and Annapolis. I have thought a great deal over the matter, and discussed it at great length with Mother. I feel on the one hand that I ought to give you my best advice, and yet on the other hand I do not wish to seem to constrain you against your wishes. If you have definitely made up your mind that you have an overmastering desire to be in the Navy or the Army, and that such a career is the one in which you will take a really heart-felt interest—far more so than any other—and that your greatest chance for happiness and usefulness will lie in doing this one work to which you feel yourself especially drawn— why, under such circumstances, I have but little to say. But I am not satisfied that this is really your feeling. It seemed to me more as if you did not feel drawn in any other direction, and wondered what you were going to do in life or what kind of work you would turn your hand to, and wondered if you could make a success or not; and that you are therefore inclined to turn to the Navy or Army chiefly because you would then have a definite and settled career in life, and could hope to go on steadily without any great risk of failure. Now, if such is your thought, I shall quote to you what Captain Mahan said of his son when asked why he did not send him to West Point or Annapolis. "I have too much confidence in him to make me feel that it is desirable for him to enter either branch of the service."

I have great confidence in you. I believe you have the ability and, above all, the energy, the perseverance, and the common sense, to win out in civil life. That you will have some hard times and some discouraging times I have no question; but this is merely another way of saying that you will share the common lot. Though you will have to work in different ways from those in which I worked, you will not have to work any harder, nor to face periods of more discouragement. I trust in your ability, and especially your character, and I am confident you will win.

In the Army and the Navy the chance for a man to show great ability and rise above his fellows does not occur on the average more than once in a generation. When I was down at Santiago it was melancholy for me to see how fossilized and lacking in ambition, and generally useless, were most of the men of my age and over, who had served their lives in the Army. The Navy for the last few years has been better, but for twenty years after the Civil War there was less chance in the Navy than in the Army to practise, and do, work of real consequence. I have actually known lieutenants in both the Army and the Navy who were grandfathers—men who had seen their children married before they themselves attained the grade of captain. Of course the chance may come at any time when the man of West Point or Annapolis who will have stayed in the Army or Navy finds a great war on, and therefore has the opportunity to rise high. Under such circumstances, I think that the man of such training who has actually left the Army or the Navy has even more chance of rising than the man who has remained in it. Moreover, often a man can do as I did in the Spanish War, even though not a West Pointer.

This last point raises the question about you going to West Point or Annapolis and leaving the Army or Navy after you have served the regulation four years (I think that is the number) after graduation from the academy. Under this plan you would have an excellent education and a grounding in discipline and, in some ways, a testing of your capacity greater than I think you can get in any ordinary college. On the other hand, except for the

THEODORE ROOSEVELT JR.
*and his blue macaw ("Eli Yale"),*
*c. 1902.*

profession of an engineer, you would have had nothing like special training, and you would be so ordered about, and arranged for, that you would have less independence of character than you could gain from them. You would have had fewer temptations; but you would have had less chance to develop the qualities which overcome temptations and show that a man has individual initiative. Supposing you entered at seventeen, with the intention of following this course. The result would be that at twenty-five you would leave the Army or Navy without having gone through any law school or any special technical school of any kind, and would start your life work three or four years later than your schoolfellows of to-day, who go to work immediately after leaving college. Of course, under such circumstances, you might study law, for instance, during the four years after graduation; but my own feeling is that a man does good work chiefly when he is in something which he intends to make his permanent work, and in which he is deeply interested. Moreover, there will always be the chance that the number of officers in the Army or Navy will be deficient, and that you would have to stay in the service instead of getting out when you wished.

THEODORE JR. *on stilts at the door of Sagamore Hill, c. 1904.*

I want you to think over all these matters very seriously. It would be a great misfortune for you to start into the Army or Navy as a career, and find that you had mistaken your desires and had gone in without really weighing the matter.

You ought not to enter unless you feel genuinely drawn to the life as a life-work. If so, go in; but not otherwise.

Mr. Loeb told me to-day that at 17 he had tried for the army, but failed. The competitor who beat him in is now a captain; Mr. Loeb has passed him by, although meanwhile a war has been fought. Mr. Loeb says he wished to enter the army because he did not know what to do, could not foresee whether he would succeed or fail in life, and felt the army would give him "a living and a career." Now if this is at bottom your feeling I should advise you not to go in; I should say yes to some boys, but not to you; I believe in you too much, and have too much confidence in you.

# INAUGURAL ADDRESS
Saturday, March 4, 1905

---

**AFTER SERVING OUT MCKINLEY'S TERM** (in as decisive a manner as if he'd won the position in his own right), Roosevelt was re-elected to the Presidency in 1904. His inaugural celebration was the largest and most diverse of any in memory: cowboys, Native Americans (including the Apache Chief Geronimo), coal miners, soldiers, and students stood shoulder to shoulder as the oath of office was administered by Chief Justice Melville Fuller. Roosevelt's inaugural address is measured and optimistic, and undoubtedly inspired confidence in those who elected him.

My fellow-citizens, no people on earth have more cause to be thankful than ours, and this is said reverently, in no spirit of boastfulness in our own strength, but with gratitude to the Giver of Good who has blessed us with the conditions which have enabled us to achieve so large a measure of well-being and of happiness. To us as a people it has been granted to lay the foundations of our national life in a new continent. We are the heirs of the ages, and yet we have had to pay few of the penalties which in old countries are exacted by the dead hand of a bygone civilization. We have not been obliged to fight for our existence against any alien race; and yet our life has called for the vigor and effort without which the manlier and hardier virtues wither away. Under such conditions it would be our own fault if we failed; and the success which we have had in the past, the success which we confidently believe the future will bring, should cause in us no feeling of vainglory, but rather a deep and abiding realization of all which life has offered us; a full acknowledgment of the responsibility which is ours; and a fixed determination to show that under a free government a mighty people can thrive best, alike as regards the things of the body and the things of the soul.

Much has been given us, and much will rightfully be expected from us. We have duties to others and duties to ourselves; and we can shirk neither. We have become a great nation, forced by the fact of its greatness into relations with the other nations of the earth, and we must behave as beseems a people with such responsibilities. Toward all other nations, large and small, our attitude must be one of cordial and sincere friendship. We must show not only in our words, but in our deeds, that we are earnestly desirous of securing their good will by acting toward them in a spirit of just and generous recognition of all their rights. But justice and generosity in a nation, as in an individual, count most

My Fellow Citizens:

No people on earth have more cause to be thankful than ours; and this

*should be reverently* ~~can be~~ said in a spirit not of boastfulness *(in our own strength)* but of gratitude to the Giver

of Good who has blessed us with the conditions that have enabled us to

achieve so large a measure of well-being and of happiness.  To us as a

*It has been granted* ~~has come to fortunate~~

people ~~it has been given~~ to lay the foundations of our national life in a

great ~~virgin~~ *new* continent.  We are the heirs of the ages, and yet

we have had to pay few of the penalties which in old countries are exacted

*A copy of* **THEODORE ROOSEVELT'S INAUGURAL ADDRESS** *with his emendations, March 4, 1905.*

*opposite:* **THEODORE ROOSEVELT** *delivering his second inaugural address in front of the Capitol, Washington, D.C., March 4, 1905.*

when shown not by the weak but by the strong. While ever careful to refrain from wrongdoing others, we must be no less insistent that we are not wronged ourselves. We wish peace, but we wish the peace of justice, the peace of righteousness. We wish it because we think it is right and not because we are afraid. No weak nation that acts manfully and justly should ever have cause to fear us, and no strong power should ever be able to single us out as a subject for insolent aggression.

Our relations with the other powers of the world are important; but still more important are our relations among ourselves. Such growth in wealth, in population, and in power as this nation has seen during the century and a quarter of its national life is inevitably accompanied by a like growth in the problems which are ever before every nation that rises to greatness. Power invariably means both responsibility and danger. Our forefathers faced certain perils which we have outgrown. We now face other perils, the very existence of which it was impossible that they should foresee. Modern life is both complex and intense, and the tremendous changes wrought by the extraordinary industrial development of the last half century are felt in every fiber of our social and political being. Never before have men tried so vast and formidable an experiment as that of administering the affairs of a continent under the forms of a Democratic republic. The conditions which have told for our marvelous material well-being, which have developed to a very high degree our energy, self-reliance, and individual initiative, have also brought the care and anxiety inseparable from the accumulation of great wealth in industrial centers. Upon the success of our

*An* INVITATION TO THE INAUGURATION *of Theodore Roosevelt as President of the United States, 1905.*

experiment much depends, not only as regards our own welfare, but as regards the welfare of mankind. If we fail, the cause of free self-government throughout the world will rock to its foundations, and therefore our responsibility is heavy, to ourselves, to the world as it is to-day, and to the generations yet unborn. There is no good reason why we should fear the future, but there is every reason why we should face it seriously, neither hiding from ourselves the gravity of the problems before us nor fearing to approach these problems with the unbending, unflinching purpose to solve them aright.

Yet, after all, though the problems are new, though the tasks set before us differ from the tasks set before our fathers who founded and preserved this Republic, the spirit in which these tasks must be undertaken and these problems faced, if our duty is to be well done, remains essentially unchanged. We know that self-government is difficult. We know that no people needs such high traits of character as that people which seeks to govern its affairs aright through the freely expressed will of the freemen who compose it. But we have faith that we shall not prove false to the memories of the men of the mighty past. They did their work, they left us the splendid heritage we now enjoy. We in our turn have an assured confidence that we shall be able to leave this heritage unwasted and enlarged to our children and our children's children. To do so we must show, not merely in great crises, but in the everyday affairs of life, the qualities of practical intelligence, of courage, of hardihood, and endurance, and above all the power of devotion to a lofty ideal, which made great the men who founded this Republic in the days of Washington, which made great the men who preserved this Republic in the days of Abraham Lincoln.

**T. ROOSEVELT, JR., THE STAR.**

Saves Harvard Freshmen from Defeat Worse than 5 to 0.

(Special to The World.)

WORCESTER, Mass., Oct. 28.—Harvard's freshmen were defeated in a football game this afternoon by the Worcester Academy. The score was 5 to 0 and it would have been bigger had it not been for Theodore Roosevelt, jr. Jones had got through the entire Harvard eleven and was headed for a touchdown, but young Roosevelt caught him after a hard run and brought him down with a neat tackle.

This was young Roosevelt's first game for Harvard and he was one of the star performers. He showed he was game all through and played left end for all there was in it. He made several pretty tackles.

**THE WORLD: SUNDAY, OCTOBER 29, 1905.**

At Harvard T played football on the Freshman team & on the 2nd Eleven, although he weighed less than 130 pounds, until he broke his ankle (v. picture being helped off the field.)

# MAKING FOOTBALL
# MORE SPORTING

Football began as a college sport in the mid-nineteenth century, and it was a rugged affair, featuring gang-tackling, slugging, and unsportsmanlike behavior on the field and behind the scenes. Nevertheless, Roosevelt was a fan of the game, believing that it built young bodies and strengthened character through its emphasis on teamwork and perseverance. (Ten of the Rough Riders who fought behind him in Cuba listed their occupations as "football player" in their enlistment documents.)

The number of injuries and deaths caused by the game grew year by year; in 1905, eighteen young men were killed and 159 severely hurt on the football field. Roosevelt, who was well into his second Presidential term by this time and burdened with affairs domestic and foreign, was nevertheless greatly troubled by this fact and—as was his tendency—charged in to rectify the situation. On October 9, 1905, he summoned representatives from the top Ivy League schools to the White House and read them the riot act. If they couldn't curb the brutality rampant in the sport, he'd abolish the game with an Executive Order.

His ultimatum didn't come a moment too soon—the American people were losing interest in football because of its violence and fatalities. Chastened, the coaches formed the American Football Rules Committee and set about making the game safer and more fair. It may sound only faintly hopeful, but by 1906, the game suffered "only" six fatalities—and five of them occurred during fistfights.

That year, the committee changed its name, first to the Intercollegiate Athletic Association of the United States and ultimately to the National Collegiate Athletic Association, the name by which it is known today.

If Roosevelt hadn't taken the lead in reforming the game, it's likely there would be no football. In commemoration of that fact, the NCAA annually confers its highest honor—the Theodore Roosevelt Award ("Teddy")—on a graduate from an NCAA institution who earned a varsity letter in college and who ultimately became a distinguished citizen of national reputation. Past winners include four former Presidents: Dwight D. Eisenhower, Gerald R. Ford, George H. W. Bush, and Ronald Reagan.

*A scrapbook page showing the* HARVARD FOOTBALL TEAM, *Theodore Roosevelt Jr. being helped off the field with a broken ankle at a Harvard football game, and Ted Jr. sitting, October 1905.*

# 6.

# PRESERVATION AND EXPANSION

**R**OOSEVELT HAD MADE IT CLEAR that he would use his one and only full term in office to cement U.S. interests abroad, while at the same time signing legislation to safeguard the country's wilderness areas.

In 1905, halfway around the world, Japan won a decisive victory in its war with Russia and officially inquired as to whether Roosevelt would be willing to help broker peace with its adversary. Both Roosevelt and Czar Nicholas II agreed to his participation in the talks, which took place in Portsmouth, New Hampshire, in August. A peace treaty was signed by the two nations on September 5, and for his part in the negotiations, Roosevelt would be awarded the Nobel Prize for Peace—and the distinction of being the first American to win one in any field.

As Roosevelt looked ahead to his departure from the presidency, he must have been thinking about his legacy, and what his final acts as Chief Executive should be. He made numerous court appointments and reorganized his Cabinet. He reached a "gentlemen's agreement" with Japan, under which all segregation of Japanese schoolchildren in the United States would cease in exchange for tighter restrictions on immigration. He signed the proclamation establishing Oklahoma as the 46th state in the Union.

During the summer of 1907, Roosevelt threw his active support behind William Taft as his successor, rather than his own Vice President, Charles Fairbanks. This left Fairbanks little choice but to withdraw

*overleaf:* **PRESIDENT ROOSEVELT** *standing next to an elephant he killed in Africa, 1909.*

*opposite:* **PRESIDENT THEODORE ROOSEVELT** *on a steam shovel during construction of the Panama Canal, 1906.*

*left:* **SCRIBNER'S MAGAZINE COVER** *for October 1909 featured Theodore Roosevelt's first African article "African Game Trails," which was serialized over the course of a year.*

*right:* **DINNER ADDRESS** *for Roosevelt's Nobel Peace Prize acceptance, 1906.*

*below:* **PRESIDENT THEODORE ROOSEVELT** *standing with Russian and Japanese envoys aboard the presidential yacht,* The Mayflower, *August 5, 1905.*

3

want is just exactly what the Cuban people themselves want, that is, a

the Island,

continuance of order within, and peace and prosperity, so that there shall

be no shadow of an excuse for any outside intervention. ~~I mention that~~

~~just to show you that you have not given the Nobel Prize to a man who has~~

~~merely spoken of peace and justice, and did not try to live up to his~~

~~words.~~

We acted along the same general lines

~~To a lesser extent, we tried to do the same~~ thing in the case of S an

We intervened only so far as to prevent the need

of taking possession of the Island.

Domingo. None of you will know of this, so I will just tell you briefly

when

what it was that we did. The Republic of S an Domingo, in the West Indies,

the Island, while I was President

had suffered from a good many revolutions. In one particular period ~~that~~

there were

I had to deal with, it was a little difficult to know what to do, because

~~we had~~ two separate governments in the island, and a revolution going on

against each, and a number of dictators, under the title of President,

had seized power at different times, had borrowed money at exorbitant

and Americans,

rates of interest from Europeans, and had pledged the custom houses of the

to different countries;

different towns, and the chief object of each revolutionary was to get

hold of the custom houses. Things got to such a pass that it became

evident that certain European powers would land and take possession of

THE GREAT WHITE FLEET
*returns from its world trip to Chesapeake Bay, February 22, 1909.*

from the race for the Republican nomination. (What goes around comes around. Fairbanks would later support Taft's successful re-election bid against Roosevelt.)

By the final year of his term, Roosevelt's profligate use of his presidential power and advocacy of progressive policies had caused a severe rift with his more conservative colleagues. Another result of his aggressive anti-trust activities was the collapse of several key financial institutions, causing nationwide financial panic. To avert a run of bank failures, Roosevelt approved the acquisition of Tennessee Coal and Iron by U.S. Steel, a move that undoubtedly rankled the "trust buster," but, along with the issuance of $150 million in new government bonds, succeeded in turning the economy around.

Perhaps to avert attention from the economy, and certainly to put the rest of the world on notice, Roosevelt decided to rattle his sword one last time. He ordered 16 battleships on an around-the-world cruise in a show of American strength, seeing them off personally from the port at Hampton Roads, Virginia, and welcoming them home a few months later. For his part, Taft sailed to victory in November with 321 electoral votes to William Jennings Bryan's 162.

With his presidency at an end, Roosevelt turned his attention to a different kind of wildlife: he embarked on a long-anticipated safari in Africa, with a party that included his son Kermit and several world-renowned big-game hunters. Charged with bringing back specimens for the Smithsonian Institution and American Museum of Natural History and partially subsidized by Andrew Carnegie, Roosevelt and his party bagged elephant, rhinoceros, hippopotamus, buffalo, giraffe, zebra, and more than 20 species of antelope. In all, the party is said to have killed or trapped more than 11,000 animals. The Smithsonian could barely handle the shipments that arrived; it took years to mount all of the specimens, and many were sent on to other museums.

Roosevelt's support of Taft had sealed the election, but it now seemed that Taft's agenda, and his brand of progressivism, differed markedly from Roosevelt's own. The first blow to Roosevelt's confidence in Taft came when he learned, while on safari, that Taft had dismissed Gifford Pinchot, a staunch conservationist and the close friend Roosevelt had appointed head of the Forestry Service.

Once back in the States, Roosevelt found it hard to sit on the sidelines of the political arena after so much time center stage. Taking advantage of his new platform—he'd become a contributing editor to *The Outlook*—he wrote numerous pieces taking issue with Taft's positions and tactics, inciting the left wing of the party against the more cautious and less politically nimble Taft. In 1910, Roosevelt gave an electrifying speech in Osawatomie, Kansas, one of the most radical of his career, in which he attacked the judiciary and threw down the gauntlet to Taft. The infighting within the party took its toll: Democrats overtook Congress in the 1910 midterms, and Taft's re-election was in serious jeopardy.

Belatedly, Roosevelt tossed his hat back into the Presidential ring, declaring his candidacy for the nomination on February 12, 1912. Always an effective campaigner, he tore through 21 states that spring and won 9

*above left: The Smithsonian-Roosevelt* AFRICAN EXPEDITION TEAM, *1909.*

*above right:* THEODORE ROOSEVELT POSES WITH A BULL RHINOCEROS *he killed on an African savanna, c. May 1919, photographed by Kermit Roosevelt.*

out of 12 Republican primaries, including the one in Taft's home state of Ohio. But . . . the system that Roosevelt had played so effectively against itself in the past was not on his side. Taft had the support of party leaders, and in those days, the popular vote carried less weight in primary elections; he won the delegate vote and secured the nomination.

That might have been the end of it—if Roosevelt hadn't been Roosevelt. Once he realized he couldn't win the nomination outright, he called upon his followers to march out of the convention hall and regroup in another location, joining with him to create a new Progressive Party and offer up a full slate of candidates. Thus, the "Bull Moose Party" was born, dedicated to rooting out corruption in business and politics and supporting women's suffrage, among other familiar planks—and to electing Theodore Roosevelt to spearhead the effort. Its convention was held in August, officially placing Roosevelt in the race along with his running mate, California governor Hiram Johnson. The Democrats had officially nominated New Jersey Governor Woodrow Wilson on July 2.

RHINOCEROS *from the Smithsonian-Roosevelt Expedition, 1915.*

Roosevelt campaigned hard, even taking a bullet in the process, but it was a matter of too little too late. Where a united Republican party might easily have won the day, a divided one effectively handed the election to Woodrow Wilson, who walked away with 6.3 million votes (42 percent of the total) and 435 electoral votes. With 4.1 million votes (27 percent) and 88 electoral votes, Roosevelt did beat Taft, who came away with 3.5 million votes (23 percent) and only 8 electoral votes—making it one for the record books: Taft is still the only incumbent President ever to come in third.

*above:* **A CAMPAIGN BUTTON** *made in support of Theodore Roosevelt's "Bull Moose" Party candidacy for President, 1912*

*left:* **THEODORE ROOSEVELT** *returning from Africa: "Can a Champion Come Back?" Cover of* Judge, *August 6, 1910.*

# "LADIES AND GENTLEMEN ...
# I HAVE JUST BEEN SHOT."

History nearly repeated itself on October 14, 1912, when Roosevelt fell victim to an assassin's bullet while delivering a campaign speech in Milwaukee, Wisconsin. A saloonkeeper named John Schrank shot the candidate squarely in the chest—but luck was on Roosevelt's side, aided by his own long-windedness. The bullet lost its lethal power as it passed first through his steel eyeglass case and then a folded copy of the 50-page speech he'd tucked into his breast pocket.

Stubborn and hearty as ever, Roosevelt refused to go immediately to the hospital, surmising correctly that the bullet hadn't penetrated his chest cavity. Instead, he delivered the 90-minute speech that had literally saved his life, beginning with an ad-lib suited to the moment: "Ladies and gentlemen, I don't know whether you fully understand that I have just been shot; but it takes more than that to kill a Bull Moose." It couldn't have come off better if he'd planned it as campaign stunt.

When Roosevelt did submit to an X-ray, it was determined inadvisable to remove the bullet, so it **stayed** in his chest for the rest of his life. The incident cut short his campaign effort in the crucial last two weeks leading up to the election, but it is impossible to determine how much effect that had on the outcome. (It should be noted that in solidarity, the two opposing candidates did no campaigning while Roosevelt was in the hospital. One wonders how that might be handled today.)

*top:* **BLOODSTAINED SHIRT** *worn by U.S. President Theodore Roosevelt during an assassination attempt by New York saloon keeper John F. Schrank on October 14, 1912, in Milwaukee, Wisconsin.*

*bottom: Photo of* **ROOSEVELT'S SPEECH** *with the bullet hole from when he was shot while campaigning in Milwaukee in 1912.*

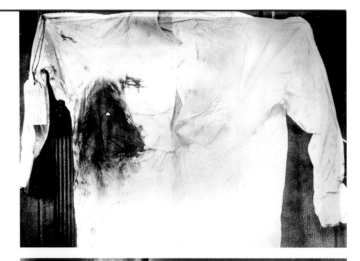

ROOSEVELT DEVOTED A GENEROUS PORTION of his autobiography (including the following excerpts) to his work on behalf of the natural world, which he undertook as passionately as any of his foreign policy efforts. We have him to thank, in large part, for the swaths of American wilderness that remain pristine for all to enjoy.

# The Natural Resources of the Nation

When Governor of New York, as I have already described, I had been in consultation with Gifford Pinchot and F. H. Newell, and had shaped my recommendations about forestry largely in accordance with their suggestions. Like other men who had thought about the national future at all, I had been growing more and more concerned over the destruction of the forests.... But Gifford Pinchot is the man to whom the nation owes most for what has been accomplished as regards the preservation of the natural resources of our country. He led, and indeed during its most vital period embodied, the fight for the preservation through use of our forests. He played one of the leading parts in the effort to make the National Government the chief instrument in developing the irrigation of the arid West. He was the foremost leader in the great struggle to coördinate all our social and governmental forces in the effort to secure the adoption of a rational and farseeing policy for securing the conservation of all our national resources. He was already in the Government service as head of the Forestry Bureau when I became President; he continued throughout my term, not only as head of the Forest service, but as the moving and directing spirit in most of the conservation work, and as counsellor and assistant on most of the other work connected with the internal affairs of the country. Taking into account the varied nature of the work he did, its vital importance to the nation and the fact that as regards much of it he was practically breaking new ground, and taking into account also his tireless energy and activity, his fearlessness, his complete disinterestedness, his single-minded devotion

GIFFORD PINCHOT (in a photograph from 1921) advocated conservation of natural resources and coined the term "conservation ethic."

to the interests of the plain people, and his extraordinary efficiency, I believe it is but just to say that among the many, many public officials who under my administration rendered literally invaluable service to the people of the United States, he, on the whole, stood first. A few months after I left the Presidency he was removed from office by President Taft. ✶ ✶ ✶

ALL THE FORESTS which belonged to the United States were held and administered in one Department, and all the foresters in Government employ were in another Department. Forests and foresters had nothing whatever to do with each other. The National Forests in the West (then called forest reserves) were wholly inadequate in area to meet the purposes for which they were created, while the need for forest protection in the East had not yet begun to enter the public mind.

Such was the condition of things when Newell and Pinchot called on me. I was a warm believer in reclamation and in forestry, and, after listening to my two guests, I asked them to prepare material on the subject for me to use in my first message to Congress, of December 3, 1901. This message laid the foundation for the development of irrigation and forestry during the next seven and one-half years. It set forth the new attitude toward the natural resources in the words: "The Forest and water problems are perhaps the most vital internal problems of the United States."

On the day the message was read, a committee of Western Senators and Congressmen was organized to prepare a Reclamation Bill in accordance with the recommendations. . . . On June 17, 1902, the Reclamation Act was passed. It set aside the proceeds of the disposal of public lands for the purpose of reclaiming the waste areas of the arid West by irrigating lands otherwise worthless, and thus creating new homes upon the land. The money so appropriated was to be repaid to the Government by the settlers, and to be used again as a revolving fund continuously available for the work.

The impatience of the Western people to see immediate results from the Reclamation Act was so great that red tape was disregarded, and the work was pushed forward at a rate previously unknown in Government affairs. Later, as in almost all such cases, there followed the criticisms of alleged illegality and haste which are so easy to make after results have been accomplished and the need for the measures without which nothing could have been done has gone by. These criticisms were in character

THEODORE ROOSEVELT AND OTHERS *in a horse-drawn wagon in front of a redwood tree in California, c. 1903.*

precisely the same as that made about the acquisition of Panama, the settlement of the anthracite coal strike, the suits against the big trusts, the stopping of the panic of 1907 by the action of the Executive concerning the Tennessee Coal and Iron Company; and, in short, about most of the best work done during my administration.

With the Reclamation work, as with much other work under me, the men in charge were given to understand that they must get into the water if they would learn to swim; and, furthermore, they learned to know that if they acted honestly, and boldly and fearlessly accepted responsibility, I would stand by them to the limit. In this, as in every other case, in the end the boldness of the action fully justified itself.

Every item of the whole great plan of Reclamation now in effect was undertaken between 1902 and 1906. By the spring of 1909 the work was an assured success, and the Government had become fully committed to its continuance. . . .

Although the gross expenditure under the Reclamation Act is not yet as large as that for the Panama Canal, the engineering obstacles to be overcome have been almost as great, and the political impediments many times greater. The Reclamation work had to be carried on at widely separated points, remote from railroads, under the most difficult pioneer conditions. The twenty-eight projects begun in the years 1902 to 1906 contemplated the irrigation of more than three million acres and the watering of more than thirty thousand farms. Many of the dams required for this huge task are higher than any previously built anywhere in the world. They feed main-line canals over seven thousand miles in total length, and involve minor constructions, such as culverts and bridges, tens of thousands in number.

What the Reclamation Act has done for the country is by no means limited to its material accomplishment. This Act and the results flowing from it have helped powerfully to prove to the Nation that it can handle its own resources and exercise direct and business-like control over them. The population which the Reclamation Act has brought into the arid West, while comparatively small when compared with that in the more closely inhabited East, has been a most effective contribution to the National life, for it has gone far to transform the social aspect of the West, making for the stability of the institutions upon which the welfare of the whole country rests: it has substituted actual homemakers, who have

DEDICATION CEREMONY *of the Roosevelt Dam in Arizona, a Salt River project of the Bureau of Reclamation, 1912.*

settled on the land with their families, for huge, migratory bands of sheep herded by the hired shepherds of absentee owners. ✶ ✶ ✶

**THE IDEA THAT THE EXECUTIVE** is the steward of the public welfare was first formulated and given practical effect in the Forest Service by its law officer, George Woodruff. The laws were often insufficient, and it became well-nigh impossible to get them amended in the public interest when once the representatives of privilege in Congress grasped the fact that I would sign no amendment that contained anything not in the public interest. It was necessary to use what law was already in existence, and then further to supplement it by Executive action. The practice of examining every claim to public land before passing it into private ownership offers a good example of the policy in question. This practice, which has since become general, was first applied in the National Forests. Enormous areas of valuable public timberland were thereby saved from fraudulent acquisition; more than 250,000 acres were thus saved in a single case. ✶ ✶ ✶

**THE CONSERVATION MOVEMENT** was a direct outgrowth of the forest movement. It was nothing more than the application to our other natural resources of the principles which had been worked out in connection with the forests. Without the basis of public sentiment which had been built up for the protection of the forests, and without the example of public foresight in the protection of this, one of the great natural resources, the Conservation movement would have been impossible. The first formal step was the creation of the Inland Waterways Commission, appointed on March 14, 1907. In my letter appointing the Commission, I called attention to the value of our streams as great natural resources, and to the need for a progressive plan for their development and control, and said: "It is not possible to properly frame so large a plan as this for the control of our rivers without taking account of the orderly development of other natural

GEORGE WASHINGTON WOODRUFF *served as Chief Law Officer of the Forest Service and as Acting Secretary of the Interior under Roosevelt, c. 1910.*

resources. Therefore I ask that the Inland Waterways Commission shall consider the relations of the streams to the use of all the great permanent natural resources and their conservation for the making and maintenance of prosperous homes." ✶ ✶ ✶

"Without the basis of public sentiment which had been built up for the protection of the forests, and with out the example of public foresight in the protection of this, one of the great natural resources, the Conservation movement would have been impossible."

THE GRAND CANYON OF THE YELLOWSTONE *by Thomas Moran, c. 1893–1901. This painting is on display at the Smithsonian American Art Museum in Washington, D.C.*

THE REPORT OF the National Conservation Commission was not only the first inventory of our resources, but was unique in the history of Government in the amount and variety of information brought together. It was completed in six months. It laid squarely before the American people the essential facts regarding our natural resources, when facts were greatly needed as the basis for constructive action. This report was presented to the Joint Conservation Congress in December, at which there were present Governors of twenty States, representatives of twenty-two State Conservation Commissions, and representatives of sixty National organizations previously represented at the White House conference. The report was unanimously approved, and transmitted to me, January 11, 1909. On January 22, 1909, I transmitted the report of the National Conservation Commission to Congress with a Special Message, in which it was accurately described as "one of the most fundamentally important documents ever laid before the American people." ✶ ✶ ✶

EVEN MORE IMPORTANT was the taking of steps to preserve from destruction beautiful and wonderful wild creatures whose existence was threatened by greed and wantonness. During the seven and a half years closing on March 4, 1909, more was accomplished for the protection of wild life in the United States than during all the previous years, excepting only the creation of the Yellowstone National Park. The record includes the creation of five National Parks—Crater Lake, Oregon; Wind Cave, South Dakota; Platt, Oklahoma; Sully Hill, North Dakota, and Mesa Verde, Colorado; four big game refuges in Oklahoma, Arizona, Montana, and Washington; fifty-one bird reservations; and the enactment of laws for the protection of wild life in Alaska, the District of Columbia, and on National bird reserves. These measures may be briefly enumerated as follows:

*The enactment of the first game laws for the Territory of Alaska in 1902 and 1908, resulting in the regulation of the export of heads and trophies of big game and putting an end to the slaughter of deer for hides along the southern coast of the Territory.*

*The securing in 1902 of the first appropriation for the preservation of buffalo and the establishment in the Yellowstone National Park of the first and now the largest herd of buffalo belonging to the Government.*

*The passage of the Act of January 24, 1905, creating the Wichita Game Preserves, the first of the National game preserves. In 1907, 12,000 acres of this preserve were inclosed with a woven wire fence for the reception of the herd of fifteen buffalo donated by the New York Zoölogical Society.*

*The passage of the Act of June 29, 1906, providing for the establishment of the Grand Cañon Game Preserve of Arizona, now comprising 1,492,928 acres.*

*The passage of the National Monuments Act of June 8, 1906, under which a number of objects of scientific interest have been preserved for all time.*

*Among the Monuments created are Muir Woods, Pinnacles National Monument in California, and the Mount Olympus National Monument, Washington, which form important refuges for game.*

*The passage of the Act of June 30, 1906, regulating shooting in the District of Columbia and making three-fourths of the environs of the National Capital within the District in effect a National Refuge.*

*The passage of the Act of May 23, 1908, providing for the establishment of the National Bison Range in Montana. This range comprises about 18,000 acres of land formerly in the Flathead Indian Reservation, on which is now established a herd of eighty buffalo, a nucleus of which was donated to the Government by the American Bison Society.*

*The issue of the Order protecting birds on the Niobrara Military Reservation, Nebraska, in 1908, making this entire reservation in effect a bird reservation.*

*The establishment by Executive Order between March 14, 1903, and March 4, 1909, of fifty-one National Bird Reservations distributed in seventeen States and Territories from Porto Rico to Hawaii and Alaska. The creation of these reservations at once placed the United States in the front rank in the world work of bird protection. Among these reservations are the celebrated Pelican Island rookery in Indian River, Florida; the Mosquito Inlet Reservation, Florida, the northernmost home of the manatee; the extensive marshes bordering Klamath and Malhuer Lakes in Oregon, formerly the scene of slaughter of ducks for market and ruthless destruction of plume birds for the millinery trade; the Tortugas Key, Florida, where, in connection with the Carnegie Institute, experiments have been made on the homing instinct of birds; and the great bird colonies on Laysan and sister islets in Hawaii, some of the greatest colonies of sea birds in the world.*

THE BIG STICK

"WALK SOFTLY AND CARRY A BIG STICK." That line, from a speech Roosevelt delivered in 1901 (before he was even President), would set the tone of his foreign policy strategy over the next decade—most significantly in creating the Panama Canal. In his autobiography, Roosevelt devoted a chapter to his passion for American expansion in South and Central America and elsewhere, as well as his belief in the "square deal" for all Americans, an anti-corporate stance that set him at odds with the Republican machine of his day. Always clear-eyed about his mission, Roosevelt knew even then that these two positions would comprise his political legacy.

# The Big Stick and the Square Deal

One of the vital questions with which as President I had to deal was the attitude of the Nation toward the great corporations. Men who understand and practice the deep underlying philosophy of the Lincoln school of American political thought are necessarily Hamiltonian in their belief in a strong and efficient National Government and Jeffersonian in their belief in the people as the ultimate authority, and in the welfare of the people as the end of Government. The men who first applied the extreme Democratic theory in American life were, like Jefferson, ultra individualists, for at that time what was demanded by our people was the largest liberty for the individual. During the century that had elapsed since Jefferson became President the need had been exactly reversed. There had been in our country a riot of individualistic materialism, under which complete freedom for the individual—that ancient license which President Wilson a century after the term was excusable has called the "New" Freedom—turned out in practice to mean perfect freedom for the strong to wrong the weak. The total absence of governmental control had led to a portentous growth in the financial and industrial world both of natural individuals and of artificial individuals—that is, corporations. In no other country in the world

had such enormous fortunes been gained. In no other country in the world was such power held by the men who had gained these fortunes; and these men almost always worked through, and by means of, the giant corporations which they controlled. The power of the mighty industrial overlords of the country had increased with giant strides, while the methods of controlling them, or checking abuses by them, on the part of the people, through the Government, remained archaic and therefore practically impotent. The courts, not unnaturally, but most regrettably, and to the grave detriment of the people and of their own standing, had for a quarter of a century been on the whole the agents of reaction, and by conflicting decisions which, however, in their sum were hostile to the interests of the people, had left both the nation and the several States well-nigh impotent to deal with the great business combinations. Sometimes they forbade the Nation to interfere, because such interference trespassed on the rights of the States; sometimes they forbade the States to interfere (and often they were wise in this), because to do so would trespass on the rights of the Nation; but always, or well-nigh always, their action was negative action against the interests of the people, ingeniously devised to limit their power against wrong,

A CARTOON FROM AN ISSUE OF *JUDGE* MAGAZINE *illustrates Roosevelt's "Big Stick" politics with his bust on the prow of the* Washington *battleship, 1907.*

instead of affirmative action giving to the people power to right wrong. They had rendered these decisions sometimes as upholders of property rights against human rights, being especially zealous in securing the rights of the very men who were most competent to take care of themselves; and sometimes in the name of liberty, in the name of the so-called "new freedom," in reality the old, old "freedom," which secured to the powerful the freedom to prey on the poor and the helpless.

## A WHITE HOUSE WEDDING

Perhaps one of the few situations, foreign or domestic, that Roosevelt didn't manage to dominate and control was the 1906 White House marriage of his daughter Alice to Nicholas Longworth, a Republican congressman from Ohio. The high-spirited Alice had been mesmerizing the public since Roosevelt first took office with her smoking, driving, flirtations, and general brashness. She had been toasted at the Mardi Gras in New Orleans, the Chicago Horse Show, and the St. Louis World's Fair. The head usher of the White House later wrote that she had a party every night of her stay in the executive mansion. And when Roosevelt decided to send her along on a diplomatic mission to the Philippines, her high jinks captivated the world and (just as the cunning President had planned) diverted attention away from his delicate political maneuverings in the region.

Thirty-five-year-old Nicholas Longworth had been one of the many Washington men pursuing Alice. By all accounts, though older than Alice and bald, he was entertaining company and wealthy to boot. The announcement of their impending wedding pushed all other news off the front pages and glorious gifts poured in from heads of state worldwide. Roosevelt at first announced "a small family affair," but it was a foregone conclusion that the wedding would be the event of the new century. When the great day dawned, the air was unseasonably warm, and thousands gathered outside the White House to catch a glimpse of the wedding party. They were not disappointed, nor were the hundreds of invited guests. Alice (who, reluctant to share the spotlight, had rejected the idea of bridesmaids in favor of 20 male military aids and ushers) was resplendent on her father's arm, her hair woven with orange blossoms and her 18-foot silver brocade train trailing after her. When the question came, "Who will give the bride away?" Roosevelt's response was almost inaudible. It seems his daughter had done the unimaginable: she'd momentarily upstaged her father.

ALICE ROOSEVELT LONGWORTH *in her wedding dress with her husband, Nicholas Longworth (left), and her father, Theodore Roosevelt (right), 1906.*

# VOYAGE TO PANAMA

**IN NOVEMBER 1906,** the President and Mrs. Roosevelt traveled on the naval vessel *Louisiana* to the Isthmus of Panama, where he spent some time inspecting the work being done on the Panama Canal. He wrote the following entertaining letters to his children while on that journey. You'd never know they came from a President in the midst of changing the geopolitics of the world.

On Board U.S.S. *Louisiana*,
On the Way to Panama.
Sunday, November 11, 1906.

BLESSED QUENTIN:
You would be amused at the pets they have aboard this ship. They have two young bull-dogs, a cat, three little raccoons, and a tiny Cuban goat. They seem to be very amicable with one another, although I think the cat has suspicions of all the rest. The coons clamber about everywhere, and the other afternoon while I was sitting reading, I suddenly felt my finger seized in a pair of soft black paws and found the coon sniffing at it, making me feel a little uncomfortable lest it might think the finger something good to eat. The two puppies play endlessly. One of them belongs to Lieutenant Evans. The crew will not be allowed ashore at Panama or else I know they would pick up a whole raft of other pets there. The jackies seem especially fond of the little coons. A few minutes ago I saw one of the jackies strolling about with a coon perched upon his shoulder, and now and then he would reach up his hand and give it a small piece of bread to eat. ✶ ✶ ✶

PRESIDENT ROOSEVELT AND HIS BOYS *in the White House, March, 1904. From left to right: Ted, Archie, Roosevelt, Quentin, and Kermit.*

On Board U.S.S. *Louisiana,*
Sunday, November 11, 1906.

BLESSED ARCHIE:

I wish you were along with us, for you would thoroughly enjoy everything on this ship. We have had three days of perfect weather, while this great battleship with her two convoys, the great armored cruisers, *Tennessee* and *Washington,* have steamed steadily in column ahead southward through calm seas until now we are in the tropics. They are three as splendid ships of their class as there are afloat, save only the English Dreadnaught. The *Louisiana* now has her gun-sights and everything is all in good shape for her to begin the practice of the duties which will make her crew as fit for man-of-war's work as the crew of any one of our other first-class battleships. The men are such splendid-looking fellows, Americans of the best type, young, active, vigorous, with lots of intelligence. I was much amused at the names of the seven-inch guns, which include *Victor, Invincible, Peacemaker,* together with *Skidoo,* and also one called *Tedd* and one called *The Big Stick.* ✦ ✦ ✦

**CULEBRA CUT**, *now known as Gaillard Cut, during the construction of the Panama Canal, 1904.*

On Board U.S.S. *Louisiana,*
Nov. 13.

DEAR KERMIT:

So far this trip has been a great success, and I think Mother has really enjoyed it. As for me, I of course feel a little bored, as I always do on shipboard, but I have brought on a great variety of books, and am at this moment reading

Milton's prose works, "Tacitus," and a German novel called "Jorn Uhl." Mother and I walk briskly up and down the deck together, or else sit aft under the awning, or in the after cabin, with the gun ports open, and read; and I also spend a good deal of time on the forward bridge, and sometimes on the aft bridge, and of course have gone over the ship to inspect it with the Captain. It is a splendid thing to see one of these men-of-war, and it does really make one proud of one's country. Both the officers and the enlisted men are as fine a set as one could wish to see.

It is a beautiful sight, these three great war-ships standing southward in close column, and almost as beautiful at night when we see not only the lights but the loom through the darkness of the ships astern. We are now in the tropics and I have thought a good deal of the time over eight years ago when I was sailing to Santiago in the fleet of warships and transports. It seems a strange thing to think of my now being President, going to visit the work of the Panama Canal which I have made possible.

Mother, very pretty and dainty in white summer clothes, came up on Sunday morning to see inspection and review, or whatever they call it, of the men. I usually spend half an hour on deck before Mother is dressed. Then we breakfast together alone; have also taken lunch alone, but at dinner have two or three officers to dine with us. Doctor Rixey is along, and is a perfect dear, as always.
✷ ✷ ✷

On Board U.S.S. *Louisiana,*
Nov. 14.

DEAR TED:
I am very glad to have taken this trip, although as usual I am bored by the sea. Everything has been smooth as possible, and it has been lovely having Mother along. It gives me great pride in America to be aboard this great battleship and to see not only the material perfection of the ship herself in engines, guns and all arrangements, but the fine quality of the officers and crew. Have you ever read Smollett's novel, I think "Roderick Random" or "Humphrey Clinker," in which the hero goes to sea? It gives me an awful idea of what a floating hell of filth, disease, tyranny, and cruelty a war-ship was in those days. Now every

arrangement is as clean and healthful as possible. The men can bathe and do bathe as often as cleanliness requires. Their fare is excellent and they are as self-respecting a set as can be imagined. I am no great believer in the superiority of times past; and I have no question that the officers and men of our Navy now are in point of fighting capacity better than in the times of Drake and Nelson; and morally and in physical surroundings the advantage is infinitely in our favor.

It was delightful to have you two or three days at Washington. Blessed old fellow, you had a pretty hard time in college this fall; but it can't be helped, Ted; as one grows older the bitter and the sweet keep coming together. The only thing to do is to grin and bear it, to flinch as little as possible under the punishment, and to keep pegging steadily away until the luck turns. ✳ ✳ ✳

U.S.S. *Louisiana*,
At Sea, November 20, 1906.

DEAR KERMIT:
Our visit to Panama was most successful as well as most interesting. We were there three days and we worked from morning till night. The second day I was up at a quarter to six and got to bed at a quarter of twelve, and I do not believe that in the intervening time, save when I was dressing, there were ten consecutive minutes when I was not busily at work in some shape or form. For two days there [were] uninterrupted tropic rains without a glimpse of the sun, and the Chagres River rose in a flood, higher than any for fifteen years; so that we saw the climate at its worst. It was just what I desired to do.

It certainly adds to one's pleasure to have read history and to appreciate the picturesque. When on Wednesday we approached the coast, and the jungle-covered mountains looked clearer and clearer until we could see the surf beating on the shores, while there was hardly a sign of human habitation, I kept thinking of the four centuries of wild and bloody romance, mixed with abject squalor and suffering, which had made up the history of the Isthmus until three years ago. I could see Balboa crossing at Darien, and the wars between the Spaniards and the Indians, and the settlement and the building up of the quaint walled Spanish towns; and the trade, across the seas by galleon, and over land by pack-train and river canoe, in gold and silver, in precious stones; and then the advent of the buccaneers, and of the English seamen, of Drake and Frobisher and Morgan, and many, many others, and the wild destruction they wrought. Then I thought of the rebellion against the Spanish dominion, and the uninterrupted and bloody wars that followed, the last occurring when I became President; wars, the victorious heroes of which have their pictures frescoed on the quaint rooms of the palace at Panama city, and in similar palaces in all capitals of these strange, turbulent little half-caste civilizations. Meanwhile the Panama railroad had been built by Americans over a half century ago, with appalling loss of life, so that it is said, of course with exaggeration, that every sleeper laid represented the death of a man. Then the French canal company started work, and for two or three years did a good deal, until it became evident that the task far exceeded its powers; and then to miscalculation and inefficiency was added the hideous greed of adventurers, trying each to save something from the general wreck, and the company closed with infamy and scandal.

PRESIDENT ROOSEVELT *climbing into a steam shovel with workers and others around, Gaillard Cut, Panama, November 16, 1906.*

Now we have taken hold of the job. We have difficulties with our own people, of course. I haven't a doubt that it will take a little longer and cost a little more than men now appreciate, but I believe that the work is being done with a very high degree both of efficiency and honesty; and I am immensely struck by the character of American employees who are engaged, not merely in superintending the work, but in doing all the jobs that need skill and intelligence. The steam shovels, the dirt trains, the machine shops, and the like, are all filled with American engineers, conductors, machinists, boiler-makers, carpenters. From the top to the bottom these men are so hardy, so efficient, so energetic, that it is a real pleasure to look at them. Stevens, the head engineer, is a big fellow, a man of daring and good sense, and burly power. All of these men are quite as formidable, and would, if it were necessary, do quite as much in battle as the crews of Drake and Morgan; but as it is, they are doing a work of infinitely more lasting consequence. Nothing whatever remains to show what Drake and Morgan did. They produced no real effect down here, but Stevens and his men are changing the face of the continent, are doing the greatest engineering feat of the ages, and the effect of their work will be felt while our civilization lasts. I went over everything that I could possibly go over in the time at my disposal. I examined the quarters of married and single men, white men and negroes. I went over the ground of the Gatun and La Boca dams; went through Panama and Colon, and spent a day in the Culebra cut, where the great work is being done.

There the huge steam-shovels are hard at it; scooping huge masses of rock and gravel and dirt previously loosened by the drillers and dynamite blasters, loading it on trains which take it away to some dump, either in the jungle or where the dams are to be built. They are eating steadily into the mountain, cutting it down and down. Little tracks are laid on the side-hills, rocks blasted out, and the great ninety-five ton steam-shovels work up like mountain howitzers until they come to where they can with advantage begin their work of eating into and destroying the mountainside. With intense energy men and machines do their task, the white men supervising matters and handling the machines, while the tens of thousands of black men do the rough manual labor where it is not worth while to have machines do it. It is an epic feat, and one of immense significance.

The deluge of rain meant that many of the villages were knee-deep in water, while the flooded rivers tore through the tropic forests. It is a real tropic forest,

PRESIDENT ROOSEVELT *discussing America's task with workmen at Bas Obispo, Panama Canal, November 26, 1906.*

palms and bananas, breadfruit trees, bamboos, lofty ceibas, and gorgeous butterflies and brilliant colored birds fluttering among the orchids. There are beautiful flowers, too.

All my old enthusiasm for natural history seemed to revive, and I would have given a good deal to have stayed and tried to collect specimens. It would be a good hunting country too; deer, and now and then jaguars and tapir, and great birds that they call wild turkeys; there are alligators in the rivers. One of the trained nurses from a hospital went to bathe in a pool last August and an alligator grabbed him by the legs and was making off with him, but was fortunately scared away, leaving the man badly injured.

I tramped everywhere through the mud. Mother did not do the roughest work, and had time to see more of the really picturesque and beautiful side of the life, and really enjoyed herself.

P.S. The Gatun dam will make a lake miles long, and the railroad now goes on what will be the bottom of this lake, and it was curious to think that in a few years great ships would be floating in water 100 feet above where we were.
✳ ✳ ✳

U.S.S. *Louisiana,*
At Sea, November 23, 1906.

DEAR KERMIT:
We had a most interesting two days at Porto Rico. We landed on the south side of the island and were received by the Governor and the rest of the administration, including nice Mr. Laurance Grahame; then were given a reception by the Alcalde and people of Ponce; and then went straight across the island in automobiles to San Juan on the north shore. It was an eighty mile trip and really delightful. The road wound up to the high mountains of the middle island, through them, and then down again to the flat plain on the north shore. The scenery was beautiful. It was as thoroughly tropical as Panama but much more livable. There were palms, tree-ferns, bananas, mangoes, bamboos, and many other trees and multitudes of brilliant flowers. There was one vine called the dream-vine with flowers as big as great white water-lilies, which close up

COPYRIGHT 1906
BY
WALDROP PHOTOGRAPHIC CO.
SAN JUAN, P.R.

**PRESIDENT THEODORE ROOSEVELT** *during his tour of Rio Piedras, Puerto Rico, 1906.*

tight in the day-time and bloom at night. There were vines with masses of brilliant purple and pink flowers, and others with masses of little white flowers, which at night-time smell deliciously. There were trees studded over with huge white flowers, and others, the flamboyants such as I saw in the campaign at Santiago, are a mass of large scarlet blossoms in June, but which now had shed them. I thought the tree-ferns especially beautiful. The towns were just such as you saw in Cuba, quaint, brilliantly colored, with the old church or cathedral fronting the plaza, and the plaza always full of flowers. Of course the towns are dirty, but they are not nearly as dirty and offensive as those of Italy; and there is something pathetic and childlike about the people. We are giving them a good government and the island is prospering. I never saw a finer set of young fellows than those engaged in the administration. Mr. Grahame, whom of course you remember, is the intimate friend and ally of the leaders of the administration, that is of Governor Beekman Winthrop and of the Secretary of State, Mr. Regis Post. Grahame is a perfect trump and such a handsome, athletic fellow, and a real Sir Galahad. Any wrong-doing, and especially any cruelty makes him flame with fearless indignation. He perfectly delighted the Porto Ricans and also immensely puzzled them by coming in his Scotch kilt to a Government ball. Accordingly, at my special request, I had him wear his kilt at the state dinner and reception the night we were at the palace. You know he is a descendant of Montrose, and although born in Canada, his parents were Scotch and he was educated in Scotland. Do tell Mr. Bob Fergie about him and his kilts when you next write him.

We spent the night at the palace, which is half palace and half castle, and was the residence of the old Spanish governors. It is nearly four hundred years old, and is a delightful building, with quaint gardens and a quaint sea-wall looking over the bay. There were colored lanterns lighting up the gardens for the reception, and the view across the bay in the moonlight was lovely. Our rooms were as attractive as possible too, except that they were so very airy and open that we found it difficult to sleep—not that that much mattered as, thanks to the earliness of our start and the lateness of our reception, we had barely four hours in which we even tried to sleep.

The next morning we came back in automobiles over different and even more beautiful roads. The mountain passes through and over which we went made

us feel as if we were in a tropic Switzerland. We had to cross two or three rivers where big cream-colored oxen with yokes tied to their horns pulled the automobiles through the water. At one funny little village we had an open air lunch, very good, of chicken and eggs and bread, and some wine contributed by a wealthy young Spaniard who rode up from a neighboring coffee ranch.

Yesterday afternoon we embarked again, and that evening the crew gave a theatrical entertainment on the afterdeck, closing with three boxing bouts. I send you the program. It was great fun, the audience being equally enraptured with the sentimental songs about the flag, and the sailor's true love and his mother, and with the jokes (the most relished of which related to the fact that bed-bugs were supposed to be so large that they had to be shot!) and the skits about the commissary and various persons and deeds on the ship. In a way the freedom of comment reminded me a little of the Roman triumphs, when the excellent legendaries recited in verse and prose, anything they chose concerning the hero in whose deeds they had shared and whose triumphs they were celebrating. The stage, well lighted, was built on the aftermost part of the deck. We sat in front with the officers, and the sailors behind us in masses on the deck, on the aftermost turrets, on the bridge, and even in the fighting top of the aftermost mast. It was interesting to see their faces in the light.

P.S. I forgot to tell you about the banners and inscriptions of welcome to me in Porto Rico. One of them which stretched across the road had on it "Welcome to Theodore and Mrs. Roosevelt." Last evening I really enjoyed a rather funny experience. There is an Army and Navy Union composed chiefly of enlisted men, but also of many officers, and they suddenly held a "garrison" meeting in the torpedo-room of this ship. There were about fifty enlisted men together with the Captain and myself. I was introduced as "comrade and shipmate Theodore Roosevelt, President of the United States." They were such a nice set of fellows, and I was really so pleased to be with them; so self-respecting, so earnest, and just the right type out of which to make the typical American fighting man who is also a good citizen. The meeting reminded me a good deal of a lodge meeting at Oyster Bay; and of course those men are fundamentally of the same type as the shipwrights, railroad men and fishermen whom I met at the lodge, and who, by the way, are my chief backers politically and are the men who make up the real strength of this nation.

A FEW MORE PASSAGES from Roosevelt's autobiography find him reflecting further on his legacy, both domestic and foreign. In the first, he reiterates his progressive, populist views on labor; and in the second, he answers his critics on the subject of the Panama Canal. "By far the most important action I took in foreign affairs during the time I was President related to the Panama Canal," he insists, setting forth for posterity his justification for the project. Ultimately, he relies on a quote by his Secretary of State and political ally John Hay for the final word on the subject: "The action of the President in the Panama matter is not only in the strictest accordance with the principles of justice and equity, and in line with all the best precedents of our public policy, but it was the only course he could have taken in compliance with our treaty rights and obligations."

# Social and Industrial Justice

THEODORE ROOSEVELT *at his desk, 1901.*

By the time I became President I had grown to feel with deep intensity of conviction that governmental agencies must find their justification largely in the way in which they are used for the practical betterment of living and working conditions among the mass of the people. I felt that the fight was really for the abolition of privilege; and one of the first stages in the battle was necessarily to fight for the rights of the workingman. For this reason I felt most strongly that all that the government could do in the interest of labor should be done. The Federal Government can rarely act with the directness that the State governments act. It can, however, do a good deal. My purpose was to make the National Government itself a model employer of labor, the effort being to make the per diem employee just as much as the Cabinet officer regard himself as one of the partners employed in the service of the public, proud of his work, eager to do it in the best possible manner, and confident of just treatment. Our aim was also to secure good laws wherever the National Government had power, notably in the Territories, in the District of Columbia, and in connection with inter-State commerce. . . .

# The Monroe Doctrine and the Panama Canal

*This* ILLUSTRATION FROM THE NOVEMBER 14, 1906, EDITION OF *PUCK* *Magazine shows Theodore Roosevelt, dressed as a Rough Rider, leading a group of laborers, armed with shovels, to work on the Panama Canal. The man in the background wearing a hat labeled "Jake" may refer to John F. Stevens, who took over the chief engineer position for the canal construction in 1905.*

The Monroe Doctrine lays down the rule that the Western Hemisphere is not hereafter to be treated as subject to settlement and occupation by Old World powers. It is not international law; but it is a cardinal principle of our foreign policy. There is no difficulty at the present day in maintaining this doctrine, save where the American power whose interest is threatened has shown itself in international matters both weak and delinquent. The great and prosperous civilized commonwealths, such as the Argentine, Brazil, and Chile, in the Southern half of South America, have advanced so far that they no longer stand in any position of tutelage toward the United States. They occupy toward us precisely the position that Canada occupies. Their friendship is the friendship of equals for equals. My view was that as regards these nations there was no more necessity for asserting the Monroe Doctrine than there was to assert it in regard to Canada. They were competent to assert it for themselves. Of course if one of these nations, or if Canada, should be overcome by some Old World power, which then proceeded to occupy its territory, we would undoubtedly, if the American Nation needed our help, give it in order to prevent such occupation from taking place. But the initiative would come from the Nation itself, and the United States would merely act as a friend whose help was invoked.

The case was (and is) widely different as regards certain—not all—of the tropical states in the neighborhood of the Caribbean Sea. Where these states are stable and prosperous, they stand on a footing of absolute equality with all other communities. But some of them have been a prey to such continuous revolutionary misrule as to have grown impotent either to do their duties to outsiders or to enforce their rights against outsiders. The United States has not the slightest desire to make aggressions on any one of these states. On the contrary, it will submit to much from them without showing resentment. If any great civilized power, Russia or Germany, for instance, had behaved toward us as Venezuela under Castro behaved, this country would have gone to war at once. We did not go to war with Venezuela merely because our people declined to be irritated by the actions of a weak opponent, and showed a forbearance which probably went beyond the limits of wisdom in refusing to take umbrage at what was done by the weak; although we would certainly have resented it had it been done by the strong. In the case of two states, however, affairs reached such a crisis that we had to act. These two states were Santo Domingo and the then owner of the Isthmus of Panama, Colombia. ✳ ✳ ✳

> "If any great civilized power, Russia or Germany, for instance, had behaved toward us as Venezuela under Castro behaved, this country would have gone to war at once."

**BY FAR THE MOST IMPORTANT ACTION I** took in foreign affairs during the time I was President related to the Panama Canal. Here again there was much accusation about my having acted in an "unconstitutional" manner—a position which can be upheld only if Jefferson's action in acquiring Louisiana be also treated as unconstitutional; and at different stages of the affair believers in a do-nothing policy denounced me as

having "usurped authority"—which meant, that when nobody else could or would exercise efficient authority, I exercised it. ✳ ✳ ✳

**FOR NEARLY FIFTY YEARS** we had asserted the right to prevent the closing of this highway of commerce [the Isthmus of Panama]. Secretary of State Cass in 1858 officially stated the American position as follows:

*Sovereignty has its duties as well as its rights, and none of these local governments, even if administered with more regard to the just demands of*

*In this July 1, 1902,* LETTER TO SECRETARY OF STATE JOHN HAY, *Roosevelt asserted his belief that the building of the Panama Canal would be one of the most significant achievements of the twentieth century.*

*other nations than they have been, would be per-*
*mitted, in a spirit of Eastern isolation, to close*
*the gates of intercourse of the great highways of*
*the world, and justify the act by the pretension*
*that these avenues of trade and travel belong to*
*them and that they choose to shut them, or, what*
*is almost equivalent, to encumber them with such*
*unjust relations as would prevent their general use.*

We had again and again been forced to intervene to protect the transit across the Isthmus, and the intervention was frequently at the request of Colombia herself. The effort to build a canal by private capital had been made under De Lesseps and had resulted in lamentable failure. Every serious proposal to build the canal in such manner had been abandoned. The United States had repeatedly announced that we would not permit it to be built or controlled by any old-world government. Colombia was utterly impotent to build it herself. Under these circumstances it had become a matter of imperative obligation that we should build it ourselves without further delay.

I took final action in 1903. During the preceding fifty-three years the Governments of New Granada and of its successor, Colombia, had been in a constant state of flux; and the State of Panama had sometimes been treated as almost independent, in a loose Federal league, and sometimes as the mere property of the Government at Bogota; and there had been innumerable appeals to arms, sometimes of adequate, sometimes for inadequate, reasons. ✳ ✳ ✳

. . . [F]ROM THE BEGINNING there had been acceptance of our right to insist on free transit, in whatever form was best, across the Isthmus; and that towards the end there had been a no less universal feeling that it was our duty to the world to provide this transit in the shape of a canal—the resolution of the Pan-American Congress was practically a mandate to this effect. Colombia was then under a one-man government, a dictatorship, founded on usurpation of absolute and irre-

sponsible power. She eagerly pressed us to enter into an agreement with her, as long as there was any chance of our going to the alternative route through Nicaragua. When she thought we were committed, she refused to fulfill the agreement, with the avowed hope of seizing the French company's property for nothing and thereby holding us up. This was a bit of pure bandit morality. It would have achieved its purpose had I possessed as weak moral fiber as those of my critics who announced that I ought to have confined my action to feeble scolding and temporizing until the opportunity for action passed. I did not lift my finger to incite the revolutionists. The right simile to use is totally different. I simply ceased to stamp out the different revolutionary fuses that were already burning. When Colombia committed flagrant wrong against us, I considered it no part of my duty to aid and abet her in her wrongdoing at our expense, and also at the expense of Panama, of the French company, and of the world generally. There had been fifty years of continuous bloodshed and civil strife in Panama; because of my action Panama has now known ten years of such peace and prosperity as she never before saw during the four centuries of her existence—for in Panama, as in Cuba and Santo Domingo, it was the action of the American people, against the outcries of the professed apostles of peace, which alone brought peace. We gave to the people of Panama self-government, and freed them from subjection to alien oppressors. We did our best to get Colombia to let us treat her with a more than generous justice; we exercised patience to beyond the verge of proper forbearance. When we did act and recognize Panama, Colombia at once acknowledged her own guilt by promptly offering to do what we had demanded, and what she had protested it was not in her power to do. But the offer came too late. What we would gladly have done before, it had by that time become impossible for us honorably to do; for it would have necessitated our abandoning the people of Panama, our friends, and turning them over to their and our foes, who would have wreaked vengeance on them precisely because they had shown friendship to us. Colombia was solely responsible

for her own humiliation; and she had not then, and has not now, one shadow of claim upon us, moral or legal; all the wrong that was done was done by her. If, as representing the American people, I had not acted precisely as I did, I would have been an unfaithful or incompetent representative; and inaction at that crisis would have meant not only indefinite delay in building the canal, but also practical admission on our part that we were not fit to play the part on the Isthmus which we had arrogated to ourselves. I acted on my own responsibility in the Panama matter. John Hay spoke of this action as follows: "The action of the President in the Panama matter is not only in the strictest accordance with the principles of justice and equity, and in line with all the best precedents of our public policy, but it was the only course he could have taken in compliance with our treaty rights and obligations."

PRESIDENT THEODORE ROOSEVELT *posing in a steam shovel at Culebra Cut, Panama Canal, November, 1906.*

# LETTER HOME FROM A TRIP DOWN THE MISSISSIPPI RIVER

**BY THE FALL OF 1907,** when Roosevelt wrote to his son from a stern-wheeler on the Mississippi, he had announced his support of Taft as the next president and was operating as something of a "lone wolf," having alienated many of his colleagues in the party. He must have found some satisfaction in the fact that he could still attract a sizable and devoted crowd when he traveled.

On Board U.S.S. *Mississippi*,
October 1, 1907.

PRESIDENT THEODORE ROOSEVELT AND CHIEF FORESTER GIFFORD PINCHOT *aboard the steamer* Mississippi *on the trip of the Inland Waterways Commission down the Mississippi River, October 1907.*

DEAR KERMIT: . . .

After speaking at Keokuk this morning we got aboard this brand new stern-wheel steamer of the regular Mississippi type and started down-stream. I went up in the *Texas* and of course felt an almost irresistible desire to ask the pilot about Mark Twain. It is a broad, shallow, muddy river, at places the channel being barely wide enough for the boat to go through, though to my inexperienced eyes the whole river looks like a channel. The bottom lands, Illinois on one side and Missouri on the other, are sometimes over-grown with forests and sometimes great rich cornfields, with here and there a house, here and there villages, and now and then a little town. At every such place all the people of the neighborhood have gathered to greet me. The water-front of the towns would be filled with a dense packed mass of men, women, and children, waving flags. The little villages have not only their own population, but also the farmers who have driven in in their wagons with their wives and children from a dozen miles back—just such farmers as came to see you and the cavalry on your march through Iowa last summer.

It is my first trip on the Mississippi, and I am greatly interested in it. How wonderful in its rapidity of movement has been the history of our country, compared with the history of the old world. For untold ages this river had been flowing through the lonely continent, not very greatly changed since the close of the Pleistocene. During all these myriads of years the prairie and the forest came down to its banks. The immense herds of the buffalo and the elk wandered along them season after season, and the Indian hunters on foot or in canoes trudged along the banks or skimmed the water. Probably a thousand

years saw no change that would have been noticeable to our eyes. Then three centuries ago began the work of change. For a century its effects were not perceptible. Just nothing but an occasional French fleet or wild half savage French-Canadian explorer passing up or down the river or one of its branches in an Indian canoe; then the first faint changes, the building of one or two little French fur traders' hamlets, the passing of one or two British officers' boats, and the very rare appearance of the uncouth American backwoodsman.

Then the change came with a rush. Our settlers reached the head-waters of the Ohio, and flatboats and keel-boats began to go down to the mouth of the Mississippi, and the Indians and the game they followed began their last great march to the west. For ages they had marched back and forth, but from this march there was never to be a return. Then the day of steamboat traffic began, and the growth of the first American cities and states along the river with their strength and their squalor and their raw pride. Then this mighty steamboat traffic passed its zenith and collapsed, and for a generation the river towns have dwindled compared with the towns which took their importance from the growth of the railroads. I think of it all as I pass down the river.

October 4. . . . We are steaming down the river now between Tennessee and Arkansas. The forest comes down a little denser to the bank, the houses do not look quite so well kept; otherwise there is not much change. There are a dozen steamers accompanying us, filled with delegates from various river cities. The people are all out on the banks to greet us still. Moreover, at night, no matter what the hour is that we pass a town, it is generally illuminated, and sometimes whistles and noisy greetings, while our steamboats whistle in equally noisy response, so that our sleep is apt to be broken. Seventeen governors of different states are along, in a boat by themselves. I have seen a good deal of them, however, and it has been of real use to me, especially as regards two or three problems that are up. At St. Louis there was an enormous multitude of people out to see us. The procession was in a drenching rain, in which I stood bareheaded, smiling affably and waving my drowned hat to those hardy members of the crowd who declined to go to shelter. At Cairo, I was also greeted with great enthusiasm, and I was interested to find that there was still extreme bitterness felt over Dickens's description of the town and the people in "Martin Chuzzlewit" sixty-five years ago.

# FINAL
# FRONTIER

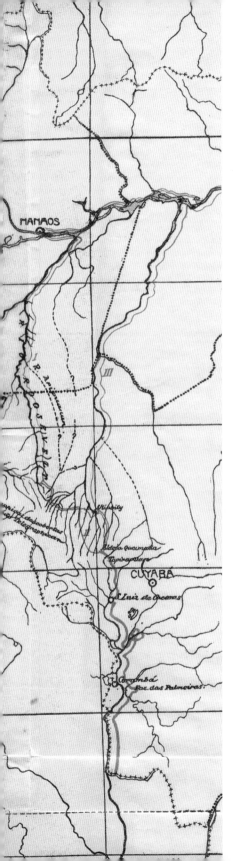

IN HIS LIFE AFTER THE WHITE HOUSE, Roosevelt had no shortage of interests to occupy his time—and though he was no longer as "vigorous" as he'd once been, adventure remained his top priority.

In October 1913, he and Edith set sail for South America, visiting Brazil, Uruguay, Argentina, and Chile, before he set off across the Andes on horseback (now with Kermit) and traveled through Argentina and Paraguay to southern Brazil—where the *real* adventure was to begin! It was there that he joined a Brazilian expedition led by Colonel Candido Rondon planning to explore the uncharted waters of the Rio da Duvida (River of Doubt). Their intention was to work their way to its headwaters, hunting jaguars, boar, and other animals along the way, then trace the river north all the way to the Amazon.

In addition to Roosevelt and Kermit, the group included a naturalist from the American Museum of Natural History, a doctor, and 16 paddlers and porters. Setting off in early December, the height of the rainy season, the travelers reached the river on February 27, 1914, and started down. It proved to be a horrific trip for Roosevelt, who, in addition to suffering from severe dysentery, sustained a leg injury that resulted in painfully infected abscesses. In a state of feverish delirium, he alternated between reciting Coleridge's "Kubla Khan" and urging Kermit to leave him behind as the accident-plagued party's supplies dwindled and several other men perished.

*overleaf:* **THEODORE ROOSEVELT'S EXPLORATION TEAM** *in Brazil, 1913.*

*opposite:* **THEODORE ROOSEVELT** *kneeling beside a slain jaguar during a hunt on the Rio Taquari in Brazil, 1913.*

*left:* **MAP OF THE ROOSEVELT-RONDON EXPEDITION** *in Brazil, 1914.*

With the constant attention of Kermit and the doctor, Roosevelt survived the trip—but he had contracted malaria, lost more than 50 pounds, and could barely walk when he finally made it back to New York on May 19. He would suffer the physical consequences of that adventure for the rest of his life, and it is generally believed that his death was hastened by it. The Brazilian government would rename the river Rio Roosevelt in his honor.

With the world at war, Roosevelt did not lose his interest in politics—or his insistence on airing his views. His *America and the World War,* published in early 1915, roundly criticized President Wilson for his lack of military preparedness and his soft touch in dealing with the civil war in Mexico as well as his insufficiently firm stand against the Germans in Europe.

Roosevelt declined the opportunity to run as the Progressive Party's candidate for President in 1916, endorsing Republican Charles Evan Hughes and continuing to assail Wilson's administration on every front. Nevertheless, Wilson managed to land a second term.

THEODORE ROOSEVELT, *by Pirie MacDonald.*

The United States officially declared war on Germany on April 6, 1917, and Roosevelt, weakened though he was, could no longer stand by. Four days later, he met with the President to request permission to raise a volunteer division and lead them into battle in France, much as he had done in Cuba two decades earlier. No doubt wisely, Wilson declined his offer. But the next generation of Roosevelts did step into the fray: Ted and Archie went to France as commissioned officers; Kermit joined the British forces in Mesopotamia; and Quentin, Roosevelt's youngest and favorite, left for France in July, having trained as a fighter pilot.

Forced to confine his participation in the war effort to speaking and writing, Roosevelt remained a thorn in Wilson's side, criticizing him for everything from failing to properly equip the troops to attempting to suppress his critics. The former President remained active in other arenas as well, continuing to fight for the social causes he'd dedicated himself to and becoming a guiding spirit to the Boy Scouts of America.

THE ROOSEVELT FAMILY, *1918. Back left to right: Richard Derby, husband of Ethel Roosevelt; Eleanor Butler Alexander Roosevelt, wife of Ted Jr.; and Kermit Roosevelt; Archie Roosevelt in front. Theodore Jr. received a Medal of Honor, and Archie, who was discharged with full medical disability in 1917, received a Croix de Guerre from the French government. Quentin was shot down and killed near Rheims in 1918.*

# A MAN OF NATURE

There was nothing more precious to Roosevelt than the natural wonders of the world. After overcoming childhood health problems, he spent much of his life camping, fishing, hunting, exploring, studying, and enjoying the outdoors. While President, he designated an unprecedented:

- ✳ 150 National Forests
- ✳ 51 Bird Reservations
- ✳ 5 National Parks
- ✳ 18 National Monuments
- ✳ 4 National Game Preserves
- ✳ 21 Reclamation Projects

In all, he provided Federal protection for almost 120 million acres of American land—equivalent to the total area of the East Coast states from Maine to Florida!

THEODORE ROOSEVELT *on horseback, c. 1900–10.*

# HISTORY AS LITERATURE

American Historical Association—Boston, Mass.

December 27, 1912

IN DECEMBER OF 1912—a month after Roosevelt and his Bull Moose Party lost the election to Woodrow Wilson (and two months after being shot in the chest while campaigning)—Roosevelt did become president once more: of the American Historical Association. A condensed version of his address to that group on the occasion of his election reveals his dizzying erudition and breadth of knowledge in the fields of literature, philosophy, and art, as well as history and science. In a way, these ruminations circle back to the young Roosevelt's conversations with his father about the merits of a future in science versus business, law, or politics. Ultimately, he left no discipline aside in his lifelong thirst for enlightenment.

There has been much discussion as to whether history should not henceforth be treated as a branch of science rather than of literature. As with most such discussions, much of the matter in dispute has referred merely to terminology. Moreover, as regards part of the discussion, the minds of the contestants have not met, the propositions advanced by the two sides being neither mutually incompatible nor mutually relevant. There is, however, a real basis for conflict in so far as science claims exclusive possession of the field.

There was a time—we see it in the marvellous dawn of Hellenic life—when history was distinguished neither from poetry, from mythology, nor from the first dim beginnings of science. There was a more recent time, at the opening of Rome's brief period of literary splendor, when poetry was accepted by a great scientific philosopher as the appropriate vehicle for teaching the lessons of science and philosophy. There was a more recent time still—the time of Holland's leadership in arms and arts—when one of the two or three greatest world painters put his genius at the service of anatomists.

In each case the steady growth of specialization has rendered such combination now impossible. Virgil left history to Livy; and when Tacitus had become possible Lucan was a rather absurd anachronism. The elder Darwin, when he endeavored to combine the functions of scientist and poet, may have thought of Lucretius as a model; but the great Darwin was incapable of such a mistake. The surgeons of to-day would prefer the services of a good photographer to those of Rembrandt—even were those of Rembrandt available. No one would now dream of combining the history of the Trojan War with a poem on the

wrath of Achilles. Beowulf's feats against the witch who dwelt under the water would not now be mentioned in the same matter-of-fact way that a Frisian or Frankish raid is mentioned. We are long past the stage when we would accept as parts of the same epic Siegfried's triumphs over dwarf and dragon, and even a distorted memory of the historic Hunnish king in whose feast-hall the Burgundian heroes held their last revel and made their death fight. We read of the loves of the Hound of Muirthemne and Emer the Fair without attributing to the chariot-riding heroes who "fought" over the ears of their horses" and to their fierce lady-loves more than a symbolic reality. The Roland of the Norman trouvères, the Roland who blew the ivory horn at Roncesvalles, is to our minds

wholly distinct from the actual Warden of the Marches who fell in a rear-guard skirmish with the Pyrenean Basques.

As regards philosophy, as distinguished from material science and from history, the specialization has been incomplete. Poetry is still used as a vehicle for the teaching of philosophy. Goethe was as profound a thinker as Kant. He has influenced the thought of mankind far more deeply than Kant because he was also a great poet. Robert Browning was a real philosopher, and his writings have had a hundredfold the circulation and the effect of those of any similar philosopher who wrote in prose, just because, and only because, what he wrote was not merely philosophy but literature. The form in which he wrote challenged attention and provoked admiration. That part of his work which some of us—which I myself, for instance—most care for is merely poetry. But in that part of his work which has exercised most attraction and has given him the widest reputation, the poetry, the form of expression, bears to the thought expressed much the same relation that the expression of Lucretius bears to the thought of Lucretius. As regards this, the great mass of his product, he is primarily a philosopher, whose writings surpass in value those of other similar philosophers precisely because they are not only philosophy but literature. In other words, Browning the philosopher is read by countless thousands to whom otherwise philosophy would be a sealed book, for exactly the same reason that Macaulay the historian is read by countless thousands to whom otherwise history would be a sealed book; because both Browning's works and Macaulay's works are material additions to the great sum of English literature. Philosophy is a science just as history is a science. There is need in one case as in the other for vivid and powerful presentation of scientific matter in literary form.

This does not mean that there is the like need in the two cases. History can never be truthfully presented if the presentation is purely emotional. It can never be truthfully or usefully presented unless profound research, patient, laborious, painstaking, has preceded the presentation. No amount of self-communion and of pondering on the soul of mankind, no gorgeousness of literary imagery, can take the place of cool, serious, widely extended study. The vision of the great historian must be both wide and lofty. But it must be sane, clear, and based on full knowledge of the facts and of their interrelations. Otherwise we get merely a splendid bit of serious romance-writing, like Carlyle's "French Revolution." Many hard-working students, alive to the deficiencies of this kind of romance-writing, have grown to distrust not only all historical writing that is romantic, but all historical writing that is vivid. They feel that complete truthfulness must never be sacrificed to color. In this they are right. They also feel that complete truthfulness is incompatible with color. In this they are wrong. The immense importance of full knowledge of a mass of dry facts and gray details has so impressed them as to make them feel that the dryness and the grayness are in themselves meritorious.

These students have rendered invaluable service to history. They are right in many of their contentions. They see how literature and science have specialized. They realize that scientific methods are as necessary to the proper study of history as to the proper study of astronomy or zoology. They know that in many, perhaps in most, of its forms, literary ability is divorced from the restrained devotion to the actual fact which is as essential to the historian as to the scientist. They know that nowadays science ostentatiously disclaims any connection with literature. They feel that if this is essential for science, it is no less essential for history.

There is much truth in all these contentions. Nevertheless, taking them all together, they do not indicate what these hard-working students believed that they indicate. Because history, science, and literature have all become specialized, the theory now is that science is definitely severed from literature and that history must follow suit. Not only do I refuse to accept this as true for history, but I do not even accept it as true for science.

Literature may be defined as that which has permanent interest because both of its substance and its form, aside from the mere technical value that inheres in a special treatise for specialists. For a great work of literature there is the same demand now that there always has been; and in any great work of literature the first element is great imaginative power. The imaginative power demanded for a great historian is different from that demanded for a great poet; but it is no less marked. Such imaginative power is in no sense incompatible with minute accuracy. On the contrary, very accurate, very real and vivid, presentation of the past can come only from one in whom the imaginative gift is strong. The industrious collector of dead facts bears to such a man precisely the relation that a photographer bears to Rembrandt. There are innumerable books, that is, innumerable volumes of printed matter between covers, which are excellent for their own purposes, but in which imagination would be as wholly out of place as in the blue prints of a sewer system or in the photographs taken to illustrate a work on comparative osteology. But the vitally necessary sewer system does not take the place of the cathedral of Rheims or of the Parthenon; no quantity of photographs will ever be equivalent to one Rembrandt; and the greatest mass of data, although indispensable to the work of a great historian, is in no shape or way a substitute for that work.

History, taught for a directly and immediately useful purpose to pupils and the teachers of pupils, is one of the necessary features of a sound education in democratic citizenship. A book containing such sound teaching, even if without any literary quality, may be as useful to the student and as creditable to the writer as a similar book on medicine. I am not slighting such a book when I say that, once it has achieved its worthy purpose, it can be permitted to lapse from human memory as a good book on medicine, which has outlived its usefulness, lapses from memory. But the historical work which does possess literary quality may be a permanent contribution to the sum of man's wisdom, enjoyment, and inspiration. The writer of such a book must add wisdom to knowledge, and the gift of expression to the gift of imagination.

The work of the archeologist, the work of the anthropologist, the work of the palaeo-ethnologist—out of all these a great literary historian may gather material indispensable for his use. He, and we, ought fully to acknowledge our debt to the collectors of these indispensable facts. The investigator in any line may do work which puts us all under lasting obligations to him, even though he be totally deficient in the art of literary expression, that is, totally deficient in the ability to convey vivid and lifelike pictures to others of the past whose secrets he has laid bare. I would give no scanty or grudging acknowledgment to the deeds of such a man. He does a lasting service; whereas the man who tries to make literary expression cover his ignorance or misreading of facts renders less than no service. But the service done is immeasurably increased in value when the man arises who from his study of a myriad dead fragments is able to paint some living picture of the past.

This is why the record as great writers preserve it has a value immeasurably beyond what is merely lifeless. Such a record pulses with immortal life. It may recount the deed or the thought of a hero at some supreme moment. It may be merely the portrayal of homely every-day life. This matters not, so long as in either event the genius of the historian enables him to paint in colors that do not fade. The cry of the Ten Thousand when they first saw the sea still stirs the hearts of men. The ruthless death scene between Jehu and Jezebel; wicked Ahab, smitten by the chance arrow, and propped in his chariot until he died at sundown; Josiah, losing his life because he would not heed the Pharaoh's solemn warning, and mourned by all the singing men and all the singing women—the fates of these kings and of this king's daughter, are part of the common stock of knowledge of mankind. They were petty rulers of petty principalities; yet, compared with them, mighty conquerors, who added empire to empire, Shalmaneser and Sargon, Amenhotep and Rameses, are but shadows; for the deeds and the deaths of the kings of Judah and Israel are written in words that, once read, can not be forgotten. The Peloponnesian War bulks of unreal size to-day because it once seemed thus to bulk to a master mind. Only a great historian can fittingly deal with a very great subject; yet because the qualities of chief interest in human history can be shown on a small field no less than on a large one, some of the greatest historians have treated subjects that only their own genius rendered great.

The true historian will bring the past before our eyes as if it were the present. He will make us see as living men the hard-faced archers of Agincourt, and

GENERAL GRANT RECONNOITERING THE CONFEDERATE POSITION. FROM A SKETCH MADE AT THE TIME.

ILLUSTRATION OF GENERAL ULYSSES S. GRANT *from* Hero Tales from American History, *by Theodore Roosevelt and Henry Cabot Lodge, published in 1895.*

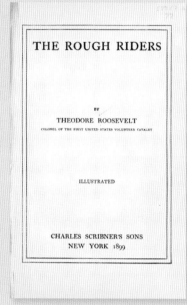

*Title page for the first edition of Roosevelt's* THE ROUGH RIDERS, *published in 1899.*

THE ROUGH RIDERS

BY

THEODORE ROOSEVELT

COLONEL OF THE FIRST UNITED STATES VOLUNTEER CAVALRY

ILLUSTRATED

CHARLES SCRIBNER'S SONS
NEW YORK 1899

the war-worn spearmen who followed Alexander down beyond the rim of the known world. We shall hear grate on the coast of Britain the keels of the Low-Dutch sea-thieves whose children's children were to inherit unknown continents. We shall thrill to the triumphs of Hannibal. Gorgeous in our sight will rise the splendor of dead cities, and the might of the elder empires of which the very ruins crumbled to dust ages ago. Along ancient trade-routes, across the world's waste spaces, the caravans shall move; and the admirals of uncharted seas shall furrow the oceans with their lonely prows. Beyond the dim centuries we shall see the banners float above armed hosts. We shall see conquerors riding forward to victories that have changed the course of time. We shall listen to the prophecies of forgotten seers. Ours shall be the dreams of dreamers who dreamed greatly, who saw in their vision peaks so lofty that never yet have they been reached by the sons and daughters of men. Dead poets shall sing to us the deeds of men of might and the love and the beauty of women. We shall see the dancing girls of Memphis. The scent of the flowers in the Hanging Gardens of Babylon will be heavy to our senses. We shall sit at feast with the kings of Nineveh when they drink from ivory and gold. With Queen Maeve in her sun-parlor we shall watch the nearing chariots of the champions. For us the war-horns of King Olaf shall wail across the flood, and the harps sound high at festivals in forgotten halls. The frowning strongholds of the barons of old shall rise before us, and the white palace-castles from whose windows Syrian princes once looked across the blue Ægean. We shall know the valor of the two-sworded Samurai. Ours shall be the hoary wisdom and the strange, crooked folly of the immemorial civilizations which tottered to a living death in India and in China. We shall see the terrible horsemen of Timur the Lame ride over the roof of the world; we shall hear the drums beat as the armies of Gustavus and Frederick and Napoleon drive forward to victory. Ours shall be the woe of burgher and peasant, and ours the stern joy when freemen triumph and justice comes to her own. The agony of the galley-slaves shall be ours, and the rejoicing when the wicked are brought low and the men of evil days have their reward. We shall see the glory of triumphant violence, and the revel of those who do wrong in high places; and the broken-hearted despair that lies beneath the glory and the revel. We shall also see the supreme righteousness of the wars for freedom and justice, and know that the men who fell in these wars made all mankind their debtors.

Some day the historians will tell us of these things. Some day, too, they will tell our children of the age and the land in which we now live. They will portray the conquest of the continent. They will show the slow beginnings of settlement, the growth of the fishing and trading towns on the seacoast, the hesitating early ventures into the Indian-haunted forest. Then they will show the backwoodsmen, with their long rifles and their light axes, making their way with labor and peril through the wooded wilderness to the Mississippi; and then the endless march of the white-topped wagon-trains across plain and mountain to the coast of the greatest of the five great oceans. They will show how the land which the pioneers won slowly and with incredible hardship was filled in two generations by the overflow from the countries of western and central Europe. The portentous growth of the cities will be shown, and the change from a nation of farmers to a nation of business men and artisans, and all the far-reaching consequences of the rise of the new industrialism. The formation of a new ethnic type in this melting-pot of the nations will be told. The hard materialism of our age will appear, and also the strange capacity for lofty idealism which must be reckoned with by all who would understand the American character. A people whose heroes are Washington and Lincoln, a peaceful people who fought to a finish one of the bloodiest of wars, waged solely for the sake of a great principle and a noble idea, surely possess an emergency-standard far above mere money-getting.

Those who tell the Americans of the future what the Americans of to-day and of yesterday have done, will perforce tell much that is unpleasant. This is but saying that they will describe the arch-typical civilization of this age. Nevertheless, when the tale is finally told, I believe that it will show that the forces working for good in our national life outweigh the forces working for evil, and that, with many blunders and shortcomings, with much halting and turning aside from the path, we shall yet in the end prove our faith by our works, and show in our lives our belief that righteousness exalteth a nation.

**ROOSEVELT'S EXPLOITS IN BRAZIL** proved the most harrowing of his long and eventful life, but out of that trip came one of his most enduringly popular books: *Through the Brazilian Wilderness.* The excerpts that follow provide some details and a taste of his perspective on the journey. Roosevelt had a knack for storytelling: the action sequences are as thrilling as fiction while the descriptions of his surroundings are vividly detailed, as befits a natural scientist. On the subject of what he was feeling during the darkest periods of the journey, however, Roosevelt remains characteristically opaque.

## The Start

One day in 1908, when my presidential term was coming to a close, Father Zahm, a priest whom I knew, came in to call on me. Father Zahm and I had been cronies for some time, because we were both of us fond of Dante and of history and of science—I had always commended to theologians his book, "Evolution and Dogma." He was an Ohio boy, and his early schooling had been obtained in old-time American fashion in a little log school; where, by the way, one of the other boys was Januarius Aloysius MacGahan, afterward the famous war correspondent and friend of Skobeloff. Father Zahm told me that MacGahan even at that time added an utter fearlessness to chivalric tenderness for the weak, and was the defender of any small boy who was oppressed by a larger one. Later Father Zahm was at Notre Dame University, in Indiana, with Maurice Egan, whom, when I was President, I appointed minister to Denmark.

On the occasion in question Father Zahm had just returned from a trip across the Andes and down the Amazon, and came in to propose that after I left the

presidency he and I should go up the Paraguay into the interior of South America. At the time I wished to go to Africa, and so the subject was dropped; but from time to time afterward we talked it over. Five years later, in the spring of 1913, I accepted invitations conveyed through the governments of Argentina and Brazil to address certain learned bodies in these countries. Then it occurred to me that, instead of making the conventional tourist trip purely by sea round South America, after I had finished my lectures I would come north through the middle of the continent into the valley of the Amazon; and I decided to write Father Zahm and tell him my intentions. Before doing so, however, I desired to see the authorities of the American Museum of Natural History, in New York City, to find out whether they cared to have me take a couple of naturalists with me into Brazil and make a collecting trip for the museum.

Accordingly, I wrote to Frank Chapman, the curator of ornithology of the museum, and accepted his invitation to lunch at the museum one day early in June. At the lunch, in addition to various naturalists, to my astonishment I also found Father Zahm; and as soon as I saw him I told him I was now intending to make the South American trip. It appeared that he had made up his mind that he would take it himself, and had actually come on to see Mr. Chapman to find out if the latter could recommend a naturalist to go with him; and he at once said he would accompany me. Chapman was pleased when he found out that we intended to go up the Paraguay and across into the valley of the Amazon, because much of the ground over which we were to pass had not been covered by collectors. He saw Henry Fairfield Osborn, the president of the museum, who wrote me that the museum would be pleased to send under me a couple of naturalists, whom, with my approval, Chapman would choose.

The men whom Chapman recommended were Messrs. George K. Cherrie and Leo E. Miller. I gladly accepted both. The former was to attend chiefly to the ornithology and the latter to the mammalogy of the expedition; but each was to help out the other. No two better men for such a trip could have been found. Both were veterans of the tropical American forests. Miller was a young man, born in Indiana, an enthusiastic with good literary as well as scientific training. He was at the time in the Guiana forests, and joined us at Barbados. Cherrie was an older man, born in Iowa, but now a farmer in Vermont. He had a wife and six children. Mrs. Cherrie had accompanied him during two or three years of their early married life in his collecting trips along the Orinoco. Their second child was born when they were in camp a couple of hundred miles from any white man or woman. One night a few weeks later they were obliged to leave a camping-place, where they had intended to spend the night, because the baby was fretful, and its cries attracted a jaguar, which prowled nearer and nearer in the twilight until they thought it safest once more to put out into the open river and seek a new resting-place. Cherrie had spent about twenty-two years collecting in the American tropics. Like most of the field-naturalists I have met, he was an unusually efficient and fearless man; and willy-nilly he had been forced at times to vary his career by taking part in insurrections. Twice he had been behind the bars in consequence, on one occasion spending three months in a prison of a certain South American state, expecting each day to be taken out and shot. In another state he had, as an interlude to his ornithological pursuits, followed the career of a gun-runner, acting as such off and on for two and a half years. The particular revolutionary chief whose fortunes he was following finally came into power, and Cherrie immortalized his name by naming a new species of ant-thrush after him—a delightful touch, in its practical combination of those not normally kindred pursuits, ornithology and gun-running.

In Anthony Fiala, a former arctic explorer, we found an excellent man for assembling equipment and taking charge of its handling and shipment. In addition to his four years in the arctic regions, Fiala had served in the New York Squadron in Porto Rico during the Spanish War, and through his service in the squadron had been

THEODORE ROOSEVELT AND SON KERMIT, *c. 1910.*

brought into contact with his little Tennessee wife. She came down with her four children to say good-by to him when the steamer left. My secretary, Mr. Frank Harper, went with us. Jacob Sigg, who had served three years in the United States Army, and was both a hospital nurse and a cook, as well as having a natural taste for adventure, went as the personal attendant of Father Zahm. In southern Brazil my son Kermit joined me. He had been bridge building, and a couple of months previously, while on top of a long steel span, something went wrong with the derrick, he and the steel span coming down together on the rocky bed beneath. He escaped with two broken ribs, two teeth knocked out, and a knee partially dislocated, but was practically all right again when he started with us. ✳ ✳ ✳

THE TRIP I PROPOSED TO TAKE can be understood only if there is a slight knowledge of South American topography. The great mountain chain of the Andes extends down the entire length of the western coast, so close to the Pacific Ocean that no rivers of any importance enter it. The rivers of South America drain into the

Atlantic. Southernmost South America, including over half of the territory of the Argentine Republic, consists chiefly of a cool, open plains country. Northward of this country, and eastward of the Andes, lies the great bulk of the South American continent, which is included in the tropical and the subtropical regions. Most of this territory is Brazilian. Aside from certain relatively small stretches drained by coast rivers, this immense region of tropical and subtropical America east of the Andes is drained by the three great river systems of the Plate, the Amazon, and the Orinoco. At their headwaters the Amazon and the Orinoco systems are actually connected by a sluggish natural canal. The headwaters of the northern affluents of the Paraguay and the southern affluents of the Amazon are sundered by a stretch of high land, which toward the east broadens out into the central plateau of Brazil. Geologically this is a very ancient region, having appeared above the waters before the dawning of the age of reptiles, or, indeed, of any true land vertebrates

*A photo taken by Kermit Roosevelt of the* **BRAZILIAN LANDSCAPE,** *1913.*

on the globe. This plateau is a region partly of healthy, rather dry and sandy, open prairie, partly of forest. The great and low-lying basin of the Paraguay, which borders it on the south, is one of the largest, and the still greater basin of the Amazon, which borders it on the north, is the very largest of all the river basins of the earth.

In these basins, but especially in the basin of the Amazon, and thence in most places northward to the Caribbean Sea, lie the most extensive stretches of tropical forest to be found anywhere. The forests of tropical West Africa, and of portions of the Farther-Indian region, are the only ones that can be compared with them. Much difficulty has been experienced in exploring these forests, because under the torrential rains and steaming heat the rank growth of vegetation becomes almost impenetrable, and the streams difficult of navigation; while white men suffer much from the terrible insect scourges and the deadly diseases which modern science has discovered to be due very largely to insect bites. The fauna and flora, however, are of great interest. The American museum was particularly anxious to obtain collections from the divide between the headwaters of the Paraguay and the Amazon, and from the southern affluents of the Amazon. Our purpose was to ascend the Paraguay as nearly as possible to the head of navigation, thence cross to the sources of one of the affluents of the Amazon, and if possible descend it in canoes built on the spot. The Paraguay is regularly navigated as high as boats can go. The starting-point for our trip was to be Asuncion, in the state of Paraguay.

My exact plan of operations was necessarily a little indefinite, but on reaching Rio de Janeiro the minister of foreign affairs, Mr. Lauro Müller, who had been kind enough to take great personal interest in my trip, informed me that he had arranged that on the headwaters of the Paraguay, at the town of Cáceres, I would be met by a Brazilian Army colonel, himself chiefly Indian by blood, Colonel Rondon. Colonel Rondon has been for a quarter of a century the foremost explorer of the Brazilian hinterland. He was at the time in Manaos, but

THEODORE ROOSEVELT *in Rio de Janeiro before the Roosevelt–Rondon Scientific Expedition to the Amazon River, 1913. Dr. Lauro Severiano Müller, Foreign Minister of Brazil and military engineer is to the right of Roosevelt.*

*Roosevelt's* BRAZILIAN EXPEDITION, *1913.*

his lieutenants were in Cáceres and had been notified that we were coming.

More important still, Mr. Lauro Müller—who is not only an efficient public servant but a man of wide cultivation, with a quality about him that reminded me of John Hay—offered to help me make my trip of much more consequence than I had originally intended. He has taken a keen interest in the exploration and development of the interior of Brazil, and he believed that my expedition could be used as a means toward spreading abroad a more general knowledge of the country. He told me that he would co-operate with me in every way if I cared to undertake the leadership of a serious expedition into the unexplored portion of western Matto Grosso, and to attempt the descent of a river which flowed nobody knew whither, but which the best-informed men believed would prove to be a very big river, utterly unknown to geographers. I eagerly and gladly accepted, for I felt that with such help the trip could be made of much scientific value, and that a substantial addition could be made to the geographical knowledge of one of the least-known parts of South America. Accordingly, it was arranged that Colonel Rondon and some assistants and scientists should meet me at or below Corumbá, and that we should attempt the descent of the river, of which they had already come across the headwaters.

I had to travel through Brazil, Uruguay, the Argentine, and Chile for six weeks to fulfill my speaking engagements. Fiala, Cherrie, Miller, and Sigg left me at Rio, continuing to Buenos Aires in the boat in which we had all come down from New York. From Buenos Aires they went up the Paraguay to Corumbá, where they awaited me. The two naturalists went first, to do all the collecting that was possible; Fiala and Sigg travelled more leisurely, with the heavy baggage. ✳ ✳ ✳

OUR TRIP WAS NOT INTENDED as a hunting-trip but as a scientific expedition. Before starting on the trip itself, while travelling in the Argentine, I received certain pieces of first-hand information concerning the natural history of the jaguar, and of the cougar, or puma, which are worth recording. The facts about the jaguar are not new in the sense of casting new light on its character, although they are interesting; but the facts about the behavior of the puma in one district of Patagonia are of great interest, because they give an entirely new side of its life-history."Our trip was not intended as a hunting-trip but as a scientific expedition."

> "Our trip was not intended as a hunting-trip but as a scientific expedition."

There was travelling with me at the time Doctor Francisco P. Moreno, of Buenos Aires. Doctor Moreno is at the present day a member of the National Board of Education of the Argentine, a man who has worked in every way for the benefit of his country, perhaps especially for the benefit of the children, so that when he was first introduced to me it was as the "Jacob Riis of the Argentine"—for they know my deep and affectionate intimacy with Jacob Riis. He is also an eminent man of science, who has done admirable work as a geologist and a geographer. At one period, in connection with his duties as a boundary commissioner on the survey between Chile and the Argentine, he worked for years in Patagonia. It was he who made the extraordinary discovery in a Patagonian cave of the still fresh fragments of skin and other remains of the mylodon, the aberrant horse known as the onohipidium, the huge South American tiger, and the macrauchenia, all of them extinct animals. This discovery showed that some of the strange representatives of the giant South American Pleistocene fauna had lasted down to within a comparatively few thousand years, down to the time when man, substantially as the Spaniards found him, flourished on the continent. Incidentally the discovery tended to show that this fauna had lasted much later in South America than was the case with the corresponding faunas in other parts of the world; and therefore it tended to disprove the claims advanced by Doctor Ameghino for the extreme age, geologically, of this fauna, and for the extreme antiquity of man on the American continent.

# Up the Paraguay

CATTLE ON THE UPPER PARAGUAY RIVER, *photographed by Kermit Roosevelt, 1914.*

At noon on the twelfth [of December] we were at the Brazilian boundary. On this day we here and there came on low, conical hills close to the river. In places the palm groves broke through the belts of deciduous trees and stretched for a mile or so right along the river's bank. At times we passed cattle on the banks or sand-bars, followed by their herders; or a handsome ranch-house, under a cluster of shady trees, some bearing a wealth of red and some a wealth of yellow blossoms; or we saw a horse-corral among the trees close to the brink, with the horses in it and a barefooted man in shirt and trousers leaning against the fence; or a herd of cattle among the palms; or a big tannery or factory or a little native hamlet came in sight. We stopped at one tannery. The owner was a Spaniard, the manager an "Orientál," as he called him-

self, a Uruguayan, of German parentage. The peons, or workers, who lived in a long line of wooden cabins back of the main building, were mostly Paraguayans, with a few Brazilians, and a dozen German and Argentine foremen. There were also some wild Indians, who were camped in the usual squalid fashion of Indians who are hangers-on round the white man but have not yet adopted his ways. Most of the men were at work cutting wood for the tannery. The women and children were in camp. Some individuals of both sexes were naked to the waist. One little girl had a young ostrich as a pet.

Water-fowl were plentiful. We saw large flocks of wild muscovy ducks. Our tame birds come from this wild species and its absurd misnaming dates back to the period when the turkey and guinea-pig were misnamed in similar fashion—our European forefathers taking a large and hazy view of geography, and including Turkey, Guinea, India, and Muscovy as places which, in their capacity of being outlandish, could be comprehensively used as including America. . . .

On the Brazilian boundary we met a shallow river steamer carrying Colonel Candido Mariano da Silva Rondon and several other Brazilian members of the expedition. Colonel Rondon immediately showed that he was all, and more than all, that could be desired. It was evident that he knew his business thoroughly, and it was equally evident that he would be a pleasant companion. He was a classmate of Mr. Lauro Müller at the Brazilian Military Academy. He is of almost pure Indian blood, and is a Positivist—the Positivists are a really strong body in Brazil, as they are in France and indeed in Chile. The colonel's seven children have all been formally made members of the Positivist Church in Rio Janeiro. Brazil possesses the same complete liberty in matters religious, spiritual, and intellectual as we, for our great good fortune, do in the United States, and my Brazilian companions included Catholics and equally sincere men who described themselves as "libres penseurs." Colonel Rondon has spent the last twenty-four years in exploring the western highlands of Brazil, pioneering the way for telegraph-lines and railroads. During that time he has travelled some fourteen thousand miles, on territory most of which had not previously been traversed by civilized man, and has built three thousand miles of telegraph. He has an exceptional knowledge of the Indian tribes and has always zealously endeavored to serve them and indeed to serve the cause of humanity wherever and whenever he was able. Thanks mainly to his efforts, four of the wild tribes of the region he has explored have begun to tread the road of civilization. They have taken the first steps toward becoming Christians. It may seem strange that among the first-fruits of the efforts of a Positivist should be the conversion of those he seeks to benefit to Christianity. But in South America Christianity is at least as much a status as a theology. It represents the indispensable first step upward from savagery. In the wilder and poorer districts men are divided into the two great classes of "Christians" and "Indians." When an Indian becomes a Christian he is accepted into and becomes wholly absorbed or partly assimilated by the crude and simple neighboring civilization, and then he moves up or down like any one else among his fellows.

THEODORE ROOSEVELT AND COLONEL RONDON *posing with their deer catch at Matto Grosso, Brazil, 1913–14.*

# The Headwaters of the Paraguay

*The STEAMER that took Theodore and Kermit Roosevelt and the rest of the expedition members up the Paraguay River into Brazil, 1913.*

Only a limited number of the naturalists who have worked in the tropics have had any experience with the big beasts whose life-histories possess such peculiar interest. Of all the biologists who have seriously studied the South American fauna on the ground, Bates probably rendered most service; but he hardly seems even to have seen the animals with which the hunter is fairly familiar. His interests, and those of the other biologists of his kind, lay in other directions. In consequence, in treating of the life-histories of the very interesting big game, we have been largely forced to rely either on native report, in which acutely accurate observation is invariably mixed with wild fable, or else on the chance remarks of travellers or mere sportsmen, who had not the training to make them understand even what it was desirable to observe. Nowadays there is a growing proportion of big-game hunters, of sportsmen, who are of the Schilling, Selous, and Shiras type. These men do work of capital value for science. The mere big-game butcher is tending to disappear as a type. On the other hand, the big-game hunter who is a good observer, a good field naturalist, occupies at present a more important position than ever before, and it is now recognized that he can do work which the closest naturalist cannot do. The big-game hunter of this type and the outdoors, faunal naturalist, the student of the life-histories of big mammals, have open to them in South America a wonderful field in which to work.

# Up the River of Tapirs

hortly before noon—January 16—we reached Tapirapoan, the headquarters of the Telegraphic Commission. It was an attractive place, on the river-front, and it was gayly bedecked with flags, not only those of Brazil and the United States, but of all the other American republics, in our honor. There was a large, green square, with trees standing in the middle of it. On one side of this square were the buildings of the Telegraphic Commission, on the other those of a big ranch, of which this is the headquarters. In addition, there were stables, sheds, outhouses, and corrals; and there were cultivated fields near by. Milch cows, beef-cattle, oxen, and mules wandered almost at will. There were two or three wagons and carts, and a traction automobile, used in the construction of the telegraph-line, but not available in the rainy season, at the time of our trip.

Here we were to begin our trip overland, on pack-mules and pack-oxen, scores of which had been gathered to meet us. Several days were needed to apportion the loads and arrange for the several divisions in which it was necessary that so large a party should attempt the long wilderness march, through a country where there was not much food for man or beast, and where it was always possible to run into a district in which fatal cattle or horse diseases were prevalent. Fiala, with his usual efficiency, took charge of handling the outfit of the American portion of the expedition, with Sigg as an active and useful assistant. Harper, who like the others worked with whole-hearted zeal and cheerfulness, also helped him, except when he was engaged in helping the naturalists. The two latter, Cherrie and Miller, had so far done the hardest and the best work of the expedition. They had collected about a thousand birds and two hundred and fifty mammals. It was not probable that they would do as well during the remainder of our trip, for we intended thenceforth to halt as little, and march as steadily, as the country, the weather, and the condition of our means of transportation permitted. I kept continually wishing that they had more time in which to study the absorbingly interesting life-histories of the beautiful and wonderful beasts and birds we were all the time seeing. Every first-rate museum must still employ competent collectors; but I think that a museum could now confer most lasting benefit, and could do work of most permanent good, by sending out into the immense wildernesses, where wild nature is at her best, trained observers with the gift of recording what they have observed. Such men should be collectors, for collecting is still necessary; but they should also, and indeed primarily, be able themselves to see, and to set vividly before the eyes of others, the full life-histories of the creatures that dwell in the waste spaces of the world.

THEODORE ROOSEVELT AND THE EXPEDITION PARTY *on horseback in Brazil, 1913.*

# The River of Doubt

On February 27, 1914, shortly after midday, we started down the River of Doubt into the unknown. We were quite uncertain whether after a week we should find ourselves in the Gy-Paraná, or after six weeks in the Madeira, or after three months we knew not where. That was why the river was rightly christened the Dúvida.

We had been camped close to the river, where the trail that follows the telegraph line crosses it by a rough bridge. As our laden dugouts swung into the stream, Amilcar and Miller and all the others of the Gy-Paraná party were on the banks and the bridge to wave farewell and wish us good-by and good luck. It was the height of the rainy season, and the swollen torrent was swift and brown. Our camp was at about 12°1′ latitude south and 60°15′ longitude west of Greenwich. Our general course was to be northward toward the equator, by waterway through the vast forest.

We had seven canoes, all of them dugouts. One was small, one was cranky, and two were old, waterlogged, and leaky. The other three were good. The two old canoes were lashed together, and the cranky one was lashed to one of the others. Kermit with two paddlers went in the smallest of the good canoes; Colonel Rondon and Lyra with three other paddlers in the next largest; and the doctor, Cherrie, and I in the largest with three paddlers.

THEODORE ROOSEVELT *in a dugout canoe on the River of Doubt, which was later renamed Rio Roosevelt, 1913.*

The remaining eight camaradas—there were sixteen in all—were equally divided between our two pairs of lashed canoes. . . .

"On February 27, 1914, shortly after midday, we started down the River of Doubt into the unknown."

The paddlers were a strapping set. They were expert rivermen and men of the forest, skilled veterans in wilderness work. They were lithe as panthers and brawny as bears. They swam like waterdogs. They were equally at home with pole and paddle, with axe and machete; and one was a good cook and others were good men around camp. They looked like pirates in the pictures of Howard Pyle or Maxfield Parrish; one or two of them were pirates, and one worse than a pirate; but most of them were hard-working, willing, and cheerful. They were white, or, rather, the olive of southern Europe,— black, copper-colored, and of all intermediate shades. In my canoe Luiz the steersman, the headman, was a Matto Grosso negro; Julio the bowsman was from Bahia and of pure Portuguese blood; and the third man, Antonio, was a Parecís Indian.

The actual surveying of the river was done by Colonel Rondon and Lyra, with Kermit as their assistant. Kermit went first in his little canoe with the sighting-rod, on which two disks, one red and one white, were placed a metre apart. He selected a place which commanded as long vistas as possible up-stream and down, and which therefore might be at the angle of a bend; landed; cut away the branches which obstructed the view; and set up the sighting-pole—incidentally encountering maribundi wasps and swarms of biting and singing ants. Lyra, from his station up-stream, with his telemetre established the distance, while Colonel Rondon with the compass took the direction, and made the records. . . .

. . . The trees were stately and beautiful. The looped and twisted vines hung from them like great ropes. Masses of epiphytes grew both on the dead trees and the

ROOSEVELT AND RONDON *scouting the countryside at Navaite on the River of Doubt, 1913.*

living; some had huge leaves like elephants' ears. Now and then fragrant scents were blown to us from flowers on the banks. There were not many birds, and for the most part the forest was silent; rarely we heard strange calls from the depths of the woods, or saw a cormorant or ibis. . . .

. . . Our canoes were moored to trees. The axemen cleared a space for the tents; they were pitched, the baggage was brought up, and fires were kindled. The woods were almost soundless. Through them ran old tapir trails, but there was no fresh sign. Before nightfall the surveyors arrived. There were a few piums and gnats, and a few mosquitoes after dark, but not enough to make us uncomfortable. The small stingless bees, of slightly aromatic odor, swarmed while daylight lasted and crawled over our faces and hands; they were such tame, harmless little things that when they tickled too much I always tried to brush them away without hurting them. But they became a great nuisance after a while. It had been raining at intervals, and the weather was overcast; but after the sun went down the sky cleared. The stars were brilliant overhead, and the new moon hung in the west. It was a pleasant night, the air almost cool, and we slept soundly. ✶ ✶ ✶

KERMIT, AS USUAL, was leading in his canoe. It was the smallest and least seaworthy of all. He had in it little except a week's supply of our boxed provisions and a few tools; fortunately none of the food for the camaradas. His dog Trigueiro was with him. Besides himself, the crew consisted of two men: João, the helmsman, or pilot, as he is called in Brazil, and Simplicio, the bowsman. Both were negroes and exceptionally good men in every way. Kermit halted his canoe on the left bank, above the rapids, and waited for the colonel's canoe. Then the colonel and Lyra walked down the bank to see what was ahead. Kermit took his canoe across to the island to see whether the descent could be better accomplished on the other side. Having made his investigation, he ordered the men to return to the bank he had left, and the dugout was headed up-stream accordingly. Before they had gone a dozen yards, the paddlers digging their paddles with all their strength into the swift current, one of the shifting whirlpools of which I have spoken came down-stream, whirled them around, and swept them so close to the rapids that no human power could avoid going over them. As they were drifting into them broadside on, Kermit yelled to the steersman to turn her head, so as to take them in the only way that offered any chance whatever of safety. The water came aboard, wave after wave, as they raced down. They reached the bottom with the canoe upright, but so full as barely to float, and the paddlers urged her toward the shore. They had nearly reached the bank when another whirlpool or whirling eddy tore them away and hurried them back to midstream, where the dugout filled and turned over. João, seizing the rope, started to swim ashore; the rope was pulled from his hand, but he reached the bank. Poor Simplicio must have been pulled under at once and his life beaten out on the boulders beneath the racing torrent. He never rose again, nor did we ever recover his body. Kermit clutched his rifle, his favorite 405 Winchester with which he had done most of his hunting both in Africa and America, and climbed on the bottom of the upset boat. In a minute he was swept into the second series of rapids, and whirled away from the rolling boat, losing his rifle. The water beat his helmet down over his head and face and drove him beneath the surface; and when he rose at last he was almost drowned, his breath and strength almost spent. He was in swift but quiet water, and swam toward an overhanging branch. His jacket hindered him, but he knew he was too nearly gone to be able to get it off, and, thinking with the curious calm one feels when death is but a moment away, he realized that the utmost his failing strength could do was to reach the branch. He reached, and clutched it, and then almost lacked strength to haul himself out on the land. Good Trigueiro had faithfully swum alongside him through the rapids, and now himself scrambled ashore. It was a very narrow escape. Kermit was a great comfort and help to me on the trip; but the fear of some fatal

KERMIT ROOSEVELT, *on the Brazilian expedition, 1913.*

accident befalling him was always a nightmare to me. He was to be married as soon as the trip was over; and it did not seem to me that I could bear to bring bad tidings to his betrothed and to his mother.

Simplicio was unmarried. Later we sent to his mother all the money that would have been his had he lived. The following morning we put on one side of the post erected to mark our camping-spot the following inscription, in Portuguese:

"IN THESE RAPIDS DIED POOR SIMPLICIO."

On an expedition such as ours death is one of the accidents that may at any time occur, and narrow escapes from death are too common to be felt as they would be felt elsewhere. One mourns sincerely, but mourning cannot interfere with labor. We immediately proceeded with the work of the portage. From the head to the tail of this series of rapids the distance was about six hundred yards. A path was cut along the bank, over which the loads were brought. The empty canoes ran the rapids without mishap, each with two skilled paddlers.

One of the canoes almost ran into a swimming tapir at the head of the rapids; it went down the rapids, and then climbed out of the river. Kermit accompanied by João, went three or four miles down the river, looking for the body of Simplicio and for the sunk canoe. He found neither. But he found a box of provisions and a paddle, and salvaged both by swimming into midstream after them. He also found that a couple of kilometres below there was another stretch of rapids, and following them on the left-hand bank to the foot he found that they were worse than the ones we had just passed, and impassable for canoes on this left-hand side. ✳ ✳ ✳

IT WAS A VERY BAD THING to lose the canoe, but it was even worse to lose the rope and pulleys. This meant that it would be physically impossible to hoist big canoes up even small hills or rocky hillocks, such as had been so frequent beside the many rapids we had encountered. It was not wise to spend the four days necessary to build new canoes where we were, in danger of attack from the Indians. Moreover, new rapids might be very near, in which case the new canoes would hamper us. Yet the four remaining canoes would not carry all the loads and all the men, no matter how we cut the loads down; and we intended to cut everything down at once. We had been gone eighteen days. We had used over a third of our food. We had gone only 125 kilometres, and it was probable that we had at least five times, perhaps six or seven times, this distance still to go. We had taken a fortnight to descend rapids amounting in the aggregate to less than seventy yards of fall; a very few yards of fall makes a dangerous rapid when the river is swollen and swift and there are obstructions. We had only one aneroid to determine our altitude, and therefore could make merely a loose approximation to it, but we probably had between two and three times this descent in the aggregate of rapids ahead of us. So far the country had offered little in the way of food except palm-tops. We had lost four canoes and one man. We were in the country of wild Indians, who shot well with their bows. It behooved us to go warily, but also to make all speed possible, if we were to avoid serious trouble.

The best plan seemed to be to march thirteen men down along the bank, while the remaining canoes, lashed two and two, floated down beside them. If after two or three days we found no bad rapids, and there seemed a reasonable chance of going some distance at decent speed, we could then build the new canoes—preferably two small ones, this time, instead of one big one. We left all the baggage we could. We were already down as far as comfort would permit; but we now struck off much of the comfort. Cherrie, Kermit, and I had been sleeping under a very light fly; and there was another small light tent for one person, kept for possible emergencies. The last was given to me for my cot, and all five of the others swung their hammocks under the big fly. This meant that we left two big and heavy tents behind. A box of surveying instruments was also abandoned. Each of us got his personal belongings down to one box or duffel-bag—although there was only a small diminution thus made; because we had so little that the only way to make a serious diminution was to restrict ourselves to the clothes on our backs.

The biting flies and ants were to us a source of discomfort and at times of what could fairly be called torment. But to the camaradas, most of whom went barefoot or only wore sandals—and they never did or would wear shoes—the effect was more serious. They wrapped their legs and feet in pieces of canvas or hide; and the feet of three of them became so swollen that they were crippled and could not walk any distance. The doctor, whose courage and cheerfulness never flagged, took excellent care of them. Thanks to hi, there had been among them hitherto but one or two slight cases of fever. He administered to each man daily a half-gram—nearly eight grains—of quinine, and every third or fourth day a double dose.

ON THE RIVER, *Brazil, 1913.*

# To the Amazon and Home;
# Zoological and Geographical Results of the Expedition

Our adventures and our troubles were alike over. We now experienced the incalculable contrast between descending a known and travelled river, and one that is utterly unknown. After four days we hired a rubberman to go with us as guide. We knew exactly what channels were passable when we came to the rapids, when the canoes had to unload, and where the carry-trails were. It was all child's play compared to what we had gone through. We made long days' journeys, for at night we stopped at some palm-thatched house, inhabited or abandoned, and therefore the men were spared the labor of making camp; and we bought ample food for them, so there was no further need of fishing and chopping down palms for the palmtops. The heat of the sun was blazing; but it looked as if we had come back into the rainy season, for there were many heavy rains, usually in the afternoon, but sometimes in the morning or at night. The mosquitoes were sometimes rather troublesome at night. In the daytime the piums swarmed, and often bothered us even when we were in midstream.

For four days there were no rapids we could not run without unloading. Then, on the 19th, we got a canoe from Senhor Barboso. He was a most kind and hospitable man, who also gave us a duck and a chicken and some mandioc and six pounds of rice, and would take no payment; he lived in a roomy house with his dusky, cigar-smoking wife and his many children. The new canoe was light and roomy, and we were able to rig up a low shelter

TRAVELING BY CANOE, *Brazil, 1913.*

under which I could lie; I was still sick. At noon we passed the mouth of a big river, the Rio Branco, coming in from the left; this was about in latitude 9°38´. Soon afterward we came to the first serious rapids, the Panela. We carried the boats past, ran down the empty canoes, and camped at the foot in a roomy house. The doctor bought a handsome trumpeter bird, very friendly and confiding, which was thenceforth my canoe companion.

We had already passed many inhabited—and a still larger number of uninhabited—houses. The dwellers were rubbermen, but generally they were permanent settlers also, homemakers, with their wives and children. Some, both of the men and women, were apparently of pure negro blood, or of pure Indian or south European blood; but in the great majority all three strains were mixed in varying degrees. They were most friendly, courteous, and hospitable. Often they refused payment for what they could afford, out of their little, to give us. When they did charge, the prices were very high, as was but just, for they live back of the beyond, and everything costs them fabulously, save what they raise themselves. The cool, bare houses of poles and palm thatch contained little except hammocks and a few simple cooking utensils; and often a clock or sewing machine, or Winchester rifle, from our own country. They often had flowers planted, including fragrant roses. Their only live stock, except the dogs, were a few chickens and ducks. They planted patches of mandioc, maize, sugarcane, rice, beans, squashes, pineapples, bananas, lemons, oranges, melons, peppers; and various purely native fruits and vegetables, such as the kniabo—a vegetable-fruit growing on the branches of a high bush—which is cooked with meat. They get some game from the forest, and more fish from the river. There is no representative of the government among them—indeed, even now their very existence is barely known to the governmental authorities; and the church has ignored them as completely as the state. When they wish to get married they have to spend several months getting down to and back from Manaos or some smaller city; and usually the first christening and the marriage ceremony are held at the same time. They have merely squatter's right to the land, and are always in danger of being ousted by unscrupulous big men who come in late, but with a title technically straight. The land laws should be shaped so as to give each of these pioneer settlers the land he actually takes up and cultivates, and upon which he makes his home. The small homemaker, who owns the land which he tills with his own hands, is the greatest element of strength in any country. ✳ ✳ ✳

AT THE RUBBERMAN'S HOUSE.

WE SPENT A LAST NIGHT under canvas, at Pyrineús' encampment. It rained heavily. Next morning we all gathered at the monument which Colonel Rondon had erected, and he read the orders of the day. These recited just what had been accomplished: set forth the fact that we had now by actual exploration and investigation discovered that the river whose upper portion had been called the Dúvida on the maps of the Telegraphic Commission and the unknown major part of which we had just traversed, and the river known to a few rubbermen, but to no one else, as the Castanho, and the lower part of the river known to the rubbermen as the Aripuanan (which did not appear on the maps save as its mouth was sometimes indicated, with no hint of its size) were all parts of one and the same river; and that by order of the Brazilian Government this river, the largest affluent of the Madeira, with its source near the 13th degree and its mouth a little south of the 5th degree, hitherto utterly unknown to cartographers and in large part utterly unknown to any save the local tribes of Indians, had been named the Rio Roosevelt.

We left Rondon, Lyra, and Pyrineus to take observations, and the rest of us embarked for the last time on the canoes, and, borne swiftly on the rapid current, we passed over one set of not very important rapids and ran down to Senhor Caripe's little hamlet of São João, which we reached about one o'clock on April 27, just before a heavy afternoon rain set in. We had run nearly eight hundred kilometres during the sixty days we had spent in the canoes. Here we found and boarded Pyrineus's river steamer, which seemed in our eyes extremely comfortable. In the senhor's pleasant house we were greeted by the senhora, and they were both more than thoughtful and generous in their hospitality. Ahead of us lay merely thirty-six hours by steamer to Manaos. Such a trip as that we had taken tries men as if by fire. Cherrie had more than stood every test; and in him Kermit and I had come to recognize a friend with whom our friendship would never falter or grow less.

ROOSEVELT WRITING *at camp, Brazil, 1913.*

Early the following afternoon our whole party, together with Senhor Caripe, started on the steamer. It took us a little over twelve hours' swift steaming to run down to the mouth of the river on the upper course of which our progress had been so slow and painful; from source to mouth, according to our itinerary and to Lyra's calculations, the course of the stream down which we had thus come was about 1,500 kilometres in length—about 900 miles, perhaps nearly 1,000 miles—from its source near the 13th degree in the highlands to its mouth in the Madeira, near the 5th degree. Next morning we were on the broad sluggish current of the lower Madeira, a beautiful tropical river. There were heavy rainstorms, as usual, although this is supposed to be the very end of the rainy season. In the afternoon we finally entered the wonderful Amazon itself, the mighty river which contains one tenth of all the running water of the globe. It was miles across, where we entered it; and indeed we could not tell whether the farther bank, which we saw, was that of the mainland or an island. We went up it until about midnight, then steamed up the Rio Negro for a short distance, and at one in the morning of April 30 reached Manaos. ✳ ✳ ✳

HERE WE FOUND MILLER, and glad indeed we were to see him. He had made good collections of mammals and birds on the Gy-Paraná, the Madeira, and in the neighborhood of Manaos; his entire collection of mammals was really noteworthy. Among them was the only sloth any of us had seen on the trip. The most interesting of the birds he had seen was the hoatzin. This is a most curious bird of very archaic type. Its flight is feeble, and the naked young have spurs on their wings, by the help of which they crawl actively among the branches before their feathers grow. They swim no less easily, at the same early age. Miller got one or two nests, and preserved specimens of the surroundings of the nests; and he made exhaustive records of the habits of the birds. Near Megasso a jaguar had killed one of the bullocks that were being driven along for food. The big cat had not seized the ox with its claws by the head, but had torn open its throat and neck.

Every one was most courteous at Manaos, especially the governor of the state and the mayor of the city. Mr. Robiliard, the British consular representative, and also the representative of the Booth line of steamers, was particularly kind. He secured for us passages on one of

ROOSEVELT'S GROUP OF EXPLORERS *dining on the steamer, Brazil, c. 1913–14.*

"THE CAMARADAS, *gathered around the monument erected by Colonel Rondon. From a photograph by Cherrie," originally published in* Through the Brazilian Wilderness, *1914.*

the cargo boats of the line to Para, and thence on one of the regular cargo-and-passenger steamers to Barbadoes and New York. The Booth people were most courteous to us.

I said good-by to the camaradas with real friendship and regret. The parting gift I gave to each was in gold sovereigns; and I was rather touched to learn later that they had agreed among themselves each to keep one sovereign as a medal of honor and token that the owner had been on the trip. They were a fine set, brave, patient, obedient, and enduring. Now they had forgotten their hard times; they were fat from eating, at leisure, all they wished; they were to see Rio Janeiro, always an object of ambition with men of their stamp; and they were very proud of their membership in the expedition.

Later, at Belén, I said good-by to Colonel Rondon, Doctor Cajazeira, and Lieutenant Lyra. Together with my admiration for their hardihood, courage, and resolution, I had grown to feel a strong and affectionate friendship for them. I had become very fond of them; and I was glad to feel that I had been their companion in the performance of a feat which possessed a certain lasting importance.

On May 1 we left Manaos for Belén-Para, as until recently it was called. The trip was interesting. We steamed down through tempest and sunshine; and the towering forest was dwarfed by the giant river it fringed. Sunrise and sunset turned the sky to an unearthly flame of many colors above the vast water. It all seemed the embodiment of loneliness and wild majesty. Yet everywhere man was conquering the loneliness and wresting the majesty to his own uses. We passed many thriving, growing towns; at one we stopped to take on cargo. Everywhere there was growth and development. The change since the days when Bates and Wallace came to this then poor and utterly primitive region is marvellous. One of its accompaniments has been a large European, chiefly south European, immigration. The blood is everywhere mixed; there is no color line, as in most English-speaking countries, and the negro and Indian strains are very strong; but the dominant blood, the blood already dominant in quantity, and that is steadily increasing its dominance, is the olive-white.

Only rarely did the river show its full width. Generally we were in channels or among islands. The surface of the water was dotted with little islands of floating vegetation. Miller said that much of this came from the lagoons such as those where he had been hunting, beside the Solimoens—lagoons filled with the huge and splendid Victoria lily, and with masses of water hyacinths. Miller, who was very fond of animals and always took much care of them, had a small collection which he was bringing back for the Bronx Zoo. An agouti was so bad-tempered that he had to be kept solitary; but three monkeys, big, middle-sized, and little, and a young peccary formed a happy family. The largest monkey cried, shedding real tears, when taken in the arms and pitied. The middle-sized monkey was stupid and kindly, and all the rest of the company imposed on it; the little monkey invariably rode on its back, and the peccary used it as a head pillow when it felt sleepy.

Belén, the capital of the state of Para, was an admirable illustration of the genuine and almost startling progress which Brazil has been making of recent years. It is a beautiful city, nearly under the equator. But it is not merely beautiful. The docks, the dredging operations, the warehouses, the stores and shops, all tell of energy and success in commercial life. It is as clean, healthy, and well policed a city as any of the size in the north temperate zone. The public buildings are handsome, the private dwellings attractive; there are a fine opera-house, an excellent tramway system, and a good museum and botanical gardens. There are cavalry stables, where lights burn all night long to protect the horses from the vampire bats. The parks, the rows of palms and mango-trees, the open-air restaurants, the gay life under the lights at night, all give the city its own special quality and charm. Belén and Manaos are very striking examples of what can be done in the mid-tropics. The governor of Para and his charming wife were more than kind. ✳ ✳ ✳

ON MAY 7 WE BADE GOOD-BY to our kind Brazilian friends and sailed northward for Barbados and New York.

Zoologically the trip had been a thorough success. Cherrie and Miller had collected over twenty-five hundred birds, about five hundred mammals, and a few reptiles, batrachians, and fishes. Many of them were new to science; for much of the region traversed had never previously been worked by any scientific collector.

> "No piece of work of this kind is ever achieved save as it is based on long-continued previous work."

Of course, the most important work we did was the geographic work, the exploration of the unknown river, undertaken at the suggestion of the Brazilian Government, and in conjunction with its representatives. No piece of work of this kind is ever achieved save as it is based on long-continued previous work. As I have before said, what we did was to put the cap on the pyramid that had been built by Colonel Rondon and his associates of the Telegraphic Commission during the six previous years. It was their scientific exploration of the chapadão, their mapping the basin of the Juruena, and their descent of the Gy-Paraná that rendered it possible for us to solve the mystery of the River of Doubt.

# CONCLUSION

I N 1918 THE WAR CAME HOME, to the Roosevelts, as it did to thousands of American families. First, Archie was critically wounded by shrapnel and sent home. Then came tragedy: on July 14, Quentin died when his plane was shot down near Rheims. He had been flying for less than six weeks.

Roosevelt's own death came quietly, less than six weeks later. On January 6, 1919, he suffered a coronary embolism and died in his sleep, leaving behind a legacy so large and varied that historians are still studying it, debating it, and taking its measure.

Several years before his death, Roosevelt and his wife Edith selected the Youngs Memorial Cemetery, nearby their Oyster Bay home, as their final resting place. They chose a plot on a hillside with a view of the harbor they loved. (Roosevelt knew the property well, and had long been impressed by the variety of bird life found there.) He was laid to rest on a cold, snowy day, and one of the last to leave when the brief service ended was his one-time political adversary, former President William Howard Taft, by all accounts deeply moved by the occasion. After her death in 1948, Edith Roosevelt was buried alongside her husband, and in time, two of the Roosevelt children were buried there as well:

PALLBEARERS CARRY THE FLAG-DRAPED CASKET *containing the body of President Theodore Roosevelt to its final resting place in the Young Memorial Cemetery at Oyster Bay, New York, January 7, 1919.*

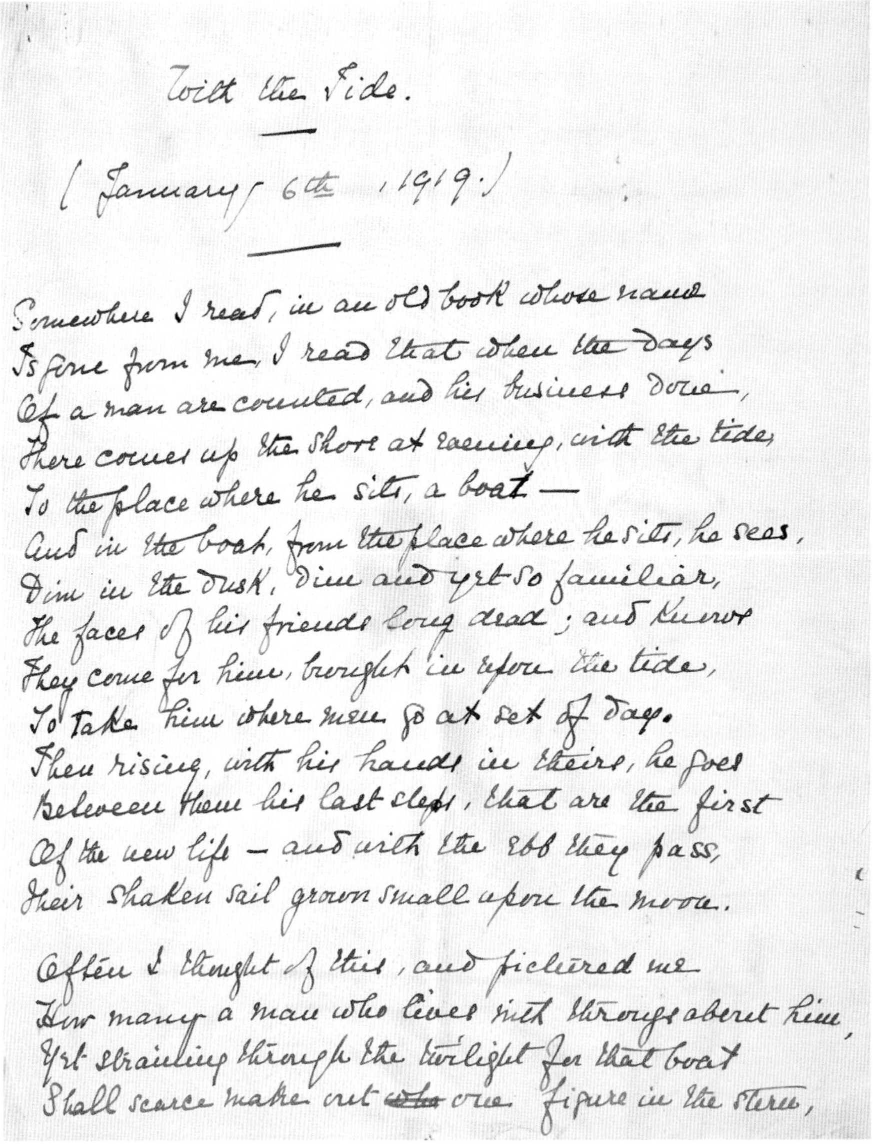

With the Tide.

(January 6th, 1919.)

Somewhere I read, in an old book whose name
Is gone from me, I read that when the days
Of a man are counted, and his business done,
There comes up the shore at evening, with the tide,
To the place where he sits, a boat —
And in the boat, from the place where he sits, he sees,
Dim in the dusk, dim and yet so familiar,
The faces of his friends long dead; and knows
They come for him, brought in upon the tide,
To take him where men go at set of day.
Then rising, with his hands in theirs, he goes
Between them his last steps, that are the first
Of the new life — and with the ebb they pass,
Their shaken sail grown small upon the moon.

Often I thought of this, and pictured me
How many a man who lives with throngs about him,
Yet straining through the twilight for that boat
Shall scarce make out ~~who~~ one figure in the stern,

**EDITH WHARTON, COUSIN OF EDITH ROOSEVELT,** *penned With the Tide, a eulogy for Theodore, January 6, 1919. The start of the eulogy is shown here.*

Ethel (1977), who had devoted herself to the preservation of Sagamore Hill; and Archie (1979), who had been wounded in two world wars but outlived all of his brothers. The remaining children lie in distant places: Quentin (1918) and Ted (1944) in the American National Battlefield Monument Cemetery in St. Laurent-sur-mer, France; Kermit (1943) in Fort Richardson National Cemetery near Anchorage, Alaska; and Alice (1980) at Rock Creek Cemetery in Washington, DC.

"The old lion is dead."

---

"Death had to take Roosevelt sleeping,
for if he had been awake, there would
have been a fight."

SCULPTOR LINCOLN BORGLUM *on the scaffold below
the face of President Theodore Roosevelt on the Mount
Rushmore Memorial in the Black Hills area of Keystone,
South Dakota, April 1944.*

Castle Creek · A Temple of The Hills.

# NATURE THE HEALER

From *Theodore Roosevelt: An Intimate Biography*
by William Roscoe Thayer, 1919

**WILLIAM ROSCOE THAYER,**
*by Pirie MacDonald, c. 1920.*

**O**NCE ROOSEVELT'S DEATH, biographers, historians, and even novelists have explored his life as a whole or in parts, attempting to plumb the depths of this complex, dynamic, extroverted, yet guarded man and evaluate his role in the American story. (At least a dozen new ones are scheduled for 2011 publication.) The following excerpt comes from the first biography to be published after the Roosevelt's death in 1919, an "intimate biography" by a Harvard classmate named William Roscoe Thayer. Best known for his studies of Italian history, Thayer nevertheless offers a unique perspective—a personal assessment of the development of Roosevelt's character, and an answer, perhaps, to some of his critics. The book became an immediate bestseller.

A PERFECT BIOGRAPHY would show definitely the interaction between mind and body. At present we can only guess what this interaction may be. In some cases the relations are evident, but in most they are vague and often unsuspected. The psychologists, whose pretensions are so great and whose actual results are still so small, may perhaps lead, an age or two hence, to the desired knowledge. But the biographer of today must beware of adopting the unripe formulas of any immature science. Nevertheless, he must watch, study, and record all the facts pertaining to his subject, although he cannot explain them. Theodore Roosevelt was a wonderful example of the partnership of mind and body, and any one who writes his biography in detail will do well to pay great heed to this

*opposite:* **SOUTH CASTLE CREEK**, *a Temple of the Hills, Black Hills, South Dakota by Franklin De Haven (detail), oil on canvas, 20th century.*

intricate interlocking. I can do no more than allude to it here. We have seen that Roosevelt from his earliest days had a quick mind, happily not precocious, and a weak body which prevented him from taking part in normal physical activity and the play and sport of boyhood. So his intellectual life grew out of scale to his physical. Then he set to work by the deliberate application of will-power to develop his body, and when he entered Harvard he was above the average youth in strength. Before he graduated, those who saw him box or wrestle beheld a fellow somewhat slim and light, but unusually well set up. During the succeeding four years he never allowed his duties as Assemblyman to encroach upon his exercise; on the contrary, he played regularly and he played hard, adding new kinds of sport to develop new faculties and to give the spice of variety. He rode to hounds with the Meadowbrook Hunt; he took up polo; and he boxed and wrestled as in his college days.

In a few years Roosevelt became physically a very powerful man. I recall my astonishment the first time I saw him, after the lapse of several years, to find him with the neck of a Titan and with broad shoulders and stalwart chest, instead of the city-bred, slight young friend I had known earlier. His body was now equal to any burden or strain which his mind might have to endure; and hence forth it is no idle fancy that suggests a perpetual competition between the two. Thanks to his extraordinary will, however, he never allowed his body to get control; but, as appetite comes with eating, so his strong and healthy muscles craved more and more exercise as he used them. And now he took a novel way to gratify them.

Ever since his first taste of camp life, when he went into the Maine Woods under the guidance of Bill Sewall and Will Dow, Roosevelt felt the lure of wild nature, and on many successive seasons he repeated these trips. Gradually, fishing and hunting in the wilderness of Maine or the Adirondacks did not afford him enough scope for his brimming vigor. He decided to go West, to the real West, where great game and Indians still survived, and the conditions of the few white men were almost as primitive as in the days of the earliest explorers. When the session of 1883 adjourned, he started for North Dakota, then a territory with a few settlers, and among the Bad Lands on the Little Missouri he bought an interest in two cattle ranches, the Chimney Butte and the Elkhorn. The following year, after the Presidential campaign which placed Cleveland in the White House, Roosevelt determined, as we saw in the letters I have quoted, to abandon the East for a time and to devote himself to a ranchman's life. He was still in deep grief at the loss of his wife and of his mother; there was no immediate prospect of usefulness for him in politics; the conventions of civilization, as he knew them in New York City, palled upon him; a sure instinct whispered to him that he must break away and seek health of body and heart and soul among the remote, unspoiled haunts of primeval Nature. For nearly two years, with occasional intervals spent in the East, the Elkhorn Ranch at Medora was his home, and he has described the life of the ranchman and cow-puncher in pages which are sure to be read as long as posterity takes any interest in knowing about the transition of the American West from wilderness to civilization. He shared in all the work of the ranch. He took with a "frolic welcome" the humdrum of its routine as well as its excitements and dangers. He says that he does not believe that there was ever any more attractive life for a vigorous young fellow than this, and assuredly no one else has glorified it as Roosevelt did with his pen. At one time or another he performed all the duties of a ranchman. He went on long rides after the cattle, he rounded them up, he helped to brand them and to cut out the beeves destined for the Eastern market. He followed the herd when it stampeded during a terrific thunderstorm. In winter there was often need to save the wandering cattle from a sudden and deadly blizzard. The log cabin or "shack" in which he dwelt was rough, and so was the fare; comforts were few. He chopped the cottonwood which they used for fuel; he knew how to care for the ponies; and once at least he passed more than twenty-four hours in the saddle without sleep. According to the best standards, he says, he was not a fine horseman, but it is clear that he could do everything with a horse which had to be done, and that he never stopped from fatigue. When they needed fresh meat, he would shoot it. In short, he held his own under all the hardships and requirements demanded of a cowboy or ranchman. To adapt himself to these wild conditions of nature and work was, however, only a part of his experience. Even more dangerous than pursuing a stampeding herd at night over the plains, and plunging into the Little Missouri after it, was intercourse with some of the lawless nomads of that pioneer region. Nomads they were, though they might settle down to work for a while on one ranch, and then pass on to another; the sort of creatures who loafed in the saloons of the little villages and amused them selves by running amuck and shooting up the town. These men, and indeed nearly all of the pioneers, held the man from the civilized East, the "tenderfoot," in scorn. They took it for granted that he was a weakling, that he had soft ideas of life and was stuck-up or affected. Now Roosevelt saw that in order to win their trust and respect, he must show himself equal to their tasks, a true comrade, who accepted their code of courage and honor. The fact that he wore spectacles was against him at the outset, because they associated spectacles with Eastern schoolmasters and incompetence. They called him "Four Eyes," at first with derision, but they soon discovered that in him they had no "tenderfoot" to deal with. He shot as well as the best of them; he rode as far; he never complained of food or tasks or hardship; he met every one on equal terms. Above all, he left no doubt as to his courage. He would not pick a quarrel nor would he avoid one. Many stories of his prowess circulated; mere heckling, or a practical joke, he took with a laugh; as when some of the men changed the saddle from his pony to a bucking bronco.

But he knew where to draw the line. At Medora, for instance, the Marquis de Mores, a French settler, assumed the attitude of a feudal proprietor. Having been the first to squat in that region he regarded those who came later as interlopers, and he and his men acted very sullenly. They even carried their ill-will and intimidation to the point of shooting. In due time the Marquis discovered cause for grievance against Roosevelt, and he sent him a letter warning the newcomer that if the cause were not removed the Marquis knew how one gentleman settles a dispute with another. Roosevelt despised dueling as a silly practice, which would not determine justice between disputants; but he knew that in Cowboy Land the duel, being regarded as a test of courage, must not be ignored by him. Any man who declined a challenge lost caste and had better leave the country at once. So Roosevelt within an hour dispatched a reply to the surly Marquis saying that he was ready to meet him at any time and naming the rifle, at twelve paces' distance, as the weapon that he preferred. The Marquis, a formidable swordsman but no shot, sent back word, expressing regret that Mr. Roosevelt had mistaken his meaning: in referring to "gentlemen knowing how to settle disputes," he meant that of course an amicable explanation would restore harmony. Thenceforward, he treated Roosevelt with effusive courtesy. Perhaps a chill ran down his back at the thought of standing up before an antagonist twelve paces away and that the fighters were to advance towards each other three paces after each round, until one of them was killed.

So Theodore fought no duel with either the French Marquis or with any one else during his life in the West, but he had several encounters with local desperadoes. One cold night in winter, having ridden far and knowing that he could reach no refuge for many hours, he unexpectedly saw a light. Going towards it, he found that it came from a cabin which

*Theodore Roosevelt's* **MALTESE CROSS "OUTFIT"** *out on a cattle round-up, near Medora, North Dakota, c. 1885.*

served as saloon and tavern. On entering, he saw a group of loafers and drinkers who were apparently terrorized by a big fellow, rather more than half drunk, who proved to be the local bully. The function of this person was to maintain his bullyship against all comers: accordingly, he soon picked on Roosevelt, who held his peace as long as he could. Then the rowdy, who grasped his pistols in his hands, ordered the "four-eyed tenderfoot" to come to the bar and set up drinks for the crowd. Roosevelt walked deliberately towards him, and before the bully suspected it, the "tenderfoot" felled him with a sledgehammer blow. In falling, a pistol went off wide of its mark, and the bully lay in a faint. Before he could recover, Roosevelt stood over him ready to pound him again. But the bully did not stir, and he was carried off into another room. The crowd congratulated the stranger on having served him right.

At another place, there was a "bad man" who surpassed the rest of his fellows in using foul language. Roosevelt, who loathed obscenity as he did any other form of filth, tired of this bad man's talk and told him very calmly that he liked him but not his nastiness. Instead of drawing his gun, as the bystanders thought he would do, Jim looked sheepish, acknowledging the charge, and changed his tone. He remained a loyal friend of his corrector. Cattle-thieves and horse-thieves infested the West of those days. To steal a ranchman's horse might not only cause him great annoyance, but even put his life in danger, and accordingly the rascals who engaged in this form of crime ranked as the worst of all and received no mercy when they were caught. If the sheriff of the region was lax, the settlers took the matter into their own hands, enrolled themselves as vigilantes, hunted the thieves down, hanged those whom they captured, and shot at sight those who tried to escape. It happened that the sheriff, in whose jurisdiction Medora lay, allowed so many thieves to get off that he was suspected of being in collusion with them. The ranch men held a meeting at which he was present and Roosevelt told him in very plain words their complaint against him and their suspicions. Though he was a hot-tempered man, and very quick on the trigger, he showed no willingness to shoot his bold young accuser; he knew, of course, that the ranchmen would have taken vengeance on him in a flash, but it is also possible that he recognized the truth of Roosevelt's accusation and felt compunctions.

Some time later Roosevelt showed how a zealous officer of the law—he was the acting deputy sheriff—ought to behave. He had a boat in which he used to cross the Little Missouri to his herds on the other side. One day he missed the boat, its rope having been cut, and he inferred that it must have been stolen by three cattle-thieves who had been operating in that neighborhood. By means of it they could easily escape, for there was no road along the river on which horsemen could pursue them. Notwithstanding this, Roosevelt resolved that they should not go free. In three days Bill Sewall and Dow built a flat, water-tight craft, on which they put enough food to last for a fortnight, and then all three started downstream. They had drifted and poled one hundred and fifty miles or more, before they saw a faint column of smoke in the bushes near the bank. It proved to be the temporary camp of the fugitives, whom they quickly took prisoners, put into the boat, and carried another one hundred and fifty miles down the river to the nearest town with a jail and a court. Going and coming, Roosevelt spent nearly three weeks, not to mention the hardships which he and his trusty men suffered on the way; but he had served justice, and Justice must be served at any cost. When the story be came known, the admiration of his neighbors for his pluck and persistence rose; but they wondered why he took the trouble to make the extra journey, in order to deliver the prisoners to the jail, instead of shooting them where he overtook them.

I chronicle these examples of Roosevelt's courage among the lawless gangs with whom he was thrown in North Dakota, because they reveal several qualities which came to be regarded as peculiarly Rooseveltian during the rest of his days. We are apt to speak of "mere" physical courage as being inferior to moral courage; and doubtless there are many heroes unknown to the world who, under the torture of disease or the poignancy of social injustice and wrongs, deserve the highest crown of heroism. Men who would lead a charge in battle would shrink from denouncing an accepted convention or even from slighting a popular fashion. But after all, the instinct of the race is sound in revering those who give their lives without hesitation or regret at the point of deadly peril, or offer their own to save the lives of others.

Roosevelt's experience established in him that physical courage which his soul had aspired to in boyhood, when the consciousness of his bodily inferiority made him seem shy and almost timid. Now he had a bodily frame which could back up any resolution he might take. The emergencies in a ranchman's career also trained him to be quick to will, instantaneous in his decisions, and equally quick in the muscular activity by which he carried them out. In a community whose members gave way to sudden explosions of passion, you might be shot dead unless you got the drop on the other fellow first. The anecdotes I have repeated, indicate that Roosevelt must often have outsped his opponent in drawing.

We learn from them, too, that he was far from being the pugnacious person whom many of his later critics insisted that he was. Having given ample proof to the frontiersmen that he had no fear, he resolutely kept the peace with them, and they had no desire to break peace with him. Bluster and swagger were foreign to his nature, and he loathed a bully as much as a coward. If we had not already had the record of his. three years in the Legislature, in which he surprised his friends by his wonderful talent for mixing with all sorts of persons, we might marvel at his ability to meet the cowboys and ranchmen, and even the desperadoes, of the Little Missouri on equal terms, to win the respect of all of them, and the lifelong devotion of a few. They knew that the usual tenderfoot, however much he might wish to fraternize, was fended from them by his past, his traditions, his civilized life, his instincts; but in Roosevelt's case, there was no gulf, no barrier.

Even after he became President of the United States, I can no more imagine that he felt embarrassment in meeting any one, high or low, than that he scrutinized the coat on a man's back in order to know how to treat him.

To have gained solid health, to have gained mastery of himself, and to have put his social nature to the severest test and found it flawless, were valid results of his life on the Elkhorn Ranch. It imparted to him also a knowledge which was to prove most precious to him in the unforeseen

*This* FREDERIC REMINGTON PAINTING *depicts Roosevelt's capture of two men trying to steal his boat on Elkhorn Ranch and accompanied an article written by Roosevelt that appeared in the May 1888 issue of* Century Magazine.

future. For it taught him the immense diversity of the people, and consequently of the interests, of the United States. It gave him a national point of view, in which he perceived that the standards and desires of the Atlantic States were not all-inclusive or final. Yet while it impressed on him the importance of geographical considerations, it impressed, more deeply still, the fact that there are moral fundamentals not to be measured by geography, or by time, or by race. Lincoln learned this among the pioneers of Illinois; in similar fashion Roosevelt learned it in the Bad Lands of Dakota with their pioneers and exiles from civilization, and from studying the depths of his own nature.

# BIBLIOGRAPHY

## WORKS BY THEODORE ROOSEVELT EXCERPTED IN *A PASSION TO LEAD*

*Hunting trips of a ranchman, sketches of sport on the northern cattle plains.* New York: G.P. Putnam [c1885].

*Rough Riders.* New York: C. Scribner's Sons, 1905, [c1899]

*Strenuous life; essays and addresses.* New York: Century, 1902.

*Theodore Roosevelt, an Autobiography.* New York: C. Scribner's Sons, 1913.

*Theodore Roosevelt's letters to his children*; ed. by Joseph Bucklin Bishop. New York: C. Scribner's Sons, 1919.

*Through the Brazilian Wilderness.* New York: C. Scribner's Sons, 1914.

*Winning of the West: an account of the exploration and settlement of our country from the Alleghanies to the Pacific.* New York: Putnam, 1907.

## ALSO BY THEODORE ROOSEVELT

*Abraham Lincoln.* New York: Collier's, 1909.

*Address of President Roosevelt at Hampton Institute.* Hampton, Va.: Hampton Institute Press, 1906.

*African game trails, an account of the African wanderings of an American hunter-naturalist, by Theodore Roosevelt; with more than two hundred illustrations from photographs by Kermit Roosevelt and other members of the expedition, and from drawings by Philip R. Goodwin.* New York, C. Scribner's Sons, 1910.

*America and the World War.* New York: C. Scribner's Sons, 1915.

*American big-game hunting; the book of the Boone and Crockett club*; ed. by Theodore Roosevelt, George Bird Grinnell. New York: Forest and Stream Pub. Co., 1893.
*American ideals : and other essays, social and political.* New York; London: G.P. Put-nam's; Knickerbocker Press, 1897, 1907.
*Book-lover's holidays in the open.* New York: C. Scribner's Sons, 1916.

*Essays on practical politics.* New York & London: G.P. Putnam's Sons, 1888.

*Fear God and take your own part.* New York: George H. Doran Company, 1916.

*Foes of our own household; The great adventure; Letters to his children.* New York: C. Scribner's Sons, 1926.

*Great adventure; present-day studies in American nationalism.* New York: C. Scribner's Sons, 1918.

*Hero tales from American history, or, The Story of some Americans who showed that they knew how to live and how to die.* with Henry Cabot Lodge. Philadelphia: Gebbie and Co., 1903.

*History as literature, and other essays.* Port Washington, N.Y.: Kennikat Press 1967, c1941.

*Life-histories of African game animals, by Theodore Roosevelt and Edmund Heller; with illustrations from photographs, and from drawings by Philip R. Goodwin; and with forty faunal maps ...:* New York: C. Scribner's Sons, 1914.

*Naval War of 1812: or, The History of the United States Navy during the Last War with Great Britain, to which is appended an account of the battle of New Orleans.* New York; London: G.P. Putnam's Sons, the Knickerbocker Press, 1882.

*Oliver Cromwell.* New York: C. Scribner's Sons, 1919.

*Outdoor pastimes of an American hunter.* New York: C. Scribner's Sons, 1905.

*Realizable ideals.* Freeport, N.Y.: Books for Libraries Press, 1969.

*Works of Theodore Roosevelt.* New York: C. Scribner's Sons, 1926.

## ADDITIONAL SOURCES

Auchincloss, Louis, and Arthur M. Schlesinger. *Theodore Roosevelt: The 26th President, 1901–1909* (The American Presi-dents Series). New York: Times Books, 2002.

Brinkley, Douglas. *The Wilderness Warrior: Theodore Roosevelt and the Crusade for America.* New York: Harper Perennial, 2010.

Dalton, Kathleen. *Theodore Roosevelt: A Strenuous Life.* New York: Vintage, 2004.

Di Silvestro, Roger L. *Theodore Roosevelt in the Badlands: A Young Politician's Quest for Recovery in the American West.* New York: Walker & Company, 2011.

Donald, Aida D. *Lion in the Whitehouse: A Life of Theodore Roosevelt.* New York: Basic Books, 2007.

Jeffers, H. Paul. *Roosevelt the Explorer: T.R.'s Amazing Adventures as a Naturalist, Con-servationist, and Explorer.* New York: Taylor Trade Publishing, 2003.

McCullough, David. *Mornings on Horse-back: The Story of an Extraordinary Family, a Vanished Way of Life, and the Unique Child Who Became Theodore Roosevelt.* New York: Simon & Schuster, 1982.

Milkis, Sidney M. *Theodore Roosevelt, the Progressive Party, and the Transformation of American Democracy.* Lawrence, KS: University Press of Kansas, 2009.

Millard, Candice. *The River of Doubt: Theo-dore Roosevelt's Darkest Journey.* New York: Anchor Books, 2006.

Miller, John J. *The Big Scrum: How Teddy Roosevelt Saved Football.* New York: Harper-Collins, 2011.

Miller, Nathan. *Theodore Roosevelt: A Life.* New York: Quill/William Morrow, 1994.

Morris, Edmund. *Colonel Roosevelt.* New York: Random House, 2010.

Morris, Edmund. *The Rise of Theodore Roos-evelt.* New York: Random House, 2010.
Morris, Edmund. *Theodore Rex.* New York: Random House, 2002.

Riis, Jacob A. *Theodore Roosevelt, the citizen.* New York: London, Macmillan, 1904.

# ART CREDITS

Cover: Theodore Roosevelt by Pirie MacDonald, Courtesy of George Eastman House, International Museum of Photography and Film

Back cover: Colonel Theodore Roosevelt in his Rough Rider uniform by Benjamin J. Falk, 1898, 520.3-010. Theodore Roosevelt Collection, Harvard College Library

**Theodore Roosevelt Collection, Harvard College Library:**
*Special thanks to Wallace Finley Dailey, Curator, Theodore Roosevelt Collection, Harvard College Library, for his invaluable assistance with providing images for this book.*

p. vi: 520.3-002
pp. xiv–1: 520.12-013
p. 2: 560.11-018
p. 4, right: 520.11-005
p. 5: 520.11-007
p. 6: 520.12-002
p. 11, left: 560.11-021
p. 15: 520.12-003
p. 21: 560.14-004
p. 24: 560.14-093
pp. 26–27: 520.14-007
p. 28: 560.14-097
p. 29: 560.14-102
p. 33: 560.14-095
p. 34, top: 560.14-062
p. 37: 560.14-098
pp. 38–39: 560.14-046
p. 40, top: 560.14-001d
p. 43, top: 560.14-195
p. 43, bottom: 560.14-194
p. 46: 560.14-054
pp. 48–49: 560.14-023
p. 52: 520.23-008
p. 55, left: Roosevelt R500.R67-017
p. 55, right: Roosevelt R335.R67r3
p. 56: 520.21-002
p. 58: 520.21-001
p. 62: 520.21-003
p. 64, left: 560.21-001
p. 64, right: Roosevelt R500.R67-025
p. 65: 520.22-002
p. 66, right: 560.52 1905-129
p. 69: Roosevelt R500.P69a-018
p. 72: 520.23-007
p. 74: 520.23-001
p. 75, left: Roosevelt R560.3.EL64-002
p. 75, right: Roosevelt R560.3.EL64-003
p. 77: 560.3-027
pp. 78–79: 560.3-006

p. 80
p. 84: 560.3-024
p. 85: Roosevelt R560.3.B17-031
p. 86: Roosevelt R560.3.EL64-009
pp. 88–89: Roosevelt R560.3.Scr7-036
p. 90: 560.3-035
p. 92, right: 560.3-096
pp. 100–101: 560.3-008
p. 102: 560.3-013
p. 103: Roosevelt R560.3.EL61-007
p. 104
p. 105: 560.3-014
p. 107: Roosevelt R560.3.EL61-058
pp. 110–111:560.3-005
p. 112: 560.3-094
p. 114: Roosevelt R560.3.EL64-019
p. 116: 560.3-018a
p. 117: 560.3-021
p. 119: Roosevelt R560.3.Scr7-011
pp. 120–121: 560.3-022
p. 122: Roosevelt R560.3.EL64-030
p. 123: Roosevelt R560.3.Scr7-008
p. 124, top: Roosevelt R560.3.B17-006
p. 124, bottom: Roosevelt R560.3.B17-004
p. 125: Roosevelt R560.3.Scr7-012
p. 126: Roosevelt R560.3.EL64-085
p. 128: Roosevelt R560.3.Scr7-017
p. 130: Roosevelt R560.3.EL61-022
p. 132: Roosevelt R560.3.EL64-018
p. 136
p. 138: 560.3-032
p. 139: Roosevelt R560.3.EL64-020
p. 141: Roosevelt R560.3.Scr7-022
p. 143: 560.3-095
p. 144: Roosevelt R560.3.Scr7-029
p. 145: Roosevelt R560.3.Scr7-032
pp. 146–147: Roosevelt R560.3.Scr7-030
p. 149: Roosevelt R560.3.Em3-061
p. 152: Roosevelt R560.3.Em3-054
p. 158: Roosevelt R560.3.Em3-073
p. 161: Roosevelt R560.3.Scr7-042
p. 162: Roosevelt R560.3.EL61-003
p. 165: Roosevelt R560.3.Em3-062
p. 167: Roosevelt R560.3.Scr7-038
p. 170: Roosevelt R560.3.Em3-071
p. 171: 560.3-031
p. 174, top: Roosevelt R560.3.Em3-055
p. 174, bottom: Roosevelt R560.3.Em3-077
p. 175: 560.3-068
p. 177: Roosevelt R560.3.EL64-074
p. 178: Roosevelt R560.3.EL64-077
p. 181: Roosevelt R560.3.EL64-012
p. 182: 560.3-059
p. 185: 560.3-044
p. 186: Roosevelt R560.3.EL61-064
p. 188: Roosevelt R560.3.EL61-059
p. 189: Roosevelt R560.3.EL61-098a
p. 191: Roosevelt R560.3.EL61-039
p. 192: 560.3-102

p. 194: 560.3-105
p. 195: Roosevelt R560.3.Em3-000d
p. 196: 560.3-015
p. 199: 560.3-133
pp. 200–201: 560.41-033
p. 205: 560.41-057
p. 210: 520.41-001
p. 221: 560.41-031a
p. 233: 560.41-045
p. 236: 560.42-002
p. 245: Roosevelt R500.R67-013
p. 254: Roosevelt R500.R67-074
p. 267: 560.52 1909-005
p. 271, bottom
p. 281: Roosevelt R500.P69a-083
p. 282: 560.52 1906-061
p. 285: 560.52 1906-043
p. 286: 560.52 1906-040
p. 308: Roosevelt R560.6.C71-079
p. 344: 520.12-016
p. 347: 560.14-096a
p. 348: 560.14-081

**Theodore Roosevelt Collection, Houghton Library, Harvard University:**
p. 3: MS Am 1834 (120)
p. 10: MS Am 1454 (288, no. 3), Courtesy of the Theodore Roosevelt Association
p. 13, left & right: MS Am 1454.36, Courtesy of the Theodore Roosevelt Association
p. 25, left: MS Am 1834 (959)
p. 31: MS Am 1834 (218)
p. 76: MS Am 1541 (310)
pp. 82–83: MS Am 1834 (593)
p. 266, right: MS Am 1454.50 (155)

**Library of Congress:** pp. 212 (all), 311, 312 and book illustrations from *Through the Brazilian Wilderness*: pp. 301, 320, 321, 325, 327, 331, 334

**Library of Congress Prints and Photographs Division:** pp. ii, 8, 16, 18, 19, 20, 36, 53, 54, 66 (left), 91, 129, 208, 225, 231, 237, 238 (left), 239 (top & bottom), 240, 241, 242, 243, 246–247, 248, 251, 253, 256, 260, 264, 272, 273, 274, 275, 288, 292, 296, 298–299, 302, 304, 305, 307, 314, 316, 317, 318 (top & bottom), 322, 323, 324, 328, 330, 332, 333, 339

**All other Picture Sources:**
p. x: The Art Archive/National Archives, Washington, DC
p. 4, left: The Granger Collection, New York
p. 9: Courtesy of Special Collections, Fine Arts Library, Harvard University
p. 11, right: Smithsonian Institution Archives, SIA2009-1582

p. 23: Museum of Fine Arts, Houston, Texas, USA/Hogg Brothers Collection, Gift of Miss Ima Hogg/The Bridgeman Art Library

p. 25, right: Theodore Roosevelt Papers, Library of Congress Manuscript Division

p. 30: AP Photo

p. 32: Print Collection, Miriam and Ira D. Wallach Division of Art, Prints and Photographs, The New York Public Library, Astor, Lenox and Tilden Foundations.

p. 34, bottom: National Park Service, Theodore Roosevelt National Park

p. 40, bottom: Buffalo Bill Historical Center, Cody, Wyoming, U.S.A.; Gift of The Coe Foundation, 84.67

p. 44: Private Collection/Photo © Christie's Images/The Bridgeman Art Library

pp. 50–51: Jacob A Riis/Hulton Archive/Getty Images

pp. 60–61: Theodore Roosevelt Jr. Papers, Library of Congress Manuscript Division

p. 70: (Roosevelt's signature) John Hay Papers, Library of Congress Manuscript Division

p. 92, left: National Portrait Gallery, Smithsonian Institution/Art Resource, NY

p. 93: National Portrait Gallery, Smithsonian Institution/Art Resource, NY

p. 94: Telegram from Captain Charles D. Sigsbee, Commander of the USS Maine, to the Secretary of the Navy, 02/15/1898 - 02/15/1898; RG 45: Naval Records Collection and Library, entry 500 Area File of the US Navy, 1775-1910, Area 10, box 16; National Archives and Records Administration, Washington, D.C.

p. 96: Letter to President William McKinley from Annie Oakley, 04/05/1898 - 04/05/1898; Item from Record Group 94: Records of the Adjutant General's Office, 1762 – 1984. (www.archives.gov ARC Identifier 300369)

p. 98: © Bettmann/Corbis

p. 135: National Archives (111-SC-82177)

p. 151: National Guard Image Gallery, Painting by Mort Kunstler, 1984

p. 154: National Archives (111-SC-98352)

pp. 156–157: Courtesy Frederic Remington Art Museum, Ogdensburg, New York

p. 168: Armed Forces History Division, National Museum of American History, Smithsonian Institution.

p. 173: National Archives (111-RB-1744)

p. 202: White House Historical Association (White House Collection): 56

p. 203: Kean Collection/Archive Photos/Getty Images

p. 204: Collection of The New-York Historical Society, 2026

p. 206, top: The Granger Collection, New York

p. 206, bottom: Division of Political History, National Museum of American History, Smithsonian Institution.

p. 207: © North Wind Picture Archives

p. 217: Private Collection/Peter Newark American Pictures/The Bridgeman Art Library

p. 226: Picture Collection, The New York Public Library, Astor, Lenox and Tilden Foundations.

p. 230: Art Resource, NY

p. 234: MPI/Archive Photos/Getty Images

p. 238, right: AP Photo/The Hannah Lindahl Children's Museum

p. 244: White House Historical Association (White House Collection): 512

p. 249: Private Collection/Art Resource, NY

p. 250: Courtesy of U.S. Geological Survey Photographic Library, (ID: Arnold, R. 168)

p. 257: Theodore Roosevelt Papers, Library of Congress Manuscript Division

p. 258: Library of Congress Rare Book and Special Collections Division. Printed Ephemera Collection

pp. 262–263: © Bettmann/Corbis

p. 265: Art and Architecture Collection, Miriam and Ira D. Wallach Division of Art, Prints and Photographs, The New York Public Library, Astor, Lenox and Tilden Foundations.

p. 266, left: George Eastman House/Underwood & Underwood/Getty Images

p. 268, left: Smithsonian Institution Archives, SIA2009-1371

p. 268, right: © Corbis

p. 269: Smithsonian Institution Archives, NHB-28234

p. 270, left: Snark/Art Resource, NY

p. 270, right: Collection of The New-York Historical Society, 2002.1.3729

p. 271, top: Photo by Harlingue/Roger Viollet/Getty Images

p. 276: Smithsonian American Art Museum, Washington, DC/Art Resource, NY

p. 278: Snark/Art Resource, NY

p. 280: © Corbis

p. 291: Adoc-photos/Art Resource, NY. Detail of photograph.

p. 293: John Hay Papers, Library of Congress Manuscript Division

p. 295: © Bettmann/Corbis

p. 300: © Corbis

p. 303: Courtesy of George Eastman House, International Museum of Photography and Film

p. 336: © Bettmann/Corbis

p. 338: Kermit Roosevelt Papers, Library of Congress Manuscript Division

p. 341: AP Photo

p. 342: Private Collection/Phillips, Fine Art Auctioneers, New York, USA/The Bridgeman Art Library

p. 343: Courtesy of Harvard University Archives, HUP Thayer, W. R. (11)

p. 351: White House Historical Association (White House Collection): 658

# INDEX

Page numbers in **bold** indicate illustrations.